LOUIS NAPOLEON:

IS HE TO BE

THE IMPERIAL CHIEF

OF

AND

THE ANTICHRIST?

BY

DAVID N. LORD.

NEW YORK:
FRANKLIN KNIGHT,
1866.

JOHN J. REED, PRINTER,

43 Centre Street, N. Y.

PREFACE.

Is Louis Napoleon one of the line of monarchs represented by the seventh head of the wild beast of the Apocalypse? Is he to become the imperial master of the old Western Roman empire? Is he to be the great agent in the restoration of the Jews? Is he to persecute the witnesses, and consign them to martyrdom? Is he to be the Antichrist, and to perish at the advent of Christ?

Is the Son of God in two, three or four years, to come in the clouds, and enter on his millennial reign?

Inquiries like these have been put forth for several years in Great Britain, and lately in the United States, and in Canada, and answered by their authors with great assurance in the affirmative; and a considerable body of persons have been drawn to accept them, and adjust to them their expectations of the future.

How large the curiosity is that is felt in this country in regard to them, is seen from the fact that near twenty thousand copies of the chief work—in its successive forms—in which they have been presented, have been distributed here. No confutation of them, so far as I am aware, has appeared.

Those who desire a knowledge of their import, will find in this volume a statement, on the one side, of their principal elements, and proofs of their groundlessness and error; and on the other, a brief exhibition of the teachings of the Scriptures in respect to the great events that are to precede, attend, and follow Christ's second coming, in which the views presented of the closing scenes of the present dispensation, and the peculiarities of that which is then to be introduced, differ much from those that are generally entertained.

CONTENTS.

INTRODUCTION.

CHAPTER I.

CHAPTER II.

CHAPTER III.

CHAPTER IV.

CHAPTER V.

CHAPTER VI.

CHAPTER VII.

CHAPTER VIII.

CHAPTER IX.

CHAPTER X.

CHAPTER XI.

CHAPTER XII.

CHAPTER XIII.

CHAPTER XIV.

CHAPTER XV.

CHAPTER XVI.

CHAPTER XVII.

CHAPTER XVIII.

CHAPTER XIX.

CHAPTER XX.

CHAPTER XXI.

CHAPTER XXII.

CHAPTER XXIII.

CHAPTER XXIV.

CHAPTER XXV.

CHAPTER XXVI.

CHAPTER XXVII.

CHAPTER XXVIII.

INTRODUCTION.

The French Revolution awakened a fresh attention to the Prophecies—Mr. Faber and Mr. Frere maintained that Napoleon Buonaparte or his Dynasty was the Power represented by the Seventh Head of the Wild-beast of the Apocalypse.

THE French Revolution, which burst like a tempest on the world toward the close of the last century, and the long train of wars and conquests under Buonaparte, by which Holland, Italy, Egypt, Switzerland, Prussia, Bavaria, Spain, Portugal, and other territories, were brought under his sway, impressed many persons in Great Britain with the feeling, that events so extraordinary, and so likely to exert an important influence on the whole circle of the civilized nations, must have a place in the revelations of the Scriptures, respecting the great actors and catastrophes that are to precede and attend the second coming of Christ. The question arose: "To which of the great powers symbolized in Daniel and John, that were to trample down the nations, and steep the earth in slaughter, does Napoleon belong?" And as he is not individually depicted in those prophets, and as most of the great actors whom they foreshow, had already passed from life, it was assumed that he must be of that succession of conquerors and tyrants, that are represented by the wild-beast of seven heads and ten horns, that emerged from the sea, Rev. xiii. 1, and that are to go on in their career, till the coming of the Son of God in the clouds.

Among the first who assigned him a place under that symbol, were Mr. Faber and Mr. Frere; Mr. Faber maintaining that Buonaparte was denoted by the seventh head of the beast, which received a death-wound, and was healed, *Sac. Cal. vol. iii. p.* 115, *edition* 1844: and Mr. Frere, that he was at first symbolized by the seventh head of that monster, but was at length represented by an eighth head, *Comb. View, p.* 105; *edition* 1815.

The persuasion that Buonaparte filled the sphere ascribed to him by Mr. Faber, seems gradually to have met a large acceptance. It was not only held by Mr. Frere, who published his Combined View in 1814; but others soon followed in their train. A still larger number became converts to their theory in the period from the expulsion of Charles X., in 1830, to the fall of Louis Philippe, in 1848; and since the assumption of the imperial sceptre by Louis Napoleon, it has been reasserted by a large group of authors with great earnestness, and connected with other peculiar views that are fraught with important errors: such as that the symbolical and chronological prophecies have a double fulfillment; that the seventieth week of Daniel is yet future; that Louis Napoleon is the Antichrist; that he is the personage foreshown Dan. ix. 27, who was to confirm a covenant with many of the Jews; that he is to aid that people in returning to their national land; that he is to persecute and slay the witnesses; that he is to perish in the battle of Armageddon; and finally, that Christ's coming in the clouds would take place in 1865–1866, or at the latest, within two, three or four years from the present time.

Their chronology is also an important element in their system: as they attempt to determine the period occupied by the four great empires; the commencement and close of the twelve hundred and sixty days; the epoch of the seventh trumpet, and other important dates and events. The question whether the scheme of these writers is truthful or not, turns therefore on the question, first, whether their theory of the wild-beast is valid or not; as it is upon that that all their representations respecting Napoleon Buonaparte and Louis Napoleon proceed: and next on the question whether their chronology is accurate: as if their system of dates and times is mistaken, their whole scheme of constructions falls with it; and finally, the character of the other parts of their system is to be determined by the teachings of the Scriptures and facts of history which they respect. If they are shown to be mistaken, their overthrow will complete the confutation of the theories they maintain respecting the wild-beast, the Buonapartes, and the age and epochs of the world.

I shall, therefore, proceed first, to show the inaccuracy and groundlessness of their theory of the wild-beast: next, to confute their estimates of the dates and periods of Daniel and John: thirdly, to point out their errors in respect to the principles on which the prophecies are to be interpreted, and confute their misrepresentations of Daniel and John: and finally, to present a view of the great predictions of the divine word that are yet to be fulfilled, and indicate the order as far as may be, in which they are to meet their accomplishment.

CHAPTER I.

Mr. Faber's View of the Wild-beast of Seven Heads—He failed to verify it—He mistook the class of Rulers who were represented by the Sixth Head of that Symbol—He erred in respect to the Head which preceded the Sixth, the Deadly Wound inflicted on the Seventh Head, and its Restoration to Power.

THE question that first demands consideration is, whether the views presented by these writers of the wild-beast of seven heads and ten horns, are in harmony with the teachings of the Apocalypse and Daniel, or irreconcilable with them. I shall direct my argument against Mr. Faber, without citing other authors; inasmuch as those who hold that Napoleon Buonaparte and Louis Napoleon, are represented by the seventh head of the beast, or the beast itself in its last form, build their conclusion on essentially the grounds on which he founds his. After stating that the classes of rulers, represented by the first five heads of the beast, were Kings, Consuls, Dictators, Decemvirs, and Military Tribunes, he presents his theories respecting the sixth and seventh heads, in the following passage:

"The chronologically sixth ruling head was the Triumvirate. This rose with Pompey, Crassus and Cæsar, in the year A. C. 59; sank into quiescence in the year A. C. 48, when, after the death of Crassus and Pompey, Cæsar was declared by the Senate and people, consul for five years, and dictator for one; awoke to activity in the year A. C. 43, with Anthony, Lepidus, and Octavius, and became extinct in the year A. C. 27, when at the call of Augustus, the first head, or the Roman imperial kingship, awoke after its long slumber of near five centuries.

"The chronological seventh ruling head, was the Francic kingship, or emperorship. Since this head, though it was the seventh in the order of origination, immediately succeeded the first head, inasmuch as the five other heads had fallen in the time of John, while the first head was then in active existence; it will be necessary to note the vicissitudes of the first head, until that first head finally fell in the year A. C. 1806, so that we may be brought in regular course to the rise of the seventh head.

"The chronological first head, arose with Romulus in the year A. C. 753, and after a long quiescence which commenced in the year A. C. 508, it awoke to activity in the year A. C. 27, when by the Senate and people, the principality of the whole of the empire was conferred on Octavius Cæsar, with the name of Augustus, which was ever afterwards borne by him and his successors."

"There are writers," he says, who assume "that the head in St. John's time, fell, when Augustulus was deposed, and when the Imperial Dignity was extinguished in the West. That assumption, however, rests upon no solid foundation. The *western* line of the Roman Emperors did indeed expire with Augustulus; but the *office* or dominant authority of the Roman Kingship, or Emperorship, was not then abolished, or did not then fall. On the contrary it continued to subsist with much vigor in the *eastern* division of the empire.

"The dignity thus evidently not extinct by the deposition of Augustulus, continued in the eastern part of the empire, until Constantinople was taken by the Turks in the year A. D. 1453.

It was then abolished in the east, as it had before been suppressed in the west. But this event did not produce its ultimate fall.

"If we revert to the west, we shall find that though it had been suppressed by Odoacer, throughout that division in the year A. D. 476, it was restored by the powerful sovereign of France, in the year A. D. 800, when Charlemagne, in the church of St. Peter, was solemnly proclaimed, the most pious Augustus, crowned by God, the great and pacific emperor of the Romans. In consequence of this transaction, the empire was now once more ruled by two Roman emperors . . . jointly as before, constituting that first head of the wild-beast which arose in the person of Romulus.

"From the year 800 to the year 1453, with the exception of the interregnum which occurred when the western imperial dignity was transferred from France to Germany, the first head, continued to represent two dynasties." *Sacred Cal. vol. iii. pp.* 115–117.

The steps by which Mr. Faber reached his conclusion in respect to the seventh head, and the Buonapartes, thus were, 1st. The hypothesis that the Roman rulers symbolized by the sixth head of the beast, were the Triumvirate, which, he held, fell in the year B. C. 27. 2d. The assumption that the head that followed the sixth, instead of the seventh, which was the next in order, was the *first*, the kingly; which he maintained, after having fallen in B. C. 508, rose again to a new life in the year B. C. 27, and continued in supremacy, through near eighteen centuries, to A. D. 1806. 3d. The representation that the line of supreme rulers, which he asserts the revived head represented, was first the imperial series from Augustus to Augustulus, who was dethroned in A. D. 476. Next the imperial line of the eastern empire, from the fall of Augustulus, to the coronation of Charlemagne in A. D. 800. Thirdly, that eastern line jointly with Charlemagne and his lineage, and subsequently the line of Otho of Germany, from A. D. 800, to the fall of the eastern empire in 1453. Fourthly, The line of Otho from 1453, to the abdication of the imperial title by Francis of Austria, in 1806. On the fall of that supposed sixth head, Mr. Faber held that the seventh head rose into power, and had its foreshadowed agent in Napoleon Buonaparte. The defeat of that emperor at Waterloo, in 1815, he alleged, was the event denoted by the deadly wounding of the seventh head; and the healing of the wound, he maintained took place in the usurpation of the throne of France by Louis Napoleon in December, 1851, and reigning on it under the title of emperor. Every one of these hypotheses, and representations, I shall now show, is without authority, and in open contradiction to the Scriptures, and to the facts of history.

1. Mr. Faber offers no proof that the Triumvirate was the order of Roman Rulers symbolized by the sixth head of the beast. This first and most fundamental postulate in his theory, is left wholly without support. Not a solitary consideration does he allege that yields it any color of authority. The

mere fact that the Triumvirate was invested with a supreme and despotic rule for a short period, both before and after Cæsar's death, is no proof that it was so diverse in nature from all the preceding forms of the government, as to entitle it to be represented exclusively of all others, by one of the heads. It manifestly had no such peculiarity; but was in principle, identical with the dictatorship, which it exactly resembled in the nature and absoluteness of its authority. The corner stone of Mr. Faber's theory thus rests upon a gratuitous assumption.

2. His representation that the Triumvirate was a wholly new, and the sixth form of the Roman government, is in contradiction to the testimony of Tacitus, who treats the power of the Triumvirate, Pompey, Crassus and Cæsar, and of Lepidus, Antony and Octavius, as of too unsettled a character, and of too short a duration to be regarded as a fixed form of rule; and exhibits the empire under Augustus, as that which succeeded to the military tribuneship. "The power of Pompey and Crassus quickly passed to Cæsar; and the arms of Lepidus and Antony, yielding to Augustus, he received the *empire* under the title of *Prince*." *Annal. lib. i. cap.* 1. Whatever settled rule prevailed during those triumvirates, was indisputably of the nature of the dictatorship, and if referred to one of the heads of the beast as its representative, it should be to the third, the symbol of that power, which was first instituted

in the year B. C. 497, and was several times revived, as in the person of Camillus, B. C. 389, of Sylla B. C. 82, and of Cæsar B. C. 45.

3. He disregards the distinction between the falling of a head of the wild beast, and the interception of a head from its activity for a moment, by a death-wound. The falling of a head, which was its drooping and sinking from the erect attitude it maintained when in power, plainly denoted the loss of its vital energies and cessation from its functions, as the ruling head of the animal. The posture it took by falling, was that of lifelessness. There accordingly is no hint in the history of the wild beast in the Apocalypse, that either of the heads that had fallen, had risen to life and power again; or that either of the two remaining heads would, or could, if they fell, be restored to a new life. The head that was healed, was a head, not that had fallen, but that had received a death-wound that for a moment stunned it, and intercepted its functions; but that still, the symbol implies, was not actually dead, but in a condition in which it was susceptive of healing, and actually received a restoration to health and activity, and in a way that was suited to its nature. This consideration refutes Mr. Faber's imagination, that the head that was revived from a death-wound, was a head, not that had been merely wounded by a deadly blow, but a head that had actually died by a natural disease, or a stroke of violence.

4. He gives no proof whatever that it was, as he affirms, the first head of the symbol, that was revived from a death-wound. There is not a hint in the prophecy that yields any support to that assumption. And Mr. Faber alleges nothing to sustain it. The pretexts by which he affects to justify it, that εἷς, one, in the expression, "the one is," is employed as the ordinal first, instead of the cardinal one, is wholly groundless and against, the general usage of the New Testament. The language of the passage is, οἱ πέντε ἔπεσαν, ὁ εἷς ἐστὶν, ὁ ἄλλος οὔπω ἦλθε; in which οἱ, the article prefixed to πέντε, indubitably distinguishes the five meant, as the first five in the series: not *a* five, or *some* five out of the heads, that had had a period of activity. The article also prefixed to εἷς, "the one," distinguishes that head from all the others: as that also before ἄλλος, "the other," discriminates that from the other six. It is the first five in the series therefore, demonstrably, that had fallen, not merely five in number, without any indication which they were; and in like manner, the ὁ εἷς, "the one"—*i. e.*, the one that now is—in supremacy, is the sixth. Mr. Faber's attempt to convert the cardinal one, into the ordinal first, so as to make it affirm that "the first in the series, now is," instead of the one that now is, is not only without authority, but is a gross violation of the passage.

5. The imperial office as held by Augustus and his successors, differed widely from that of the kings, in

its powers, prerogatives, and exemption from restraint in the exercise of an arbitrary and despotic rule. The kings reigned over but a small population, and a narrow territory, and were held under powerful restrictions by the fundamental laws of the state, and by a proud and jealous aristocracy. The great conquests by that people, of territories out of Italy, did not take place till ages after the line of kings had been supplanted by the consulate, and other forms of administration. But the emperors, instead of such petty chiefs, wielded a greater power for ages, than was ever exercised by any other line of monarchs; reigned over more numerous subjects, and a wider empire; and held all within their domains, subject in the most absolute manner to their despotic will. A head of the beast, therefore, that was suited in its size and elevation to serve as a symbol of the kings, who were little better than the chiefs of a tribe of banditti, had no adaptation to represent the superior power, the greater magnificence, and the wider and more resistless and arbitrary sway of the emperors. To suppose, as Mr. Faber assumes, that the same head was employed as the symbol of officials that differed so widely in power, prerogatives, and splendor, is to suppose that the head had no special suitableness to the function which it was to fill, and is thence to contradict the wisdom of adaptation, that marks all the symbols of the Apocalypse, to the ends for which they were employed.

6. He holds that there were two heads of the beast that were revived from a death-stroke, and restored to power; the first after a death of near five centuries; and the seventh from a death-wound, which he affirmed it received at the battle of Waterloo. But in this he offers a direct contradiction to the prophecy, which gives no intimation that more than one was restored, after a death-stroke, to a new life and fresh activity. The whole representation implies, that that event was altogether unparalleled in the annals of the beast. Why should they who dwell on the earth, wonder, when they behold the beast that was, and is not, and yet again is, if that seeming solecism is not in the predicted instance, a peculiarity to it; if a like transition from death to life, had been repeatedly witnessed in the career of the rulers of the state? In thus interpolating a second revived head, of which the prophecy knows nothing, to give a color of truth to his theory, Mr. Faber shows again that he had no legitimate means for its support.

The first two great postulates of his theory, that the Triumvirate was the order of rulers represented by the sixth head; and that the first head, after a death of centuries, was revived to a new life, and reigned from the accession of Augustus, to the abdication of the title of emperor of the Romans, by Francis of Austria in 1806, are thus wholly groundless and false; and with them, the whole fabric reared by him with so much pretence and labor, falls to the ground.

7. It is clear, therefore, that the head that symbolized the class of rulers who were exercising the government of the empire, at the time of the Vision, was not a head that had before fallen, and been recalled to a fresh life; but was the sixth, in the order of the heads, which we know from the date of the revelation, was the imperial Pagan, in the person of Domitian. And this, moreover, is made indubitable by the expression employed by the Apostle to indicate the head that was then in power. His words, *ὁ εἷς ἐστίν*, "the one that now is," defines it as being *then* in power, and exercising the sway of the empire. As therefore the epoch of the revelation was the reign of Domitian, and the year A. D. 95 or 96; it is as specific a definition of the supreme power of the period as the Pagan imperial, as though it had been embodied in the most direct and explicit terms.

CHAPTER II.

Mr. Faber is equally unsuccessful in his endeavor to prove that neither the Powers denoted by the Sixth, nor by the Seventh Head, held the Supreme Rule of the Empire during the Imperial Pagan and Christian Lines, from the Accession of Augustus to the Fall of the Western Empire.

The powers that were in supremacy at the date of the vision, in which the Apostle beheld the wild beast, and witnessed its death-wound, and its restoration, were indubitably the line of Pagan emperors, of which Augustus was the first, and Galerius and Maximian, with the Cæsars, appointed by them the last. When did that head fall? Was there, in fact, no fall of a head, as Mr. Faber contends, till the abdication of Francis of Austria, at a distance of more than eighteen hundred years? Or did the sixth fall, at the fall of the Pagan line of emperors, and give place to the seventh head, as the symbol of the Christian imperial line, commencing with Constantine, and terminating at the abdication of Augustulus, and fall of the western empire? Mr. Faber endeavored by the most fallacious pretexts, and bold misrepresentations, to make out that no head fell during that period. But his efforts were vain, and only served to show the unsoundness of the principles on which he proceeded, and the unreliableness of his judgment.

1. He totally overlooked the fact that the wild beast of seven heads and ten horns of the Apocalypse, ch. xiii. and xvii., was *a prophetic symbol*, or representative of the *future only* from the time when the beast rose from the sea. The five first heads that had already fallen, most certainly *were retrospective* merely, each of its own period of power which had already passed; not *predictive* of the rulers who were to exercise the supremacy during the remainder of that age and the ages that were to follow, till it should reach its final fall. This fact is self-evident, and it shows that none of the first five that had fallen, could rise again to life, and resume the government of the empire. Their return to life and activity in their old sphere, as heads, during which they reigned, was as inconsistent with their having fallen, and lost their functions, as the return of the *time* during which they reigned, was inconsistent with its having already passed; and as a re-entrance on life of the identical subjects over whom they had exercised their authority, was impossible. It is in contradiction to the fact that they were fallen, and therefore merely representative of the *past*, not predictive of the future, to suppose that any one of them should recover itself from its fall, and resume its functions as a living, erect, and ruling head. But Mr. Faber unfortunately saw nothing of this. He

assumed that a fallen and defunct head, might as well fill the place of a living and acting one, as a head that had not fallen, but was in the full career and vigor of its official life. He was accordingly wholly unaware, or regardless, of the contradiction which he offered to the symbol, when he assumed and asserted that one of the fallen heads rose from its death-swoon, after a lapse of five hundred years, and assumed again the reins of the empire, which had for such a period fallen from its grasp.

But it is equally true, that the sixth and seventh heads of that symbol, which had *not* fallen at the time of the *vision*, were not predictive of any agency of their own that was to be future, at the rise of the beast from the sea, but were merely representative, like the five fallen heads, of what *when the beast should emerge from the deep*, would already have come to pass. They most certainly could not be prophetic of any event that had taken place *before* the beast's emergence; as it was at that epoch that it entered on its existence in the form it then bore. To suppose that those heads were symbols of powers and acts that were to take place after the rise of the beast from the sea, would be to suppose that they were not only prophetic of future agents and events, *after* the period of their agency had passed, but that they were symbols of a set of agents and acts that differed in time and nature from those which they had symbolized in their proper period before the beast received the new form it took at that epoch, and assumed the place which the dragon had before held as the symbol of the Roman rulers from Romulus to the fall of the western empire. For why should events be again predicted as *futurities*, which had already been represented by the sixth and seventh heads of the dragon, and had had their verification in the fall of the sixth head at the overthrow of the Pagan line of emperors; and the fall of the seventh at the dethronement of Augustulus? It is clear, therefore, that the predictive office of that symbol, was confined to the agents, acts, and events in the Roman empire, which had their being *after* the rise of the beast from the sea; and this is an unanswerable proof that the sixth and seventh heads did not have their period after the fall of the western empire, but before. For on the emergence of the beast from the sea, the diadems were no longer on the *heads* of the symbol, but on the *horns*. As those badges were the symbols of supreme power, the loss of them by the heads, showed that all the heads had run their career, and fallen from their authority; while the presence of the diadems on the horns, showed with equal explicitness, that the supreme power had passed to the kings, whom the horns represented. No certainty can be more absolute, therefore, than that the fall of the sixth and seventh heads took place before the beast's emergence from the sea: not as Mr. Faber contends, at the distance of centuries after the diademed horns entered on their career, as the sovereigns of the western Roman empire. And this single consideration again overturns the whole structure of the theory Mr. Faber has reared at such an expenditure of pompous assertions, and groundless pretences.

2. There was no point entitled to a more thorough and impartial consideration by Mr. Faber, than the question whether the head representing the Pagan imperial line, did not fall, at the fall and extinction of that line on the death of Galerius, Maximian, Maxentius, Maximin, and Licinius, who were the last of the Pagan princes; and who perished either shortly before, or during the struggle between the Pagan and Christian parties, in which Constantine rose to supreme power. But he takes no notice of it whatever. Why was it kept from the eyes of his readers? Was it because he saw that a candid exhibition of that great revolution, would be likely to lead them to distrust the validity of the theory he was so strenuous to maintain? The fact that the Pagan line of emperors was swept from the throne, at that epoch; and that it was succeeded by a nominally Christian line, which continued down to the fall of the western empire, is indisputable. It is indisputable, also, that that change was an event of the greatest significance in the political as well as the religious world. As that class of rulers, marked by such peculiarities, was struck from existence, and

a new line, in many respects of a wholly dissimilar character, and opposite policy, especially in the sphere of religion, rose in its place; what is so probable as that the sixth head of the beast, which had been the symbol of the Pagan emperors, should also fall from its place, and be succeeded by the seventh head, as the symbol of the new dynasty? No modification of the government in the preceding stages of its career, approached in greatness and momentousness, that which was wrought by Constantine. In all the previous variations of the supreme rule, the changes lay chiefly in the classes of persons who exercised the government. The great principles of the ruling power, and the most important features of its policy, were in all the six forms the government had assumed, essentially the same. But on the accession of Constantine to the throne, a new and all-pervading element was introduced, by the recognition and legalization of Christianity, the nationalization of the Church, and the assumption by the monarch, of authority over the faith, the worship, and the rights of God's people, that in a degree reversed the fundamental principles and aims of the government, and gave birth to a train of events, that had no parallel in greatness and significance, in the previous history of the empire. What can be more contradictious and preposterous, than to suppose that two such diverse, and in their leading principles and aims, directly opposite lines of princes, should or could be symbolized by the same head, and that a Pagan head of the beast? It is to suppose that the representative bears no analogy to that which it denotes, but is wholly arbitrary and meaningless. Mr. Faber, however, saw nothing, it would seem, of this. To his eyes the head that represented the Pagan kings, Numa, Tarquin, and the other chiefs of the first ages of the Roman state, or that stood for Nero, Diocletian, and Galerius, was as well adapted to be the symbol of Constantine, Gratian and Theodosius, as it was of those ancient worshipers of false gods, or those later persecutors of the children of the Almighty, and conspirators against the spread and existence of his kingdom on the earth.

3. He in like manner passed the question whether the seventh head of the beast did not rise into power at the fall of the Pagan line of supreme rulers, and become the symbol of the new nominally Christian line, which commenced with Constantine, and continued until the fall of the western empire, and transition of the supreme power from the last head of the beast to its horns. Yet there was no question entitled in a higher measure to his most impartial consideration. That the imperial line of Christian emperors, commencing with Constantine, was the line symbolized by the seventh head, is indeed not only thus probable, but is indubitably certain, from the fact, that that line received a deadly wound from the sword, and yet after a brief space, was revived

again, and continued down to the fall of Augustulus, and overthrow of the western empire. The title to the throne passed, according to the laws of the empire, from Constantine to his descendants or relatives. But that prince himself, before he was summoned from life, put to death his oldest son, and several other members of his own and his father's family. After his decease, two of his brothers, two sons of one of his brothers, the husband of one of his sisters, and five other relatives, were put to death by Constantius, his oldest surviving son. Of Constantine's other sons that outlived him, Constantine was slain in battle in the year 340; and Constans was assassinated in 350. Soon after, Nepotianus, a cousin of Constantine, and Gallus, a brother of Julian, were put to death. Consequently, on the decease, in 361, of Constantine's remaining son Constantius, Julian, the Apostate, was the only surviving male of the family, who had a title to the sceptre. He accordingly, having already been made Cæsar, and being declared Augustus by the army of the west, of which he had the command, succeeded to the throne without obstruction; and publicly renouncing Christianity, and adopting Paganism as his religion, put an end for a time to the reign of the line denoted by the seventh head; though he failed to revive and reinstate the sixth. The line denoted by the seventh head thus received a deadly wound by a sword. After the lapse, however, of eighteen months, Julian fell in a battle with the Persians; and with him, Paganism, losing the power it had regained; on the election by the army of Jovian, a Christian chief, to the imperial throne, the line of Christian princes symbolized by the wounded and restored head, again obtained the sceptre, and held it till the fall of Augustulus, and the extinction of the western empire. As these events thus present an exact correspondence to the symbol, they are unquestionably its fulfillment. And this is confirmed by the fact, that no other death-wound was ever given to the seventh head of the beast from which it recovered. If another such death-wound was inflicted on it, its period must have been between the assumption of the throne of the empire by Constantine, when the seventh head succeeded to the sixth, and the fall of Augustulus, when it fell and passed from its sphere as an active power in the western empire. But there is not another group of events in the annals of the emperors of that period, that has the slightest title to be regarded as the fulfillment of the prediction.

4. Though Mr. Faber asserts, with great confidence, that no fall of a head of the beast took place at the fall of Augustulus and extinction of the western empire, he presents no considerations that yield any support to his representation, but contents himself with alleging that though the imperial line of the western empire then came to its end, the extinction of that line involved no fall of a head of the beast;

because another imperial line still subsisted in the east. He says:

"The *western* line of the Roman emperors did indeed expire with Augustulus; but the *office* or *dominant authority* of the Roman kingship, or emperorship, which is the thing typified by the head existing in the time of St. John, was *not* then abolished; or in the phraseology of the Apocalypse, did *not* then fall. On the contrary, it still continued to subsist with much vigor in the *eastern* division of the empire, represented by the leonine, ursine and leopardine parts of the symbol.

"So far was the Roman emperorship from *falling* by the abdication of Augustulus, that no other change was produced in the constitution of the regal head, except this: instead of two emperors, eastern and western, who had governed the divided empire since the death of Theodosius, the world again beheld, though with diminished territory, a sole emperor of the Romans."—*Sac. Cal., vol. iii., pp.* 116, 117.

In this pretext he tacitly assumes, that on the abdication of Augustulus, the emperor of the eastern empire became, by virtue of that act, the emperor of the west, with all the rights, prerogatives and honors that had belonged to Augustulus. Otherwise he could not be the emperor of the west: and therefore could not be symbolized as such by the head of the beast that had been the representative of Augustulus. How could Zeno of Constantinople, be the imperial monarch of the western empire, if he had none of the rights, none of the titles and dignities, none of the prerogatives, none of the power and dominion that belonged to the imperial office, while held by the fallen monarch of Rome? How could Zeno be represented by the same head of the beast as had been the symbol of Augustulus, if he had none of the prerogatives, and exercised none of the functions, which it was the office of that head to symbolize? But what can be more mistaken and absurd than to imagine that the abdication of Augustulus wrought such a stupendous change in the relations of Zeno, as to invest him with all the rights and possessions which the fallen monarch of the west had just laid down? Augustulus, by his abdication, transferred his rights and prerogatives exclusively to Odoacer, to whom he yielded his office, and of whom he became a subject; not to Zeno, with whom he had no communication, and who had no personal interest in the transaction. The pretence, therefore, that no fall of a head of the beast that had been the symbol of Augustulus, took place when that emperor fell, because another emperor still retained his throne in the eastern empire, though he had no dominion and exercised no functions in the west, is wholly solecistical and false. Consequently the continuance of the eastern imperial line, after the dissolution of the western empire, is no proof that there was not a fall of a head and of the seventh head of the wild beast, at the fall of Augustulus; and Mr. Faber fails in his attempt to prove that no such fall then took place.

But beyond this, the fall of Augustulus, and extinction of his empire, was *itself* a direct and indubitable proof, that the head of the beast that had been his representative, also fell with him. For the fall of the western imperial *line* is as direct and positive a proof of the fall of the *symbol* that had represented it, as the fall of the *symbol* is of the fall of the *line* of which it had been the representative. To suppose it otherwise, is to suppose that no fixed and infallible connection exists between the symbol, and that which it symbolizes. If an imperial dynasty that has been symbolized by the seventh head of the wild beast may fall and sink into extinction; and yet no change takes place in the symbol that answers to that fall; then manifestly no correspondence in acts and events subsists between them; and the conditions and catastrophes of the symbol are no index to the conditions and catastrophes of the line it represents; nor the condition of the line it represents, any key to the condition of the symbol. But instead of this, the fall of the line of monarchs denoted by the seventh head, is as infallible a sign that that head fell also at the same moment, as the fall of a head when beheld by John in the vision, was to him, that the line of rulers it denoted, was to fall at the moment which was to answer in the fulfillment to that act of the symbol. And this Mr. Faber himself in effect admits. For the dates to which he refers the fall of the first, second, third, fourth, and fifth heads of the beast, are the dates of the *fall* of the *orders* of rulers, which those heads severa y represented. He in all cases takes the *discontinuance* of a line of rulers, as a proof of the fall, at the same moment, of the head that had symbolized it; and the entrance of a new order of rulers on their functions, as a proof that its date was the date of the rise of the new head which was the representative of that line. By Mr. Faber's own mode, therefore, of determining the fact and the time of the rise and fall of the heads of the wild beast, the fall of Augustulus was a full and infallible proof that the head that had been his symbol, fell also at the same moment with himself.

And that the head that then fell was the seventh, I have already shown, first by the fact, that six orders of rulers had run their career before it rose into power; next, that the class that immediately preceded it, was the Pagan imperial; thirdly, that it was itself the Christian imperial, and entitled, from its peculiarity, and the vastness and momentousness of its acts, and its influence on the world for ages, to be represented by a separate head; and finally, by the distinctive and indubitable mark that it had received a death-wound by a sword, from which it was revived, and reinstated in its power; and next by the equally infallible token, that it must have fallen when the imperial line of the west fell, and the diadems were transferred from the heads of the beast to its horns, inasmuch as it had no function after that time; and that was the time when Augustulus abdicated his throne. It was the time also when the beast with the ten diademed horns rose from the sea; and also was the time of the extinction of the western empire. The confutation of Mr. Faber's theory, that no head of the beast fell at the fall of Augustulus and of his empire, is thus as absolute, as it is in the power of language to express.

CHAPTER III.

Mr. Faber fails equally, in his Theory, that there was a Line of Emperors in the Western Empire, from Augustulus to Napoleon Buonaparte and Louis Napoleon, that was represented by a Head of the Wild Beast.

1. He first assigns that office to the imperial line of Constantinople, affirming in the passage I have already cited, that on the fall of Augustulus, the western empire still had an imperial head, in the line of monarchs on the throne of the eastern empire; and that that line was symbolized by a head of the beast. But the supposition is wholly without ground, and solecistical. It is clear, *first*, that Zeno, the emperor of the east, and his successors on the Constantinopolitan throne, could not be symbolized by a head of the wild beast as the emperors of the western empire, unless they were truly such. To suppose them represented by a head, as emperors of the west, when they were not such, would be to suppose the symbol to be a misrepresentation and contravention of the truth. It is equally clear that those princes could not be emperors of the western empire, unless that empire was still in existence. That their office might be a reality, the empire of which they were the masters, must also be a reality. Otherwise, the office and title

would be but empty shadows. But that indispensable requisite to their holding imperial power over the western empire did not exist. That empire was no longer in being. Its territory had passed from the jurisdiction of the powers symbolized by the heads of the wild beast; and its population had ceased to stand in the relation to it of subjects. Those princes, therefore, could not by any possibility hold the place of genuine and authoritative sovereigns to that population. A symbolization of them as emperors of such a nonexisting empire, would have been a mockery, and cannot have taken place.

Next.—Nor had they any title or right by which they could legitimately claim jurisdiction over that territory, or the nations that occupied it. The emperors of the east had no title by virtue of their office as emperors of their own imperium, to jurisdiction over the western empire. Their right to reign, was simply a right to reign over the domains that were exclusively theirs. Nor did a right arise to them to claim and assume the jurisdiction of the west, from the fact that the imperial line of the west had lost its rights and power, and passed out of existence as rulers. No compact existed between the two lines, by which on the failure of one of them, the jurisdiction of that which was left vacant, should pass as an inheritance to the other line. No pretext is made by Mr. Faber that the eastern emperor became heir of the western, on the fall of Augustulus, by virtue of a treaty between the two parties, or because of a condition to that effect inserted in the decree by which the two divisions of the empire were separated from each other, and constituted two distinct and independent sovereignties.

Thirdly.—The eastern emperors did not acquire a title to the jurisdiction of the west, by any act of Augustulus. That prince surrendered his empire and throne to the king of the Heruli; not to Zeno, of Constantinople.

Fourthly.—Neither Zeno nor his immediate successors resorted to any measures to possess themselves of the western empire by force, on the ground that they inherited a title to it from Augustulus or his predecessors. No attempt was made by any of the eastern emperors to reduce the western empire, or any part of it, to submission to their power, till the reign of Justinian, and fifty-seven years after the fall of Augustulus; and no absolute conquest was made by him, except in Africa and Sicily, till near twenty years later; while the title to the territory which he acquired in those wars, was the title exclusively of conquest, not of hereditary right.

As then it is thus apparent that the eastern emperors had no title whatever to the throne of the west when vacated by Augustulus, it is indubitably certain that Zeno and his successors cannot have been emperors in any sense of the west; and equally certain, therefore, that they cannot have been symbolized as such by a head of the beast. The supposition is self-contradictious. How could a head of the beast have symbolized them as emperors of the west, when they in fact were not such in any respect, either truly or nominally; when they had no title to the sovereignty of the west; when they made no claim to jurisdiction over it; and when they exercised none of the functions that belonged to its sovereignty? It plainly would have been a false symbolization, and therefore cannot have been made in the visions of the Apocalypse. The supposition of such a representation is the greatest of solecisms. A head of the beast could no more represent a line of monarchs, when no line of monarchs existed, or was to exist, that answered to the head as a symbol, than it could be the symbol of any other nonentity.

Thus Mr. Faber blundered at every step of his attempt to show that the imperial line of the east was at the same time the imperial line of the west. He overlooked the fact, that there was no longer a western Roman empire. He disregarded the fact, that the emperors of the east had no jurisdiction or title to sovereignty over the west. He left out of sight the fact, that a head of the beast which was exclusively a symbol of the western line of emperors, could not possibly be a symbol of the eastern line in the same, or in any other relation. His whole imagination that the emperors of the east were also emperors of the west, is thus a consummate misconception, a sheer monstrosity. They were no more emperors of the western Roman empire, at the fall of Augustulus, and through the ages that followed, than they were of Southern Africa, Hindostan, Thibet, or China.

Did the seventh head of the wild beast then, fill no office as a symbol of the supreme rulers of the eastern empire? None whatever; the answer indubitably is. That head was the symbol simply of the last imperial line of the western empire; and on the fall of that line, its functions as a symbol terminated. It most certainly could not have been the symbol in any sphere of the imperial line of the east, after the division of the old empire into distinct and independent sovereignties. Because, first, it is a solecism to suppose a head of the beast could have symbolized a line of emperors as having jurisdiction over the west, when no line existed that had any sovereignty over it; and next, because the eastern line, at the division of the domains into two separate realms, of necessity, in acceding to that act, abdicated all its former right and title to a jurisdiction over the west: while by the same necessity, the line of the western empire, in assenting to that division of the old domains, abdicated all its former right and title to jurisdiction over the east. Such a renunciation of claims over each other, and limitation of the authority of each to its own special domains, was an essential element in the great act by which the two divisions were constituted separate and independent sovereignties.

Mr. Faber thus wholly fails in his attempt to prove that a line of imperial princes was perpetuated in the western empire for ages after the fall of Augustulus, by the imperial line that continued to reign for near a thousand years at Constantinople.

2. His representation that Charlemagne was constituted emperor of the western Roman empire in the year A.D. 800, by the act of Leo, is equally mistaken and contradictory to fact.

He offers indeed no direct proof that that prince was invested with that office. He simply alleges the fact that a crown was placed on Charlemagne's head by Leo, and that he was saluted by the people as emperor of the *Romans.* He offers nothing to show that the crowning was legal and authoritative, nor that Charlemagne was constituted, or declared emperor of *the western Roman empire;* inasmuch as the crowning, and proclamation were of a wholly different character. In order that Charlemagne might be constituted emperor of the western Roman empire, it was necessary either that he should have inherited the title and prerogatives of that office, from a predecessor, who had a right to transmit them to him; or else that the pope who placed the crown on his brow, and proclaimed him emperor, should have authority by virtue of his priestly office, to confer on him the crown of the western empire, and to give with it all its titles and dignities. If the investiture was legitimate, the right or act that conferred it, must also have been legitimate and legal. But Charlemagne did not derive a title to the name and prerogatives of emperor, from an ancestor, nor from a predecessor. He had no imperial ancestor on the throne of France. He had no imperial predecessor on that throne nor in Italy. He obtained the dominion of Italy by conquest, in place of receiving it as a bequest from the Lombard king whom he vanquished. It is equally certain that he was not constituted emperor of the western Roman empire by the act of pope Leo, in crowning him, and denominating him emperor. First because the pope had no control of the imperial crown, and authority to confer it on Charlemagne, or any other individual. To suppose that he had, would be to suppose that the claim set up by his successors to an absolute supremacy over all civil princes, and right to invest them with regal dominion, or divest them of it at their pleasure, was legitimate. But Leo had no such power. His act was accordingly as illegitimate as to the conveyance of rights and prerogatives, as a crowning and salutation as emperor by any other individual could have been.

Next because the act of Leo was wholly gratuitous, and unauthorized by Charlemagne himself. That prince so far from having dictated or sanctioned the measure, was taken by it with surprise, and regarded the officiousness and audacity of the pope with displeasure. At least such is the view given of the transaction by Dean Milman.

"The Christmas of the last year of the eighth century arrived. Charles and all his sumptuous court, the nobles and people of Rome, and the whole clergy, were present at the high service of the nativity. The Pope himself chanted the mass. The full assembly were wrapt in profound devotion. At *the close*, the Pope arose, advanced towards Charles, with a splendid crown in his hands, placed it on his brow, and proclaimed him 'Augustus.' Charles and his son Pepin *humbly submitted* to the ratification of this important act, as anointed by the Pope.

"Was this a sudden and unconcerted act of gratitude, a magnificent adulation by the Pope, to the unconscious and hardly consenting emperor? What rights did it convey? In what, according to the estimate of the times, consisted the imperial supremacy? To these questions history returns but vague and doubtful answers."—*Latin Christ., vol. ii.*, American Edition, p. 458–459.

Dean Milman, in proof that the crowning was unpremeditated by Charles, and the mere work of the pope, cites a passage from a writer of the age, who relates that "Charlemagne declared that holy as was the day, the Lord's nativity, *if he had known the intention of the pope*, he would not have entered the church." Sigonius admits that such statements were made by writers, but dissents from them, and represents the coronation as welcome to Charles. It can scarcely be believed, however, that he can have been ambitious of receiving the imperial title and diadem from a pope of Leo's tarnished reputation: For he had been publicly accused of the most infamous crimes; and the king had gone to Italy for the express purpose of arraigning and judging him; and it was only by an artifice of the clergy that Leo escaped a trial in which he would at least have been discredited by the most ignominious imputations. For on the arraignment of the parties before the tribunal, the bishops who were assessors with the king, rose and disclaimed the right to sit in judgment on the pope, on the pretext, that as he was the supreme pontiff, and held absolute jurisdiction over all others, he was necessarily exempt from judgment by others, and the sole arbiter of his own cause. And on that representation, the bare protestation by the pope of his innocence was accepted as a sufficient proof that the charges against him were false.*

But the act of the pope was illegal and invalid, even if the king had anticipated and acquiesced in it. For whence had Leo the power to constitute Charles emperor of the Romans? Not by virtue of his pontificate. To suppose that he had power to confer that office, is to suppose that he had equal power to take it away, and thence that the emperor in place of an independent prince, became by his inauguration his mere vassal. If Charles himself had the power to constitute himself emperor, he could not have invested the pope with authority to make him such, for that would have involved an equal power

*Sigonius De Regno Ital. an. 801, pp. 157, 159.

in the pope at his will to divest him of his title and crown; and would have weakened his prerogatives and tarnished his dignity instead of augmenting them. The coronation was accordingly in fact a dishonor to Charles, for instead of a magnificent gift, it implied that he had not become emperor by virtue of his ancestry, nor by his conquests; but owed the title and dignity to the generosity or subservience of the pope. No legitimate heir or claimant of an imperial empire and throne, would consent to such an illegal and unauthoritative inauguration, instead of an investiture by legitimate officials, and the usual and impressive forms of such a ceremony, that is to affect in the most intimate manner the rights both of rulers and of subjects. It is to trifle to exhibit such a sham investiture, as having the force of a legal and authoritative transaction, that carried with it the resuscitation of an empire that had passed from existence, and the gift of the rights, powers and dignities of an imperial rule over it. But thirdly, the investiture of Charlemagne by the pope, illegitimate and empty of power as it was, was not an investiture with the title of emperor of *the western Roman empire;* but simply of the Roman population of the capitol and the neighboring territory that had been conquered by Charlemagne from the Lombards. The language of Anastatius, whose account of the transaction is quoted by Baronius and Pagi, is as follows:—

"Then the pontifex with his own hands, crowned him with a costly crown; and the faithful Romans, seeing the great favor which he cherished toward the church and the Pope, unanimously with a loud voice exclaimed, 'Life and victory to Charles, the most pious Augustus, crowned by God great and pacific emperor.'* He was then thrice saluted by the crowd, and proclaimed Emperor of the *Romans*."

The title given him, thus was not emperor of the western Roman empire; but simply emperor of the Romans; that is, of the population of Rome itself and the neighboring territory which he had conquered from the Lombards. It was a mere appropriation to him, therefore, of a new title; not a conveyance to him of any new prerogative, or authority, either over the western empire at large, or over Italy, France, Germany, or any other territory which he had inherited or conquered. The account given of the transaction by the Annalista Lambecianus, cited by Pagi, is the same. Sigonius also exhibits the act as originating with Leo, and as involving nothing more than the appropriation to Charlemagne of the imperial title. The aim of Leo in the measure, he represents was, to place that prince in an attitude toward the papacy and the Catholic church, that

*Exclamaverunt; Carolo, piissimo Augusto, a Deo coronato magno pacifico imperatori, Vita, et Victoria! Ante sacram confessionem beati Petri, ter dictum est; et constitutus est, imperator Romanorum. Annales a. 800.

would prompt him to act a more effective part as its patron and protector.*

This is confirmed also by Pagi, who repels the representation by Baronius, that the imperial power was transferred by the act of Leo, from the Greeks to the Franks. Thus he says:—

"Baronius wrote inaccurately when he affirmed that the imperium was transferred by Leo to Charles. Bellarmine falls into the same error in saying that the western empire was transferred from the Greeks to the Franks. The term, 'transference' does not justly express the transaction. For Irene, the empress of the east, neither relinquished nor lost any of her rights. Besides, the western imperium was extinct, and could not therefore be transferred to any other prince, but could only be renewed; which was exactly what Leo did, as is seen from the coin issued by Charles, which bore the inscription, 'Renovation of the Empire.'†

In accordance with this, Sigonius represents the imperial *title*, which had failed more than three hundred years before, as simply renewed, or brought again into use by the act of Leo."‡

These testimonies thus effectually set aside Mr. Faber's pretext that Charlemagne was constituted

*Ut catholicum eundem, ac potentissimum regem, firmum simul, ac fidum Christianis atque ipsi Romanæ Ecclesiæ, tutorem et patronem pararet. De Regno. It. a 800, p. 158.

†Vox enim, translatione, rem gestam non bene explicat. Preterea Imperium occidentale extinctum erat, idioque in aliquem principem, transferri non poterat, sed tantum renovari, quod et reapse præstitit Leo.

‡Sigonius inquit; hunc dignitatis imperitoriæ *titulum* cum in Momyllo Augustulo, ultimo occidentalis Imperatore, ante trecentos annos, sub regnum Gothorum in Italia defecisset, in eodem occidente Pontifex renovavit. De Regno Italiae A.D. 801.

the emperor of the western Roman empire as Honorius, Valentinian III., and others were down to Augustulus. He received nothing but the mere name of emperor of the Romans, and that was conferred in an illegal and unauthoritative way. There was no reconstruction of the western Roman empire. There was no change of dominion or authority. All the territory, population and rulers of the Gothic kingdoms that were not embraced in what Charles inherited from his father, or had conquered by his sword in Italy, Germany, or elsewhere, remained as independent of him after his coronation as it was before.

3. Mr. Faber fails in like manner to present any proof of his representation that Otho, king of Germany, was constituted the imperial head of the western Roman empire by being crowned by the pope in A.D. 962, and simply saluted as emperor, by the clergy and people of Rome.

It was simply as the monarch of his own inherited or acquired dominions in Germany, and conquests in Italy, that he was declared emperor. That is the specific representation of Sigonius, Baronius, Pagi, and Gibbon. Not a syllable is uttered by them implying that he was inaugurated as the imperial head of the western empire. Such a pretext is a gross affront to truth. Did Otho ever attempt to assert a title to that empire? Did he ever claim in virtue of his inauguration at Rome to be the emperor of France,

Great Britain, Spain, Portugal, Northern Africa, or Sicily? There was no one from whom he could inherit such a title. There was no one who could give him the rights and powers of such a headship of the empire. Otho himself, notwithstanding the title he received, was nothing more than one of the kings descended from the Gothic tribes, who conquered the western empire from the Romans, and transmitted it to their posterity. He had no more imperial authority over the kingdoms of the monarchs who were contemporary with him in the other parts of the western empire, than those monarchs had over him and his domains.

4. Mr. Faber is equally unsuccessful in his attempt to prove that Napoleon Buonaparte was the emperor of the western Roman empire, and as such was the personage symbolized by the seventh head of the beast. It certainly behooved him, in order to give any color of truth to his theory, to sustain this step in it by the most indubitable proofs. Not the shadow of evidence, however, does he allege to verify it. He utters nothing to sustain it but a tissue of statements and assertions that have not the remotest bearing on the point he affects to establish by them.

"We shall find," he says, "that in every particular the Francic emperorship minutely answers to the prophetic character of the seventh head. In May, 1804, Napoleon Buonaparte assumed the official title of emperor of the French."—Vol. iii., p. 124. But that is not the title which Honorius, Valentinian iii. and others down to Augustulus bore: nor is it any more equivalent to the title, emperor of the western Roman empire, than the title emperor of Morocco, Brazil, or Mexico is. What can transcend the error of thus assuming that being emperor of one of the Gothic kingdoms, is identical with being invested with supreme authority over them all? Was Buonaparte emperor of Great Britain? Was he emperor of Spain, of which Joseph Buonaparte was king? Was he emperor of Sicily, of which Murat was monarch? Was he emperor of Westphalia, the throne of which Jerome occupied? Or of Holland, of which Lucien held the sceptre? They were indeed dependents and subservients; but they did not belong to the empire of France, and he was not their emperor, any more than he was emperor of Thibet or Kamskatka.

Mr. Faber proceeds. "In March, 1805, he became king of Italy." But that was not to become the imperial head of the old western empire. Did Mr. Faber hold that in becoming king of Italy, he became the monarch of all the other western kingdoms, which were once subject to the imperial line at Rome? Or if he held that preposterous notion, how did Buonaparte's assuming the title of King of Rome, prove that in his wholly different office as emperor of France, he was the personage symbolized by the seventh head of the wild beast? Can any conclusion be at a greater distance from the premise from which it is drawn?

He adds: "In August, 1806, the first Roman head fell by the abdication and abolition of the official title of emperor of the Romans." But the emperor of Austria, who renounced that title, derived by him from Otho, was not the emperor of the western Roman empire, any more than Otho himself was; and could not, and did not, in fact abdicate it. The imperial title which he renounced was simply the title "Emperor of the *Romans*," and indicated merely that he was the emperor of his own special empire. The reason, moreover, which he gave for his abdication was, not that he had been deprived of his dominions in Italy, but that a share of his territories in Germany had been wrested from him by the Confederation of the Rhine. His language is:

> "Being convinced of the impossibility of discharging any longer the duties which the imperial throne imposed upon us, we owe it to our principles to abdicate a crown, which could have no value in our eyes, when we were unable to discharge its duties, and deserve the confidence of the Princes, electors of the empire. Therefore it is, that considering the bonds which unite us to the empire as dissolved by the Confederation of the Rhine, we renounce the imperial crown, and by these presents, absolve the Electors, Princes and States, members of the supreme tribunal, and other magistrates, from the duties which unite them to us as their legal chief."—*Alison's Hist. Vol. V. p.* 690.

The office which he resigned thus, was not that of emperor of the western Roman empire, of which he neither possessed the jurisdiction, nor held the title;

but was simply his office as the imperial head of the dominions he had held in Germany, where the electors, princes, and states, he absolved from their allegiance, had their place. What can transcend the truthlessness and folly of the pretence, that the surrendry of that imperial title, was the abdication of the title and office of emperor of the western Roman empire, held by Honorius, Valentinian III, and Augustulus?

But how, even on Mr. Faber's theory, did the abdication of Francis of Austria, carry to Napoleon Buonaparte a title to the emperorship of the western Roman empire? Did the emperor of Austria formally transfer it to him? Not at all. Did he resign it that it might be assumed by Napoleon? No. Did his relinquishing the title, naturally and necessarily invest Napoleon with the right of assuming it? Not in the least. Did Buonaparte in fact ever assume the title? Never, nor ever uttered a whisper, implying that he thought himself entitled to arrogate it. How then could the abdication by Francis of the imperial throne of Germany, prove that Buonaparte was the emperor of the western Roman empire? And how beyond that, could it prove that Buonaparte was the person that was symbolized by the seventh head of the wild beast of the Apocalypse?

He proceeds: "In February, 1810, it was decreed that the papal states should be united to the French empire; that of that empire, Rome should rank as the second city; that the prince imperial should take the title of King of Rome; and that the emperors after having been crowned in Notre Dame, at Paris, should before the tenth year of their reign, be also crowned in that of St. Peter's at Rome."—Vol. iii. p. 124. But how did that decree that the Papal states should be united to France, prove that Napoleon was the imperial head of the western Roman empire? Or, how did it demonstrate that he was the person symbolized by the seventh head of the beast? Or how does the decree that Rome should be the second city in rank in the empire, and that the imperial prince should bear the title of the King of Rome, prove that Napoleon was the personage represented by the seventh head of the wild beast? What can surpass the recklessness and folly of attempting to establish a point of such interest by considerations like these, that have not the remotest bearing on it? If the fulfillment of these decrees was a condition of Buonaparte's being the party symbolized by the head of the beast, the argument was very unfortunate for Mr. Faber; as the marks, he here employs to identify Napoleon as the power represented by the seventh head of the beast, wholly failed. The imperial prince never became the King of Rome; nor was Buonaparte ever crowned in St. Peter's at Rome. Before these decrees were carried into effect, he was struck from his throne, and from life, and was soon after followed into the invisible world by his son. Of what more reprehensible perversion of acts and events was a writer ever guilty, than that to which Mr. Faber here descended?

And finally, he is equally mistaken and absurd, in his pretext that Buonaparte, as represented by the seventh head of the beast, met at Waterloo the catastrophe, which is symbolized by the deadly wound of that head. There is no correspondence between the events. Buonaparte was not put to death by a sword on the field of Waterloo. He was not divested of his imperial title and authority, by his defeat on that battle-ground. So far was he from it, that he retreated to Paris, and there, after some delay, abdicated his throne, surrendered himself into the hands of the English, and was conveyed to St. Helena, where at the distance of seven years he died a natural death. The event which Mr. Faber alleges to prove that Napoleon was the emperor denoted by the seventh head of the beast, thus instead of verifying that pretext, confutes it.

5. It is scarcely necessary to add, that he failed in like manner to present any proof of the assertion advanced in his tract on the subject, issued in 1853, that Louis Napoleon, by his usurpation of supreme power, became the imperial chief of the western Roman empire; and as such, is symbolized by the seventh head of the wild beast. He offers nothing except empty pretexts, and confident asseverations to support that preposterous persuasion. Intoxicated with self-elation, at the imagined confirmation of his

theory, he did not descend to the task of proving it, but contented himself with blowing the trumpet of the far-seeing and demi-semi-prophetic perspicacity he imagined he had exhibited, in prognosticating the assumption of the French sceptre by the nephew of Napoleon. As Napoleon Buonaparte himself did not become the imperial chief of the western empire of the Romans, by becoming the imperial head of the empire of France; how did the fact that Louis Napoleon seized the sceptre of France, any more constitute him the imperial head of the old western empire? How did his elevation of himself to the throne of France, invest him with the titles and prerogatives of the ancient emperors of the west, any more than the elevation of Louis XVIII, Charles X, and Louis Philippe to the French throne, after Buonaparte's overthrow, invested them with those ancient titles and prerogatives? The pretext is too self-subverting and preposterous to require any farther refutation.

Thus every step in the long train of assumptions, and assertions on which Mr. Faber reared his theory, is false, and in open contradiction both to the prophecy, and to history. Of what portentous falsifications and solecisms is it made up? No power represented by the seventh head of the beast, has been in existence for near fourteen centuries; and none is ever again to appear in the territory of the western Roman empire, or any where else on the earth. The sovereignty of the western imperium, instead of remaining in the hands of an imperial line after the fall of Augustulus, passed to the ten Gothic kings, who erected kingdoms for themselves out of the old western empire which they had conquered; and it has been held by them from that time to the present day. And that transition of the supreme rule, from a line of emperors, like those denoted by the sixth and seventh heads of the wild beast, to kings, is clearly foreshown in the Apocalypse, ch. xiii. 1., by the absence of the crowns from the heads of the beast, and their presence on the ten horns. No apology, therefore, exists for the monstrous misrepresentation and caricature of both the prophecy and of history of which Mr. Faber was guilty in the structure of his theory. It bears the marks of a deliberate and unscrupulous figment, and deserves the severe censure of all who revere the word of God, and appreciate the importance of truthful statements of the great facts of history that intimately touch the interests of his kingdom.*

* This feature of Mr. Faber's theory of the wild beast, will occasion no surprise to those who are aware that he laid it down in his Sac. Calender of Prophecy, as a fundamental rule in the treatment of the Apocalypse, that the expositor should begin his work *by framing a theory of the great train of agents, acts, and events which the Revelation foreshows*, and determine their *nature*, their *order*, and their *connexions* with each other, *independently of, and antecedently to, any interpretation of the symbols themselves.* He only followed his own supreme rule, therefore, when he set aside or misrepresented the teachings of the prophecy, and the facts of history, and substituted the fictions of his imagination in their place. See his S. Cal. first edition, vol. i., p. 327.

CHAPTER IV.

Mr. Faber's Chronological Theory is also erected in a large degree on Supposititious Grounds, and Misrepresents alike the Word of God and the Facts of History.

THE next important element in the scheme of these writers, is their chronology of the four great empires of Daniel, and of the 2300, 1260, 1290, and 1335 days, and other periods, that are expressly foreshown as the measures of certain acts, or conditions of some of the symbols of Daniel and John. Among them, Mr. Faber holds a leading place. It is marked, however, by the same defects;—inconsistency with those prophecies and with the facts of history,—as characterize his speculations respecting the beast of seven heads. His theory is—that the times of the Gentiles, commenced with the birth of Nebuchadnezzar, and are to extend through two thousand five hundred and twenty years; that the twelve hundred and sixty years, and forty-two months of Daniel and John, are the last half of that period; that they had their commencement at the delivery of the saints into the power of the little horn of Dan. vii. 25, and that they are to terminate somewhere between 1863 and 1875; when, according to him, the present dispensation is to end, the powers denoted by the wild beast are to be destroyed, and a new and more benign economy is to be instituted.

As in the structure and support of his theory respecting the wild-beast, and other symbols of Daniel and John, he proceeds on the most unhesitating assurance that his chronological dates and periods to which he adjusts his constructions of those prophecies, are correct; it is manifest that in order to the verification of his constructions, his calendar of times and dates, should be sustained by the most indubitable proofs. For to convict it of great and fatal errors, will be to overthrow again the whole fabric of his theory respecting the most important symbols, and predictions of which he treats. I shall proceed, therefore, to show that the main grouuds on which he builds his Calendar of prophetic times, is supposititious and false. I shall confine myself mainly to his theory, inasmuch as his scheme is substantially that which is held by the writers whose speculations I am to notice on other topics.

After stating that "in the prophecies of Daniel and John we find several different numbers specified, as the measures of certain chronological periods," he adds:

"These numbers are, three times and a half, 42 months, 1260 days, 2300 days, 1290 days, 1335 days; 70 weeks, 21 days, 5 months, 10 days, three days and a half, and a day, a month, and a year.

"Of such numbers, the three times and a half, the 42 months, and the 1260 days, are mutually equivalent; those terms expressing only, in varied phraseology, one and the same period: for if we reckon a time, or a year to contain 360 days; 42 months, or 1260 days will be exactly equal to three such years and a half.

"By a similar mode of reduction, 5 months are equal to 150; 70 weeks to 490 days; and with a variation which will in this instance be accounted for, a day, and a month, and a year conjointly to 396 days.

"Hence when the various numbers are homogeneously expressed by days, they will stand as follows: 1260 days, 2300 days, 1290 days, 1335 days, 490 days, 21 days; 150 days, 10 days, three days and a half, and 396 days.

"*To these numbers we must add another*, which is the root of all those smaller numbers that are included in it; a number specified indeed by the prophet Daniel, but specified only after a mystical or typical fashion. The number to which I allude is seven times, or 2520 days.

"This radical and perfect number is produced, by the duplication of the broken and imperfect number three times and a half; and we shall find in the sequel, that it comprehends in its own ample term, not only its two moities, or the two imperfect numbers of three times and a half respectively, but likewise the twelve hundred and ninety days, the seventy weeks, the five months, the 10 days, the 21 days, the three days and a half, the day and the month and the year, and by far the greater part of the 2300 days. Such being the case, the 7 times, or the 2520 days constitute a measure that may well be denominated, *the sacred Calendar of Prophecy*; and for the purpose of practical application, this measure is made, as we shall hereafter see, *the gage or span of the great Metalic Image;* whether that image be viewed as chronologically progressive through four mighty successive empires, or as geographically completed in the last mighty empire of the Romans. The measure of seven times, being thus made the chronological measure of the succession of the four Gentile empires, we find our Lord alluding to it under the significant appellation of THE TIMES OF THE GENTILES.

"The seven times or the 2520 days, which constitute the Times of the Gentiles, or the Sacred Calendar of prophecy, are followed by a season of blessedness, which is said by Daniel to begin at the commencement of a period of 1335 days." *Sac. Cal.*, vol. i. 2 edition, pp. 27, 28.

I proceed now to show that his Calendar is built on a supposititious foundation, and not only has no authority from the Scriptures, but is in contradiction to their plain and indubitable teachings.

1. The corner stone on which his chronological edifice rests, is the assumption and assertion that "seven times" are given in the prophecy of Daniel, ch. iv. 16, 23, 32, as the gage or span of the great "Metalic Image;" and the measure of the period denominated by Christ, the times of the Gentiles. But that assumption is mistaken in every respect.

First. No such number as 2520 years is mentioned in that prophecy. This Mr. Faber himself admits, and he proposes to *add* that period to those which are given in that prophet, that he may have a number that will meet the demands of the Calendar he was about to frame, as "a gage" of the great image, and measure of the times of the Gentiles. He laid the foundation, therefore, as I shall show, of the structure he was about to rear with a consciousness that it was an assumption or theory for which he had no express warrant.

Next. But that is not the only reprehensible feature of his procedure; for he founds his representation that such a period is indicated in Daniel, on the false pretext that the seven times, ch. iv. 16, 23, 32, which are given as the period during which Nebuchadnezzar was to be driven from his court and dwell with the beasts of the field; are also given as a measure of the period symbolized by the great image. He says that number is specified by the prophet Daniel, but specified only after a mystical or typical fashion. The number is seven times, or 2520 days." That, however, is not only without authority, but is a gross misrepresentation of the words. To say that "the seven times" are used in a mystical or typical fashion, is to say that they are employed in the same relation as the twelve hundred and sixty days, and a time, times, and a half, are used, namely as symbols of a number of years, that corresponds to the number of days that are employed as the representative. For there is no other mode in which periods of time are used in a mystical way, as representatives of periods that differ from themselves, while they bear to them an analogy. But the seven times of Daniel iv, are not employed in that relation. They are expressly given as the period of Nebuchadnezzar's degradation from his regal station and banishment among the beasts of the field; and exclusively as the measure of that period. This will appear indubitably true as I advance in the analysis of the passage. That Mr. Faber wholly misrepresents the words, when he ascribes to them the office of a symbol, used on the principle of analogy, is seen from the facts;

First, That the words "seven times" of our version, answer exactly to the terms of the original, seven being a numeral, and *iddanin*, fixed and well-known periods of time; and mean, therefore, it is universally admitted, and by Mr. Faber himself, seven solar years. Vol. ii. pp. 23, 24.

Secondly, The seven times are not given as the measure in any sense of the age of the image. No such period nor any other exists in that vision, as literally or symbolically the measure of the ages during which the career of the four empires denoted by the four metals were to continue. There is no chronological element whatever in the dream. The periods through which the several dynasties symbolized in it were to exist, are concealed. There is nothing in the dream or the interpretation of it that can be made the ground of any determination respecting them; and this significant fact Mr. Faber well knew: for if the vision of the image presents any key to the range of time through which the four dynasties were to exist, why did he resort to the vision of the fourth chapter, which has no reference to that of the second, to wrench from it if he could some clue to what God has chosen to conceal? To take the seven times of Nebuchadnezzar's degradation, chapter iv., as the measure of the duration of the powers represented by the image, is therefore arbitrary, and a palpable violation of the prophecy. Mr. Faber can no more make them the measure of the image, than he can the 2300 days of the eighth chapter, or the time, times, and half a time of the twelfths.

Third, But beyond this, the terms "seven times" are not even applied to the *tree itself*, which was the great symbol of the vision, and the symbol of Nebuchadnezzar: nor are they applied to the stump and roots of the tree, which, as symbols of Nebuchadnezzar's continued life, were to be preserved from destruction, to show that he should be kept in life through his degradation, and at length be reinstated in his kingdom. They are applied exclusively to Nebuchadnezzar himself. It was not necessary to apply them to the tree in order to put a limit to the period in which the roots and stump were to remain in the ruin to which they were reduced; inasmuch as the office of the tree as a symbol, in being cut down, was simply to represent Nebuchadnezzar's dethronement; and the object of the preservation of the roots and stump in life, was to show that Nebuchadnezzar was to be kept in life till the time came for his restoration to his reason and his throne. The roots, stump, and stem, were not, at the end of his chastisement, to be restored to the life, greatness, and strength, in which they had flourished before the trunk was cut down, and its branches hewn off, in order to show that Nebuchadnezzar should in like manner be restored to his reason, his manliness, and the dignities and prerogatives of his regal office. His restoration to his senses, and to his throne were predicted without a symbol, in simple, unfigurative language. "And whereas they commanded to leave the stump of the tree-roots; thy kingdom shall be sure unto thee, after that thou shalt have known that the heavens do rule." The narrative of the fulfillment of the vision is in like manner given in simple language, without either symbol or figure. "At the same time my reason returned unto me, and for the glory of my kingdom, mine honor and brightness returned unto me; and my counsellors and my lords sought unto me, and I was established in my kingdom." The seven times thus, are not applied to the great symbols of the vision, to indicate the period during which the stem, and its roots should continue in their ruin; but are predicated exclusively of Nebuchadnezzar, in the vision itself, in its interpretation, and in the account given of its fulfillment. The language of the holy one who came down from heaven was, "Let *his heart* be changed from *man's*, and let a beast's heart be given unto *him;* and let seven times pass over *him.*" And in like manner in the explanation of the dream, the times are predicated only of Nebuchadnezzar. "This is the interpretation, O king; and this is the decree of the Most High, which is come upon my lord the king. They shall drive thee from men, and thy dwelling shall be with the beasts of the field, and they shall make thee to eat grass as oxen, and they shall wet thee with the dew of heaven; and *seven times shall pass over thee*, till thou know that the Most High ruleth in the kingdom of men, and giveth it to whomsoever he will." This predication of the seven times, exclusively of the person who was represented by the symbol of the vision, and its application to him alone, in the vision, interpretation, and history of the fulfillment, show in the most decisive manner, that that period was not used as a symbol, on the principle of analogy, to represent years by days, but was employed in its literal meaning, to denote seven natural years. Interpretations indeed are always given in simple language, never in symbols, which would themselves require interpretation, as much as that which they were employed to explain.

Fourth. Mr. Faber's construction implies, moreover, that the "seven times" are used with a double meaning; first, as literal, natural years, in their office as the measure of Nebuchadnezzar's degradation; and next, as a symbol on the principle of analogy, to denote a period that corresponds in the number of its years to the number of days embraced in seven years. For as they unquestionably are used in their literal sense in their application to Nebuchadnezzar, to express the period during which his humiliation was to continue; if they are also employed, as Mr. Faber affirms, to denote a period of 2520 years, they must have a double sense. Mr. Faber accordingly ascribes to them that two-fold meaning; and gives his sanction to the doctrine maintained by many of the writers who follow him in his theory of the wild beast, and in his chronology; that the chronological predictions generally have a double signification, and are to have a double accomplishment. But that is wholly unauthorized, and is a consummate misrepresentation and caricature of the prophecies; as I shall show in a later chapter.

Fifth. Mr. Faber, in assuming that the seven times of Nebuchadnezzar's humiliation, are symbols of the 2520 years, which he avers are the period through which the career of the four great empires is to extend, assumes that Nebuchadnezzar was himself, in his insanity, divestiture of power and degradation to the condition of a beast, a symbol of the rulers of those four empires through the period of 2520 years, during which he represents that their reign is to continue. For if he is not the symbol of those rulers; how can the period of his degradation be the symbol of an analogous period through which they were to be subjected to some similar condition? If his time represents theirs, nothing can be more certain than that he himself is their symbol, and his condition a symbol of their condition. If he did not stand in that relation to them, no connection could subsist between the seven years of his humiliation, and the 2520 years of their corresponding subjection to evil. Mr. Faber, indeed, not only assumes that Nebuchadnezzar was their symbol, but openly maintains it. Thus he says:

"The golden head is positively declared to be Nebuchadnezzar *himself*, in his quality of sovereign of the first empire. THOU *art this head of gold.* Hence the rise of the golden head is not the commencement of the Babylonian empire, like the ascent of the first great beast from the troubled seas, but the epoch is specifically limited to the age of the individual king, Nebuchadnezzar, so that the rise of the golden head is the rise of that particular monarch; and as the symbol is borrowed from the human form which is born and lives and dies, the rise of the golden head must coincide with the birth of Nebuchadnezzar, who is himself accordingly *the type or federal representative, or animating principle* of the four empires collectively shadowed out by the image. The true date, therefore, from which the age of the statue must be calculated as the Grand Prophetic Calendar, is the birth of the individual king, Nebuchadnezzar. Thou art this head of gold."—*Sac. Cal., vol. ii. p.* 6.

"The head of gold, as we are assured by Daniel, is Nebuchadnezzar himself. Hence, as the image, is an image of a man; and as the man, Nebuchadnezzar is the head or principle of the image, the human image in which according to the laws of nature the head is first protruded, must synchronize with the birth of *its type* the individual Nebuchadnezzar."—*Sac. Cal., vol. ii. pp.* 7, 8.

He thus openly asserts that Nebuchadnezzar was "the type or representative of the four empires shadowed out by the image;" and attempts to prove it by the fact that the image was a symbol of a succession of supreme rulers, of whom Nebuchadnezzar was the first. But how does the fact that Nebuchadnezzar was one of the personages symbolized by the image, show that he was in his place a type or symbol of the image and all that it denoted, any more than the fact that his successors, Evil Merodach his son, and Neriglissar his son-in-law, and Nabonadius his grandson, were also among those represented by the image, and by its golden head as well as himself? If his belonging to the train of monarchs whom the image represented, made him a symbol of the image and all that it denoted, then for the same reason every one in the succession of rulers of the four empires must have been a symbol of the image and all that it represented; and Mr. Faber confutes himself by proving that no such distinction belonged to Nebuchadnezzar as he assigns to him. If Mr. Faber's assumption is legitimate, Nebuchadnezzar stood on exactly the same level as every other supreme ruler in the four empires.

But what can transcend the senselessness of the pretext to which he resorts to prove that Nebuchadnezzar filled the symbolic office he ascribes to him, namely, that because the image was of the human form, it must be considered as originating in a birth!

The image presented itself to Nebuchadnezzar in a dream under the all-directing providence of the Almighty. It was not born of a mother. Who ever before imagined that mental conceptions and statues and pictures of the human form, beheld in dreams, or seen by the bodily eyes, are by the laws of nature born of mothers! Or who ever before gravely assumed and maintained that such mental conceptions and material statues and pictures must be considered as dated at the birth of the persons whom they represent! It is not consistent with the laws of nature, it seems, on Mr. Faber's theory, that imaginations or images should be formed of human beings in mature life! Such are the silly expedients on which he relies to give a color of truth to his lawless and self-confuting attempt to prove that Nebuchadnezzar was a symbol of the image, and all that was represented by it.

But in that pretext he implies and assumes that Nebuchadnezzar truly filled the office he ascribes to him; and thereby exhibits him as symbolizing the image and the rulers it represents, not only in the successful part of his career, but also in the catastrophes and indignities with which he was smitten. For his loss of his reason, his expulsion from his throne and his capital, and his degradation to the condition of a brute, must have been personated by him as to befall those whom he symbolized; as much as he represented them in his pre-eminence in genius, and his activity and splendor as a monarch and conqueror; and the period of his humiliation was a prophecy that the dishonors and miseries that were to befall them were to continue through the analogous period of two thousand five hundred and twenty years. And that implies that each one of the long line of those rulers was to be subjected to a degradation like that of the monarch of Babylon through a period of that length. For Nebuchadnezzar, if their symbol, must represent them, not in a mass, as though but a single individual; but as a series of individuals, each of whom was to suffer dethronement, insanity, and degradation to a level with the beasts for a period, as much longer than seven years, as 2520 years are longer than 2520 days. But what greater violation of the divine word was ever perpetrated, than that which Mr. Faber's construction thus involves? Or what more effective confutation of his boasted calendar of the prophecies, could he have devised? If each of the long line of rulers symbolized by the great image, some of whom probably have not yet entered into life, are to pass through a period of 2520 years of catastrophes and disgraces, before they reach the end of their career, his great almanac of the times of the Gentiles, instead of ending as he held in 1863, has 2500, 2600, and perhaps a longer course to run before it will arrive at its close.

Such are the overwhelming proofs that his chronology is founded on a supposititious ground. There is no such period known to the prophecy of Daniel, as 2520 years. Nebuchadnezzar is not employed as a symbol of the rulers of the four great empires denoted by the metalic Image. The dethronement and degradation of Nebuchadnezzar are not used in it as symbols of similar humiliations and disgraces that were to befall the rulers of those empires: and this is not only clear from the prophecy itself, but is placed beyond doubt, by the fact that no such catastrophes as overwhelmed the monarch of Babylon, have been experienced by the other individuals of the line denoted by the image. Mr. Faber's whole theory in respect to the "seven times," is thus a sheer fiction, got up for the purpose of framing a scheme of chronology, that should have the air of great exactitude, and be capable by false constructions of a seeming corroboration from the revelations that are recorded in Daniel.

2. He falls into equal errors and self-confutations, in his attempt to prove that the fictitious period of 2520 years, is the span of the great metalic image, or measure of the duration of the four great lines of rulers of the Gentile nations, symbolized by the image, and by the four great beasts of Daniel. He presents his theory in the following passages:—

"It is manifest that the sacred calendar, and great almanac of prophecy, is a prophetic chronology of times measured by the succession of Daniel's four principal kingdoms. Such being the case, the *length* of the sacred calendar, is the duration of those four kingdoms, under their scriptural aspect; or the duration of the life of the image, reckoned from the commencement of the golden head. . . . But the golden head is declared to be the individual Nebuchadnezzar himself. Therefore the great almanac commences with the *birth* of that prince. The *precise* year of his birth, *history does not determine;* but as the epoch of his reign and of his victories is well known, we may be sure from our knowledge of this epoch, that he must have been born in the course of the ten years, which elapsed between the years 658 and 646 before the Christian era. Hence it will follow that the great almanac of prophecy commenced at some point between those two years."—*Sac. Cal., Vol. i., pp.* 68, 69.

Here are several very important errors and self-contradictions. In the first place, he now represents his great calendar of 2520 years, as commencing at the *birth* of Nebuchadnezzar. But in his theory respecting the "seven times," he as explicitly exhibits the beginning of the seven years of Nebuchadnezzar's *exile* from his *palace* and *court*, as the commencement of the 2520 years. The seven times, he asserts, were the span of the great image, and measure of the duration of the four great empires. Here is a difference of eighty seven years, between his two dates; and as neither of them can be determined with exactness, and as it is indubitably certain, that neither of them was the commencement of the period of the image, his dates themselves, and their contradiction to each other vitiates the whole series of his calculations respecting the true place of the events that have followed to the present time. Whether he reckons the events of the first twelve hundred and sixty years from the birth of Nebuchadnezzar, or from his degradation to the condition of a brute; every one of them will be assigned to a wrong year; and whether he reckons from either of those dates to the beginning of his second twelve hundred and sixty years, his calculations will be equally uncertain and deceptive. Each of his estimates of the beginning of his great period, is thus wholly supposititious and demonstrably false.

In the next place. By his own admission, the precise year of the birth of Nebuchadnezzar, is unknown and indeterminable. He holds that it may have taken place in any one of the ten years that intervened between 658 and 646 before the Christian era. Every event the date of which is to be determined by its distance from his birth, is of course therefore involved in equal uncertainty. An almanac founded on such mere imaginary and false grounds, cannot be of any authority. To denominate it a sacred calendar of prophecy, is an offence to truth and decorum. In the third place. Mr. Faber offers a direct contradiction to the divine Word and to history, in referring the commencement of the four kingdoms to the birth of Nebuchadnezzar. That prince was not born the monarch of Babylonia, nor did he enter on that office until he was formally inaugurated as king a short time before the death of his father, which took place, it is generally held, within a year of his accession to the throne. His vision of the great image took place in the third year of his reign as sole monarch, probably in B.C. 602. The prophecy accordingly exhibits him, at the time of the vision, as the king of Babylonia, and in possession of all the powers and prerogatives that belong to a despotic monarch. No allusion is made to his birth, to his infancy or childhood, or to his becoming sole monarch on the decease of his father. "This is the dream, and we will tell the interpretation thereof before the king. Thou O king art a King of kings; for the God of heaven hath given thee a kingdom, power, and strength, and glory; and wheresoever the children of men dwell, the beasts of the field, and the fowls of the heaven, hath he given into thine hand, and hath made thee ruler over them all. Thou art this head of gold." Ch. ii. 36–38. It, therefore, was not until the time of the vision itself, or at least, not till he became the sole monarch of his empire, that the period began during which the head of gold represented him as the monarch of Babylon, and the time commenced, during which the rulers denoted by the image, were to exercise their sway. It was at the distance, therefore, from the latest year in which Mr. Faber holds it could have occurred, of at least forty years. He, however, refers it in his table of dates to the year 657 before Christ, which is fifty-three or four years before the date of the vision. This discrepancy with the prophecy again vitiates the whole series of his dates that depend on it, and postpones the close of his 2520 years half a century beyond the time to which he refers it.

3. The reason that Mr. Faber assigned the birth of Nebuchadnezzar to the interval between B. C. 658 and 646, was simply to place it back far enough to admit 1260 years after it, before the 1260 of Daniel vii. 25, commenced. His estimate of the date of Nebuchadnezzar's birth has no ground in history, but is in direct contradiction to Berosus, who as quoted by Josephus in Antiq. Judæorm, book x. c. xi., represents Nebuchadnezzar as only of mature age, instead of forty or fifty years at his father's death: and exhibits the death of the father as the effect of sickness, not of old age, as Mr. Faber maintains. Thus:

"When his father heard that the person who had been appointed Satrap in Egypt, Coele Syria and Phœnicia, had revolted from him, being himself still disabled by illness, he entrusted a part of the forces to his son Nebuchadnezzar, now of a mature age, and sent him against him. And Nebuchadnezzar meeting the rebel and making battle, conquered him, and from this beginning reduced the territory under his rule. But it happened about that time, that the father—Nabopolassar—having contracted a disease, died in the city of Babylon after he had reigned twenty-one years. And Nebuchadnezzar, on being apprised with little delay, of the death of his father, and having arranged affairs in Egypt and the neighboring regions, and given command that the Jewish, Phœnician, Syrian, and Egyptian captives should be conducted under a powerful guard to Babylon, he himself, with a few attendants, proceeded across the desert, to that city."*

The expression *εν ἡλικία,* here plainly denotes mature age, in contradistinction from such youthfulness as would have disqualified Nebuchadnezzar for the important command with which he was entrusted. The word sometimes denotes youth, sometimes mature age, as in the expression in John ix. 21., "he is of age, ask him," the meaning of which is, he is no longer a child; he has reached a time of life in which

* *Μέμνηται δὲ αὐτοῦ τῶν πράξεων καὶ Βηρωσσὸς ἐν τῆ τρίτη τῶν Χαλδαίκων ἱστοριῶν, λέγων οὕτως. Ακούσας δὲ ὁ πατὴρ αὐτοῦ Ναβουχοδονόσορος, ὅτι ὁ τεταγμένος σατράπης ἓν τε Αἰγύπτω, δὲ τοῖς περὶ τὴν Κοίλην Συρίαν, δὲ τὴν Φοινίκην τόποις ἀποστάτης αὐτοῦ γέγονεν, οὐ δυνάμενος αὐτὸς ἔτι κακοπάθειν, συστήσας τῶ υἱῶ Ναβουχοδονοσόρω ὄντι ἐν ἡλικία μέρη τινὰ τὴς δυνάμεως ἔπεμψεν ἐπ' αὐτὸν. Συμμίξας δὲ Νεβουχοδονόσορος τῶ ἀποστάτη καὶ παραταξάμενος αὐτοῦ τε ἐκράτησε; καὶ τὴν χώραν ἐκ ταύτης τῆς ἀρχῆς ὑπὸ τὴν αὐτοῦ Βασιλείαν ἐποιήσαται. Τῶ δὲ πατρὶ τῶ Νεβουχοδονοσόρω συνήβη κατ' αὐτὸν καιρὸν ἀῤῥωστήσαντι ἐν τῆ Βαβυλωνίων πόλει μεταλλάξαι τὸν βίον, ἔτη βασιλευσάντι εἴκοσι ἑν. Αἰσθόμενος δὲ μετ' οὐ πολὴν χρόνον τὴν τοῦ πατρὸς τελευτὴν Ναβουχοδονοσόρου, καὶ καταστήσας τὰ κατὰ τὴν Αἰγύπτον πράγματα, καὶ τὴν λοιπὴν χώραν, καὶ τοὺς αἰχμαλώτους Ἰουδαίων τὲ δε Φοινίκων, δὲ Σύρων, δὲ τῶν κατὰ τὴν Αἰγύπτον ἐθνῶν, ... αὐτὸς ὁρμήσας ὀλιγοστὸς διὰ τοῦ ἐρήμου παρεγένεται εἰς Βαβυλῶνα.—Josephus, Ant. Jud.,* lib. x. c. xi.

he is capable of giving a suitable answer to your questions. The expression, he is of age, in our idiom, is of the same import; denoting simply that he of whom it is affirmed has passed out of childhood and youth, and arrived at such maturity as to fit him to act for himself. That this is the true meaning of the word, Mr. Faber was unquestionably aware; but he attempts to conceal his misrepresentation of it as denoting forty or fifty years of age by saying, "it is ambiguous, but the context sufficiently determines the import;" and proceeds to wrench it into a direct confirmation of his theory. He says, "It seems then, according to Berosus, that the elder Nebuchadnezzar was a *very old and infirm man when he* made his son colleague, and that the younger Nebuchadnezzar was at that time in mature age. Hence, if we suppose the father to have been between seventy and eighty years old at the time of his death, and the son (agreeably both to the age of his father, and to the phraseology of Berosus), to have been from forty to fifty years old at the time of his association in the empire; we shall make the birth of Nebuchadnezzar to have occurred some time between the years before Christ 658, and 646." *Sac. Cal. Vol. ii. pp.* 8, 9.

Here are thus two palpable misrepresentations fabricated for the purpose of giving an air of truth to his arbitrary theory in respect to the birth of Nebuchadnezzar: first, in the pretext that according to Berosus, Nabopolassar was a very old and infirm—

that is—decrepit man at the appointment of his son as colleague. There is not a hint in Berosus to that effect: Instead, he expressly says that Nabopolassar was in ill health, and that he had contracted a disease of which he died. But old age is not a disease; nor is the fact that a person dies of a disease, as of a fever, any proof or sign that he is old and infirm. Berosus accordingly confutes Mr. Faber in place of yielding him any support. Next. He is guilty of a falsification of the expresson ἐν ἡλικία, in mature age,in representing it as showing from the context, that Nebuchadnezzar in being of mature age, was forty or fifty years old. The object of Berosus in applying to him that term, manifestly was merely to show that he was not so young as to be inadequate to the command of the army and government of the provinces, with which he was intrusted. Had he been forty or fifty years old, it would have been a reflection on him to have said that he was of age: as it would have implied that he was tardy in reaching a competency for the high office he was called to fill. Such are the unscrupulous artifices to which Mr. Faber resorted to give an aspect of truth to the most unpardonable fictions on which he built his chronology.

He falls into an error also, in his representation that the times of the Gentiles are identically the same in their commencement and duration, as the period of the four great empires symbolized by the image. It is not a point indeed of much moment, except as it exemplifies the inaccuracy and unreliableness that mark his speculations generally in respect to periods and events. There is nothing in the words of Christ respecting the times of the Gentiles, nor in any part of the Old or New Testament, that implies that the period designated by those words, is the same in beginning and duration, as the period of the four great empires. The prediction, "And Jerusalem shall be trodden down by the Gentiles, till the times of the Gentiles shall be completed;" implies that they are a period that derives a special characteristic from the supremacy of the Gentiles over the people of Israel; and that they are foreshown in the ancient prophets, in predictions that are to have a specific fulfillment. The times of the Gentiles will reach their end when the great events take place which it is predicted in the Old Testament, are to mark their close. But no intimation is given that they are identically the same, as the times of the four great Gentile empires. So far from it, they are clearly foreshown in the Pentateuch, in a form that renders it manifest that they began centuries before Nebuchadnezzar was represented by the golden head of the image. The great characteristic of the times of the Gentiles, is, that they are the times in which the Gentiles were to domineer over the people of Israel, conquer their territory, demolish their cities, and carry them captive into distant lands, where they were to hold them in a degrading and torturing bondage, till the time of their redemption. But those characteristics have not been confined to the period of the four great empires. They began far earlier in the invasion of Israel by the neighboring nations, and exercise over them of a despotic and crushing rule, while they remained in their own land. "And if ye shall despise my statutes, or if your soul abhor my judgments, so that ye will not do all my commandments; I also will do this unto you: ye shall sow your seed in vain, for your enemies shall eat it; and ye shall be slain before your enemies; they that hate you shall reign over you; and I will bring a sword upon you that shall avenge the quarrel of my covenant; and ye shall be delivered into the hand of the enemy; and I will destroy your high places, and cut down your images; and I will make your cities waste, and bring your sanctuaries into desolation." Levit. xxvi. 15–31. All these were evils with which they were to be smitten by foreign nations while they continued in their own land. Then follow predictions of their being carried into exile; and the occupation of their desolated inheritances by enemies and foreigners: "And I will bring the land into desolation, and your enemies who dwell therein shall be astonished at it. And I will scatter you among the heathen, and will draw out a sword after you; and your land shall be desolate, and your cities waste," vs. 32, 33. There are similar predictions also, Deut. xxviii. 36, 49, 64. "The Lord shall bring thee, and thy king which thou shalt set over thee, unto a nation which neither thou nor thy fathers have known, and there shalt thou serve other gods, wood, and stone. The Lord shall bring a nation against thee from far, from the end of the earth, as the eagle flieth; a nation whose tongue thou shalt not understand. And he shall besiege thee in all thy gates, until thy high and fenced walls come down wherein thou trustedst throughout all thy land. And the Lord shall scatter thee among all people, from the one end of the earth, even unto the other; and there thou shalt serve other gods which neither thou, nor thy fathers have known;—wood and stone." These predictions of conquests and oppressions by enemies while they continued in possession of their land, unquestionably had a large fulfillment before the commencement of the period of the four great empires. It is equally indubitable that the predictions of their being carried into captivity by nations whose gods of wood and stone they should serve, had their accomplishment before the Babylonian exile; inasmuch as the effect of that terrible chastisement was to recall them from the worship of idols. And we know that they had a fearful verification in the ten tribes who, after repeated invasions, were carried into exile, partly one hundred and thirty-eight, and partly one hundred and nineteen years before the powers symbolized by the image began their career; and losing their knowledge of Jehovah, soon became the worshipers of the gods of the Gentiles, with whom they seem to have become indistinguishably intermixed. It is not to be supposed that that captivity of the ten tribes by the Assyrians, and abandonment by the Most High as his people, that have now continued for more than twenty-five centuries, and proved a far more fatal infliction, than what befell the tribes of Judah, Benjamin, and Levi under the Babylonians and Romans, were not contemplated in the denunciations of evil on them in Leviticus and Deuteronomy. Instead, as those stupendous inflictions formed a chief part of the chastenings with which it was the purpose of God that they should be smitten by the hands of the Gentiles, their period is unquestionably included in the times of the Gentiles. And this is rendered indubitable by the revelations that are made in the Old Testament, that at the time when the domination of the Gentiles is to come to its end, the ten tribes are to be recalled to their ancient land, and to their relations to God as his chosen people, as surely as the tribes of Judah, Benjamin and Levi are. When the Redeemer comes to Sion and turns away ungodliness from Jacob, *all Israel* shall be saved. Romans xi. 26.

Mr. Faber is, therefore, wholly mistaken in his representation that the times of the Gentiles are limited to the period of the four great empires; and the pompous parade he makes of the important place he assigns them in his almanac of prophecy, is an unfortunate exemplification of the want of accuracy that reigns throughout his speculations in reference to the prophesies.

5. He is mistaken in his judgment of the date of the delivery of the times, the laws, and the saints into the power of the little horn.

The question whether the date to which Mr. Faber refers the delivery of the saints, and the times, and laws into the hands of the little horn of Daniel vii. 25, is important, as on it the truth or falsehood turns of his estimates of all the subsequent events which he reckons from that act; especially the time when, as he holds, the period symbolized by the twelve hundred and sixty days, is to end.

He refers the investiture of the pope and his hierarchies—the power symbolized by the horn—with authority over the laws and the saints, to the year A.D. 604: and chiefly on the assumption that in that year, on the seeming conversion of Ethelbert, king of Kent, the whole of the kings of the kingdoms into which the western Roman empire was divided, had embraced the Catholic faith, and yielded their assent to the claims which were made by the pope and his clergy, to supreme authority in religion. But the delivery of the laws and saints into the hands of the pope and his hierarchies, did not take place in the conversion of the monarchs and princes to belief in the Catholic religion; nor in their simply assenting to the lofty claims of the Romish ecclesiastics to authority over the faith and worship of the church; but was a *decretive* or *legislative* act of the monarchs and princes of each kingdom, to whom the power belonged, by which the Catholic church was legalized and made the ally and instrument of the state, and the officials of the church were invested with special rights, and clothed with authority to enforce their doctrines and ceremonies on their subjects by penalties. This is clear from the fact, that the assumed right of the church to persecute dissentients, was derived in all cases, from the civil power; and that power was in all instances, the executor of the decrees of the pope, the hierarchies, and the synods, against the property, the liberty, and the lives of those who were sentenced by them to punishment. But the legalization, and nationalization of the church in a state did not necessarily take place immediately on the conversion of the monarch and his court. It perhaps was not then anticipated, nor contemplated by them until some special exigency called for their intervention, to give effect to the will of the church. That the Catholic church was not nationalized in Kent, in England, in the year A.D. 604, by being made the state church, and invested with power to persecute, is abundantly certain; *first*, from the consideration that there is no record in the histories of the period, of any such act on the part of Ethelbert and his court: Instead, the king's measures were merely those of *toleration* and *friendliness* to Augustin and his associates. Though he retained for a time, his attachment to his Pagan deities, he gave the missionaries liberty to remain in the kingdom and to preach their doctrines to his people; promised them protection; made provision for their support; and appropriated to their use an ancient monastery of the Britons: In the course of the next year the king professed himself a convert to the new religion, and with many of his subjects received the rite of baptism. But no laws were passed investing Augustin and his compeers with power to compel those who continued to be Pagans to unite in the Catholic worship, nor to punish them for their persistence in their idolatry. Both classes were tolerated by the government. Nor were any measures resorted to by the king, to compel the native British Christians, of whom there were many, to conform in their faith and worship to the doctrines and observances of the Catholic party. There were no doctrinal differences between them to be the occasion of controversy and persecution. The only point on which they were not in agreement with each other, related to Easter. *Next*, That there was no nationalization of the church in Kent at that period, is clear, moreover, on Mr. Faber's own theory, from the consideration that, if the delivery of the laws and the saints into the power of the horn, had been consummated at that epoch, the twelve hundred and sixty years of the horn's supremacy and persecution of the true worshipers, would have terminated in the year 1863. For he dated the commencement of the Gentile period in the year 657, before Christ, and as expressly assigned its completion to the year 1863. But we know that that period did not terminate in that year. No persecution and slaughter of the witnesses, which are immediately to follow the close of the twelve hundred and sixty years, took place at that time; no signals appeared that the times of the Gentiles, which Mr. Faber held were to expire at the same moment, had reached their end. The non-occurrence of these, as well as many other events that are to precede, or attend the close of the twelve hundred and sixty years, demonstrates, in the most emphatic manner, that his theory in regard to the beginning and end of the domination of the papal power over the true worshipers, is totally mistaken; a sheer, and undisguised figment, without any authority from the word of God, and against the most indubitable facts of history. *Thirdly.* That there was nothing beyond a mere toleration of the Catholic church, during the reign of Ethelbert, which continued to the year 616; is clear also from the fact that paganism was equally permitted and protected during that period; and that his son Eadbald, who succeeded him on the throne, for a time renounced the Catholic religion and reverted to paganism, without any change of the laws. The worship of idols was as consistent, therefore, with the laws of the kingdom as the profession was of the Catholic faith. This is confirmed by the fact, that Redwald the king of East Anglia, who succeeded Ethelbert as Bretwalda of the Angles, was so far from a true faith in the Catholic religion, that he undertook to blend the two worships in the same temple; by placing an altar of Woden by the side of an altar dedicated to the God of the Christians. Nothing can be more certain, therefore, than that there was then no law of the realm that gave the Catholics an exclusive right to offer worship, or any precedence in rank or privilege over those enjoyed by the worshipers of idols. And this toleration of both religions continued for a long period; as is manifest, from the fact, that Edwin of Northumbria, who succeeded Redwald as Bretwalda, and held the office seventeen years, continued in the practice of paganism during most of that period; that it was not till the reign of Oswald, who next held the office of Bretwalda, that the Northumbrians were generally led to embrace the Catholic faith; and that paganism did not fall till the death of Penda, the king of Mercia, in A.D. 655, when under the auspices of Oswio then Bretwalda, the Mercians were converted, and the homage of idols was in the main discontinued; except in the small realm of Sussex, which had never been unpaganized; and of Kent which had long before returned from its nominal conversion under Augustin, to its former addiction to the worship of idols. It is indisputable therefore that there was no general conversion either of the rulers or the people of England to the Romish church, until after the middle of the seventh century; and no nationalization of the church and investiture of it with the power that was given to the little horn, until after that date. When that investiture took place, or when the persecution of dissentients from the Catholic faith commenced, there are no means of determining. The war of the horn on the witnesses of Jesus began probably in some of the other kingdoms of western Europe at an earlier day than in England, but what the date was of the first persecution, is unknown and indeterminable. The time accordingly, when the twelve hundred and sixty years, which are the period of the horn's persecuting career, began, is not only unknown, but is shrouded beyond the possibility of discovery, until it shall be indicated by the occurrence of the events, which it is foreshown are to signalize its close. Mr. Faber's attempt to prove that it had its beginning in the year A.D. 604, is indubitably, therefore, an entire failure, and stamps his scheme again as a consummate misrepresentation and caricature alike of the Word of God and the facts of history.

I might point out other fatal errors in his chronology, but it is unnecessary. I have shown by ample proofs that the whole of his calculations respecting the great prophetic periods, and the time when the present dispensation is to close, are wholly false. It will be seen in the chapters that follow, that with his chronology the speculations fall also which he and others found on it respecting Louis Napoleon, and the agencies and catastrophes which they prognosticate of him as the imagined seventh head of the beast, the patron and persecutor of the Jews, and the Antichrist, who is to perish at the battle of Armageddon.

To verify the foregoing statements respecting the conversion of the Angles, by quotations, would require too much space. They are founded on the testimony of Bede in his Hist. Gentis Anglorum. I give a few passages.

1. That Ethelbert merely *tolerated* Augustin and his monks is seen from Book i., c. 25. "We are not disposed to molest you, but rather to receive you with hospitality, and supply you with the food you need: Nor will we prevent any from joining you whom you are able to win by your preaching."

2. He engaged that no one should be compelled to embrace the new faith. Those only were to enter the Christian society, who were prompted to it by conviction and desire. Book i., c. 26.

3. On the death of Ethelbert in A.D. 616, Eadbald his son who succeeded to the sceptre, refused to accept the Christian faith. At the same time the

sons of Saberct, who held the throne of the East Saxons, openly gave leave to their subjects to worship idols, and drove the bishops and their adherents from the kingdom. Book ii., c. 5.

4. The Saxon princes refusing obedience to Eadbald, Redwald the king of East Anglia became Bretwalda, or head of the heptarchy: and renouncing the faith in Christianity he had once professed, undertook to unite paganism and the Christian worship in the same temple, by placing a small altar for victims to demons, by the side of that on which oblations were to be presented to Christ. Book ii., c. 15.

5. Edwin of Northumbria, who succeeded Redwald as Bretwalda, did not embrace the Christian faith until the eleventh year of his reign and the sixth before his death in A.D. 633. Book ii. c. 14, 15, 20.

6. On the death of Edwin, Oswald a Christian prince, succeeded to the throne of Northumbria and becoming Bretwalda, induced a large share of the Northumbrians to renounce idolatry and join in the worship of Christ. Book iii., c. 1, 2.

7. On the death in A.D. 640, of Eadbald, the son of Ethelbert, and a pagan, Earconberct inherited the sceptre, and was the first of the Anglo kings who renounced and destroyed the idols through his whole kingdom. Book iii., c. 8.

8. In A.D. 653, the Eastern Saxons, who had renounced the Christian faith, under Sigberct accepted it again. Book iii., c. 22.

9. On the death of Oswald, Oswio of Northumbria became Bretwalda, and conquering Penda, the Pagan chief of the Mercians, in A.D. 655, and incorporating the territory in his own dominions, the Mercians abandoned their idols, and joined the ranks of the church. Book iii., c. 24.

10. In A.D. 665, Sigher, king of the Eastern Saxons, among whom Christianity was introduced under Ethelbert, renounced the Christian faith, and with his nobles undertook to restore the deserted temples of Paganism, and renew the worship of images. Book iii., c. 30.

11. At length in A.D. 669, the races of the Angles, generally, wherever settled, embraced the Catholic rule of life; that is, asceticism, monkery, and the homage of relics; and observed the canonical mode of celebrating Easter: And Theodore, the archbishop, was the first to whom all the churches of the Angles gave the fraternal hand. Never before were there happier times from the first arrival of the Angles in Britain. Book iv., c. 2.

12. Ædilred, king of the Mercians, in A.D. 676, invaded and devastated Canterbury, desecrated the churches and monasteries, and put the population of a considerable city to the sword. He and his army must, therefore, have been contemners and enemies of the Christians. Book iv., c. 12.

13. In A.D. 681, Vilfrid, who had been driven from York, his bishopric, and for a time left England,

at length returned and established himself in the province of the South Saxons, and converted that people who had before lived in the practice of idolatry, to the worship of Jehovah. Book iv., c. 13.

14. In A.D. 686, through the labors of Vilfrid, the population of the small island Vecta, which had before been wholly devoted to idolatry, were won to the faith of the gospel. Book iv., c. 16.

Ninety years thus passed from the arrival of Augustin in Kent, before the struggle between Paganism and the Catholic faith reached its close. When the new doctrine obtained a commanding supremacy and gave its character to the religion of the nation, it is not possible to decide: It plainly was not till late in the seventh century

CHAPTER V.

The principal writers who have embraced Mr. Faber's theory respecting the wild beast; and his chronology; and who hold with him that Louis Napoleon is symbolized by the seventh head of the beast, and is to be the Antichrist.

For my knowledge of some of the writers who cherish these false views, I am indebted to Mr. Baxter's volume, entitled "Louis Napoleon, the destined Monarch of the World, and Personal Antichrist;" fourth edition, issued by Appleton & Co., and other publishers, in 1863. He gives the names of more than twenty authors who have treated of the theme. With the most important of them I am familiar, and shall directly cite their pages. Mr. Frere, in his "Combined View of the Prophecies," printed in 1814, six years after Mr. Faber's first publication on the subject, and issued again in 1815, expressed the belief that Napoleon Buonaparte was the seventh head of the wild beast. On the fall and death of that personage, and assumption of the French sceptre by Louis Napoleon, he pronounced him an eighth head of the beast, and with an affectation of prophetic foresight, attempted to foreshow what were to be the great events of his career and its final catastrophe. Dr. Burgh, a clergyman of the English Establishment, published in 1830–1832, a series of Lectures on the Second Advent, in which he maintained that the seventieth week of Daniel was still future; and that the prince that was to come, instead of Titus, is "the last enemy of the Jewish people, the last invader of the holy city, and the Antichrist." A volume of Lectures on the Hopes of the Church was given to the public by J. Darby, in 1842, in which he advocates the futurist, or literal day interpretation of the great periods of the prophesies; and maintains that Daniel's seventieth week is still future, and is to be the last in this dispensation. Sir Edward Denny published in 1845, "A Companion to the Chart of the Seventy Weeks," in which he advances the same views respecting the seventieth week; but holds that the prince that was to come, is the power that is symbolized by the little horn of the beast; and will profess himself to be the Messiah of the Jews: and will perish at the battle of Armageddon. In 1846 S. P. Tregelles, D.D., the editor of Bagster's editions of the Scriptures, published a volume on Daniel, in which he asserts the futurity of Daniel's seventieth week, denies that the periods of time given in the prophesies of Daniel and John, are employed in the relation of analogy, as symbols of larger periods than they themselves literally express; and not only affirms that the prince who was to come, has not appeared on the earth; but avows his belief that all the great acts of the Messiah, spoken of in Dan. ix. 24, "to finish transgression; to make an end of sin; to make reconciliation for iniquity; and to bring in everlasting righteousness," are still *future*. In 1846 Mr. H. Kelsall put forth a volume on Antichrist, in which he advances essentially the same views of the seventieth week of Daniel, of the prince that was to come, and of the part he is to act as Antichrist. The Rev. C. Maitland issued, in 1849, a volume on "The Apostolic School of Interpretation," in which he unfolds at large essentially the same theory. In 1849, the Rev. B. W. Newton published a volume on "The Prospects of the Ten Kingdoms," and in 1863 a second edition, in which he advocates substantially the same views, and treats at length of the main questions which the theory involves. In 1857–8 a still more important work, in three volumes, was presented to the public by Mr. Beale, a Cambridge Master of Arts, under the title of "Armageddon;" in which the most positive and ultra of the views of the party are asserted, respecting "the year day fulfillment of the prophesies that relate to the papal Antichrist and the Gentile church, and their subsequent literal day accomplishment in Louis Napoleon the Personal Antichrist, and the Jewish church;" and other topics that belong to the general theme. Another voluminous writer on the subject, the Rev. R. A. Purdon, a clergyman of the Church of England, has published a monthly pamphlet on prophetic subjects for several years, and was among the first to announce distinctly and confidently that Louis Napoleon is the person who is to reveal himself as the Antichrist; his original declaration to that effect having been made in December, 1849, after the election of Louis Napoleon to the presidency of the republic of France. His subsequent writings have been devoted largely to the evolution and support of his views respecting the political and spiritual dominion, which he persuades himself that emperor is to acquire throughout the world.

I might enlarge this catalogue of writers who have embraced the great features of this system, and treated it in its chief aspects; but these are enough to show that it has in a degree been before the churches in Great Britain for more than half a century; and that within the last twenty years it has been largely and earnestly discussed, and has attracted the interest and concurrence of a considerable body of readers. I present a few passages to indicate the attitudes in which they present the subject, and the confidence with which they affirm and argue; and the extraordinary self-possession with which they run into the most discreditable blunders, and put forth the most unfortunate misrepresentations.

The following passages are from Mr. Frere's Comb. View, issued in 1814, and republished in the following year:—

"I conceive that Buonaparte will not only revive the title of emperor of the Romans, but will actually make Rome the place of his residence. This difficulty 'respecting the seventh and eighth head of the beast,' does not arise from the prophecy's being yet unaccomplished, but from an erroneous interpretation having been given to the symbol of the beast of the bottomless pit, by means of which the passage is made to represent the Roman *empire* as becoming a *king:* whereas nothing can be more intelligible than this prophecy, when the new meaning" —advanced by Mr Frere—"is adopted; for it then declares that *the spiritual beast of infidelity*, the infidel power of the Apocalypse embodied in an individual, or the infidel king of Daniel, having been the seventh head of the Roman empire as king of Italy, will also be the eighth head in another capacity, and probably therefore with the title of emperor of Rome."

He adds in a note. "This prophecy which leads us to infer that Buonaparte will become emperor of Rome, is so confirmed by other circumstantial prophetic evidence, that I do not hesitate to avow my conviction of the certainty of the event; although he is at this time so situated (in Elba,) as in appearance to render such an event highly improbable. Having, however, more than a year ago, *foreseen* and *declared* from the prophetic writings, the reverses which France would undergo, and which she has since sustained, as well as the termination of her tyrannical career, and the future removal of the empire of Buonaparte from France to Italy, I see nothing in his present circumstances but what has a direct tendency to the accomplishment of the prophecies so understood. Three or four years will show how far I am correct in my views, and I wish now to record my opinion that it may hereafter become an evidence of the clearness and precision of the prophetic writings."—P. 105–6.

This is written with the air of one who deems himself raised up by Providence, and endowed with a prophetic foresight, that he might make known to the church the import of an important symbol, of which it had lost the true meaning; and apprise it of the approach of great events, as they were about to take place. He reveals that feature of delusion, without reserve, in the preface of his Three Letters republished in 1859.

"The present critical state of the times and the excitement prevailing in men's minds, while looking for the things that are coming on the earth, naturally induce the author of the following pages to make another attempt to call the attention of the church, and of the public, to the result of his *prophetic labors*, which have enabled him principally through the means of a new system of apocalyptic arrangement, and the adoption of a more stringent rule of interpretation, than commentators have hitherto followed, *not only to make known during the last forty-five years the general course of predicted events*, but also at every critical period, to verify the truth of his system, by calling attention to the particular prophecy next about to receive its fulfillment."—P. 1.

This presumptuous and boastful spirit, which had its origin on the one side, in a profound ignorance of the teachings of the divine Word, and the principles on which it is to be interpreted; and on the other, in a blind and towering self-conceit; reigns in a great measure through his writings. Instead of any indications that he enjoyed special divine guidance, his vaunted predictions bespeak an extraordinary measure of misapprehension and infatuation; and had met, long before the republication of his letters, in 1859, from the events of Providence, the most overwhelming confutation. Thus Napoleon Buonaparte never became emperor of the Romans; and never made Rome his capitol nor his residence. There is no "spiritual beast of infidelity" spoken of in the Apocalypse; nor an "infidel power" exhibited there as "embodied in an individual;" neither is there any intimation in that prophecy that "the seventh head of the Roman empire as king of Italy," is also to become "an eighth head in another capacity." There is no allusion in the Apocalypse to a seventh, an eighth, or any other head of the Roman empire; nor to an eighth head of the wild beast. No eighth head is ever to rise on that symbol. Mr. Frere mistakes a head for the eighth king, who is to be represented by the beast in its last form. Napoleon Buonaparte was not an infidel king, as Mr. Frere represents. The renunciation of Christianity by the French legislature and nation, took place before he rose to power; and instead of concurring in it, on his gaining the throne, he felt so deeply the necessity of a State religion, that he re-nationalized the Catholic church, that he might employ it as an ally in the education and control of his people, who he saw if left without religion, would neither have the intelligence nor the conscience that are requisite to an effective and stable government. These consummate blunders are specimens of the utter want of an accurate knowledge of the prophesies which Mr. Frere affects to interpret by a special gift of inspiration; and of the wild misrepresentations of the facts of history, that mark his volumes on these subjects.

The following citation is from Sir E. Denny's Companion to the Chart of Seventy Weeks, quoted by Mr. Baxter:—

"This great septenary period is divided into three distinct parts: Seven weeks; threescore and two weeks; and one week; the first two of which follow in due continuous order, without interruption. Whereas, between the last two, namely, the three score and two weeks, and the one week, a long interval occurs; these last two being separated, the one from the other, by the whole period of Israel's dispersion.

"The period of sixty-nine weeks begins B. C. 457; and as to the point in history when it was to end, we find that sixty-nine weeks out of the seventy, should elapse before the Messiah should be come; that is, I believe, before he should be offered to Israel. I feel no hesitation in placing the end of this period, namely, the seven weeks, and threescore and two weeks, just at the point where John the Baptist began to tell of him who was coming, *before* he actually appeared on the scene.

"And after the threescore and two weeks, shall Messiah be cut off, but not for himself. On hastily reading this passage, one would naturally suppose that the Lord was cut off at the *close* of this period. But in these words the preposition *after* is indefinite. We do not read *immediately* after; as if at the end of the period exactly. It was at the termination of this period that John the Baptist appeared as the prophet—the Elias of his day—announcing the coming Messiah. Between Messiah's announcement by John, and his death, an interval elapsed of seven years—or a week—divided into two equal parts; the first three years and a half being the time of John's mission:—the next that of Jesus Christ himself.

"This *unnoticed week*, as I term it, of the Messiah's rejection, is left *an utter blank* in the prophecy. . . The week of proffered blessing, was, as it were, altogether *cancelled and blotted out.* The one week of this prophecy will come in *at the end of the Christian dispensation*, to complete the full term of seventy weeks, and to supply the place of *the forfeited week.*

"The last week of Daniel, thus detached from the rest, being the great crisis in the history of the world, previous to the setting up of the kingdom, the period of Israel's ripened apostasy, will be one of deep and awful interest, of unparalleled judgment: and between this and the forfeited week, there will be a sort of moral *coincidence*, as well as of palpable *contrast:* inasmuch, as one was the period when the true Messiah came forth and was rejected; the other will be a time when the *false Messiah* will rise and be received by the Jews as the hope of their nation". . "And *the people* of the prince that shall come, shall destroy the city. The prince that shall come on the other hand, is the last head or king of this very same people: the same as the little horn which Daniel beheld in his vision come forth out of the head of the great Roman beast; who in the last day, when Israel shall have filled up their sin, in owning him *as their king* —their *promised Messiah*, will be used as a scourge more fearful by far than Nebuchadnezzar or Titus, or any of those who have trodden Jerusalem down from the very beginning. Such is the one who in the latter day will arise, and as we read in the prophecy, will enter into a covenant for one week with the deluded nation of Israel, who will *present himself* to them, and be *received* as *the expected Messiah;* and then in the end, be used as a means of chastising that nation, who slew the Lord when he came."—*Cited by Mr. Baxter*, pp. 195–199.

Here is a singular group of defects and errors. It is an important indication of the inaccuracy of his views, that they rest for their support on his mere advocacy of them. No authentic and decisive proofs are alleged by him to verify any one of them. They are merely assumed and asserted, not demonstrated; though he professes to found them on the express word of God. But beside the omission of legitimate proofs, he falls into palpable mistakes on every one of the chief points which he advances.

1. Thus he represents the whole period of Israel's dispersion as intervening between the sixty and two weeks and the seventieth week; although the ten tribes were carried into exile more than seven centuries and a half before Christ's crucifixion. The two tribes were also led captive to Babylon more than six hundred years before his death. If Sir Edward refers to the dispersion of the Jews by the Romans under Titus; not an hour of that period was included in the week in which Christ closed his mission on the cross. It was not till near thirty years after, that Jerusalem was captured, and those who survived the siege were sold into slavery, and distributed into different parts of the empire.

2. He is mistaken in assigning to John the Baptist a ministry of three years and a half; and representing it as wholly antecedent to Christ's ministry. The period of John's ministry was but about a year and a half; and his imprisonment was also for a like time, or near that period. Only three years, therefore, intervened between the commencement of his

4*

mission and his death; and two years to two and a half of that period were concurrent with Christ's ministry.* This misrepresentation is of moment, as it is a specimen of the manner in which the facts of history are wrested, to suit the exigencies of this theory. The object of the statement that John's ministry began after the sixty-ninth week had reached its end, and that it extended through three and a half years, was to open the way for the pretext that the death of Christ did not take place till after the close of the seventieth week: that he might affirm, as he does, that that week was "cancelled and blotted out." For if the sixty-ninth week had expired, when John began his mission, and Christ's ministry began at the termination of his, at the close of the first half of the fourth year, and continued till the seventh year had passed, as that year was, in the order of time, the four hundred and ninetieth, it is plain that Christ cannot have been crucified until after the seventieth week. But that is in the most direct contradiction to the testimony of the Evangelists, who represent his crucifixion as taking place under Pontius Pilate, and in the fourth year before that to which that procurator's death is referred by the Roman historians; and therefore in the seventieth week.

3. Some of his expressions imply that he admits that the Messiah was in truth put to death; yet in

* See Robinson's Harmony of the Gospels, pp. 7-10, and pp. 189, 196.

his denial, on the one side, that his crucifixion took place in the week that followed the sixty-ninth; and his assertion on the other, that the preposition *after*, in the expression "and after sixty and two weeks shall Messiah be cut off," is *indefinite*, and does not mean, in the seventieth week that directly followed the sixty-ninth, he exhibits it as uncertain when his death did take place. But that is equivalent to representing that we in fact have no evidence that he was really put to death. For we have no proof of his crucifixion, except that first of the New Testament, which refers his death to the reign of Tiberius, and the procuratorship of Pontius Pilate, both of whom died in the fourth year after the date which the Gospels assign to his crucifixion; and next, of later Greek and Roman writers, whose testimony renders it clear that his crucifixion took place at the close of the first half of his thirty-fourth year; which was the end of the first half of Daniel's seventieth week. To deny or impeach the truth of this representation, is in effect to deny, not only that we have any means of determining the date of Christ's crucifixion, but that we have any certainty that he was ever subjected to death on the cross.

4. He gives no proof of his representation, that the prince who he holds is to come at the close of this dispensation, is to be a *false Messiah;* and is to present himself to the Jews, and be received by them in that character. There is not the slightest intima-

tion in Daniel that the prince who was to come, and whose people were to destroy the Sanctuary, and the city, was to be a false Messiah, and was to be received by them, as their promised Deliverer and King. No one could frame a more groundless and arbitrary fiction. Nor is there any intimation in the Scriptures, that the eighth king, who is also called the beast in its last form, or that the man of Sin and Son of perdition, is to be a false Messiah, and to be received as such, by either Jews or Gentiles. So far from it, that great conspirator is expressly exhibited on the one hand, as claiming that he is himself God, and exalting himself, as above the Most High; and on the other, as waging a direct war on the Redeemer and his armies, in the hope of striking his kingdom from the earth. His aim, indeed, is, by exterminating Christ's party, to prove that there *is no Messiah* of the Jews, nor Saviour of the Gentiles, but that he himself holds the supreme dominion of the world.

I might point out other errors in the passages I have quoted; but the proofs I have given that he is involved in the most extraordinary and fatal mistakes in all his principal views, are sufficient to show that he is at a very unfortunate distance from a just knowledge of the subjects he attempts to treat.

The following passage is from Mr. Kelsall's volume on Antichrist, published in 1846:

"At first the Prince, Antichrist, makes a treaty or covenant with the Jews for one seven, or hebdomad—the last of the seventy weeks of Daniel ix. 27; but after making this seven years' covenant, he will break it in the midst, and cause the sacrifice and oblation to cease; after which the period for the exercise of his open blasphemy exactly corresponds with the time, times and half, of Daniel vii., at the commencement of which, the abomination of desolation is to be set up, and the worship of him and his image continue until the time of fulfillment. The abomination of desolation is probably the image, endowed by Satan with the power of speech and breath, or life (Rev. xiii. 15). . . . This is the point of time when Antichrist breaks his covenant in the midst of seven years, and when the two witnesses (Rev. xi. 3) make their appearance in Jerusalem. Forty-two months are therefore left for the completion of these wonders. About the same time as the two witnesses (probably Elias and Moses), there will appear in Jerusalem a false prophet, who will be empowered to perform astonishing miracles. He will cause an image of Antichrist to be set up in the sanctuary, which by the agency of Satan, he will be enabled to endow with life and speech. This image seems to be typified in Daniel iii. He will require every man to worship this image, and to receive a mark in his forehead, or on his right hand, as a token that he acknowledges Antichrist as God, and he will cause to be put to death all who refuse to receive the mark."—*Baxter*, *pp.* 208, 209.

We have here another exemplification of the wild and preposterous manner in which this school of writers misrepresent and pervert the Scriptures, in order to give their groundless system a color of support from their teachings.

1. After the manner of those I have before quoted, he gives not a syllable of confirmation to any one of his statements. They are uttered as though they

were known to be true, beyond the possibility of confutation. His simple asseveration is presented as a sufficient warrant for the reader's implicit acquiescence in them. If he was in possession of such ample evidence that they are taught in the divine word, why did he withhold it from those whom he addresses, and confine himself to mere, unsupported assertion?

2. He has no authority in the prophecy, for his representation, that the Prince who was to come, was to *make* a treaty with the Jews. The language of the prophet is: "And he (the Messiah) shall *confirm the covenant* with many for one week." There is no intimation that while he was to *confirm the covenant*—which, in order to such an act, must already have been in existence—he was also to make another covenant with the Jewish people, and therefore in respect to a different subject from that which was to be verified by fresh proofs of its validity and acceptableness. This notion that a new covenant was to be framed, is a mere fiction of the writer.

3. He has not the slightest ground in the prophecy, for his representation that at the end of the three years and a half, or at any other time, the personage who was to confirm the covenant, or according to Mr. Kelsall, make a new compact, was or is to break it. There is not a hint in the passage that the covenant that was to be confirmed, was to be broken, either by the maker of it, or by the Jewish people. So far

from it, the language directly precludes the supposition of its breach during the week of its verification. For it was to be confirmed for *one week*, that is, for *the whole*, and through the whole of the week ;—not merely at its commencement. The confirmation was to be for the last half of the week, as absolutely as for the first. The representation that the covenant was to be broken at the end of three years and a half, is thus a sheer fiction, in contravention of the express words of the passage. It stamps its authors and propagators therefore with the guilt of a deliberate interpolation in the text, in order to give it a shape that would enable them to employ it as a means of verifying their theory. It is not a *perversion* of its words; but first a rejection of their plain grammatical sense; and then *the ascription* to them of a prediction, of which there is not a trace in them.

4. He falls into an unfortunate error, in regard to the image, Rev. xiii. 14, which he affirms is to be set up in the Sanctuary in Jerusalem; and made an object of worship. He plainly imagines that that image which the two horned beast caused its vassals to make, was and is a real material image, that is capable of being transported from Italy to Palestine, and there set in a temple and made an object of worship. No blunder could bespeak a profounder ignorance of the nature and meaning of that symbol. The image which the two horned beast commanded his subjects to make, and which John beheld, was a mere

visionary symbol; framed after the pattern of the wild beast of seven heads and ten horns, of ch. xiii. 1–8: when under the sway of its seventh head. It was an image, the prophet represents *to the first wild beast which was healed of a death wound;* that is, it was modeled after the shape of that beast in trunk and limbs; and, with an erect and ruling head. And it was the symbol of an ecclesiastical organization that corresponded in its great outline, to the civil government of the empire under its seventh head as is seen from the acts of legislation and persecution it exerted. What priestly organization then, did the pope and his state hierarchy denoted by the two horned beast, prompt the population of the ten kingdoms to erect, that answered in its general features, to the structure of the civil empire, during the reign of Jovian and his successors to Theodosius? The reply is: The imperial Catholic hierarchy formed of the hierarchies of the several kingdoms, by their union in one vast structure, with the pope as its head; which rose at length by lies and frauds, to an absolute supremacy over the empire, and exercised the tyrannical and imperious acts that are ascribed to it by the prophet. The worship of this image of the wild beast, which the crowd was required to pay, was a prostrate acquiescence in the false pretexts of the monster—as the minister of God, and virtual ascription, to it thereby in its faith and obedience, of the power and prerogatives of the Most High which were arrogated by it. This mere visionary symbol, which no more had a substantive existence on the earth, than the wild beast itself, after which it was modeled, Mr. Kelsall mistakes for a real material image; and represents that it is to be transported to Jerusalem, and installed there in a Jewish temple as an object of worship! Into what more consummate delusion could he have fallen? What more unpardonable fiction could he have framed, and endeavored to interpolate in a text which treats exclusively of the great and peculiar acts of Christ?

5. He has no authority whatever for the representation, that the two witnesses are to appear in Palestine. The prophecy exhibits the empire of the ten horned wild beast, and of the image, or imperial Catholic hierarchy, as the scene of their testimony and slaughter; and represents their dead bodies as lying unburied in the broad place of the great city Babylon, which is also the symbol of the imperial Catholic hierarchy of the ten kingdoms.

6. His pretext that at the same time, a false prophet is to appear at Jerusalem, who will be empowered to perform astonishing miracles, is an equal fiction. There is no prediction in Daniel or John, that such a prophet is to present himself in that city at the close of the present dispensation. The unclean spirits who go forth to the kings to gather them to the great battle are to work portents; but their scene is to be the ten kingdoms of the west, and their pe-

riod anterior to the gathering of the kings and their armies in Palestine. The Man of Sin also, and Son of perdition, is to come after the working of Satan, with all power and signs and lying wonders; but his chief sphere is also to be at the west. There is no intimation in the prophets that a false prophet is to appear at Jerusalem immediately before the overthrow of Antichrist, and work great miracles for the purpose of persuading the Jews to worship an image of Antichrist which is to be set up in the temple, and which Satan is to "endow with the power of life and speech." That monster is a fiction framed by Mr. Kelsall, or those from whom he borrowed it, for the purpose of embellishing the theory with an unexpected prodigy, that should startle the credulous and excitable whom they wish to win to faith in their theory.

I add a passage from the Rev. R. A. Purdon, who holds that Napoleon Buonaparte was the power symbolized by the seventh head of the beast; and that Louis Napoleon is the Antichrist:

"There can no longer be a doubt that some terrible lesson is preparing for the nations of Europe, and that *the empire* of Napoleon is to be *revived.* We do not speak of the *title* of emperor; but the actual *empire* of Napoleon in its full territorial extent. Louis Napoleon has already laid the foundation of his power, with a depth and solidity, that is truly superhuman. In 1815, Napoleon I. fell, and not only was his empire broken up, but his name and family were annihilated in France. . . . His nephew has arisen, and struck the record out of the book of Europe. He has taken up the empire where the allies broke it off; Napoleon is to be again as if he had never ceased to be. His name, his empire, his ideas, his principles, his very eagles are all to be revived. The interregnum of thirty-five years, is to be even as a dream when one awaketh. But perhaps it will be said that we are traveling too fast; that not a particle of the *empire* has yet in May, 1852, been revived. We believe that the revival of the empire is as certain as if it had been already effected: that it is *predestined*, and that the whole creation could not prevent it. Louis Napoleon, we believe, will regain year after year *all the provinces of the fallen empire* from North to South, and will add to them, what Napoleon I. never could do, the Turkish provinces in the east.

"The eighth head is of the seven; and as we believe that Napoleon I. was the seventh head, it appears that from his family the eighth head will take its rise. . . The deadly wound of the seventh head was received, when Napoleon was defeated in battle, and sent to die at St. Helena: the healing of the deadly wound will be fully accomplished, when his representative and nephew, has assumed the dominion of the empire of Napoleon." —*Baxter*, *pp.* 230, 231.

These are mere expressions of opinion founded on the usurpation of the imperial sceptre by Louis Napoleon in December, 1851: and the false notion that Napoleon Buonaparte was the personage denoted by the seventh head of the beast; and thence that Louis Napoleon is the eighth head of that symbol: though no eighth head is attributed to it in the Apocalypse. They are mere repetitions of what had been proclaimed by Mr. Faber and Mr. Frere thirty to forty years before, and frequently reheralded by them and their followers in the interval, and as often shown by events to be mistaken. They are of no significance, except as they serve to apprise the reader of the unhesitating confidence with which this school of speculatists contemplate their favorite views, and the extraordinary facility with which they persuade themselves that they find the shapeless births of their disordered imaginations, drawn in characters of light, on the pages of revelation.

More than twelve years have passed since Mr. Purdon penned the passage I have cited. Yet of his confident prognostications that Louis Napoleon was to regain every portion of the empire of the first Buonaparte, that lay out of France; and to extend his conquests also over the Turkish provinces of the East—Egypt, Syria, and Mesopotamia, not one has been verified. Louis Napoleon has not extended his domains to the Rhine; he has not conquered Italy; neither Spain, nor Portugal has been brought to submission to his sceptre. He has not reconquered Switzerland. He has not become master of Bavaria. Prussia has not been overrun by his armies, and crushed into subjection to his rule: nor Austria, Saxony, or any part of Poland. His only enlargement of territory is the acquisition of Nice, and Savoy that belonged to Sardinia. His only important wars have been for the protection of the Turkish empire from the ambitious aims of Russia, and for the liberation of Italy from the power of Austria and of

Rome, and aiding it to erect itself into an empire founded on the will of the people, and characterized by religious toleration and free institutions. His lawless attempt to conquer Mexico is likely to prove unsuccessful.

What more effective confutation of his sanguine predictions could have befallen Mr. Purdon? Yet his disappointments have not been greater or more disparaging to his foresight, than those that have rendered the predictions of every other writer of this class, the object of ridicule and reprobation, from Mr. Faber and Mr. Frere, to those who are now building on the same false theories, and repeating the same misrepresentations of the divine word. The only event of any moment that has answered to their predictions, is the assumption by Louis Napoleon of the throne of France, which was known to be meditated by him, and expected by thousands long before it took place or was predicted by Mr. Purdon. Their anticipations in regard to the career he was to run, have not met with the slightest verification. Their faith however in their scheme, instead of being diminished by this disastrous experience, appears to retain its strength, and utter itself in as loud tones of assurance, as at any former period; though every sign in the posture of the world is against them, and the time itself has advanced to a point at which their chronology forbids their looking for a verification of their scheme in the future.

This chapter, which orginally closed with the remarks on Mr. Purdon's prognostications, was written in August, 1864. Within the last three months, events have occurred that change the attitude of several of the kingdoms of Europe towards each other in a manner that strikes all parties with surprise and astonishment; and no one perhaps more than Louis Napoleon himself. For while he was affecting to act in a degree as the arbiter of events, such a defeat of Austria took place, and such a triumph of Prussia, as to destroy the balance of power, and create a rival that may prove a match for France, and place him and his empire, should a conflict arise between them, in a measure in jeopardy.

This was an issue, probably, he had not anticipated. He was at least interpreted as assuming that Austria and Prussia would be so equally balanced, that the effect of their contest with each other would only be to exhaust their strength, and sooner or later present to him an opportunity to interpose, and dictate to them such terms of peace as should so augment his power and limit and weaken theirs, as to give him in a higher measure than he had before attained, the lofty position of master of western Europe.

When disappointed in this expectation by the sudden and far-reaching victories of Prussia, he was reported to have been so reluctant wholly to lose the prize he had hoped to grasp, that he intimated to the court at Berlin, that he should look for a rectification of the boundary of France, to countervail the large accessions Prussia has made to her territory. In place, however, of designating, as was asserted, the Prussian provinces on the left of the Rhine as the object of his wishes, his proposal it is now stated, is much more moderate; contemplating only the cession of a small district from Prussia, and a still less important transfer from Bavaria and Holland; and this having been declined by Prussia, he is said to have acquiesced, and in order to counteract false reports, to have intimated that it is not his purpose to urge his solicitations by force.

Whether this is a final relinquishment of a design to absorb those or other territories in his empire; or is a mere device for a delay that may enable him to draw an expression from the French nation in favor of war for that domain, and make a fuller preparation for the strife, there are yet no means of determining. If he absolutely abandons the project of annexation by force, or by diplomacy, and resigns the purpose of enlarging his territory; that will itself confute the pretext of Faber, Frere, Darby, Purdon, Tregelles, Newton, and others, that he is to become the imperial chief of the ten kingdoms, and the Antichrist who is to conquer the Turkish provinces in Syria, restore the Jews, erect a temple in Jerusalem, and set himself in it as an object of worship.

If in place of relinquishing his ambitious schemes,

he merely waits for some crisis in German affairs that may favor his plans, and embarks in a war of aggrandizement, he cannot be certain of success: he may meet a disastrous defeat, and be compelled to surrender portions of his territory to Prussia, instead of appropriating hers to himself: and thereby lose his prestige and power in such a degree as may prove not only a barrier to other projects of aggression, but endanger the stability and perpetuation of his throne.

Should he, however, resume and succeed in a purpose of extending his territory to the Rhine, it will prove no verification of Mr. Purdon's prediction that he is to expand his dominion over Holland, Belgium, Saxony, parts of Poland, and other regions in that direction; nor that he is to reconquer Italy, Spain and Portugal, and incorporate them in his empire. Nor should he reduce them all to the condition of dependencies, would he thereby present any ground for the prognostication that he is to conquer the eastern domains of the Turks, become the Antichrist, be the restorer of the Jews, extort a worship from his subjects, and perish at Armageddon. Whatever else may happen, as the predictions that are to be treated in later chapters of this work are unfolded, it will be seen with the most ample certainty, that he is to meet his doom, long before the hour arrives when Antichrist reveals himself, and the tragedy of the present dispensation reaches its close.

CHAPTER VI.

Their Theory of a League by Louis Napoleon with the Jews in reference to their Restoration to their National Land—Mr. Baxter's Views of its Date—Sir Edward Denny's Statements respecting its Time, and its Stipulations—Dr. Tregelles' Views of its Object and Period—Mr. Beal's Estimate of its Date, and the Period through which its Engagements are to extend.

THE first and most important event, according to Mr. Baxter and several of the writers whom he cites, that is to mark the career of Napoleon III, is to be the formation of a league between him and the Jews for the period of seven years, in reference to their return to their national land. He says:

"The seven years' covenant, which is to be made between Louis Napoleon and the Jews, exactly seven years and two and a half months before the end of this Dispensation, constitutes *the starting point* of the twenty leading events" (that are to signalize that period).

"During the first three and a half years of the seven, twelve out of twenty important events occur. And during the second three and a half years of the seven, together with the additional two and a half months (Dan. xii. 12), the remaining eight of the twenty take place.

"If the Covenant is made before October in 1863, then the seven years and two and a half months will of course extend from 1863 to 1870; and the first three and a half years will be from 1863 to 1866–7; and the second three and a half years with the two and a half months, will be from 1866 to 1870. But if the covenant should be made between October 16, 1863, and October 16, 1864, then the seven years and two and a half months would extend from 1863–4 to 1870–71. The fact of 1871–2 seeming, from the prophetic dates, to be the end of this dispensation, makes it exceedingly probable that the covenant will be made in 1864–5; but still, if it is made a year or two later, the difference will be comparatively small. The evidence of the prophetic dates, as well as the circumstance that Louis Napoleon will be sixty-four years old in 1872, shows that the destruction of Antichrist, at the end of this dispensation, cannot be much later than 1872, and consequently the covenant cannot be made much later than 1864–5. As it is absolutely certain, *beyond all possibility of doubt*, that Antichrist will be destroyed at Armageddon exactly seven years and two and a half months after the date of the covenant, we have only to wait till the date of the covenant is ascertained, and shall then know, almost to a day, the precise time of the consummation."—*Pp.* 69, 70.

The following passage is from Sir Edward Denny:

"The prince before named, having for the first three and a half years of his time reigned in peace over the Jews, he, now at the end of that time—that is, in the midst of the week, as we here read—throws off the mask and discovers himself. He had acted as a deceiver at first; and now, having compassed his object, he shows himself forth as a tyrant. He had set up at first, with a view to flatter his subjects, that species of worship which only would take with the Jews. But now this is all set aside; he causes the oblation and sacrifice to cease, and for the forty-two months, or three years and a half, spoken of in Revelation and Daniel, namely, the latter half of the week, he opens his mouth in blasphemies against the God of heaven, while he at the same time oppresses his people."—*Baxter, p.* 200.

Dr. Tregelles entertains the same views in regard to a covenant:

"And he (the prince who shall come) shall confirm a covenant with many for one week. . . . He makes a covenant with the multitude; that of course means the multitude of Daniel's people; they are leagued with him and he with them. This takes place three years and a half before he causes sacrifice and oblation to cease; hence it is clear that they go on, as under his patronage, for some time. This will, I believe, throw some light upon the two thousand three hundred days mentioned in chapter viii. 14. We find him, here, making a covenant for one seven years, then breaking it at the end of three years and a half; and the removal of sacrifice, etc., is so spoken of, as to connect it with the breaking of the covenant. This tends, I think, to show that one thing done in pursuance of this covenant, had been the establishment of the temple worship. The period of two thousand three hundred days, is a few months short of the whole term of the seven years—enough being included, it may be, to be allotted for those preparations, which will be needful for the worship to be set up; then follows the time during which it is carried on under his auspices; and then follow three years and a half of distinct persecuting and blasphemous power."—*Remarks on Daniel, pp.* 103, 104.

Mr. Baxter states that the author of Armageddon "considers that 1862 will most probably be the year when Louis Napoleon will make the seven years' covenant with the Jews. By Jewish reckoning, 1862 will not terminate until Nisan or Tisri—about April or September, 1863; but whenever the covenant is made, there will be only seven years and two and a half months to the end or consummation."—*Baxter*, *p.* 242.

That this theory is a fabrication, without authority from the divine word, and in open antagonism to the passage on which its authors profess to found it, one would think must be the conviction of all familiar with the Scriptures, who catch a true glimpse of its features.

1. If so important a revelation were made in the prophecy of Daniel, it would, it may justly be presumed, be in the power of these writers to demonstrate it in a clear and satisfactory manner. If God had chosen to reveal such a group of future events, he would have graven them in such intelligible characters, that they might be easily and naturally read aright. There would be no need of evading the question, whether it is directly expressed or not, in the grammatical sense of chap. ix. 26, 27; nor whether it lies couched under a symbol or symbols, in that, or any other part of the prophecy. The very first task to which those who embrace and proclaim it, would address themselves, would be to unfold the words or signs in which it is held that it is embodied, and set forth the proofs of its presence there, in a clear light. They would shrink from ascribing such a prediction to God on the mere ground of their own opinion, or of the judgment of other uninspired men. They would disdain to offer so gross an offence to their readers as to ask them to treat them as though

they were authenticated prophets, and receive the announcements which they utter, as of as high authority as though they were spoken by the lips of the Almighty. Yet not a syllable of proof is alleged by them of the truth of their representations on this subject, either from the prophecy itself, or from any other quarter! The whole is left to rest on their mere unsupported declarations. There is no pretext that there is a symbol, in the passage, in which it is enveloped. There is no attempt to unfold the philology of the prophecy, and prove that their view of its meaning is that which is expressed in its grammatical sense. It stands apart from the passage itself, as absolutely as though it were avowedly a prophecy out of their own heart. This is a sad feature of their theory, and places the reader under a direct and emphatic obligation, not to yield it his credence, until its validity as a revelation from God, is verified.

2. There not only is no direct delineation in chap. ix. 26, 27, of such a personage as Louis Napoleon, either in fact, or as these writers depict him; but there is nothing in it, that is suited to *suggest* that he is the subject of its prediction, any more than scores of other princes and potentates are. The mere fact that a prince is foreshown as to come to Judea with an army, and destroy the sanctuary and city, is of itself no proof that Louis Napoleon is that prince; any more than it is that the son of Jerome Buona-

parte, who bears the title of prince; or the imperial prince, the son of Louis Napoleon, is the person to whom the prediction refers. And those personages are no more entitled to be regarded as the subjects of the prediction, than any person of rank is, in Spain, in Italy, or in Austria. And in like manner, if the great personage of v. 27 is, as these authors affirm, the same as the prince of v. 26, there is no more ground for the assumption that Louis Napoleon is the person of whom it speaks, than there is that any one of scores and hundreds of other individuals is the party to whom the prediction refers. There is nothing in it by which Louis Napoleon can be identified as its subject, any more than there is by which any other of the numerous princes of the ten kingdoms who are contemporary with Louis Napoleon can be identified as the agent who is to exert the acts which it foreshadows. What a slender foundation for the support of such a lofty fabric! They have nothing but the word *prince*, wholly detached from its place in the passage, on which to erect their towering structure.

3. There is nothing in the present attitude of Louis Napoleon, or the posture of the other monarchies of western Europe, that indicates that he is to act the part, and within a year or two, which these authors predict of him. He is indeed at the head of a great and war-like nation, and wields by means of his power and policy, a vast influence on the neighbor-

ing kingdoms. Yet his aims are for the present professedly conservative and peaceful, rather than aggressive. If he desires to extend his empire to the Rhine, that, he implies, is the limit of his ambition. There are no signs *that he intends* soon to bring Spain, Portugal, Italy, Austria, western Germany generally, or Great Britain into subjection to his sceptre. It is not within the scope of his power, if they are true to their own independence; for united they are far stronger than he is; and they will be sure, if we may judge from the events of 1813, 1814, and 1815, to act in concert for their common defence, if he should attempt to tread them into submission to his will. Nor are there any indications that he is *soon* to extend his conquests over the east, plant his palace tent in Judea, and reveal himself there as the Antichrist. He could not engage in such an enterprise, without drawing on himself a large part of the forces of western and northern Europe. There are no events that lie more absolutely out of the sphere of likelihood, than that he should in one, two, or three years achieve the conquests, and act out the vast system of agencies, which these prophets assign to him. Western Europe must undergo a greater revolution than has ever yet befallen it; must pass through a season of unparalleled anarchy, and become the victim of a wholly different order of rulers, than has hitherto determined its destinies, before an imperial chief like Napoleon can grasp its throne, and run the career in the east which these authors assign to him.

4. The sole ground on which their persuasion respecting Louis Napoleon rests, is the false and preposterous theory fabricated by Mr. Faber, and Mr. Frere, that Napoleon Buonaparte was the personage symbolized by the seventh head of the wild beast; and that Louis Napoleon, on his seizure of the sceptre of France, either took the place of Napoleon Buonaparte as the person denoted by that head, or else was symbolized by an eighth head of the same monster, and is the power represented by the beast in its last form. But as I have shown that that theory is a mere fiction, without any authority either from the word of God, or the facts of history, their prognostications respecting the offices Louis Napoleon is to fill, and the portentous agencies he is to exert, are left without any ground whatever, except the crude and delirious vaticinations of their own minds. If their theory could not be directly refuted by the word of God and the events of his providence and the agency of man, it would, from its total want of evidence, be wholly unentitled to credence.

5. But we have the most decisive proof of their error in the consummate misrepresentations of the passage, chap. ix. 27, to which they resort to give it the air of supporting their theory. They exhibit the first act, which they hold is there foreshown of Louis Napoleon, as *making* a covenant, or entering into a

league with the Jews. They use the word *make*, *made*, or some equivalent term, signifying that the covenant or league is to be projected and formed at the beginning of the seven years through which its stipulations are to extend. That is the language employed by Dr. Tregelles. "He *makes* a covenant with the multitude; that of course means, the multitude of Daniel's people; they are *leagued* with him, and he with them. This takes place three years and a half before he causes sacrifices and oblations to cease; hence it is clear that they go on as under his patronage for some time." But that is not the true rendering of the word. The act affirmed in respect to the covenant, is the act of *confirming* it; and implies therefore that the covenant itself was already in existence before that act was exerted. The verb denotes, to give strength, to render firm; and thence exhibits that to which the strength and firmness are given, as already in being. And when the verb is applied to a *compact*, or covenant that is shown to be *unalterable* by the very act that is exerted in respect to it, it means to *confirm* it; that is, to *verify* it, *fulfill* it, and demonstrate its truth and power, by carrying its pledges into effect. To strengthen and confirm a covenant, is to make it sure that it is to continue to be what it is; not to alter it, or make a new covenant. These writers, therefore, in treating the passage as though it foreshowed that a covenant never before instituted was to be made at the time referred to, in place of being ratified and shown to be authoritative and unfailing, by its being fulfilled, totally misrepresent the transaction; and thereby overthrow their whole theory respecting it. For if the covenant is not to be *made* by the agent who is to exert the act affirmed respecting it, but being already in existence, is only to be confirmed; then it is clear that Louis Napoleon is not to fill the office these parties ascribe to him: he is not to originate the project of returning the Jews to their ancestral land; he is not to frame a league with them in regard to their migration to Palestine, and re-establishment there as an independent people; he at most, is only to confirm and carry into effect, what some one who preceded him had engaged to perform. But neither Napoleon Buonaparte, nor any other monarch of France, who preceded Louis Napoleon, entered into any such covenant with the Jews, and left it as an inheritance to him. Their whole scheme thus falls hopelessly to the ground.

6. But they perpetrate a still more flagrant outrage on the passage, in representing it as affirming that the agent who is to confirm the covenant, is in the middle of the week to break it. There is not a syllable in the passage, intimating or implying that the covenant is to be broken at the middle of the week; or at any other time. So far from it, the express language of the prediction is: "And he shall confirm the covenant with many *for one week*," that

is, for the whole of the week: not simply at its beginning and first half, but as absolutely through its last half, as through its first. This representation that the league is to be broken by the agent who confirms it, and all its just and benign provisions set at nought, is thus a stark interpolation fabricated by these writers against the clearest meaning of the passage, and in order to open the way for the representation which they build on it: that Louis Napoleon is to perpetrate a breach of his own compact, in order that he may act the part of the Man of Sin, and of Antichrist, which they ascribe to him. What an expedient to give a color of probability to a theory, which they have reared, to draw the credulous and fanatical to their train!

7. Who then is the personage who was to confirm the covenant with many for one week, and in the midst of the week cause sacrifice and oblation to cease?

Not Louis Napoleon; first, because he did not come into existence, till near eighteen hundred years after the confirmation of the covenant took place, and the legitimate offering of sacrifices ceased. Next, because the time assigned by these writers to the formation of the covenant, has passed without any accomplishment of their predictions. They have represented in a very confident manner, that the formation of the imagined league, was to take place in 1862, 1863, 1864, or 1865. Those years have passed, and no signal has appeared of any compact or negotiation, between Louis Napoleon and the Jews in regard to their migration to the holy land under his auspices. They have referred the formation of the treaty to those years, moreover, on the ground of the chronology on which they proceed, in all their constructions of the prophecy, and in conformity with which they affirm that the present dispensation is to terminate in 1868 to 1872. By their own calculations of periods, therefore, their theory in respect to Louis Napoleon is hopelessly overthrown. And thirdly, because the whole ground on which they found their prognostications in respect to him, is a wild and senseless fiction, as I have shown, at war with the divine word, and in utter disregard of the indubitable truths of history.

Nor was Titus the personage who was to confirm the covenant. He was the Roman prince, whose office was simply to go to Jerusalem with his hosts, destroy the sanctuary and city; and sweep away the Jewish nation as with a flood; for those great acts are the only acts that are foreshown of him; and their date was more than thirty years after the confirmation of the covenant, and the discontinuance of legitimate sacrifice and the close of the seventieth week.

Who then was the great being who was to confirm the covenant with many for one week; and in the midst of the week during which the covenant was kept in unfailing strength and effectiveness, cause sacrifice and oblation to cease? The answer is: The great Messenger of the Covenant who, it was foreshown in Malachi, ch. iii. 1, was at the period to which the prediction relates, to appear in the temple, and reveal himself to his true people. The covenant was the covenant of God with Adam, Abraham, Moses, and the whole Israelitish nation, respecting the redemption of men by the obedience and blood of the Messiah: and accordingly he was recognized as that messenger by Mary, Elizabeth, Zacharias, and at his presentation at the temple by Simeon, and Anna under the promptings of the Holy Spirit; and during his ministry and subsequently to his resurrection, by tens of thousands of that people. And he filled the great office ascribed to him in v. 27. He confirmed the covenant to those who listened to his voice during the three years and a half of his ministry, by announcing himself as the Son of God who had come to take away the sin of the world; by promising eternal life to all who believed on him; by working innumerable miracles, by which he demonstrated his deity; and at length, by dying on the cross to make expiation for sin. He confirmed it also, after his death, by his resurrection, by commissioning his disciples to preach the glad tidings of redemption through his blood; and by pouring out the Holy Spirit and renewing a great multitude of the Jews, and giving them assurance of their interest in his salvation by the supernatural knowledge and miraculous powers, with which they were endowed. This confirming of the covenant with many of that people, continued through three years and a half; when his disciples were directed no longer to confine the proffer of salvation to them, but to proclaim it also to the Gentiles.

It was, in consequence, accordingly, of this confirmation of the covenant which he accomplished by his ministry and death, that in the midst of the week he caused the sacrifice and oblation to cease. As he whom the sacrificial offerings typified had come and wrought the expiation by his blood which their blood foreshadowed, there was no longer a necessity for the presentation of animal sacrifices. And we find in fact, that after his resurrection those offerings were discontinued by his disciples. Not a hint appears in the Gospels, the Acts, or the Epistles that a solitary victim was presented by any believer, after his crucifixion.

All that is foreshown in this verse, thus had a full and a sublime verification in him. It must, therefore, be taken as its true fulfillment, and the only fulfillment it is to receive. To deny it, is to deny that acts and the only acts that correspond to the prediction have any title to be considered as its accomplishment: and that is to turn the prophecy into a mockery. What more shocking desecration of the passage can be conceived, than to strike from it the Redeemer, as those writers do, and substitute in his place, in the greatest and most gracious acts of his life and death—a mere man, whom these very authors depict as being, and to be, the greatest monster that ever strode the earth!

8. That the confirmation of the covenant, and the abrogation of sacrifice and oblation, took place in the last half of the seventieth week, is made certain by the indication in v. 27, that the entrance of the abomination of desolation into the courts of the temple, which Christ expressly foreshowed was to *precede* the siege of the city, was to take place after the end of the seventieth week. Verse 27, accurately translated, is the following: "And he shall confirm the covenant with many for one week; and in the middle of the week shall cause sacrifice and oblation to cease. And over the wing (the battlement) shall come the abomination of desolation; and that which is decreed, shall—until the full accomplishment—be poured upon the desolated." Here the order of the predictions shows clearly that the entrance of the abomination of desolation into the holy place—the courts surrounding the temple—was to take place at a later day than the confirmation of the covenant and discontinuance of sacrifices. And Christ accordingly, forewarned his disciples that the presence of the abomination of desolation in the holy place, would be a token that the destruction of the city was nigh; and enjoined them immediately to flee to the mountains.

He foretold also that the approach of armies toward the city from different directions, was to be a sign of its speedy destruction, and a warning to them to flee from it. These predictions thus show, in the clearest manner, that the abomination of desolation was to gain a place in the temple courts, before the siege of the city began; as otherwise the disciples of Christ would have been precluded from flight to the mountains. And this fact indicates with equal certainty, that the abomination of desolation was introduced into the sacred courts, by *the Jews themselves*, and while they held unobstructed possession of the city.

What then was the abomination of desolation; that is, execrable wickedness, or pollution, that drew after it the destruction of the temple and city? It was undoubtedly the seizure and occupation of the courts of the temple, by the vast crowd of robbers and assassins, who formed the party called Zealots, who converted it into a fortress, and made it the scene of the most bloody and the most impious crimes. Josephus himself put that construction on it; for he relates in his account of the horrible excesses of those infuriated desperadoes, that it was foreshown in an ancient oracle, that the abomination of desolation was to be the work of the Jews. And he exhibits Ananus the high priest, as lamenting in an address to the people, that the temple and courts were desecrated by that infuriate mob, who penetrated into the innermost recesses of the temple, and made that edifice and the courts, the scene of the most revolting pollution. *Bel. Jud., Book* iv. c. 3, 10. Josephus also distinctly represents that sacrilegious appropriation of the temple to the most impious uses, as taking place before the siege of the city by Titus began. *Bel. Jud., Book* iv. c. 6. 3. iv. 5. 2.

But what was the wing over which the abomination was to enter into the sacred enclosure? It was doubtless a wing or battlement of the temple court. Tacitus represents the collonades, or porticos with which the courts were surrounded as excellent bulwarks. They scaled those barriers, perhaps, or made breaches in them, by which they could have access to the temple courts, without obstruction, when the gates of the inclosure were shut.

It is clear then, from the passage itself, from the forewarnings by Christ, and from the testimony of the Jewish historian, that the abomination of desolation was introduced into the holy place a short time before the siege of the city by Titus was commenced; that it was the work of the Jews themselves; and that the horrible desecration of the temple and its courts by the sacrilegious mob called Zealots, was interpreted at the time by some of the Jews, as the fulfillment of this prophecy by Daniel. It is abundantly certain therefore that the perpetration of that atrocious outrage on the temple of God, is not, as these writers persuade themselves, reserved to Louis Napoleon. It had its accomplishment more than thirty years after the close of Daniel's seventieth week; and in a form far more impious and appalling than could have been conceived before the bloody and heaven-daring acts of the Jews which it denoted, were perpetrated.

CHAPTER VII.

These Writers deny that Christ's Work foreshown (Daniel ix. 24) has been Wrought, and affirm that it is yet Future—Mr. Baxter's and Dr. Tregelles' Views—Rev. B. W. Newton's Statements.

THESE authors allege that the predictions (Daniel ix. 24) respecting Christ's work, in putting a bar to transgression, in sealing sin, in making expiation, and in bringing in everlasting righteousness, were not fulfilled in his ministry and death at his first advent, but are still future, and are to meet their accomplishment at his second coming. Mr. Baxter states his views of the postponement of his work, originally assigned to the week that immediately followed the sixty-ninth, to a future period, in the following passage:

"The true explanation of this prophecy (Dan. ix. 24–27) appears to be that seventy weeks or years were marked off as the period of God's dealings with the Jews while nationally gathered in their own city, and were to end with their complete redemption and deliverance, as described in verse 24. Had the Jews received the Messiah, when he officially came to them at the end of the sixty-nine weeks by the Baptist's preaching, and by his own public ministry, then apparently the seventieth week would have followed continuously, and would have closed with the Son of David reigning over the house of Jacob forever.

But their rejection of Jesus caused the fulfillment of the seventieth week to be postponed, until they should be fully punished for that sin, and then the seventieth week, after running its course, will end as originally intended, with the setting up of Messiah's kingdom over Israel, and the bringing in of everlasting righteousness. Thus Israel's rejection has interposed between the sixty-ninth and seventieth week, the long interval of the Gentile dispensation, during which they are punished by their house being left unto them desolate."—*Baxter, pp.* 177, 178.

1. No proof is alleged by him, it should be noticed, of the truth of this representation. It is left to rest on his mere testimony. Was not such a novel and portentous proposition entitled to be accompanied by some evidence that it has the sanction of the divine word? Are the most momentous revelations God has made, thus to be set aside by a mere stroke of Mr. Baxter's pen?

2. He is, however, mistaken, and in a most censurable form. What ground has he for assuming that the prediction (v. 27) was conditioned for its fulfillment on the obedience of the Jewish people to the call of Christ? There is no hint to that effect in the prophecy. What better reason has he for such an assumption in respect to verse 27, than he has in regard to verses 24 and 26? He certainly has none. Such a pretext would be no more arbitrary, nor more destructive of the certainty of the predictions of those verses, than it is of the prediction of this. That pretence is, in fact, alleged by Mr. Baxter and others of

this school of writers. As therefore it assumes that none of the acts and events of Christ's mission which they foreshow have taken place—inasmuch as the Jews, as Mr. Baxter avers, did not receive, but rejected him; it implies that the whole work of redemption remains unaccomplished. What an issue for one who professes a knowledge of the prophecy so far in advance of most who study it, that they will be startled and overwhelmed with shame, when the light of its true meaning which he has attained breaks upon their eyes!

3. The predictions of the events that were to take place in the seventieth week, most certainly were not contingent on the acceptance of Christ by the Jewish people; but were absolute, like all other prophecies, and contemplated his rejection and crucifixion in the exact manner in which they took place. "Him being delivered by the determinate counsel and foreknowledge of God, ye have taken and by wicked hands have crucified and slain."—*Acts ii.* 23. That all the acts which it was foreshown men were to exert toward him, such as despising him, rejecting, mocking, and scourging him, and putting him to death, were predicted as infallibly certain, is clear, from the fact that the new Testament contains a record of their fulfillment, and express recognitions of them as verifications of those predictions. There is a like record of the accomplishment in Christ's birth, ministry, and death, of all the great acts and

events that are foreshown in the old Testament of him; and it is stated in regard to many of them, that they took the forms they bore, that they might be fulfillments of what had been predicted by the ancient prophets. To deny that those acts and events were accomplishments of the predictions in which they were foreshown, is to deny that actions and events that correspond to predictions, have any title to be considered as fulfillments of them; and that is to deny that either predictions or fulfillments have any certainty, and overthrow all ground for faith in the word of God.

4. Mr. Baxter, in representing that the events foreshown of Christ's life, and the acts of men toward him, were contingent; and that the Jews might have received him, and thereby given rise to an administration wholly different from the present, and that would have led to a like difference in the conditions and actions of men; implies that there was no intrinsic necessity that Christ should be subjected to the humiliations, wants, sorrows, and sufferings that formed the great features of his life, and which the Scriptures and reason testify were requisite to the perfection of his obedience and expiation. He was made perfect, we are taught, through suffering. It was the great obstacles he had to encounter in the unbelief, aversion, and enmity of men, and in the power and malice of Satan, that put his allegiance to a decisive test, and raised his obedience to an inten-

sity, greatness and grandeur that suited his office, as the Redeemer, and rendered his righteousness and expiation adequate for the pardon and justification of sinners. But this great fact, which appears in the most conspicuous form in every part of his life, Mr. Baxter overlooks, and in effect, assumes that an unsuffering and untried Messiah might, as far as his acts and endurances were concerned, have wrought a redemption of the world, as well as one that was tested and found invincible in his rectitude under the most numerous and most crushing temptations. What error could bespeak in louder tones the utter truthlessness of his theory, or indicate in a more decisive form his sheer inacquaintance with the great principles on which the work of redemption proceeds?

5. Instead of contemplating it as possible that the Jewish people might spontaneously receive him, and supercede the necessity of his obeying and dying in their behalf; Christ proceeded in his work on the fact that the race which he came to save, were in revolt, and engaged in open war against him, and could be reclaimed from sin and death only by his meeting the trials and bearing the sufferings that filled up his life, and thereby opening the way for the employment of the requisite agency of the Spirit and of the word, to bring them to repentance and faith.

Mr. Baxter thus fails in the reasons he gives for the postponement of the seventieth week through eighteen hundred years, and evinces, by his great errors, the untenableness of his scheme. I cite another passage from him:

"That the seventieth week is hitherto unfulfilled, clearly appears from reading in their strictly consecutive order the verses containing the prophecy. Seventy weeks are cut off, as a period, which with respect to the Jewish people, and their city Jerusalem, is to terminate with the finishing of the transgression, the making an end of sins, the bringing in of everlasting righteousness, and the anointing of the holy place. . . . All this cannot have been completely fulfilled with respect to Jerusalem and the Jews at the crucifixion; for Jerusalem has ever since been desolate, and the sins of the Jews have been had in especial remembrance; but it will be fulfilled at the restoration and conversion of the Jews, after the second advent."—P. 178.

This is an important passage, from the light it throws on their views of the nature of the acts which they hold are foreshown in the 24th verse. Nothing can be clearer than that they do not regard them as the acts of Christ in rendering obedience and dying for the expiation of sin; but hold them to be acts simply by which his work, whatever else it was when he was on the earth, is to be made available to the redemption of the Israelitish people at his second coming. I add a passage from Dr. Tregelles, in which the same view is expressed:

"The various things spoken of in verse 24, to finish the transgression, to make an end of sins, to make reconciliation for iniquity, and to bring in everlasting righteousness, are all, I believe, future. I do not regard any of them as referring strictly to the work of Christ upon the cross, (although we as believers in him, know that many of these things have a blessed application to us,) but it rather appears to me that they all belong to the time of Israel's blessing, when the preciousness of the blood of Christ shall be *applied* to those who are spared of them."—*Remarks on Daniel, p.* 97.

The same views are expressed by the Rev. B. W. Newton.

"The time of the devastation of Jerusalem by Roman armies, was not a period of which it could be said, that her sins were forgiven, and everlasting righteousness brought in. On the contrary it was a period when her sins were had in remembrance, and in consequence thereof, her people were led away captive into all nations, and scattered toward the four winds of heaven. But an hour is coming, when the blood of atonement that has been already shed, shall be *applied* to repentant Israel, when the veil shall be taken from their heart, and they shall recognize him whom they have despised, as being Jehovah their righteousness."—*Aids to Prophetic Inquiry, p.* 135.

There is thus in these writers a direct and unhesitating representation, that the predictions, Dan. ix. 24, respecting Christ's work, in shutting up transgression, sealing sin, making reconciliation for iniquity, and bringing in everlasting righteousness, were not fulfilled in his life, ministry and death, at his first advent; but are still future, and are to meet their accomplishment at his second coming. Their views, however, are wholly mistaken, and fraught with errors of the most reprehensible and fatal character.

1. This, like the other points in their system, which I have thus far controverted, is left without any proofs of its truth. One might naturally presume that in advancing a belief so extraordinary, and involving such portentous implications respecting the whole administration of the Most High, they would deem it due to the divine word itself, and to the rights of their readers, to make a full exposition of the grounds on which, they hold, it has an indubitable basis. If they build on philology, why should they not prove by examples, that the terms of the passage do not denote the great acts of obedience and expiation, they are usually held to express; but instead, signify, as they maintain, the application of Christ's sacrificial work to men by the renewing and faith-inspiring power of the Holy Spirit? If they build, not on words, but on the great principles and measures of the divine government, why do they not state those principles and measures, and show how they legitimately lead to such a construction of the passage? Not a syllable, however, do they give in explanation and justification of their procedure. They announce the import they assign to the prediction, as though nothing but their judgment was necessary to settle its meaning.

2. The reason that they offered no proofs from philology to sustain their construction, doubtless

was, that it has no ground in the language of the prophet, but is utterly foreign to its genuine and established sense. This will be seen with the most ample certainty from a simple exposition of its several expressions. "Seventy weeks are cut off (from other time) upon thy people, and upon thy holy city." This implies that that period was to be signalized by acts and allotments by God, and actions by men, that were to lead on to the consummation that was to be reached in the seventieth week.

The next clause announces the first element of that great work to which all that had gone before was preparatory. "Seventy weeks are cut off," to shut up, restrain, or put a barrier to transgression: that is, to intercept it from immediately generating the penal effects to which it exposes the guilty; and that is one of the most essential functions of expiation. Such is unquestionably the sense of the words, whether we render the verb by the terms, *shut up*, or by the word restrain. The *object* of the act denoted by the verb is *transgression*, *a violation of law* that is already in being, and the *aim* of the act is to shut up;—that is, arrest, and put a barrier to transgression, by which it shall be intercepted for a time at least, from its legal effect in generating a penalty to him who committed it. Every individual who is spared from instant punishment partakes of this benefit. It thus is not the *sinner* who is the object of shutting up or restraining, but *sin itself*, by the guilt of which he is held.

The next expression is, "To seal sin:" that is, to stamp it as being what it is, and what it is contemplated by the divine law—namely, as guilty, and meriting the punishment God denounces on it; and as inexpiable, except by the blood of the Son of God; as a document is stamped by a seal, which shows it to be what the law represents it as being. This is the only sense the act of sealing will here bear. The object of sealing sin is not to ratify it and declare it to be legitimate and in harmony with law. Such a testimony would be false, and contradictious to the aims with which Christ undertook and wrought the work of redemption. The office of sealing sin was to identify and put a mark upon it, as being what it is declared to be in the prohibitions and in the penalties of the law. And here, as before, the object of the act is, not the *sinner*, but the *sin* which he has committed.

The third expression is, "To expiate sin," or to render the verb according to its literal meaning in the original text, "to cover sin," so as to hide it from sight and preclude it from being imputed and avenged; the verb cover being employed by the Israelites by a figure from the similarity of the effect, to denote expiation—that is, atonement, satisfaction for a crime, so that it should no longer be avenged nor imputed. This is the clear and only sense the term will bear. The act of expiation, covering and removing the guilt of sin, is thus wholly different from the act of shutting it up, or precluding it for a time from giving birth to the penalty which it deserves; and wholly different from sealing sin, by which it is identified and stamped as being what it is in its nature and demerit. In this instance also, *sin* is the object of the expiating act, not the sinner, who is the author of the sin. The three acts thus form a gradation. Transgression is first intercepted from giving birth to the penalty, to which the sinner is obnoxious; next sin is stamped with a mark which shows that God regards it as of the guilt which he ascribes to it in his law; and lastly, an expiation is made for it, by which it is blotted out, that the sinner may be released from its penalty.

The act that is next expressed is: "To bring forth everlasting righteousness," that is, to render and manifest a full and spotless obedience that was to be the ground of the Messiah's own acceptance in his work, and of the free and full justification of those who, believing on him, and confiding in him, are made partakers of his salvation. And this is as essential a part of his work as the expiation of their sins was, which he made by his death. Christ is accordingly denominated "Jehovah our righteousness." No one will question the truth of this exposition. Christ is the being who exercised and displayed the righteousness; and the righteousness itself is wholly distinct from the sinner, to whom it is made the ground of justification.

Next follows the expression: "To seal vision and prophecy:" that is, to stamp them as truthful, and verify them, by fulfilling them, as a document is shown to be genuine, and authoritative by a seal that bespeaks its authenticity and truthfulness. This is unquestionably the meaning of putting a seal on vision and prophecy. It does not denote, as some have imagined, to shut up prophecy as in an impenetrable envelope, or to draw an impervious veil over vision, that its symbols may not be seen, nor its voices heard. The object of a seal is to give authority and perpetuity to the document to which it is affixed; not to debar those whose prerogatives and interests it concerns, from opening, reading, and accepting its contents. The design of the seals on the Apocalyptic scrolls, was not to intercept Christ from opening them till the contents of the scrolls were to be disclosed to the eyes of creatures; but instead, it is expressly intimated, to show that it pertained to him alone, to break the seals, and send forth the symbols: not to creatures, who were neither able to open the book nor look on the dazzling characters in which its revelations were written.

The last clause of the verse is: "And to anoint a Holy of Holies;" that is, to consecrate the heavenly sanctuary in which he was to present his blood, and offer his intercessions. And this great act was consequent on the acts previously specified, and immediately followed his ascension to heaven, after his resurrection, and the revelation of himself to his disciples; for he entered on his priestly office when he ascended to the heavenly temple, and sat down at the right hand of God; and he now there, makes intercession for us. Rom. viii. 34; Heb. vii. 25–28.

This delineation of the work of Christ in his life and death, is thus one of the most specific, the most comprehensive, and the most lofty that is anywhere drawn by the pen of inspiration. What a height and depth of meaning is comprised in the expression, to shut up, restrain, or put a bar to transgression, by *reprieving* the sinner from its avenging power, so that he may enjoy a period of probation, before he is summoned to judgment? What a breadth of significance lies couched in the words, "And to seal sin;" that is, to put a mark on it in the eyes of all creatures, that shows it to be what God represents it in his law; as unspeakably guilty, forfeiting all good, deserving death which is made its penalty, and inexpiable, except through the obedience and blood of a divine Redeemer? What expression could the Father have given of his sense of the evil of sin, that could have surpassed that which he made in surrendering his Son to the humiliation and suffering that were essential to its expiation? What other proof could the eternal Word have given to the universe, that he regards it as worthy of the doom which God pronounces on it, that could equal in greatness and awfulness that which he presented in stooping to take on himself our nature, and bear our sins on the cross? At that great spectacle there was not a bosom in God's vast kingdom, that did not throb with the profoundest feeling that sin is indeed what God declares it to be, in malevolence and demerit. And what vivid realizations must have filled every heart, that the obedience of Christ was a glorious and perfect obedience for his own justification, and for the justification of those who accept him as their Saviour, and that his death in the place of the sinner was a full expiation for sin;—all that the righteousness of God demanded; all that the necessities of the guilty required; all that was needful to the well-being of the universe? And what immeasurable significance lies in the concluding stroke in the picture, "To anoint a Holy of Holies;" that is, consecrate the scene in the heavenly realms, of which the Holy of Holies in the temple on earth was the type, Heb. ix. 11; where Christ presented his blood, and offers his intercessions? There is not a group of thoughts in the whole circle of inspiration, that transcends this in the truthfulness, fullness, and grandeur of the portraiture it presents of the work of the Redeemer.

The evidence is decisive, therefore, that these writers are wholly in error, in denying that this passage is predictive of Christ's great work in obeying and suffering in his life and death at his first advent, and maintaining that the acts which it foreshows are still future, and are to be exerted by him at his second coming.

3. They not only reject its true meaning, and ascribe to it a foreign and false import; but they completely change the subjects of the principal predictions, by striking out the objects of the acts that are foreshown, and substituting a different entity in their place, and thereby convert the prophecy into a consummate solecism. Thus the object of the first three of the predicted acts, are transgression and sin. Transgression was to be intercepted from working the immediate destruction of the offender: and sin was first to be branded with a mark that should bespeak its awful evil and desert of punishment; and then to be expiated so that it could justly be forgiven, and the sinner released from its penalty. But these objects of those great acts these writers discard; and substitute in their place the *sinner himself*, as that on which the acts expend their energy. But that entirely alters the nature of the prophecy, and converts it into a monstrosity. Thus, to shut up, restrain, or put a bar on a *sinner*, would be simply to intercept him from *acting*, and bring him as an agent to a stand; just as to put a bar to sin, would be to prevent it from giving birth to the penal effects that naturally spring from it. It would not be, as these writers perhaps imagine, to turn the sinner from sinning to obedience; but merely to stop him from acting at all; for though the *object* of the verb is

changed by them, the meaning of the *verb itself* remains what it was before; and denotes the absolute interception of that on which its force is expended, from the species of effects to which it would otherwise continue to give birth. But thus to suspend all the active functions of the sinner, would be to prevent him from knowledge, repentance, love, and faith, as completely as it would from sinning, and would place him, while that syncope remained on him, out of the possibility of salvation. Such is the first result to which their change of the objects of the verbs, leads.

Next, "To seal sinners," would be to fix on them a mark bespeaking them to be what they are in the sight of God, guilty, lost, and doomed to death; and thereby indicating that they are abandoned to the destruction which they deserve. For it would identify them as incorrigible, and reprobate; in the same manner as the office of the mark of the beast and its image, is to identify those who are to continue, after the last warning, to bear it, as the irreclaimable vassals of those powers, and doomed to perish in the same penal fires with them. Such a sealing would be a sealing to perdition, therefore, not to life. This is the second result of their falsification of the passage.

Thirdly, "To expiate sinners," is an expression without any legitimate meaning; inasmuch as sinners themselves are not the subjects of expiation, but only their sins. It implies, however, that their sins are to remain unexpiated; and thence are forever to preclude them from pardon and salvation.

Can any higher proof be conceived of the utter error of their construction of the passage, than that it leads to these false and shocking results? How mistaken and fatal the principle is on which they proceed, may be exemplified by applying it to other kindred passages in the sacred word. Thus in the sublime language of John the Baptist: "Behold the Lamb of God who taketh away the sin of the world;" if the word *sin* be stricken out, and the word *sinners* inserted in its place, not only is the object on which Christ's act is exerted, changed; but the act itself he is to exert, is to be wholly altered in its nature and effect, and become an act of destruction instead of salvation. For to take away sinners, would be to strike them to the grave, and consign them to perdition. "And the king said to the servants, 'Bind him hand and foot, and *take him away*, and *cast him into outer darkness*. There shall be weeping and gnashing of teeth.'" "Because of wrath, beware lest he take thee away with a stroke; then a great ransom cannot deliver thee." So also of many other expressions; as those in which Christ is said to have borne our sins, and been bruised for our iniquities. If sin is erased and sinful men are put in its place, the meaning becomes false and impossible: as the affirmation then is that he literally bore us, in our material nature having dimensions and weight in his own body on the tree; which is truthless and monstrous; while, on the other hand, the office he filled in suffering for our sins is wholly omitted.

4. Their construction of the passage implies, that his death was not expiatory. As the great acts foreshown of him in the verse, are indubitably those of obeying and suffering as the Messiah for the redemption of men; to deny that he in fact exerted those acts that are predicted of him, is plainly to deny that he died as an expiatory victim. If he did not in truth put a bar to transgression by his sacrifice; if he did not put a mark of condemnation on sin, on the one side, by rendering a spotless obedience; and on the other by bearing its penalty; how can it be said that his death was vicarious and expiatory? The two propositions are direct antitheses. To affirm that the sacrificial acts foreshown in the verse are yet future, is equivalent to affirming that no death as a sacrifice for the sins of men has yet been borne by the Redeemer; and to assert that, is in so many words to assert that no expiatory and redemptive work has yet been accomplished. But that is to contradict all the representations of the New Testament respecting his death. They all exhibit him as having accomplished his expiation in his death on the cross. "I delivered unto you first of all that which I also received, how that Christ died for our sins, according to the Scriptures; of which this of Daniel

was undoubtedly one of the most full and explicit. 1 Cor. xv. 3. Peter says of him: "He his own self bare our sins in his own body on the tree, that we being dead to sins, should live unto righteousness; by whose stripes we are healed." 1. ch. ii. 24. And John says of him: "Unto him that loved us and washed us from our sins in his own blood, and hath made us kings and priests unto God even his Father; to him be glory and dominion forever and ever." Rev. i. 5, 6.

5. Their representation implies that the exaltation of Christ to the right hand of the Majesty on high, was premature. For it is expressly affirmed by Paul that it was because of his divesting himself of his form of God, and taking upon himself the form of a servant, and becoming obedient unto death, that he was exalted on high, and a name was given him that is above every name, that at the name of Jesus every knee should bow of those in heaven, and those on the earth, and those under the earth; and every tongue should confess that Jesus Christ is Lord, to the glory of God the Father. If then, as these authors affirm, he did not die that obedient death on the cross, and did not make expiation for sin, nor bring in everlasting righteousness by his life and his sacrifice; what can be more certain than that his exaltation to the throne of heaven did not take place on the ground represented by the Apostle; and that he was not entitled

because of his mediatorial work, to the submission and adoration that are rendered to him in heaven! Such are some of the revolting implications that are involved in their misrepresentation of his work as it is delineated in this passage.

6. It implies that the faith of believers since his death contemplates him in a false relation. For they under the most explicit teachings of his word, accept and trust in him, as having died for their sins eighteen hundred years ago, according to the Scriptures; not as in the ages that preceded his advent in the flesh, as a Saviour who is to make expiation for their sins at some future time. If, therefore, the views of these expositors, are in harmony with truth; all believers since the first promulgation of the gospel, have essentially misapprehended his work, and built their hope in him, and paid him their homage, on a mistaken foundation. But that is false and impossible.

7. And finally, their theory implies that Christ's work of expiation is yet future; and therefore, that he is to die at his second coming. If he is to be the Saviour of men; and a spotless obedience and full expiation are to be the measures by which he is to save them; what can be more certain, on the theory of these authors, than that he is yet to obey and die for them; and that his second obedience and death are to take place at his coming again to the earth,

and entering here on his everlasting reign! I will not dwell on the senselessness and impiety of this implication.

Such are the overwhelming proofs of the groundlessness and error of their construction of this great prophecy of the Redeemer's obedience and sacrifice at his first coming.

CHAPTER VIII.

Their theory respecting the futurity of the Seventieth Week of Daniel. Mr. Baxter's views; The theory of Dr. Tregelles; Rev. B. W. Newton's representations.

These writers maintain, as some of the passages already cited show, that the last of the seventy weeks of Daniel, instead of immediately following the sixty-ninth, is disjoined from it by more than eighteen hundred years, and is still future, though to arrive and pass during the life of Louis Napoleon. I transcribe a few passages in which this theory is advanced. Mr. Baxter attaches a high importance to it, as an element of his system: and justly; as if it is overthrown, his whole scheme falls with it.

"The faith of professing Christians is about to be tested by a signal and extraordinary fulfillment of prophesy, which will be despised and rejected by those who are fools and slow of heart to believe all that the prophets have spoken; but will be distinctly understood by the wise and watchful, so as to enable them to discover the date of Christ's approaching advent. It was very generally believed by the early Christian church, that Daniel's seventieth week would be fulfilled at the time of the second advent, by the Antichrist being received by many of the Jews as their Messiah; and subsequently placing his image, the abomination of desolation, in the rebuilt Jewish temple, which would thus be defiled during the latter half week; the three and a half years of tyranny. This view was very little advocated during the dark ages of papal corruption; but during the last half century it has been extensively revived. It is thus expected that seven years before the end, Antichrist will confirm a covenant with many of the Jews for one week of seven years, and in the midst of the week will cause the sacrifice to cease even unto the end. As Louis Napoleon is clearly foreshown to be the Antichrist; and as the end appears from the chronological prophesies, to be about, or soon after 1872; therefore it now remains to be seen whether these interpretations will be proved to be true, by Napoleon making a seven years' covenant, about, or soon after 1864–5."—*Louis Napoleon*, pp. 175, 176.

Dr. Tregelles holds, in like manner, that the seventieth week is yet future, and is to coincide in date with the time, times, and half a time of Daniel vii. 25, which he refers to the close of the present dispensation.

"This series of years has run on unhinderedly, from the issuing of the edict to the cutting off of Messiah, but at this part of the vision there are various events spoken of, before the one remaining week comes into notice at all. And the city and the sanctuary shall the people destroy of a prince who shall come. This refers I have no doubt to the destruction of Jerusalem by the Romans. . . . The prince who shall come, is the last head of the Roman power, the person concerning whom Daniel had received so much previous instruction.

"The vision gives us no intimation about the times of the events which belong to the interval. We only find at the cutting off of Messiah, *one seven years* is unaccomplished. This '*reserved week*,' as some have aptly called it, belongs to the time of the prince who shall come."—*Remarks*, p. 102.

"The seventy weeks when distributed into portions, will then stand thus:—

I. From the edict to the building of the wall..................... 49 years.

II. From the building to Messiah the Prince and his cutting off...... 434 "

[*Then an interval of unmarked length.*]

III. The period of the covenant of the prince that shall come........ 7 " 490."—p. 105.

He thus represents the seventieth week as "unaccomplished" at Messiah's death; holds that it is thrown forward for a period whose length is unknown, but is not less than eighteen hundred years; and is to be signalized when it comes, by the presence of the prince who is be the last head of the Roman power.

The Rev. B. W. Newton advances the same views.

"The seventy hebdomads of *years* mentioned in this passage, are distributed into three divisions.

"The *first* consists of seven hebdomads, that is, 49 years.

"The *second* of sixty-two hebdomads, " " 434 "

"The *third* of one hebdomad, " " 7 "—490

"The first of these divisions of forty-nine years, commenced when the commandment went forth to restore and to build Jerusalem.

"The second division of four hundred thirty-four years, commenced with the completion of the wall, and extends to the cutting off of Messiah. After threescore and two hebdomads—434 years, shall Messiah be cut off.

"The third division of seven years, will commence when 'the prince that shall come,' that is, Antichrist 'shall make a covenant with the multitude'; and ends by wrath being sent upon the Desolator, and blessing on Jerusalem.

"The course of the hebdomads shall not be resumed until Israel, under a covenant formed with Antichrist, shall again assume a *national* existence in Jerusalem."—*Aids to Prophetic Inquiry, pp.* 135–137.

I might cite similar representations from other writers, but these may be taken as expressing the views that are common to the party.

1. In regard to this important element of their system, it might reasonably have been presumed, that they would make some strenuous, and if practicable, scholarly effort, to demonstrate its truth. To take the liberty again of interpolating a groundless notion into the word of God, and demand for it the authority of inspiration, without uttering a syllable either to justify or palliate it, is an extraordinary offence, not only against God, but against man. They do not affect to allege any direct proof from the chapter itself of the futurity of the seventieth week. The only considerations they offer to corroborate their theory, are drawn from other parts of Daniel, and are as unauthoritative and mistaken, as their notion is that the events foreshown as to take place in the seventieth week, are still future.

2. This omission of proof from chap. ix. 24–27, was itself, however, the effect of necessity; as there is not a hint in those verses, that the seventieth week was not to be the week that was immediately to suc-

ceed the sixty-ninth. And this absence from the predictions of the passage of any intimation, direct or indirect, that the seventieth week was not immediately to follow the sixty-ninth, but was to be separated from it by an interval of many centuries, is itself a decisive signal of the error of their theory. For this is a prophecy in which certain times are given, for the express purpose of indicating the epochs when the events foreshown in it were to take place. How then is it to be assumed, that in such a revelation, in which the periods were essential elements, God should disclose only those of them that are of the least significance, and subservient to others that are to follow; and leave the most numerous and the most important, wrapt in a depth of darkness and uncertainty that must necessarily baffle and confound his children? The supposition is derogatory to his truth and his wisdom. The object in here giving *first*, the whole period of the weeks; *next*, the several divisions into which they were distributed; and then indicating the events that were to take place at the beginning of the first; and at the beginning and close of the second; plainly was, that it might be known first, from what event the first division was to be dated: and then from what epochs the second and third were to be reckoned. That was the natural effect of the division, and of the designation of the event, that was to mark the beginning of the first; and the date and event, that were to identify the commencement of the second: and finally the great acts that were to bespeak the close of the sixty-two weeks and the presence of the seventieth.

Thus, the decree of Artaxerxes indicated the beginning of the first division, and the building of the wall and city, as the great event that signalized that period. The rebuilding, and the close of the 49 years from the date of the decree, indicated the commencement of the second period, in immediate continuity with the seven preceding weeks. Reckoning from that date, the termination of the sixty and two weeks, was determinable without the designation of the acts by which it was marked, though it was doubtless identified, to such as understood it, by the baptism of Jesus; the descent of the Spirit on him; the public recognition of him as his Son by the Father; and the open identification of him by John as the Lamb of God who was to take away the sin of the world. The announcement that after the sixty and two weeks Messiah should be cut off, identified the period of his death as the seventieth week: and the prediction that he should confirm the covenant for one week, in the middle of which he should cause sacrifice and oblation to cease, showed that his death was to take place at that point in the seventieth week. To deny it, is to deny that it was the object of the division of the weeks into groups, and the prediction of events that were to mark their dates, and their periods, to make known the periods and epochs when the great events of the prophecy were to take place; and is therefore to contradict the most peculiar and distinctive feature that is sculptured on its face. According to these writers, there is not a solitary hint, when the great events foreshown, v. 24, are to take place! If it were so, the pretence that a chronology of the periods and dates, is inserted in the prophecy, would plainly be a misrepresentation. For what chronology of the whole period and its great series of acts and events would the dates and periods of the two first divisions form? They owe their whole significance to their relation to the remaining division. If the time and the events of the third are unknown, the knowledge of the date of the decree of Artaxerxes authorizing the rebuilding of Jerusalem, and that forty-nine years would pass before the wall of the city would be completed, would be of little consequence, even while the period was revolving; and would lose all its special importance to the generations that followed that age. The bare announcement that after the first division, a period of sixty-two weeks was to follow in immediate continuity with the seven weeks without any prediction of the events in which they were to terminate, would be but a mockery. Their theory is thus not only unverified by them, but is in palpable contradiction to the structure of the passage, and to the object for which the chronology is given of its great periods and events.

3. But they not only disregard the structure of the prophecy; they contravene the express representation it presents, that the reason that the seventy weeks were cut off from other time, was, that they were to be the period of the great events that were to reach their climax, in the crucifixion of Christ, and the confirmation of the covenant with Israel. "Seventy weeks are cut off, *upon thy people, and upon thy holy city,* to put a bar to, and restrain transgression; and to seal sin; and to expiate iniquity; and to bring forth everlasting righteousness; and to seal vision and prophecy; and to anoint a Holy of Holies." This is thus an express announcement that the seventy weeks were separated in their relation to the Jewish people, and their holy city, from other time, in order that they might be, and because they were to be the period, in which the Messiah was to appear and accomplish his sacrificial work for the redemption of men. And they are exhibited as cut off *as a whole*, and at *one stroke;* not in parcels, and by successive acts. If they had been cut off by successive acts, in two periods separated from each other by a vast series of ages, the description would unquestionably have been in conformity with that fact. Why should the Spirit of truth frame the representation in such a manner, as to indicate that the weeks were to be a continuous series; if they were not to be such? Why should their disseverance from each other by ages, be concealed; and the

people of the covenant thereby be involved in inexplicable doubt and perplexity? The supposition of such a procedure is an impeachment of his rectitude and benignity, and is against the very letter of the narrative. The weeks were cut off as one period, and at one stroke. Their division into groups was by a subsequent act, and was in order to indicate the parts of the series in which the great events, that were to lead on to the consummation, were to fall. Thus, the first great event that was to be in order to that consummation was, the rebuilding of Jerusalem. That is indicated in the decree itself of Artaxerxes, and in the prophecy; and the seven weeks, the first division of the seventy are designated as its period. The building of the walls of the city also, and re-erection of dwellings, which were authorized by the decree of Artaxerzes given to Nehemiah, were indispensable conditions to all that was to follow in the sixty and two weeks, and in the seventieth; in order to the protection of the inhabitants from the enemies by whom they were surrounded; in order to the public celebration of the sacrificial rites, and the stated offering of worship; in order to the religious education of the people, their preservation from relapses to idolatry, and their nurture in that knowledge and belief of the great purposes of God in respect to their redemption, by which they should be kept in expectation of the coming of the Messiah. The commencement of that first period, was given in the prophecy itself, and the great event also, that was to take place at the close of the second division. "Know therefore and understand that from the going forth of the commandment to restore and to build Jerusalem, unto Messiah the Prince, shall be seven weeks, and three score and two weeks." The rebuilding of the wall of the city took place we know from Nehemiah, before the expiration of the first of the seven weeks. The re-erection of dwellings continued, doubtless, through the whole period, and the complete reorganization of the community, and re-establishment over them of the laws by which they were to regulate their conduct as God's people, we learn from Nehemiah, did not take place till the close, or near the close of the forty-ninth year, from the date of the Persian monarch's decree.—Neh. xiii.

The prophecy presents no indication, what the great events that were to signalize the sixty-two weeks, the second period were to be. We know however from the cutting off of the seventy weeks in order to the coming, ministry and sacrifice of the Messiah, that the sixty and two weeks, like the first seven, were to be the period of events that would contribute in a conspicuous manner to a preparation for those of the seventieth week: which was to be the time of Christ's ministry and death. And we learn from history, that many of the great measures of Providence, and acts of men, that had their place in that time, filled a most important office in generating that posture both of the Jewish and the Gentile world, which marked the period of Christ's birth, ministry, and death. Among them was the conquest of the Persian empire by the Greeks; the more favorable condition in which the Jews in Palestine and the neighboring countries were placed; their far larger intercourse with the east and the west; the multiplication of their colonies, especially in Asia Minor and Greece; the use of the Greek language to which they became addicted; and the diffusion and use of that language through all the countries that were comprised in the Greek empire, or had a large commercial intercourse with its maratime cities. This was an event of the utmost significance, as the language of the Greeks became the chief vehicle of communicating the Gospel both to Jews and Gentiles, especially at the west; and was the tongue in which the inspiring Spirit embodied the discourses of our Lord, the history of his life, his preaching and his crucifixion, and the revelations made by him of his purposes respecting the future. That the conquest of Palestine and the neighboring countries by the Greeks, was to exert a vast influence on the condition of the Jews, is clearly foreshown indeed, in Daniel's eighth, tenth and eleventh chapters.

Another event fruitful of a vast train of effects of the most important and benign character, during this period, was the translation of the Hebrew Scriptures into Greek, by which the knowledge of the Old Testament was placed within the reach of the Gentile population of the empire who were familiar with that language.

A third event of immeasurable moment in the great series that was to lead on to that condition of the Jewish and of the Gentile world, that distinguished the time of Christ's birth and life, was the conquest of the Greek empire by the Romans. Out of it sprung the arbitrary and cruel rule of Herod the great, the Procuratorship of Pontius Pilate, and the sway of Herod Antipas and Herod Agrippa. From it resulted in a great measure the civil and religious condition of the Jewish people, the ambition of the rulers, and the malice of the priests, which issued in the rejection and crucifixion of the Son of God. This conquest was also foreshown in the prophecies of Daniel, and many of the great acts of the new power, especially its overthrow of the Jewish state, and its antagonism to the Prince of princes were predicted, and a vivid picture drawn of the vast influences it was to exert for ages.

All these events, though not enumerated in Daniel's ninth chapter, contributed in the most direct and effective manner, to place the Jewish community and Gentile population of the Roman empire in that attitude in which they stood at the birth, ministry, and death of Christ.

Another note of time is presented in the announcement that "from the going forth of the commandment to restore and to build Jerusalem, unto Messiah the prince, shall be seven weeks, and threescore and two weeks:" and this indicates in the most distinct and definite manner, the event that on the one side was to mark the close of the sixty-ninth week, and on the other, the commencement of the seventieth. The expression "unto the Messiah, the Prince," refers, not to his birth, but to his baptism, recognition by the Father as his beloved Son, and command that those to whom he was sent, should hear him; and his entrance on his trial in the wilderness and on his ministry to the Jews. This is certain from the chronology. Four hundred and eighty-three years had elapsed from the date of the decree to his entrance on his ministry; and no more. To regard the event at which the sixty-ninth week terminated, as his birth would involve an error of thirty years: as therefore there is no event subsequent to his public identification as the Messiah by the Father and the Spirit, the open announcement of him as the Lamb of God by the Baptist, and his own avowal of himself as the Son of God and the Saviour of the world, to which it could with any propriety be referred, it is certain that the event at which the sixty-ninth week ended, was Christ's public manifestation by God and by himself as the Son of the Most High, and the promised Prince of Israel.

This declaration demonstrates, therefore, in the

most definitive manner, on the one hand, that the death of Christ did not take place in the sixty-ninth week, for that week ended at his entrance on his ministry; and on the other, that the period of his ministry and death was the seventieth week; and, as his ministry extended through only three years and a half, that the date of his death was at the distance of three years and a half from the close of the sixty-ninth week; and this is confirmed by the representation that in the midst of the one week he should cause sacrifice and oblation to cease; setting aside by his vicarious death the necessity and obligation any longer to offer the sacrifice, whose office was simply to typify him. There thus is not the slightest room left for doubt, whether his ministry and death had their place in the seventieth week. There is not a single point in the chronology of the chapter that is more demonstrably clear and incontrovertible than this. The theory of these writers is, accordingly, not only unsupported by the prophecy, but is against its plainest and most indubitable specifications of its dates and times.

4. That is confirmed by the prediction, v. 26, "And after the three score and two weeks shall Messiah be cut off." This is in harmony with the fact already revealed, that the sixty-nine weeks were to close, and the seventieth begin at the epoch of his entrance on his ministry. It is equivalent, therefore, to a specific denial that he died during the sixty-ninth, or any pre-

vious week; and to an explicit affirmation that his death was to take place in the seventieth week. As it was after the sixty-ninth week, and there was but one week of the seventy remaining, its period was, by the unequivocal definitions of the text, the seventieth week. And these clear specifications, these repeated determinations of the time, as in that week, and nowhere else, were doubtless designed, among other ends, to place in the hands of the priests, teachers and people, ample means of identifying the great epochs of the prophecy as they occurred, and to guard them and the generations that followed, against delusion by the false Christs who were to rise soon after the promulgation of the Gospel, and proclaim them selves the Messiah promised in this ancient prophet.

5. All this is confirmed by the chronology of the period. As we know from the prophecy itself that the epoch of his manifestation to Israel, and entrance on his ministry, was the termination of the sixty-ninth week, and beginning of the seventieth, v. 25; and as we know that he entered on his ministry in his thirty-first year, Luke iii. 23, we know that seven years added to the thirty that had passed before his baptism, extended to the thirty-eighth from his birth. And this accords with the chronology of the sixty-nine weeks of Daniel himself; the statements of the Gospels and Acts, and the testimony of secular historians; and places it beyond doubt that his ministry and death had their periods in the seventieth week.

The date to which the twentieth of Artaxerxes is on the most authoritative grounds referred, is the four hundred and fifty-fifth year, before the first of the current Christian era. It is admitted by writers generally that Christ's birth took place at least three years earlier than the date that has been assigned to it by Archbishop Usher and others. Let us assume that our Saviour's birth occurred in the four hundred and fifty-third year from the date of the decree, from which the seventy weeks are reckoned. That would be the four hundred and fifty-third year of the four hundred and ninety: add to that the thirty years that intervened between his birth and his baptism, and they make 483 years. Add then the three and a-half years of his ministry, and the like period of the confirmation of the covenant after his crucifixion, and they make 490 years, the exact number embraced in the period denoted by the seventy weeks.

This Dr. Tregelles rejects, and expresses the belief that the ministry and death of Christ had their place in the sixty-ninth week, on the assumption that the public manifestation of himself as the Messiah, referred to in v. 25, did not take place till his entrance into Jerusalem, four days before his last Passover. But that is a groundless and most unwarrantable assumption. Christ had been publicly recognized and proclaimed by the Father himself as his Son, three years and a-half before; had been pointed out by John the Baptist as the Lamb of God; and had, in the first year of his teaching, been acknowledged by Nathaniel as the Son of God and the King of Israel; had openly avowed his deity and Messiahship to Nicodemus; and in his discussions with the Jewish teachers and rulers had apprised them that it was by faith in him alone that they could obtain admission to his kingdom; and it was the clearness and fullness of these assertions of his Messiahship, and the confirmation of their truth presented in his great and numerous miracles, that had wrought the exulting convictions in the minds of the crowd that attended him in his entry into Jerusalem, by which they were led to shout hosannahs to him as the Son of David, their promised Messiah, and pronounce blessings on him as the great messenger who had come in the name of the Lord. There was no more explicit and emphatic exhibition of himself on that occasion as the Son of David, nor any higher manifestation of his divine power, than marked his ministry at every stage from his recognition by John, Nathaniel and Nicodemus at its commencement, to the hour of his entry into the city when his followers had become so numerous, and so open in their homage as to alarm the priests and rulers, and prompt them to consummate the conspiracy against his life which they had secretly cherished, through near the whole course of his teaching.

Dr. Tregelles also endeavors to elude the proof furnished by v. 27, that the Redeemer's death took place in the seventieth week; by alleging that the personage who was to confirm the covenant with many for one week, instead of the Messiah, was the prince mentioned, v. 26, who with his army was to destroy the city and sanctuary.

"This destruction is here said to be wrought by a certain people, not by the prince who shall come, but by his people: this refers, as I believe, to the Romans as the last holders of undivided Gentile power:—They wrought the destruction long ages ago;—the prince who shall come, v. 26, is the last head of the Roman power, the person concerning whom Daniel had received so much previous instruction. And he the prince who shall come, shall confirm a covenant with many for one week." —*Pp.* 102, 103.

But here, in the first place, is a misrepresentation of the passage. There is no intimation in it, as Dr. Tregelles implies, that the people, that is, the army of the prince, was to destroy the city wholly independently and irrespectively of him. The supposition is solecistical, as it assumes that the Roman legions had no commander. But so far was that from being the fact, it was the prince himself, it is expressly said, who was to come to the city, and therefore at the head of his legions, while no formal notice is given that his warrior host should come. That is only implied in the acts it is foreshown they were after their arrival to exert. The plain meaning of the expression therefore is, that the prince who was to come, should by his army, destroy the city and the sanctuary. Who then was that prince? He is spoken of as already predicted, and known therefore to the reader. The language is not,—*a* prince shall come,—of whom the reader had had no intimation before; but, *the* prince who, as already foreshown, is to come. The answer is undoubtedly, it is the prince, or line, symbolized by the sixth horn of the goat, ch. viii. 9, 23, 24, who it is predicted, "should destroy the mighty and the holy people;" as that horn was indubitably the symbol of the line of Roman Rulers, who conquered Macedonia in the year 168 before Christ, and subsequently extending their dominion over the whole of the Greek empire, held possession of Palestine at the birth and crucifixion of our Lord. The text confutes therefore, instead of sustaining his construction.

In the next place, he admits that the Romans under Titus—then a prince, and subsequently emperor—marched to Jerusalem and beseiged, captured and destroyed it, according to the letter of v. 26. But that exhausts the scope of the prediction. He, however, assumes that there is to be another destruction of the Jewish city and sanctuary, and a fierce persecution of the people by the personage whom he calls the last head of the Roman power. He proceeds perhaps on Mr. Baxter's theory, that there is to be a double fulfillment of the prophesies of Daniel and John. Whether it be so, or not, he is wholly mistaken. There most certainly is no prediction in v. 27 that there is to be another desolation of the city by the Romans, or any other people, beside that foreshown, v. 26. Nor is there any prediction in Isaiah or Zechariah of such a catastrophe. The picture drawn by each of those prophets represents the city as still *standing*, after the second advent of Christ and destruction of the hostile Gentile hosts. The people of the city are to flee into the valley opened by the removal of the Mount of Olives, half toward the north, and half toward the south, at the moment of Christ's descent, Zech. xiv. 4, 5; while the overthrow of walls and battlements and towns, foretold by Isaiah, is ascribed to Jehovah's arising to shake terribly the earth. Ch. ii. 14–21.

In the third place, his assumption that the personage who was to confirm the covenant for one week with many of the Jews, was the prince of v. 26, whose hosts were to destroy the city, and that that prince is still future, and is to be the last head of the Roman power, is not only groundless, but is in total contravention of the usages of language, and the laws of our nature. For according to Dr. Tregelles, what the passage affirms is, that the people of a prince *who was not himself to come until* 1800 *years had revolved*, should destroy the city and the sanctuary. But that implies that that prince was already in life, and was to continue in it through that vast period. Otherwise the people who were to destroy the city, could not be his people. It is absurd and solecistical to speak of a people, as the people of a prince, who is not in existence, and is not to come into being till a vast series of ages has passed. Such a non-existence could have no authority over them. He could have no power to exert acts in reference to them. He would be, as respects them, as mere a nonentity, as he would be, if he were never to have a being. When a series of monarchs reign over the same nation through a succession of generations, the people are the people of each individual monarch in the line,—only while he holds the sceptre over them. The subjects of Queen Victoria of England, are exclusively those who are contemporaries with her, and live under her sway. She is not the queen of the English people of the generation that lived under the rule of Henry VIII., Elizabeth, James I., the Charleses, or any of her predecessors, who passed from life before their birth who constituted the nation, when she assumed the throne. Her subjects became her people, only when she became their sceptred head. The people of Louis Napoleon, are those exclusively who live under his rule. He is not the monarch of the generation over which Henry IV. reigned. He is not the prince of the French people that lived under the sceptre of Louis XIV. He is not the monarch of the generation that was contemporaneous with Louis XV.; nor even of those, except they still survive, who were the subjects of his relative the first Napoleon. Yet this self-evident truth, Dr. Tregelles with astonishing inconsideration disregards, and assumes that Antichrist, who is not yet revealed, was the chief of the Roman host in the siege and destruction of Jerusalem in the seventieth year of the Christian era, and attempts in violation of the most indubitable laws of thought and language, to fasten that preposterous sense on the words of the prophecy, that he may bend it into harmony with his mistaken theory.

He affirms that "the prince who was to come," was "the last head of the Roman power." If that were true, he was indisputably a Roman in his lineage, and must therefore have been in life at the latest, before the fall of the last head of that power, at the overthrow of the western Roman empire. There has been no head of the western empire since the abdication of Augustulus. All the present civil rulers of the kingdoms that occupy the territory of that imperium, are of Gothic descent, and they, and they alone, or others of the same lineage, are to hold the sceptres of those realms till the Son of God comes, and puts an end to their rule.

The prince, in verse 26, is not, as Dr. Tregelles represents, the antecedent of "he," supplied by the translators, in the expression: "He shall confirm the covenant with many for one week." If it were, it would prove that Titus the Roman prince, who conquered the city, was the person who confirmed the covenant with many for one week, inasmuch as he, as I have shown, was the chief who commanded the legions by which the city and sanctuary were destroyed. This is seen also from the fact, that there was no covenant in existence between Titus and many of the Jews to be confirmed by him; nor was any made and confirmed with any portion of that people after the siege commenced. Not a trace of such a transaction exists on the records of that period by Josephus, or the Latin historians; nor is the supposition of a league between them compatible with the narratives given by those writers, of the unyielding obstinacy and delirious infatuation of the chiefs and factions that reigned in the city throughout its investment. And finally, this is placed beyond doubt by the fact that the covenant that was confirmed, was the covenant of God with his ancient people; and the Being who confirmed it, was the Messenger of the Covenant, the Lord Jesus Christ, who made the expiation for sin, and rendered the obedience that were to be the grounds of pardon and salvation to men.

The reason that the prediction of the overthrow of the city and sanctuary was interposed between the prophecy of his death and the prophecy of his confirming the covenant, doubtless was, that the Jewish people might be apprised that Christ was not to enter on his reign as the king of that people immediately after his resurrection. This is obvious from the expression, "Messiah shall be cut off; but there is nothing to him. And (even) the city and the sanctuary, the people of the prince who shall come will lay waste; and the end shall be with a flood; and unto the end, war, a decree of desolations." The expression, "and it is not to him," or, "there is nothing to him," is plainly elliptical, and indicates that there was something, which without this notice, Jewish believers might assume was immediately to follow his death and resurrection; but which was not then to take place. What was it, then, that belonged to him as the Messiah, that was not then to be received by him? His inauguration as the king of Zion, and entrance on his reign over Israel and over the earth, according to the prediction, Psalm ii. 6–8, "Yet have I set my king upon my holy hill of Zion. I will declare the decree: The Lord hath said unto me, Thou art my Son; this day have I begotten thee. Ask of me, and I will give thee the nations for thine inheritance, and the uttermost parts of the earth for thy possession." It was this investiture with the dominion of the earth, which the disciples thought might take place soon after his resurrection, that was postponed, in accordance with the vision of his coming in the clouds (chapter vii. 13, 14) till the time arrives of the judgment and destruction of the powers represented by the beast. This announcement that his kingdom on earth was not immediately to be given to him, but was to follow his ascent to heaven, where he is to reign till his enemies are put under his feet, was needful, doubtless, to guard his people from misconception and disappointment, and show them when the moment came that the risen Redeemer ascended to his throne in the skies, that that great measure was not a departure from the purposes God had before revealed, but was in order to their final accomplishment. And the natural place for this announcement, is that which it received, in immediate connection with the prediction of his death; and followed by the prophecy that the city in which his throne at his second coming is to be established, was in the meantime to be overthrown, and the nation swept away as by a flood. Having thus, on the one hand, indicated the postponement of Christ's reign on the earth, in conformity with the vision (ch. vii. 9–14) which exhibits his coming in the clouds, and reception of the dominion of the earth as not to take place till the power denoted by the beast has run its career, and the hour of its judgment has come; and on the other, foreshown the desolation of the city and sanctuary, and the slaughter and exile of the nation; the prophecy then as naturally returns to the confirmation of the covenant with Israel, which Christ was to give during the seventieth week, in the teachings and miracles of his ministry, in his death on the cross, in the gift of his renewing and inspiring Spirit to his disciples, by which he opened to them a full knowledge of all the ancient predictions respecting himself, and brought to their remembrance all the words of instruction and prediction they had heard from his lips. And it was equally suitable and natural, that in connection with this, it should be foreshown that the typical sacrifices were to be discontinued after his death; and finally, that after the seventy weeks had expired, the temple and its courts, in which those sacrifices had been offered, were to be polluted by abominations that would draw down a desolation that should continue till the full judgment on the nation, which had been predicted, has been accomplished.

The view I have presented of this passage, and of the whole question, respecting the seventieth week of the prophecy, is thus supported by all its language, and all that we know of the events it foreshows, from other portions of the word of God. No arbitrary assumptions are employed to give it support; no violations of the laws of thought and speech to sustain it; no contradictions to the office and work of Christ; no ascriptions of the actions of persons whose period was eighteen hundred years ago, to a being who has not yet come into existence, nor is ever to appear in our world. The theory of these writers, built up with so much labor and artifice, consequently falls to the ground.

CHAPTER IX.

Some of these Writers maintain that many of the Prophecies are to have a Double Fulfillment.

ANOTHER important element of the system held by some of these authors is the pretext that those of the prophecies of Daniel and John, of which the periods are given, are to have a two-fold accomplishment, the first extending through as many years as there are days in the symbol by which they are represented; the other extending through only as many days as there are units in the symbol itself: twelve hundred and sixty days, first denoting twelve hundred and sixty years; and next, the number of days which the words literally express. This theory is stated with less distinctness both by Mr. Baxter and by the authors whose opinions in regard to it he quotes. The following passages present the clearest of Mr. Baxter's statements in respect to it:

"The relative positions of the twenty events 'that are to occur during the final seven years and two and a half months of this dispensation,' are ascertained in many cases, by deducing the *future literal day* fulfillment of the prophecies, from their *past year day* fulfillment. These positions are here shown by giving their distance from the date of the *covenant*, as a common standard of reference."—*Preface, p. vi.*

"Futurist literal day expositors hold that the three and a half years mentioned in Daniel vii., xii., and Revelation xi., xii., xiii., as a time, times, and a-half, or forty-two months, are the three and a half years of the Antichrist's future persecution; and are identical with the latter half of Daniel's seventieth week of seven years, which commences with a seven years' covenant being made between the Antichrist and the Jews. This does not conflict with the view that there has been *a typical year day* fulfillment of that three and a half times, as 1260 years of Papal dominancy, and of the little horns of Daniel vii. and viii., as the Papal and Mahometan powers respectively."—*Baxter, pp.* 182, 183.

How generally this view is entertained by this school of authors I am not aware. It is not held by Dr. Tregelles nor by the Rev. B. W. Newton, as they maintain that neither the time, times and half a time of Daniel, nor any other periods are employed as symbols of longer times than they themselves literally denote. The theory thus is, that there are two sets of periods of which the first, like the time, times and half a time, and the 1260 days of Daniel, bears the same proportion to the second, that years bear to days; that the two sets are to terminate at the same moment; and that each of the corresponding periods, such as the twelve hundred and sixty days, and the three and a half years, are to be occupied by identically the same actors and events. The series of events for example that is foreshown as to take place during the twenty-three hundred days interpreted as symbols of twenty-three hundred years, are to be repeated again by the same actors, and in the same forms and conditions in the last twenty-three hundred literal days of the present dispensation. That this is the view held by those who advocate the notion of a double fulfillment of the prophecies, in which times are used as symbols of times, is clear, from the consideration that there cannot be "a future literal day fulfillment" of those prophecies unless it is precisely like their *past* year day fulfillment, in agents, acts, events and conditions. The sole difference between them must lie in their respective lengths. Their *likeness* is to lie in the literal fulfillment in each, of the prophecies in which days are used as symbols of years; and in the coincidence of the moment in which they are to reach their end. The truth of this representation is amply confirmed by Mr. Baxter. He says:

"It is not surprising that a few writers should have imagined that form of the periods of three and a-half years mentioned twice in Daniel, and five times in Revelation, should signify the *first half* of the final week of seven years; and others of these periods of its last half. It is a natural mistake for those to fall into who do not understand how remarkably all the periods have had a *precursory* year-day simultaneous fulfillment within twelve hundred and sixty *years*, from the year of our Lord 534 to 1794–5; and, therefore, they will all necessarily *synchronise and run parallel in their future* literal day fulfillment within 1260 days; or the last half of the seventieth week. Those literal day expositors who shirk laborious investigation, by blindly ignoring the year-day fulfillment, grope and stumble in the dark when they attempt to arrange the relative positions of the literal day seals, trumpets and vials; whereas this arrangement is discoverable in its minutest details by deducing the literal day fulfillment from the year-day fulfillment, because *the literal day fulfillment of Daniel and Revelation within* 2595 *days*, WILL BE ALMOST AN EXACT FAC SIMILE *of their year-day fulfillment within* 2595 *years*."—*Note, pp.* 247, 248.

The literal day fulfillment is thus, according to Mr. Baxter, to be an exact copy as to agents, acts and events, of the year day fulfillment, which will in the main have preceded it. He accordingly says, in another passage:

"In reading the works of literal day expositors who interpret the 1260 days three and a half times, and forty-two months, to mean 1260 literal days, or three and a half years; and of year-day expositors who interpret the same periods to mean 1260 years, the prophetic student must not be stumbled at their sometimes mutually rejecting each others views. *Each system of interpretation is, however, equally correct*, for there is *a double fulfillment of most of the prophecies of Daniel and Revelation*, primarily in years, and secondly in days."—p. 183.

If there is to be such a double fulfillment, the two must be exactly alike, as to agents, acts, events and conditions, and differ only in the length of the periods they occupy, as years differ in length from days.

But this theory of a double fulfillment of the prophecies is wholly mistaken, and fraught with immeasurable confusion and self-confutation.

1. It is a mere assumption, unsupported by even a

pretext of proof. Not a word is penned by Mr. Baxter to show that it has any authority from the word of God. The fancy entertained by him that the arrangement he proposes of the literal day seals, trumpets and vials, is easily discoverable in its minutest details, by deducing the literal day from the year day fulfillment, "*because* the literal day fulfillment of Daniel and Revelation, within 2595 *days*, will be almost an exact fac simile of their year day fulfillment within 2595 years," is no *proof* that there is to be such a literal day fulfillment. In alleging it as evidence of the truth of the theory, he assumes the identical point he affects to establish.

2. It is in total contradiction to the laws of symbolization. The general principle on which symbols are employed, is that of analogy:—things of one species or sphere being taken to represent things of another to which they bear a general resemblance. In symbolizing time, time itself of a known and specific period, is used to represent time of a longer, but an analogous length. Thus, a day of twenty-four hours, during which the earth revolves on its axis, is employed as the representative of the analogous period of a solar year, during which the earth wheels round the sun. This is the only relation in wnich time is used as a symbol of time; and the only one in which it can be used on the ground of resemblance. But this great law, the theory of a double prediction by the same symbol contradicts, by affirming that the 1260, 1290,

1335, and 2300 days, while used as representatives of years, are in the same instances used, *not* as symbols of years, but unsymbolically to denote the simple number of days which they literally express. But that is to deny that they are used as representatives of years. If it is a known and indubitable fact, that they are employed to denote the mere number of days, of which they themselves severally consist, how can it be shown that they are also used in the relation of analogy, to denote a corresponding number of years? It plainly cannot. If on the other hand, it is known from the laws of symbolization, and from the fulfillments that have taken place of the predictions in which they occur, that they are employed as symbols to represent years, instead of days, how can it then be shown that they are in the same identical instances used as days to signify periods that correspond in length to themselves? They manifestly cannot. The attempt to fix on them such a meaning, is groundless and arbitrary in the extreme.

3. If the theory is legitimate, then on the same principle, the literal day predictions, must be taken as symbolizing each another period, that is to follow itself, with another literal day fulfillment; and that literal day period of fulfillment, must be held to be the representative of a third, and so on without end. But that overturns the faith of these writers that Christ is to come at, or soon after, the close of the 1260 or 1290 years; and put an end to the times of

the Gentiles. For if, as their scheme of a double prophecy and fulfillment implies, there is to be an endless succession of the periods foreshown in Daniel and John, then indubitably either Christ is not to come at the close of the first 1260 or 1290 years, as these authors maintain, or else he is to come an infinite number of times; which is contradictory to the prophesies, and confutes and confounds in the most pitiable manner, their belief as to his coming but once; and at, or near the close of the 1260 or 1290 years. If they can prove that the 1260 days, besides symbolizing a like number of years, also foreshow another literal 1260 days like themselves; then they cannot prove that that literal 1260 days, does not also foreshow a second 1260 literal days that are immediately to follow them and be characterized by the same actors, acts, events, and conditions, as they are. And if they cannot prove that, then plainly they cannot demonstrate that there is not to be an interminable repetition of that period, and the actors and events that are to signalize it.

4. It is in the most open and senseless contradiction to the whole representation of the Scriptures on the subject. There is not an intimation in the prophesies, that indentically the same prediction is in any instance to have a double accomplishment. If it were expressly taught that judgments and chastenings foreshown in a prophecy, are to have double, and many fulfillments, there would be no means ot know-

ing when they had reached their end. If the Israelites may in virtue of the predictions in Hosea, Amos, Isaiah and other prophets, be carried into captivity a second time, and left in exile through several thousand years, who can know but that a third captivity may follow the second, and a fourth the third, and so on forever? What an impeachment of the truth and wisdom of the Most High it is, to impute to him such a method of prediction!

There are indeed many predictions in the Scriptures, that the same events *in kind* are repeatedly to occur; but not one that indentically the same event is to take place more than once. Christ foreshowed that there were to be wars, earthquakes and famines and pestilences; but they were not to be the same individual wars and earthquakes, famines and pestilences. Though resembling each other in their general characteristics, as wars and earthquakes, they were not to be identical repetitions of the first in the train, to which each belonged. The wars were to be between different nations, or at different times, under different leaders, and attended with the slaughter of different individuals. The earthquakes were not to be repetitions of each other, in the same locality, but were to have their scene "in diverse places."

There is to be but one incarnation, one ministry one crucifixion, one burial, one resurrection, one ascension and glorification of the Son of God. There is to be but one corporeal death of the same individual; one resurrection of the same individual saints to life and glory; and one resurrection of the unholy dead to shame and everlasting contempt. And so of all other events foreshown in the prophesies, whether they are revealed through symbols, or foretold in language. There is to be but one series of rulers of the western Roman empire symbolized by the beast from the sea, Rev. xiii. 1–3; there is to be but one conquest of that empire by Goths and Vandals from the north of Europe or Asia; there is to be but one irruption of Saracens from Arabia under Mahomet and diffusion over western Asia, northern Africa, and a part of Europe. There is to be but one conquest of the same territory by Seljukians, Moguls and Turks, and establishment and support of an empire for more than 800 years. The seven seals are the only seals that are to be broken; the seven trumpets are the only trumpets that are to be blown; the seven vials are the only vials that are to be poured. The inflictions foreshown under these last, are, accordingly expressly denominated "the last plagues." They are not to be duplicated, through an interminable series of years.

5. But such a repetition of that which is foreshown by Daniel and John, as this theory contemplates, is physically impossible. As well might these writers affirm that the whole solar system is to be crowded into a single ball of the dimensions of the minutest particle of matter of which it consists, as to maintain

that all the actors, acts, and events, of the last twenty-five hundred and fifty years, are to reappear in the world in the last 1260 or 1290 days of the present dispensation. How can identically the same agents, acts, events, and conditions, be repeated, and fill the several parts in the last 1260 days of this dispensation, which they filled in their first advent and career in the world? Is Nebuchadnezzar again to conquer Judea, Tyre, Egypt and Syria; build Babylon a second time, and a second time be driven from the presence of men, and dwell with the beasts of the field? Is Belshazzar again to drink wine with his courtiers in the vessels that were taken from the temple at Jerusalem; see again the handwriting on the wall, and hear his doom from the lips of Daniel? Is Cyrus again to conquer Sardis and Babylon; Cambyses to invade Egypt, slaughter its inhabitants, overthrow its temples, and deface its sculptures? Is Alexander again to rise and reduce the Median and Babylonian empire to his sceptre? Are the Romans to appear, a second time, and spread their conquests from Britain in the west, to Mesopotamia in the east; and trample down identically the same nations and the same individuals, as in their first bloody career? Are the Saracens and Turks once more to overrun western Asia and northern Africa, and repeat the slaughters and tortures on the same worshipers of idols, whom they scourged in their first invasions? Is the long succession of popes who have reigned at

Rome for more than twelve hundred years, with all their countless train of priests, monks, and unofficial subjects, to reappear and act their parts again in the ten kingdoms of western Europe? For all this, and infinitely more, is to be compressed, according to these writers, in the last twelve hundred and sixty, or twelve hundred and ninety days, of this dispensation. What a monstrous conception! These parties, however, have scarcely turned a glance, it may be presumed, to this feature of their theory, though it stands out in bold prominence on its front. Who are to be the actors in the fancied literal day-fulfillment of the predictions that have already taken place in the 1260 year-day fulfillment, if not the identical persons who acted their part in that year-day accomplishment? If they are wholly different persons, and their acts wholly different acts, they and their agency plainly cannot be a second fulfillment—though on a smaller scale, of that of the year-day that preceded it. The agents, the actions, the events, the sufferings and deaths being different, the tragedy itself is manifestly as distinct from the first as it is from any other. The whole notion is thus an absurd and revolting solecism.

CHAPTER X.

Mr. Baxter's Theory that the Symbols taken from the Material World are to Appear in their Proper Nature, in a Second Fulfillment, which he holds is to take place.

MR. BAXTER maintains that there is not only to be a double fulfillment of most of the prophecies of the Revelation, but that there is also to be a fresh symbolization of the events which they foreshow, conspicuous to the eyes of all; that is, that the symbols that were exhibited to John in vision, are to appear in the forms in which he beheld them, and exert the acts and produce the effects which he witnessed, as they filled their several spheres in his presence. Thus, he says in regard to the seventh of the twenty events, whose period he affects to determine:

"Event vii. Commencement of Astounding Physical Phenomena, such as hail and fire falling on the earth, a third part of salt and fresh water becoming blood, and a third part of the luminaries being eclipsed.—*Rev. vi.*

"This series of marvellous phenomena continues throughout the last nine months of the primary three and a half years, and is caused by the first four trumpets. As the first trumpet is believed to have been accomplished from about A.D. 250 to 365, its corresponding position in the literal-day fulfillment, will be from about the sixteenth of the ninth month of the third year, to the eleventh day of the first month of the fourth year (reckoning from the date of the covenant); and during part or the whole of this period of nearly four months, *literal hail and fire mingled with blood will be cast on the earth, and the third part of trees burnt up, and all green grass burnt up.* This plague, as well as those caused by the other trumpets and by the vials, had its counterpart in the plagues inflicted by Moses upon the Egyptians, which were evidently intended as *types* of those yet unfulfilled plagues; and a decisive and unanswerable argument is thus afforded against the objections of the unbelieving skeptic, who denies the probability of this literal fulfillment of Revelation; for it is obvious that the deliverance of the Israelites out of the hand of Pharaoh, was in all its circumstances, preëminently a type of the far greater deliverance of the Christian and Jewish church from the tyranny of the last great Antichrist of the time of the final crisis.

"And the second angel sounded, and as it were a great mountain burning with fire was cast into the sea, and the third part of the sea became blood; and the third part of the creatures that were in the sea and had life, died; and the third part of the ships were destroyed. The judgment inflicted under this second trumpet will continue nearly two months after the close of the first trumpet, and culminate in the destruction of the ships three or four months before the three and a half years' tribulation. Some brilliantly luminous object, *as it were* a burning mountain or pillar of fire, will be cast into the sea, a third part of which (that part which is adjacent to Europe) will become blood; and as a natural consequence, every living creature in the third part which is thus affected, will die, and their carcases floating upon the surface of the crimson, blood-dyed waters, and breeding pestilence by their insufferable odor, will present a spectacle of unequalled horror. All the ships, likewise that are in that same third part of the sea, will be destroyed. . . . . Subsequent intercommunication between different countries by sea, will be greatly impeded by this unexampled destruction of vessels. *Not a few of the gigantic iron-plated vessels of war which are now being constructed by France and England, will probably be among the ships thus destroyed.* A larger proportion of French war-vessels may escape, because engaged in different quarters of the globe in carrying out Napoleon's schemes of universal conquest.

" 'The great star' of the third trumpet, he holds, is also literally to fall on the rivers and fountains, and 'by its means the nauseous flavor of wormwood will be supernaturally imparted to all fresh water in the third part of the earth, within which all salt water had previously been turned into blood, and the infusion of this ingredient, will even poison many men and result in their death!'

" At the fourth trumpet, the third part of the sun, moon and stars will be darkened. . . . The date of this phenomenon which probably will last a few days, will be about 58 days before the 1260 days of infidel persecution, just as the year-date of this trumpet in 476, was 58 years before the 1260 years of papal dominancy."

" Thus the first four trumpets are foreshown to commence respectively about nine, five, three, and two months before Napoleon's three and a half years' reign as Antichrist; and the fearful sights and great signs introduced by them in the heavens above, and in the earth beneath, and in the waters under the earth, will give ample warning to mankind of the awful wars that are about to follow."—pp. 83–86.

It is a distasteful task, to transcribe passages fraught with such caricatures of the divine word. But no one can form a just estimate of the ill-judgment and presumptuousness of this writer, unless made acquainted with the perversions of the symbols into which he runs.

1. He offers not a syllable of proof from the prophecy, or from any other quarter, that the symbols of the Apocalypse are thus to appear on the earth, to the eyes of all who dwell in the scene which the predictions respect, and act out their several parts, as they acted them when exhibited to the prophet in vision. It is a sheer fiction; a bold attempt to fasten on the prophecy a vast train of agents and events of which it breathes not a whisper; and will infallibly be rebuked by the Almighty Being whose word is thus misrepresented; as he has forewarned those who add unto the things which he has revealed. "I testify unto every man that heareth the words of the prophecy of this book. If any man shall add unto these things, God shall add unto him the plagues that are written in this book."—Rev. xxii. 18.

2. The pretext that the plagues of the trumpets and vials had their counterpart in the plagues inflicted on the Egyptians, and that they were types of these Apocalyptic inflictions, is wholly groundless and in contradiction to the truth. The plagues of Egypt were nearly all unlike those of the trumpets and vials. There were no frogs in the trumpets and vials; no conversion of the dust into insects; no swarms of flies; no murrain on domesticated animals; no blains upon beasts; no locusts that de-

voured vegetation; no pitch darkness; no death of the first-born. Thus seven of the Egyptian plagues had no counterpart whatever in the trumpets and vials. Two only of the Apocalypse, were the same as those of Egypt, namely, the conversion of water into blood, and the descent of hail mingled with fire. Another resembled that of the first vial, only, in the infliction of boils and blains on *man* along with *beasts;* while the ulcers caused by the first vial, were a plague only to men. No one who writes with any proper care, would fall into such a serious misrepresentation.

He betrays an equal degree of misapprehension in the assertion that the plagues of Egypt were types of the symbols of the trumpets and vials of the Apocalypse. They cannot be types, *first,* because types are only used as representatives of things, the future existenee of which had been previously revealed. Thus animal sacrifices were instituted as types of the great future Sacrifice, the Lamb of God; but they were instituted after God had revealed to our first parents the coming of that great Being to take away by his death the sins of the world. Had not that futurity first been made known, the animal sacrifices that were to be slain, would not have been to the offerers types of the coming Redeemer; and so of all other types. But no revelation was made at the infliction of the plagues of Egypt, that they were types of future plagues that were to be inflicted on the inhabitants of the Roman empire. There was no Roman empire then in existence; and no foreknowledge was given to Moses, or any other human being, that such a people as the Romans were ever to exist. *Next,* Things to be types, must be expressly appointed by God to the office they are to fill, and that appointment must be made known to those who are required to regard them as types. Otherwise they cannot be employed in that sphere by those who are to use them. To employ them in such a relation, without divine authority, is to arrogate the prerogative of appointing types, and usurp the place that belongs only to him. And, *thirdly,* Types are never representative of mere visionary existences, but only of such as are to have a real, palpable being in the world of intelligences. Thus, the animal sacrifices of the old economy, were types of Jesus Christ who was a real person, and was to come into the world and accomplish his work as our Redeemer by his death. The high priest was in like manner in his sphere, as the offerer of typical sacrifices, the type of the great High Priest who was to offer himself as the real sacrifice and expiation for our sins. The Holy of Holies in the tabernacle, was in the same manner a type of the Holy of Holies in the heavenly temple, in which Christ presents his blood, and intercedes for his people. But the chief symbols of the Apocalypse, were not real existences, in the outer world, like the earth, the sea, the sun, and moon, but only had their being in the visions in which they were exhibited to the Apostle. To treat them as independent and living realities, and assume, that because the real waters of Egypt were turned into blood, the visionary hail fire and blood of the first trumpet, which were mere symbols, are hereafter to descend as realities on the Apocalyptic earth, is in the grossest manner to contradict their nature and sphere. Has the great metallic image beheld by Nebuchadnezzar in a dream, had any other being than in his vision? Is it hereafter to have a real existence on the earth, and meet the gaze and wonder of the inhabitants who now dwell in his desolate dominions? Are the wild beasts of Daniel and the Apocalypse, that had their being only in visions, at a future time to appear on the earth, as genuine and palpable realities, and act out again, the bloody tragedies which they exhibited to Daniel and John in the the visions in which they were beheld? Mr. Baxter predicts it. God does not.

CHAPTER XI.

Their Notion of the Covenant between Louis Napoleon and the Jews. Their Views of Antichrist drawn from Ancient Writers.

ANOTHER notion advanced by several of those writers with great confidence, is, that in virtue of a covenant to be made with Louis Napoleon seven years before the close of this dispensation, the Jews are to return to Palestine, erect a temple in Jerusalem, and recommence the offering of sacrifices according to the Mosaic ritual; but that after favoring them in that measure for three years and a half, he is then to break his covenant with them, take possession of the temple by force, preclude them from continuing the presentation of sacrifices, and setting both himself and his image in the sacred edifice, persuade or compel them to worship him as God. Thus Mr. Baxter says:—

"One of the first objects to which the Jews, who are induced by the seven years' treaty to migrate to Jerusalem, and those who are already settled there, will naturally turn their attention, will be the rëestablishment of their temple worship, and the restoration of the ceremonies, of the Mosaic ritual. In Daniel viii. 13, this is foretold to happen 2300 days before the sanctuary is cleansed (by Antichrist's destruction at Armageddon,) and as the last mentioned event takes place exactly 7 years and 2½ months after the date of the covenant, it results that the sacrifices will be commenced just 295 days, or nine months and 25 days after the date of the covenant, and at the distance of 2300 before the end of the 7 years and 2½ months (or 2595 days). The passage in Daniel viii. 13, 14, reads thus: 'How long shall be the vision concerning the daily sacrifice and the transgression of desolation, to give both the sanctuary and the host to be trodden under foot?' That is to say: How long will the period be, during which the sacrifices will be restored, and then after their removal, how long will the desolation of the sanctuary continue? The answer is, *Unto* 2300 *days; then shall the sanctuary be cleansed.* It is manifest that the sacrifices beginning 7 months and 25 days after the covenant, will only continue for 965 days, or 2 years 8 months 5 days, until the end of the first 3½ years, because in the midst of the week of 7 years, Antichrist will cause the sacrifice to cease . . . and make it desolate until the consummation, Dan. ix. 27. The period of the subsequent desolation of the temple by the setting up of Napoleon's image there, extends over the latter 3½ years of the 7 years, and the supplementary 2½ months (Dan. xii. 7–12, Rev. xi. 2, literal fulfillment). Thus 965 of the 2300 days constitute the period of the daily sacrifice; and the remaining 1335 of the 2300 days constitute the period of the desolation of the sanctuary by the substitution of the worship of Napoleon's image, instead of the sacrifices. The analogy of the year day fulfillment of the 2300 days, shows that there probably will be a partial renewal of the sacrifices 9 months after the covenant, and a partial cleansing of the sanctuary 25 days before the consummation.

"It is said that the Jews consider Mount Moriah upon which the Mahometan Mosque of Omar is now standing, to be the only proper place for the offering of their sacrifices, in virtue of its having been the consecrated site of Solomon's temple; and the fact of its being in the hands of the uncircumcised, constitutes the main impediment to the rēinstitution of their sacrificial rites. Louis Napoleon's approaching covenant with them, will probably permit the conversion of this Mosque of Omar into a Jewish temple; it will then be appropriately fitted with altars and sacrificial tables and vessels, and the daily temple services will be strictly observed, accompanied with the burning of incense, and the slaying of oxen and lambs. (Is. lxvi. 3.) It is within their temple that Napoleon is to be worshiped as God, (2 Thess. ii.) 3½ years after the date of the covenant."—*Pp.* 72, 73.

The same views are presented by Sir Ed. Denny.

"The prince before named, having for the first three and a half years of his time, reigned in peace over the Jews, he now at the end of that time throws off the mask, and discovers himself. He had acted as a deceiver at first; and now having compassed his object, he shows himself forth as a tyrant.

"This will be the time of Jacob's trouble... when the holy city shall be trodden under foot, the abomination of desolation set up, and *the image of the beast*, namely, that of the desolator himself, shall stand in the holy place, as the object of worship, and when all shall be slain who will dare to refuse to worship the idol."—*Quoted by Mr. Baxter, p.* 200.

Dr. Tregelles advances the same views in regard to the idol, and the persecution of those who refuse to worship it:

"His reign is a time of grievous and grinding oppression to Israel; his abominable idol (the image of the beast, that the false prophet causes both to speak and to breathe, Rev. xiii.), being set in the holy place, all who refuse to worship it are the objects of his wrath; death is the doom which their disobedience receives."—*Remarks on Daniel, p.* 153.

Mr. Kelsall, Mr. Beale, Mr. Newton and others, give the same sketch of Antichrist and the image.

The unvarying sameness of the views presented in these passages, the similarity of the terms in which they are expressed, their enunciation in a dogmatic form, and the absence of attempts to verify them from the Scriptures, indicate that these writers who repeat them with such exactitude, are not the original authors of them, but are copyists of one another, or of other and earlier commentators. Why else is it that they proceed in announcing their peculiarities, as though they were reciting a creed, or repeating a pater-noster, advancing exactly the same doctrines in the same order, and in the same words, without adding a fresh thought, or uttering a pulse of emotion? Though, however, most of them maintain a singular reticence in respect to the source whence they derived them, it is admitted and avowed by Dr. Burgh, Mr. Maitland, Mr. Newton, Mr. Baxter, and perhaps some others, that they are drawn from writers of the second, third and fourth centuries; while nevertheless no intimation is given that they had their origin in opinions that were wholly mistaken, and that were confuted ages since by the non-occurrence of the events which, it was held, were to form their fulfillment; and that it was for that reason that they were soon erased from the faith of the church. Nor is any question raised by them respecting the validity of the opinions which they thus adopt, and their title to be received as a true exposition of the predictions to which they refer. Their having been held by persons of eminence in the early ages of the church is treated as a proof of their truth; and the mere re-assertion of them as enough to conciliate the assent of the reader. They were taken partly from Irenæus; more largely from Hippolytus, and in a measure from Apollinarius of Laodicea. That they were held in part by Irenæus, Bishop of Lyons, in Gaul, who was a Greek, and flourished toward the close of the second century, is seen from the fact, that in his work against Heresies, he represented that the worship of Antichrist in the temple at Jerusalem was to be instituted immediately before Christ's second advent, and was to be the abomination of desolation foretold, Daniel ix. 27. He says:

"But not only through the things that are spoken, but also through those that are to take place under Antichrist, it will be shown that being an apostate and a robber, he wishes to be adored as God; and instead of a servant resolves to be proclaimed a king. For assuming the boldness and art of the Devil he will come as though a rightful king; not, however, as legitamatized by subjection to God; but impious, unrighteous and without law; an apostate and a murderer, and repeating in himself the revolt of the Devil. And, indeed, while putting aside idols, in order to induce the belief that he himself is God, he sets up himself as the sole idol, that they may serve him: It is of him that the Apostle speaks, 2 Thess. ii. 3, 4. Paul thus clearly proves his apostasy, his exaltation of himself above all that is called God, or that is worshiped; that is, *above every idol*, and his attempt to show himself to be God by his tyranny.

"But I have shown already that no one was ever denominated by the Apostles God by virtue of his nature, except Him who is truly such, the Father of our Lord, by whose command that temple was built in Jerusalem, in which the Adversary will sit, aiming to show himself to be Christ."*

"And in the half of the hebdomad, he says, sacrifice and libation shall be taken away; and the abomination of desolation shall be in the temple; and unto the completion of the time the consummation shall be given upon the desolation. However, the half of the hebdomad is three years and six months."†

* Et non tantum autem per ea quae dicta sunt, sed et per ea quae erunt sub Antichristo, ostenditur, quoniam existens apostata et latro quasi Deus vult adorari, et quum sit servus, Regem se vult præconari. Ille enim omnem suscipiens diaboli virtutem, veniet quasi Rex justus, nec quasi in subjectione Dei legitimus; sed impius et injustus, et sine lege, quasi apostata, et iniquus et homicida, quasi latro diabolicam apostasiam in se recapitulans; et idola quidem seponens, ad suadendum quid ipse sit Deus, se autem extollens unum idolum serviant ipsi; de quo Apostolus in Epistola quae est ad Thessalonicenses secunda sic ait, ch. ii. 3, 4. Manifeste igitur Apostolus ostendit apostasiam ejus, et quoniam extollitur super omne quod dicitur Deus; vel quod colitur; hoc est super omne idolum, (hi enim sunt qui dicuntur quidem ab hominibus; non sunt autem Dei) et quoniam ipse se tyrannico more conabitur ostendere Deum.

Ostendimus autem in tertio libro, nullum ab Apostolis ex sua persona Deum appellari, nisi eum qui vere sit Deus, Patrem Domini nostri; cujus jussu hoc quod est in Hierosolymis, factum est Templum ob eas causas quae a nobis dictae sunt, in quo adversarius sedebit, tentans semet-ipsum Christum ostendere, sicut Dominus ait—Matth. xxiv. 15. Cum ergo videritis abominationem desolationis, quae dicta est a Daniele propheta. stantem in loco sancto,—qui legit intelligat.

† Et in dimidio hebdomadis, ait, tolletur sacrificium et libatio; et in Templum abominatio desolationis; et usque ad consummationem tem-

"And ten horns, that is, ten kings shall arise, and after them shall another rise which shall surpass in evil all that had been before him; and he shall weaken three kings, and speak against the Most High; and shall think to change times and laws, and they shall be delivered into his hand, until a time, times, and half a time; that is, through three years and six months, in which coming he shall reign over the earth."—*Book iv. c.* 25.*

"And when Antichrist shall have desolated the world, through a reign of three years and six months in his seat in the temple at Jerusalem, then the Lord shall come from heaven in clouds in the glory of the Father, and casting him and those who do his will into the lake of fire, he will introduce the just to the times of the kingdom, the rest of the holy seventh day."†

He thus held that Antichrist is to be an individual, not a dynasty or succession of men, and that he is to seat himself in the temple of God according to the prediction, 2 Thess. ii. 3–12, and exhibit himself as God; that that temple is to be at Jerusalem; that

poris, consummatio dabitur super desolationem; dimidium autem hebdomadis tres sunt anni et menses sex.—*Adversus Haereses, lib. iv., c. xxv.*

* El decem cornua Reges exsurgent; et post eos surget alius quae superabit malis omnes qui ante fuerunt, et Reges tres deminorabit, et verba adversus Altissimum Deum loquitur, et cogitabit demutari tempora et Legem, et dabitur in manu ejus usque ad tempus, tempora, et dimidium temporis; hoc est per triennium et sex menses in quibus veniens regnabit super terram.

† Quum autem vastaverit Antichristus hic omnia in hoc mundo, regnans annis tribus et mensibus sex, et sederit in templo Hierosolymis; tunc veniet Dominus de cœlis in nubibus, in gloria Patris illum quidem et obedientes ei in stagnum ignis mittens, adducens autem justis Regni tempora, hoc est requietionem septimam diem sanctificatum.—*Irenæus Adv. Haereses, lib. iv. c. xxv.*

his reign there is to extend through three years and a half; and that at its commencement he is to cause sacrifice and libation to cease. He utters no intimation, however, in these passages that Antichrist is also to set up his image, or an idol in the temple, and make that an object of worship; and the supposition of it is unnatural and self-contradictious. He is to seat *himself* in the temple, as Jehovah was seated on the Mercy seat in the holy of holies, where his presence was attested by the Shekinah, and by voices responsive to the requests by the High Priest for instruction by Urim and Thummin. Antichrist will, doubtless, in like manner, seat himself, in a sanctum, and invest himself not improbably with what will seem to beholders at a distance a supernatural light. But to set up his image, or an idol in his presence, and allow homage to be paid to that, would be to divert it from himself, and imply that he is not the Supreme and only God, as he is to claim to be.

But their views are taken in a much larger measure from Hippolytus, a Catholic bishop of the third century, who embodied them in a commentary on Daniel, which, after having slept unknown to the world for ten or twelve centuries, was disinterred from the Chisian library two centuries or more ago, and published at Gottingen, in 1774, together with the Septuagint of Daniel, and Theodotion's translation of that prophet, from Origen's Tetrapla, to which it was appended. The following are the principal passages in which he presents the constructions of Daniel adopted by these writers:

"XXII. For when the sixty-two hebdomads shall have been completed and Christ shall have come, and the Gospel shall have been every where preached, the times having been finished, then one, the last hebdomad, will be left, in which Elias will come, and Enoch, and in the middle of it, the abomination of desolation will appear, namely, Antichrist, announcng the desolation of the world. And when he shall have come, sacrifice and libation, which are now every where offered by the nations to God, shall be taken away.*

"XXXVIII. The prophet having thus narrated what has already taken place and been completed in the times (that have passed, c. xi. 1–35), now announces to us another mystery, indicating the last times. For he speaks thus: 'And there shall arise another king, bold and impudent; and he shall be exalted against every God, and shall be magnified, and shall speak proudly, and shall prosper until the wrath is completed. But Edom shall be saved from his hand, and Moab and the chief of the sons of Ammon. And he shall stretch out his hand over

*XXII. *Τῶν γὰρ ἑξήκοντα δύο ἑβδομάδων πληρωθεισῶν, καὶ Χριστοῦ παραγενομένου, καὶ τοῦ ἐυαγγελίου ἐν παντὶ τόπῳ κηρυχθέντος, ἐκκενωθέντων τῶν καιρῶν μία ἑβδομὰς περιλειφθήσεται ἡ ἐσχάτη, ἐν ᾗ πάρεσται Ἡλίας, καὶ Ἐνὼχ, καὶ ἐν τῷ ἡμίσει αὐτῆς ἀναφανήσεται τὸ βδέλυγμα τῆς ἐρημώσεως, ἕως ὁ Ἀντίχριστος ἐρήμωσιν τῷ κόσμῳ καταγγέλλων· οὗ παραγινομένου ἀρθήσεται θυσία, καὶ σπονδὴ, ἡ νῦν κατὰ πάντα τόπον ὑπὸ τῶν ἐθνῶν προσφερομένη τῷ Θεῷ· τούτων οὕτως εἰρημένων ἑτέραν πάλιν ὀπτασίαν διηγεῖται ἡμῖν ὁ προφήτης· οὐδὲν γὰρ ἕτερον ἐμερίμνησεν, εἰ μὴ ἵνα πάντα ἀκριβῶς ἐκδιδαχθῇ τὰ μέλλοντα, καὶ ἡμᾶς ἐκδιδάσκων φανῇ.*

the land; and the land of Egypt shall not be safe: for he shall have control over the hidden treasures of gold and silver and all the precious things of Egypt, and of Lybia, and of Ethiopia in all their fortified places.*

"XXXIX. These things, therefore, the prophet thus related, respecting Antichrist, who is to be without shame, eager for war, and a tyrant, who, being exalted above all kings and every God, will build the city Jerusalem and will erect a temple. Him the incorrigible will worship as God, and bend the knee to him, conceiving him to be the Christ. He will take off the two witnesses and forerunners of Christ who proclaim his glorious kingdom from heaven, as he said: 'And I will give my two witnesses, and they shall prophecy a thousand two hundred and sixty days, clothed in sackcloth. As also he had said to Daniel, I will confirm the covenant with many one week, and it shall be in the half of the week that my sacrifice and libation shall be taken away; so that the one week may be shown to be divided into two halves. For the two witnesses preaching three years and a half; then the Antichrist during the remainder of the week shall make war on the saints and devastate the world, that that which is spoken may be fulfilled—and they

* XXXVIII. *Διηγησάμενος οὖν ὁ προφήτης τὰ ἤδη συμβάντα καὶ χρόνοις τελεθέντα, ἕτερον πάλιν ἡμῖν μυστήριον καταγγέλλει, ἐσχάτων καιρῶν ποιούμενος ἔνδειξιν, λέγει γὰρ οὕτως· καὶ ἀναστήσεται ἕτερος βασιλεὺς ἀναιδὴς· καὶ ὑψωθήσεται ἐπὶ πάντα Θεὸν, καὶ μεγαλυνθήσεται, καὶ λαλήσει ὑπέρογκα, καὶ κατευθυνεῖ, μέχρις οὗ συντελεσθῇ ὀργὴ, καὶ τὰ ἑξῆς· καὶ οὗτοι διασωθήσονται ἐκ χειρὸς αὐτοῦ Ἐδὼμ, καὶ Μωὰβ, καὶ ἀρχὴ υἱῶν Ἀμμών. Καὶ ἐκτενεῖ τὴν χεῖρα αὐτοῦ ἐπὶ τὴν γῆν· καὶ ἡ γῆ Αἰγύπτου οὐκ ἔσται εἰς σωτηρίαν· καὶ κυριεύσει ἐν τοῖς ἀποκρύφοις τοῦ χρυσίου, καὶ τοῦ ἀργυρίου, καὶ πᾶσι τοῖς ἐπιθυμητοῖς Αἰγύπτου, καὶ Λιβύων, καὶ Αἰθιόπων ἐν τοῖς ὀχυρώμασιν αὐτῶν.*

shall present the abomination of desolation a thousand two hundred and ninety days.*

"XL. Daniel has spoken of two abominations; one of destruction, and one of desolation. But what is that of destruction, unless it be that which Antiochus Epiphanes set there for a time; and what is that of desolation, except that general one, when Antichrist shall have come. . . . .

"This king being saluted by the tribes (around Palestine) and honored by all, and become the abomination of desolation to the world, shall hold the supremacy through a thousand two hundred and ninety days. Happy will he be who survives and comes to the thousand three hundred and thirty-five days. For the abomination being come, and war made on the saints, whoever shall pass through his days, and approach the forty-five

* XXXIX. *Ταῦτα μὲν οὖν οὕτως ὁ προφήτης διηγεῖται περὶ τοῦ Ἀντιχρίστου, ὃς ἔσται ἀναιδὴς, πολεμοτρόφος, καὶ τύραννος, ὃς ὑπὲρ πάντας βασιλεῖς, καὶ πάντα Θεὸν ἐπαρθεὶς, οἰκοδομήσει τὴν Ἱερουσαλὴμ πόλιν, καὶ τὸν ναὸν ἀναστήσει· τούτῳ προσκυνήσουσιν ὡς Θεῷ οἱ ἀπειθεῖς, καὶ τούτῳ γόνυ κλινοῦσιν, ὑπονοοῦντες αὐτὸν εἶναι τὸν χριστόν· οὗτος ἀνελεῖ τοὺς δύο μάρτυρας, καὶ προδρόμους Χριστοῦ κηρύσσοντας τὴν ἔνδοξον αὐτοῦ ἀπ' οὐρανῶν βασιλείαν· ὡς λέγει· καὶ δώσω τοῖς δυσὶ μάρτυσί μου, καὶ προφητεύσουσιν ἡμέρας χιλίας διακοσίας ἑξήκοντα, περιβεβλημένοι σάκκους· καθὼς καὶ τῷ Δανιὴλ εἴρηκε· καὶ διαθήσει διαθήκην πολλοῖς, ἑβδομὰς μία, καὶ ἔσται ἐν τῷ ἡμίσει τῆς ἑβδομάδος, ἀρθήσεται μου ἡ θυσία, καὶ ἡ σπονδὴ, ἵνα δειχθῇ ἡ μία ἑβδομὰς εἰς δύο μεριζομένη· τῶν μὲν δύο μαρτύρων τρία ἥμισυ ἔτη κηρυσσόντων, τοῦ δὲ Ἀντιχρίστου, τὸ ἐπίλοιπον τῆς ἑβδομάδος τοὺς ἁγίους πολεμοῦντος, καὶ τὸν κόσμον ἐρημοῦντος, ἵνα πληρωθῇ τὸ εἰρημένον· καὶ δώσουσι βδέλυγμα ἐρημώσεως ἡμέρας χιλίας διακοσίας ἐνενήκοντα.*

days, a period of fifty more days arriving, the kingdom of heaven will come. For the Antichrist comes, and in the course of the fifty days that follow, the saints shall inherit the kingdom with Christ.*

XLII. "Who, then, were the two men who stood on the bank of the river, unless the law and the prophets; and who was he who stood over the water, but he himself they had formerly predicted: who in the last days, at the Jordan, was openly to be testified of by the Father, and pointed out to the people by John. They therefore ask him, knowing that all

* XL. *Δύο οὖν βδελύγματα εἴρηκε Δανιὴλ, ἓν μὲν ἀφανισμοῦ, ἓν δὲ ἐρημώσεως· τί τὸ ἀφανισμοῦ, ἀλλ' ἢ ὁ ἔστησεν ἐκεῖ κατὰ τὸν καιρὸν Ἀντίοχος; καὶ τί τὸ τῆς ἐρημώσεως, ἀλλ' ἢ καθόλου ὡς παρέσται ὁ Ἀντίχριστος; καὶ οὗτοι σωθήσονται ἐκ χειρὸς αὐτοῦ, Ἐδὼμ, καὶ Μωὰβ, καὶ ἀρχὴ υἱῶν Ἀμμὼν· οὗτοι γάρ εἰσιν οἱ συνερχόμενοι αὐτῷ διὰ τὴν συγγένειαν, καὶ βασιλέα αὐτὸν πρῶτοι ἀναγορεύοντες· οἱ μὲν Ἐδὼμ εἰσὶν υἱοὶ Ἡσαῦ οἱ κατοικοῦντες τὸ ὄρος Σηεὶρ· Μωὰβ δὲ καὶ Ἀμμὼν, οἱ ἐκ τῶν δύο θυγατέρων αὐτοῦ γεγεννημένοι, ὡς καὶ Ἡσαΐας λέγει· Καὶ πεταθήσονται ἐν πλοίοις ἀλλοφύλων θάλασσαν ἅμα προνομεύσουσι, καὶ οἱ ἀπὸ ἀνατολῶν ἡλίου, καὶ οἱ ἀπὸ δυσμῶν, καὶ βοῤῥᾶ, δώσουσι δόξαν· οἱ δὲ υἱοὶ Ἀμμὼν πρῶτοι ὑπακούσονται· οὗτος ὑπ' αὐτῶν βασιλεὺς ἀναγορευθεὶς, καὶ ὑπὸ πάντων δοξαθεὶς, καὶ βδέλυγμα ἐρημώσεως τῷ κόσμῳ γενηθεὶς, κρατήσει ἡμέρας χιλίας διακοσίας ἐνενήκοντα· μακάριος ὁ ὑπομείνας, καὶ φθάσας εἰς ἡμέρας χιλίας τριακοσίας τριάκοντα πέντε· τοῦ γὰρ βδελύγματος παραγενομένου, καὶ πολεμοῦντος τοὺς ἁγίους, ὃς ἂν ὑπερβῇ τὰς ἡμέρας αὐτοῦ, καὶ ἐγγίσῃ εἰς ἡμέρας τεσσαράκοντα πέντε, ἑτέρας ἐγγιζούσης πεντηκοστῆς, ἔφθασεν ἡ βασιλεία τῶν οὐρανῶν· ἔρχεται μὲν ὁ Ἀντίχριστος, καὶ εἰς μέρος τῆς πεντηκοστῆς, τὴν δὲ βασιλείαν οἱ ἅγιοι ἅμα Χριστῷ κληρονομεῖν μέλλουσι.*

dominion and authority are given to him; that they may learn accurately when he is to institute the judgment in the world, and when the things that have been spoken by him shall be fulfilled. And he, desiring to assure them in the most effective way, raised his right hand and his left to heaven, and swore by him who lives to eternity. Who swore? And by whom did he sware? The Son manifestly by the Father, saying: The Father lives to eternity.*

XLIII. "Therefore by his act in raising his hands, he showed that he spoke in respect to the time, times, and half a time, when the dispersion of the Israelites is to be finished, indicating the three and a half years of Antichrist. For he calls time a year, and times two years, and half a time, half a year. They are the thousand two hundred and ninety days which Daniel had spoken of before, when the tribulation shall be consum-

* XLII. *Τίνες οὖν ἦσαν οἱ δύο ἄνδρες οἱ ἑστῶτες παρὰ τὸ χεῖλος τοῦ ποταμοῦ, ἀλλ' ἢ ὁ νόμος, καὶ οἱ πρωφῆται; καὶ τίς ἦν ὁ ἑστῶς ἐπάνω τοῦ ὕδατος, εἰ μὴ αὐτὸς οὗτος περὶ οὗ αὐτοὶ πάλαι προεκήρυξαν; ὃς ἔμελλεν ἐπ' ἐσχάτων ἐπὶ τῷ Ἰορδάνῃ φανερῶς ὑπὸ τοῦ πατρὸς μαρτυρεῖσθαι, καὶ ὑπὸ Ἰωάννου τῷ λαῷ παῤῥησίᾳ δείκνυσθαι· ὁ τὸ κάστυ τοῦ γραμματέως περὶ τὴν ὀσφὺν φέρων, καὶ τὸ βαδδὶν τὸν ποικίλον χιτῶνα ἐνδεδυμένος· οὗτοι οὖν πυνθάνονται αὐτοῦ εἰδότες, ὅτι αὐτῷ ἐδόθη πᾶσα ἀρχὴ καὶ ἐξουσία· ἵνα μάθωσι παρ' αὐτοῦ ἀκριβῶς πότε μέλλει ἐπάγειν τῷ κόσμῳ τὴν κρίσιν, καὶ πότε τὰ ὑπ' αὐτοῦ λελαλημένα πληρωθήσεται· ὁ δὲ κατὰ πάντα τρόπον πείθειν τούτους βουλόμενος ἐπῆρε τὴν δεξιὰν αὐτοῦ, καὶ τὴν ἀριστερὰν εἰς τὸν οὐρανὸν, καὶ ὤμοσε κατὰ τοῦ ζῶντος εἰς τὸν αἰῶνα· τίς κατὰ τίνος ὤμοσεν; υἱὸς δηλονότι κατὰ τοῦ πατρὸς, λέγων· ὅτι ζῇ ὁ πατὴρ εἰς τὸν αἰῶνα, εἰ μὴ εἰς καιρὸν, καὶ καιροὺς, καὶ ἥμισυ καιροῦ, ἐν τῷ συντελεσθῆναι διασκορπισμὸν γνώσονται ταῦτα πάντα.*

mated, and the dispersion finished, Antichrist being come. In those days all these things shall be known; and from the time of the removal of the daily sacrifice, a thousand two hundred and ninety days are to be computed: iniquity shall abound even as the Lord said: because iniquity shall abound, the love of many shall become cold."*

XLIV. "For there is no doubt that when a sinister change takes place, dissensions will be generated. But contensions arising, love will grow cold. And the saying also: 'Happy he who shall endure, and shall come to the thousand three hundred and thirty-five days,' is instructive and consolatory; as the Lord said: 'But he that endureth unto the end, shall be saved;' for it implies that we are not by any means to expect a universal change to coldness and aversion, but that iniquity is not to be so increased, that the abomination of desolation, that is the antagonist and rival, may be able to seize (the place to which he aspires). He also said to one: '*Until evening;*' that is until the completion. And '*Until morning.*' What is morning? The day of the resurrection; for it is the beginning of another age, as the dawn is the beginning of day. For the

* XLIII. *Τὸ οὖν ἐκτεῖναι αὐτὸν τὰς δύο χεῖρας, δἰ αὐτοῦ τὸ πάθος ἔδειξε τὸ δὲ εἰπεῖν εἰς καιρὸν, καὶ καιροὺς, καὶ ἥμισυ καιροῦ ἐν τῷ συντελεσθῆναι διασκορπισμὸν, τὰ τρία ἥμισυ ἔτη τοῦ Ἀντιχρίστου ἐσήμανε· καιρὸν γὰρ λέγει ἐνιαυτὸν, καὶ καιροὺς δὲ δύο ἔτη, ἥμισυ δὲ καιροῦ ἥμισυ ἐνιαυτοῦ· αὗταί εἰσιν αἱ χίλιαι διακόσιαι ἐνενήκοντα ἡμέραι, ἃς προεῖπε Δανιὴλ ἐν τῷ συντελεσθῆναι τὸ πάθος, καὶ γενέσθαι διασκορπισμὸν παρόντος τοῦ Ἀντιχρίστου· ἐν ταῖς ἡμέραις ἐκείναις γνώσονται ταῦτα πάντα, καὶ ἀπὸ καιροῦ παραλλάξεως τοῦ ἐνδελεχισμοῦ, καὶ τὸ ἡμέραι χίλιαι διακόσιαι ἐνενήκοντα ψηφιζόμενόν ἐστι· πληθυνθήσεται ἡ ἀνομία, καθὼς καὶ ὁ δεσπότης λέγει· διὰ τὸ πληθυνθῆναι τὴν ἀνομίαν, ψυγήσεται ἡ ἀγάπη τῶν πολλῶν.*

thousand four hundred days, are the light (are to extend to the light) of the world. For when the light shall shine in the world, Christ himself having said: 'I am the light of the world,' the Sanctuary shall be cleansed. Those words the adversary has also spoken, and applied them to himself. But the holy place is not by any means to be cleansed, until he has been disarmed of his power."*

Thus nearly all the peculiar constructions of Daniel by Dr. Tregelles, B. W. Newton, Sir Edward Denny, Baxter and others, are found in Hippolytus:

1. That writer held that the proud and impious king of Daniel xi. 36, is the Antichrist; and also, like others of that age, that he is to be an individual; not a class or series of persons.

* XLIV. *Ὅτι γὰρ τῆς παραλλάξεως γενομένης τὰ σχίσματα γέγονεν, οὐκ ἀμφίβολον· τῶν σχισμάτων δὲ γενομένων πέψυκται ἡ ἀγάπη· καὶ τὸ μακάριος ὁ ὑπομείνας, καὶ φθάσας ἡμέρας χιλίας τριακοσίας τριάκοντα πέντε, ἔστι χρηστὸν, ὡς εἶπεν ὁ δεσπότης, ὁ δὲ ὑπομείνας εἰς τέλος οὗτος σωθήσεται· καθ' ὅλον τοίνυν τὴν παράλλαξιν μὴ παραδεξώμεθα, ἵνα μὴ ἡ ἀνομία πληθυνθῇ, καὶ καταλάβῃ τὸ βδέλυγμα τῆς ἐρημώσεως· τουτέστιν ὁ ἀντικείμενος· καὶ εἶπεν αὐτῷ ἕως ἑσπέρας· τουτέστι μέχρι τῆς συντελείας, καὶ πρωΐ· ὅπέρ ἐστι πρωΐ; ἡ ἡμέρα τῆς ἀναστάσεως· ἀρχὴ γάρ ἐστιν ἑτέρου αἰῶνος, ὡς ἀρχὴ ἡμέρας, ἡ πρωϊνή· τὸ δὲ ἡμέραι χίλιαι τετρακόσιαι, ἔστι φῶς κόσμου· τοῦ γὰρ φωτὸς φανέντος ἐν τῷ κόσμῳ, τοῦ εἰπόντος ἐγὼ εἰμὶ τὸ φῶς τοῦ κόσμου, καθαρισθήσεται τὸ ἅγιον ὡς εἴρηκεν, ὁ ἀντικείμενος· οὐδαμῶς γὰρ καθαρίζεται τὸ ἅγιον, μὴ ἐκείνου καταργηθέντος.*

2. He held that he is to be exalted above all kings, and is to arrogate a supremacy above God; and these are points that are authorized by the prophecy and the New Testament. But much that follows is fictitious and mistaken.

3. Such as that that king is to rebuild Jerusalem.

4. That he is to erect a temple there.

5. That he will receive in it the homage of the wicked, as though he were God.

6. That his worshipers are to regard him as the Messiah.

7. That the two witnesses are to be of the same period as Antichrist.

8. That Antichrist is to confirm a covenant with many at Jerusalem for one week.

9. That he is to take away the daily sacrifice and oblation.

10. That in the last half of the last week, he is to persecute the saints, and put the witnesses to death.

11. That he is to introduce the abomination of desolation into the temple.

12. And that while time is a year, times two years, and half a time half a year, the period denoted by the three years and a half is merely the number of days that are embraced in three and a half years; and that the 1260, 1290, and 1335 days, stand solely for the number of days which they literally express.

13. Dr. Tregelles, Mr. Baxter and others affirm expressly, that Antichrist is to make a league or compact with the Jews for seven years, and is to break it in the middle of the seventieth week. Hippolytus *implies* that he is to make a covenant with them, inasmuch as he represents that he is to confirm one, which must therefore first be made, in order that a confirmation of it may take place.

14. He implies, also, that Antichrist is to break the covenant; as he affirms that he is, in the last half of the last week, to persecute the saints and slay the witnesses of Jesus.

15. Several of the writers I have cited, exhibit Antichrist as setting up his image in the temple as an object of worship; and treat that as the abomination of desolation. Hippolytus expresses no such notion, but like Irenæus, represents Antichrist himself as the object of homage, and as the abomination that makes desolate.

It was held, however, by Apollinarius of Laodicea, that he was to set his image in the temple, as I shall show on a later page; where I shall also point out the false grounds on which that writer, Hippolytus, and others, founded their belief that the 1260 and 1290 days were the measure of Antichrist's career, and ascribed to him the erection of a temple at Jerusalem, his setting himself or his image in it, and becoming thereby the abomination of desolation.

Those ancient views are thus, in their main particulars, an exact parallel of those reproduced by these modern writers. As, however, those who have recently discussed the subject have treated it very much as though the opinions they advance were the result of their own independent inquiries, I shall proceed to scan them as I should were I not cognizant of the fact, that they are not their original authors.

CHAPTER XII.

The Error of their notion of a League between Louis Napoleon and the Jews—Their false Construction of Daniel ix. 27—The Principles on which Symbols are used—Time as a Symbol employed in the relation of Analogy.

These writers proceed in their representations on the assumption that Louis Napoleon is what they call the seventh, or as some of them hold, the eighth head of the beast from the sea. Rev. xiii. xvii. But I have shown that there is now no power answering to the seventh head of that symbol; nor is there ever again to be. Neither is there ever to be an eighth head. The imagination that he is represented by that symbol is a mere delusion.

They proceed also on the assumption, and repeat it page after page, that Louis Napoleon was to make a covenant with the Jews at the latest this or the last year, for seven years, in virtue of which that people are to return to Palestine. But I have proved that there is no ground whatever in the prophecy for such a pretense.

I will now show that there are no indications of a disposition either in Louis Napoleon or in the Jews, so far as is known, to enter into a treaty of that nature with each other; and moreover, that it is not possible, unless the most gigantic miracles are wrought, that such a stupendous measure as their theory contemplates, should be accomplished in the period assigned by these writers of seven years from 1863, 1864, or 1865.

1. There are certainly no public indications thus far, that Louis Napoleon is negotiating or contemplating a treaty with the Jews, by the stipulations of which he is to aid them in returning to their national land, reëstablishing themselves there as a distinct and sovereign people, rebuilding their temple, and reinstating their sacrificial worship. Not a whisper of such a negotiation has reached the ear of the political or ecclesiastical writers of France, England, Germany, or this country. There is not the slightest preparation in the minds of that people for such a measure. A hint that he is contemplating it, would raise a shout of ridicule from both Jews and Gentiles.

2. Before a measure of that kind can be carried into effect, either the Jews must acquire a title to the civil dominion of Palestine, and probably also to the soil; or else Louis Napoleon must be prepared to put them in possession of it by conquest. But how is he to conquer Palestine? He is not at war with the Porte. Is he to plunge into a conflict with that power, in order that he may seize Palestine and make a present of it to the Jews? He is not in the habit

of giving away territory without an equivalent. Will the Jews consent to return, if, in place of an independent nation, they are to be only the *colonists* of Napoleon, and subject to any measure of despotism which he may please to exercise over them?

3. On the supposition that Louis Napoleon should enter into such a treaty, and make arrangements to send forces to conquer Palestine that he might constitute it a dependence on France; is it likely that he would be allowed to carry out his schemes of conquest and self-aggrandizement, without obstruction? Would Turkey tamely acquiesce in the robbery of such a province, the transference of which to the hands of a powerful and ambitious people, would endanger the whole of the eastern portion of the empire? If France were master of Palestine, how long would it be before Syria, and Mesopotamia would fall into her grasp? How long before the great Mediterranean islands and the commercial ports on the northern shores of that sea, would be seized that she might be mistress of its waters? Would Russia, would England, would Austria, would Italy even, stand an unconcerned spectator of such a stride in power without interfering to check and intercept it? No man of sense will believe it. They must become the vassals of Napoleon before it can be possible. But if he is to wait till he has conquered all the great antagonist powers of Europe, Mr. Baxter's seven years from 1863, 1864, or 1865 will be likely to have

run their course before Napoleon will reach a point at which he can migrate with his forces to Palestine, to bring that region under his sceptre, that he may present it as a heritage to the Jews.

4. But suppose all this should be achieved after four, five, or six years of bloody struggles—and that the Jews of western and northern Europe should, in large numbers, be disposed to remove to Palestine under the guardianship of Louis Napoleon, the transportation of one or two millions of persons of all ages, to a land that is a desert, without crops, without herds or flocks, without forests, without mines, without roads, without cities, without habitations, without ports, is not to be the work of a few weeks, a few months, nor a few years. Ten, twelve, or fifteen would be a very moderate period for it. And who is to pay the expense of such a migration? Half, probably two-thirds, perhaps the whole of the property of a million and a half of the Jews who, would be likely to remove in the first six or eight years, would be inadequate to meet the requisite expenditure. Will Louis Napoleon empty his purse for their accommodation? Will England unbar her treasures for their relief? Will Austria or Prussia be disposed to pay enormous charges to weaken themselves and strengthen the emperor of France by transporting their subjects on a vast scale to a territory that is under his jurisdiction? These considerations are sufficient to show that whatever else may

happen, it is not within the sphere of likelihood nor possibility that the transference of such a body of human beings from the west of Europe and the south of Russia, to Palestine, in such conditions as to shield them from famine, pestilence, and death, could be accomplished in so short a period as that which remains, according to the speculations of these writers, before this dispensation will reach its close, and the Son of God reveal himself in the clouds of heaven. Whatever else may or may not take place, the predictions and asseverations of these authors cannot be verified in that brief time, nor come within many years of a verification.

5. The attempts of these writers to authenticate their theory by passages from Daniel and John, are marked by the grossest mistakes and misrepresentations.

Thus Mr. Baxter alleges, Daniel viii. 13–14, as equivalent to the question: How long will the period be, during which the sacrifices will first be *restored;* and then after their *removal* [how long will] the desolation of the sanctuary continue? No misconception could be greater. In the first place there is not a syllable in the passage in regard to a *restoration* of sacrifices. That is a sheer interpolation by Mr. Baxter and his coadjutors; and with its fall their whole construction vanishes into air.

In the next place, the prophecy, chapter viii., is not a language, but a symbolical prophecy. As the ram and goat were symbols of monarchs, and their acts were representative of acts those monarchs were to exert; as the four horns that came up in the place of the great horn that was broken; and the little horn that sprung up from beneath one of the four, were also symbols of kings; and the acts of the little horn which waxed great to the host of heaven, and cast some of the stars to the ground, and magnified itself against the prince of the host, and took away the daily sacrifice, and cast down the place of his sanctuary, are symbolical; so the daily sacrifice and the sanctuary were symbols, and only symbols. The taking away the sacrifice was also a symbol of a different act; and the casting down of the sanctuary was a symbol in like manner of a different but analogous event. That accordingly which is foreshown, is not at all, as Mr. Baxter imagines, the taking away of literal sacrifices at the temple in Jerusalem, and the casting down of the temple itself. No fancy could be more false and contradictory to the principles on which the symbols are used. But the events that are predicted through those symbols, and the acts of the little horn in regard to them, are first the analogous acts of the Roman civil and priestly power, in the empire, in taking away the expiation of Christ which the sacrifices offered on the altar typified, and substituting the Mass and other false rites and works in its place. And next, the analogous act of casting down and desecrating the edifices that were erected by true believers for the worship of God, or appropriating them to secular uses, or to the homage of creatures and idols. Mr. Baxter's construction is thus totally false. He does not even discern what the subject is of the prediction. He can no more show that the daily sacrifices and the sanctuary are used in a literal sense—not as symbols—than he can prove that the little horn, its waxing great to the host of heaven, which is interpreted as the stars, and casting some of those orbs to the ground, and stamping on them, are not symbols. Will he venture to maintain that the goat on whose head the little horn stood is hereafter to appear in Persia; and that Daniel is to be present and behold it; that that horn is to wax great, even so as to reach the stars of heaven, which are thousands of millions of miles distant, and is to cast some of them down to the earth and trample on them? He may, indeed, be guilty of that violation of the prophecy; as he asserts, without a blush, that the symbols of the seals, trumpets and vials, are all yet to manifest themselves on the earth, and act again the parts they performed when the prophet beheld them in vision; but his misconception will not divest the prophecy of its genuine meaning, nor give any color of truth to the views he maintains. Let the reader consider what revolting impossibilities and monstrosities he must accept and undertake to vindicate, if he takes this writer as his guide, who thus mutilates and falsifies the word of God, when an expedient presents itself that promises to yield him the support he needs to sustain his theory.

A similar mistake is made by Dr. Tregelles, who attempts to confirm his construction of Daniel ix. 27, by Daniel vii. Thus, he says:

"The character of this period of three years and a half is to be specially gathered from chapter vii., in which mention is made of a time, times and a half, and also from the forty and two months, 1260 days, etc., which are spoken of in the book of Revelation.

"The identity of the time, times and a half, of chapter vii., *with the last half week of this chapter*, might almost be taken for granted—the proof, however, is simple; the horn in chapter vii. acts in blasphemy and persecution, until the Lord Jesus and his people take the kingdom; the three years and a half run on to that point; here in this chapter the whole period of seventy weeks issues in the absolute and established blessing of Israel, Daniel's people;—the week of this covenant is the last portion of the seventy weeks, and the half week after the sacrifice is taken away is the latter portion of that week. Thus the period in chapter vii. and the concluding period before us run on to the same point;—they are also equal in duration; hence they begin at the same time, and are altogether identical. If we would form a just estimate of the events of the last half week, we must gather it from chapter vii.; here we have the same power in the local connexion with Jerusalem."—*Remarks on Daniel, p.* 104, *Edition of* 1864.

A most extraordinary misconception, surely! What can transcend the fallacies on which it proceeds, and the sweeping denial with which it is fraught, of the laws of the prophecy, and all the great revelations that are made in it! As Dr. Tregelles holds a high rank as a scholar in an important sphere of sacred learning, and many may acquiesce in his opinions without examiniug the grounds on which they rest, and their bearing on the teachings of the prophecy, let me invoke attention to his assumptions and reasonings in this passage. Nothing can be more evident than that he has not a true understanding of the nature and laws of symbols, but proceeds on grounds that subvert the meaning of every prediction in the seventh of Daniel; and those not less which the Spirit of God himself interprets, than those which are left unexplained. He falls into the singular error first of assuming, without proof, and against fact, that the meaning of Daniel ix. 27, *is what he affirms it is;* and *then* assumes and asserts that that meaning is identically the same as that of those portions of Daniel vii. to which he refers as proving it.

1. In respect to Dan. ix. 27, he assumes that the horn spoken of, Daniel vii. viii., is the same as the prince that was to come, Daniel ix. 26, whose period he assigns to what he holds is Daniel's seventieth week, and maintains is yet future. Having made this assumption, he then proceeds to represent, *without proof*, that what is said of the horn, ch. vii., is said of the *prince*, ch. ix. 26.

2. He next assumes and maintains that the time, times and a half of Daniel vii. are identical with the last half week of ch. ix. 27.—*Remarks, p.* 103.

3. He assumes and affirms, without proof, that the seventieth week of Daniel is the last week of this dispensation, and is yet future; and he asserts, that what is said in Daniel vii. 25, is also said in Daniel ix. 27.

4. He assumes and declares, without proof, that the blasphemies and persecutions which he ascribes to the prince, whom he holds is to make a covenant, are identically the same as to the perpetrator of them, their nature, their time, and the persons who are affected by them, as those are which are spoken of in ch. vii. as on the one hand persecuting, and on the other suffering persecution.

A number of the points he thus assumes I have already shown are not only not proved by him, nor by any who concur with him in opinion, and cannot be proved to have any authority from the prophecy, but are in utter contradiction to the most indisputable and essential of its teachings. Such are the notions that the prince who, according to Dr. Tregelles, is to make a covenant, is the same identical person or power as the little horn, Daniel vii. 9–12; that that personage is to make a covenant; and that the seventieth week of Daniel is future and is to end at the same moment as the time, times and a half of Daniel vii. 25. From all this it is clear that the question whether his construction is correct or not, turns upon the question, what the principles are on which symbols are used, and what the laws are by which they are to be interpreted? What, then, are those principles? What is the relation in which the symbols in question of Daniel vii. and viii. are used? Do they represent things exactly like themselves, or are they used on the ground of analogy to symbolize things of a different but a resembling class? If the latter is the relation in which they are used, then Dr. Tregelles' whole scheme falls. For he assumes that the time, times and a half of Daniel vii. 25 are not employed to denote a longer period than they themselves literally express; but are used to represent that identical number—namely, twelve hundred and sixty days, of which they themselves consist. For he says, and repeats the averment, that the period of Daniel vii. and the last half week of Daniel ix. 27 are exactly equivalent to each other; that they began at the same moment, run parallel with each other throughout their course, and thence terminate at the same time. He therefore specifically denies that the time, times and a half, of Daniel vii. 25, are used as symbols, on the principle of analogy, to represent a longer period than themselves. Now, if he is wrong here—totally wrong, then his whole scheme falls. If he is right, then the prophecy falls. I may justly say there is no other question in the whole sphere of hermeneutics of greater significance than this. Not only the credibility of the prophecy, but the wisdom and truth of Jehovah himself, are involved in the issue. For, as he has testified in the most specific and emphatic form in many instances, that symbols like those of Daniel vii. 7–8, 17–20, 21, 23, 24, 25, are used in the relation of a general resemblance to signify agents, acts and events of a different nature and sphere from themselves; if they are not employed in that relation, then his own testimony embodied in the interpretation given of them by the revealing Spirit is convicted of error, and the glory of his wisdom and truth are overshadowed and extinguished.

For the angel who, under the promptings of the Spirit, interpreted the symbols which the prophet had beheld, said: "These great beasts which are four, are four kings, or successions of kings, which shall arise in the earth," v. 17. The four beasts are thus explained in the prophecy itself as symbols of agents of a different order from themselves; and on the ground of analogy; for there is a general likeness between wild beasts that prey on inferior animals, and cruel and bloody tyrants who slaughter and crush their fellow men. And this interpretation given by the Spirit of God exemplifies five of the fundamental laws of symbolization; *first*, that agents always represent agents, not acts, effects, or conditions; *next*, that living agents always represent living agents; *thirdly*, that when the symbols bear an analogy to that which they represent, they are used to denote agents or things that differ from themselves; *fourthly*, that a single living agent sometimes symbolizes a great number of analogous agents, as in this instance a single beast represented thousands and myriads of human beings; and *fifthly*, that the acts of the symbols represent the acts of the agents whom the symbols denote. The angel interpreted the horns on the same principle. "And the ten horns are ten kings that shall arise; and another shall rise after them; and he shall be diverse from the first, and he shall subdue three kings." Here the symbol, the horn of a strong animal through which it exerts its power of defence and aggression, and which stands in a relation to the whole animal, like that of a king to the organized body of officials of which he is the chief, is used as a symbol, not of a mere horn like itself, but of an armed, brave, and powerful monarch, as the master of the civil and military organization of which he is the head.

In like manner, the acts of the horn that spake great things, and made war with the saints, and wore out the saints of the Most High, are symbolical, and represent acts of the persons denoted by the little horn, that are of a different kind, but are as suitable to the spirit and sphere of those persons, as the acts of the horn in the vision were to its office as a horn. The interpretation given, ch. viii., of the ram and goat, their horns and their acts, proceeds on the same principle. "The ram which thou sawest having two horns denotes the kings of Media and Persia; and the rough goat is the king of Grecia, and the great horn that is between his eyes, is the first king. Now that being broken, whereas four stood up for it, four dynasties shall stand up out of the nation, but not in his power. The little horn that sprung up under one of the four horns, and waxed great to the host of heaven, and cast down some of the stars, is also interpreted as symbolizing a king of fierce countenance that should stand up in the latter times of the four horns, be of great power, destroy wonderfully, and waste the mighty and the holy people," v. 20–25.

This, then, is beyond all question the principle on which symbols of the kind here used are employed. It is made certain not only by the analogy that obviously subsists between animals of such gigantic size, such power, and such destructive instincts, and the kings and inferior civil and military officials whom they represent; but by the testimony of God himself. It is not to be denied, therefore, set aside, nor overlooked. It cannot be set aside without an impeachment of God and his truth.

But *time*, when used as a symbol, is also employed in this relation of analogy to a greater period of time, and in this relation only. All the periods used as symbols of time are periods of days, or else weeks, months and years which are made up of days; the twenty-four hour periods of the earth's revolution on its axis, and bear an analogy to years, which are periods of the earth's movement round the sun. The fact, therefore, that days stand in that relation to years, each being determined and measured by a motion of the earth, is an indubitable proof that days when employed as symbols, are symbols of time of a greater but an analogous length. To deny it, is as unwarrantable, as it would be to deny that when a powerful, fierce and carniverous beast is employed as a symbol, it is employed as a symbol of fierce, bloody and domineering conquerors and destroyers of men.

And finally, this is confirmed by the fact that days, it is shown by the testimony of the Scriptures themselves, are in several instances used as symbols of an equal number of years. Thus Moses said: "As for you, your carcases shall fall in the wilderness, and your children shall wander in the wilderness forty years. . . After the number of the days in which ye searched the land—forty days—each day for a year; shall ye bear your iniquities."—Num. xiv. 32–34.

God employed a day for a year also in the symbolic acts which he enjoined on Ezekiel iv. 4–6: "Lie thou also upon thy left side, and lay the iniquity of the house of Israel upon it, according to the number of the days that thou shalt lie upon it, thou shalt bear their iniquity. For I have laid upon thee the years of their iniquity, according to the number of the days, three hundred and ninety days. So shalt thou bear the iniquity of the house of Israel. And when thou hast accomplished them, lie again on thy right side, and thou shalt bear the iniquity of Judah forty years. I have appointed thee a day for a year —a day for a year."

We have thus, in these three instances of the use of days, as representatives of a greater time, a specific announcement that they are employed as symbols of a corresponding number of years; and the reason undoubtedly is that a day presents an analogy to a year, that no other period bears, namely, that it is measured by a revolution of the earth on its axis; while a year is determined and measured by a revolution of the earth round the sun.

The seventy weeks of Daniel also, it is known from the events of which they were the measure, are employed as expressing a number of years that corresponds to the days of seventy weeks. Expositors and chronologers, Hebrew, Greek, Catholic and Protestant, without, so far as I am aware, an exception, put that construction on them; and its truthfulness is verified by the fact that 483 years intervened between the event from which the seventy weeks are dated—the decree of Artaxerxes Longimanus, king of Persia, in his twentieth year.—Neh. ii. 1. authorizing the rebuilding of Jerusalem—and Christ's entrance on his ministry; and three years and a half from the commencement of his ministry to his death, which took place, according to the prophecy, three years and a half before the close of the seventieth week. This Dr. Tregelles cannot deny without con tradicting the clearest teachings of the prophecy.

For if he maintains that the time, times and a half are not used as denoting a period that differs from themselves, he must for the same reason maintain that the four great beasts do not represent agents that differ from themselves, and imply that all symbols drawn from the animal and the material world, represent agents or things, acts or effects, that are an exact copy of themselves. How can he any more show that time, times, and a half, are not employed as symbols of periods that differ in length from themselves, than he can that a winged lion, a bear, a leopard, a monster brute, a ram, a goat, are not used to represent agents that differ in nature from themselves? The diversity between Nebuchadnezzar, with the subordinate officials civil and military of which he was the chief, and the winged lion, by which that vast organization of human beings was symbolized, was not greater or more imposing for such agents, than the diversity is between twelve hundred and sixty years, and the twelve hundred and sixty days which are their representative: for the period represented is three hundred and sixty times greater than that which symbolizes it. If he adheres to his construction of the times, months, and days of Daniel, he must for the same reason adhere to that principle in his interpretation of the great animal symbols of that prophet, and hold that they foreshow that identically such monsters were, or are to appear on the earth, and act the parts that are ascribed to them, and that they indicate nothing more.

Will he, then, like Mr. Baxter, take that ground? Will he affirm that a lion, having eagle's wings, will rise out of the Persian or Mediterranean Sea, and enter Babylonia; that it will employ itself in seizing and devouring all the inferior animals of Media, Assyria, Syria, Tyre, Palestine, Egypt, and western Arabia; and that its wings after a time being plucked, it will be made to stand up as a man, and a man's heart be given to it? Will he assert that the monster beast of one head and ten horns, Daniel vii., whose teeth were iron, and its nails brass, is also to appear in Italy, and act out the tragedy of violence and slaughter toward other animals, which is imputed to it? Will he hold, also, that the great red dragon of seven heads and ten horns, and a tail of such sweep as to strike stars from the firmament, will appear, standing on the moon, desiring to devour the man-child to which the woman, clothed with the sun, is about to give birth? Will he hold that the beast from the sea of Rev. xiii., having seven heads and ten horns, and on its horns ten crowns, and upon its heads names of blasphemy, is also to present itself in the western Roman empire, and exert the agency and suffer the catastrophes that are foreshown of it? And finally, will he aver that the crimson-colored beast from the abyss, with seven heads that are fallen, and ten horns that are erect, and bearing a woman clothed in scarlet and purple, will present itself in western Europe, run a bloody career, and at length be cast alive into a lake burning with fire and brimstone? Will he maintain that that is the genuine and indubitable teaching of Daniel and John, and that such a prophecy having relation chiefly to the animal world, is more worthy of the attributes of God, more indicative of his wisdom, more expressive of his power, righteousness and grace, than a revelation of the rise in the world of successions of human beings of a hideousness, ferocity, and bloodiness toward men, that resemble the fierce natures and acts of those beasts toward the weaker animals that fall in their way? That is the conclusion he must adopt, unless he abandons the ground he here occupies; as I shall hereafter make apparent by additional considerations.

CHAPTER XIII.

Dr. Tregelles' Error in regard to the Horns of Daniel vii. and viii.—They are not Symbols of the same Power; their Persecutions are not the same; nor are their Blasphemies alike—No Temple is to be built at Jerusalem by the Israelites who first return; no Sacrifices are to be offered by them—There is no Proof that the Man of Sin is to set himself in a Temple there—There is none that there is to be a Persecution of the True Worshipers in Palestine at that period.

THERE are several other errors in the passages quoted from Dr. Tregelles and other writers in the preceding chapter.

1. Dr. Tregelles is mistaken in the supposition that the little horn of Daniel vii. 8, 20, 21, and Daniel viii. 9–12, are the same. Nothing can be clearer than that they are very widely different. The little horn of the wild beast of ten horns (Daniel vii. 20, 21) grew up on the head of that *beast*, which is the symbol of the civil and military rulers of the western Roman empire; and is itself the symbol of a civil and ecclesiastical power in that empire, in the midst of the civil and military sovereignties denoted by the other ten horns. But the little horn of Daniel viii. 9–12 sprung up, not on the head of that wild beast, but upon the head of the *goat*, which is the symbol of the supreme rulers of the Greek empire. The power

accordingly represented by that little horn which sprung up under one of the four horns of the goat, and pushed it from its place, though a Roman agent, was seated *within the Grecian empire*, and was purely a civil and military power, in distinction from an ecclesiastical one, like the little horn of the ten-horned wild beast. The Roman power represented by the little horn of the goat, introduced itself into the empire of the Greeks by the conquest of Macedonia by Paulus Æmilius in the year 168 before Christ, and had its main seat in the eastern empire, under Diocletian, Galerius, and at length Constantine and his successors, for several ages. The prediction respecting its acts had its accomplishment first in the conquests that were soon made by the Romans of the whole territory that had belonged to the four Greek dynasties represented by the four horns of the goat; and next in the persecution of the true worshipers of God, for a period by the Pagan emperors; and then by those that were nominally Christian, and the preclusion from the faith of men of the sacrifice of Christ as the expiation of sin, substitution in its place of works, superstitious rites and idol worship; and destruction or desecration of the edifices in which the true people of God paid their homage to him. Many of the buildings appropriated by the pure worshipers to the service of God, were confiscated in the fourth, fifth, and following centuries, or destroyed; or such as were left undemolished, were desecrated by the introduction of images, and the observance of unlawful and impious rites. No greater persecutors ever appeared than Diocletian, Galerius, Licinius, Constantine, Constantius, Justinian, and others who had their seat, and most of them exclusively, in the eastern Roman empire, that had previously belonged to the Greeks. The eleventh horn of the wild beast, and the sixth horn of the goat, differed essentially therefore from each other. The horn of the goat was a mere civil and military power, and had its seat in the eastern Roman empire; and it was as such a power, that it magnified itself against the Prince of the host of heaven, and took away from the faith of men the expiation wrought by Christ which the daily sacrifice symbolized; and destroyed or defiled the sanctuaries in which God received a true worship. It made no pretensions to the office of vicegerent of God.

On the other hand, the eleventh horn of the beast, Daniel vii., was chiefly an ecclesiastical power, that had its seat exclusively in the western Roman empire, claiming to be the vicegerent of God, arrogating the right to dictate the faith not only of the people, but of the rulers of the ten Gothic kingdoms, and wearing out the saints by the most persistent, cruel and bloody persecution.

It is a still greater error to maintain that the prince whom Dr. Tregelles and other writers I have cited, imagine is to confirm a covenant with the

Jews, is also the same power as is denoted by the horn of the goat and of the beast. The power symbolized by the sixth horn of the goat, came into being more than two thousand years ago, and long since finished its career. The power denoted by the eleventh horn of the beast came into being a little more than twelve centuries ago, and is still in existence. The prince whom these authors hold is to confirm a covenant with the Jews in the seventieth week of Daniel, which they regard as yet future, has not yet come into existence, and never will. He is not a reality, but a mere fiction; and when the time comes that those who expect him, look for him most eagerly, and strain their eyes to catch a gleam from his diadem, he will mock at their delusion, and shrink into inanity.

2. The persecutions by the eastern and western horns, are not the same. The principles on which they proceeded were, indeed, in a large degree alike, as both arrogated the right of dictating the religion of their subjects. But the power denoted by the eastern, claimed the right as belonging to their office as civil rulers; the power symbolized by the western horn claimed to be invested by God himself with that prerogative. But their persecutions differed from each other in respect to their instigators and agents, their period, and the individuals against whom they were directed. The monarchs of the east were the authors of the persecutions in their empire.

Their war on the people of God began centuries before the western horn rose into power: and the victims of their vengeance were their own subjects. The persecutions in the west, were in the main instigated by the Popes and the Catholic clergy; and the civil powers of the ten kingdoms, were the executors of their will. Their persecutions began twelve centuries ago and continue to the present time, and the victims of their vengeance have been the subjects of the Pope himself, or of the kings who were symbolized by the other horns of the beast.

Nor can the persecutions by the prince who, according to these writers, is yet to come, be the same as those of the powers denoted by the horn of the goat and the horn of the beast.

3. The blasphemies of the horns differ also from the blasphemies that are to be uttered by the Man of Sin, whom these writers hold is to be the prince who is to make a covenant with the Jews. The blasphemies of the power symbolized by the sixth horn of the goat lay in its arrogating dominion over the worshipers of God in their relations to him, and magnifying itself against the Son of God, by legislating over his people and his laws, setting aside his expiation, and instituting false Saviours in his place. The blasphemies of the power denoted by the eleventh horn of the beast, lay essentially in its arrogating a similar authority over the population of the ten western kingdoms, setting Christ's expiation

aside, and substituting the mass in its place; claiming God's sanction of all its false doctrines and false worships, and speaking great words against the Most High. Their blasphemies thus differed in a measure from each other in kind; they were the acts of different individuals, and the times in which they were uttered were different.

But their blasphemies are still more unlike those which are to be breathed from the impious lips of the Man of Sin. For he, instead of simply claiming that he is invested by God with authority over the faith and worship of his subjects, is to deify himself, and boast that he is not only equal, but superior to Jehovah, set himself in his temple and demand from his subjects a worship of himself as God.

4. It is asserted by these writers, with great assurance, that a temple is to be built for their sacrificial rites, by the Jews, on their return to Jerusalem, and before the advent of Christ. Mr. Baxter intimates that perhaps they will fit up the mosque of Omar for the offering of sacrifices, p. 73. Mr. Newton maintains that the temple will be a new erection. "The Jews, when they return to Jerusalem, will sooner or later rebuild their temple and reinstitute their sacrifices." Cited by Mr. Baxter, p. 223. Mr. Purdon entertains the same view: "The infidel king will succeed in setting up his image by main force, in the *newly-finished temple.*" Baxter, p. 229. There is not a syllable, however, in the prophecy respecting

the erection of a new temple for sacrificial rites, or any other services connected with the worship of Jehovah. Nor is there any intimation to that effect in any other part of the prophetic Scriptures, though there are several passages that imply that there is to be a temple at Jerusalem in the last days; as Isaiah ii. 1; yet the only *prediction* of a new temple is that of Ezekiel, which is to be built in obedience to a specific command, and in conformity to a prescribed model. The persuasion that the erection of such an edifice is implied in Daniel ix. 27, is a sheer delusion. They *infer* that a temple is to be built, simply because they have assumed that sacrifices are to be offered. They quote nothing to prove it. It is a mere fiction patched on to the text, in order to conceal one of the fatal gaps that yawn in their theory.

5. Their bold and reiterated representation that sacrifices are to be offered, is equally without authority from the prophecy. They begin with the false assumption, that the seventieth week, instead of being that which immediately followed the sixty-ninth, was thrown forward more than eighteen centuries. But as sacrifices cannot be offered according to the Mosaic ritual, without a tabernacle or temple that is erected by the command of God, and consecrated to him; and as no temple now exists, it is clear that they cannot present the morning and evening victims, nor any other oblation, unless they first erect a temple. Hence these writers announce it as a cer-

tainty deduced by the most indubitable logic, that a temple is to be erected by the Jews immediately after their return. But the premise from which this conclusion is drawn, being false, the conclusion is false also. How astonishing that these authors go on reiterating statements, and assertions, page after page, that certain things are taught in the prophecy, that have their existence only in their imaginations! "Woe to the foolish prophets that follow their own spirit, and have seen nothing." Their supposition is as devoid of probability as it is of authority from the Bible. They assume that the temple which they hold is to be erected by the Jews immediately on their return, is to be truly consecrated to God, as a place of sacrificial rites. But that implies that its erection and appropriation to his service will be held by the Jews generally to be obligatory on them, and acceptable to him. That, however, is incredible. A considerable part of those who first return, will have become believers in Christ, we are expressly taught—Zech. xiii. 9.—and will not, therefore, engage in offering sacrifices that are merely typical of him, and the presentation of which was discontinued by the Apostles and early Christians from the day of his resurrection. They would regard it as involving a renunciation of him as their Saviour, and the adoption, like the Galatians, of another gospel. There is also to be a large body among them who, if without a true faith in Christ, will still have reached a strong conviction that he is their Messiah. They are to go back to their land under a general, though doubtless an inadequate conviction that they are under the special care of the God of their fathers, and that he is to reëstablish them by extraordinary means in their ancient inheritance. It is absurd to suppose that that feeling which has held possession of them in all past ages, is to have no part in prompting their return. Why should they go back, if they have no faith in the promises made to their fathers? What other conceivable motive can rise to such strength as to prompt them to a movement, involving so many deprivations, exposing them to so many dangers, and so uncertain in its issue as it must be if assured by no pledges of success from the Holy One of Israel? But those who are swayed by this general faith in God's interposition for their guidance, will not be likely to disregard the convictions and persuasions of the true believers in Christ with whom they are intermingled as members of the same families and groups. That there will also be a large body who will have no true faith, but will be under the dominion of unbelief, pride, and worldly ambition, is clearly indicated by the slaughter to which a multitude are to be consigned, and the deep repentance and the wondering faith in the blood of Jesus, with which the survivors are to be touched. Zech. xii. 10–14; xiii. 8. The sins that are to draw on them the avenging judgments by which they are to be struck to the grave, are represented as those of idol homage, and false pretences to a prophetic spirit. Zech. xiii. 1–5. Instead of worshiping Jehovah by sacrifices, many of them are to go back from their exile among pagans, like their fathers in leaving Egypt, deeply infatuated with the false gods and false faiths under which they have been nurtured; while others who openly profess to be the worshipers of the God of Israel, will act the part of the false prophets whom Christ foretold were to appear after his departure from the world.

But that this fancy that they are to offer sacrifices and resume the whole Mosaic ritual, is wholly mistaken, is seen from the consideration that they will have no descendant of Aaron who can fill the office of priest. No one was authorized by the Mosaic law to offer animal sacrifices or incense in the tabernacle or temple, except Aaron and his lineal descendants. An intrusion into the priest's office in any of its most important functions was a sacrilege, and was punished as such by the most signal inflictions. Thus Uzziah, the king, on entering the temple, and attempting to offer incense on the golden altar, was struck with leprosy, by which he was driven from his throne and banished from the society of his family and his people. That law has not been abrogated, nor will it be. The Jews, therefore, who return before Christ's advent, will not attempt to reinstate the offering of sacrifices and oblations, if for no other reason, because they will have no priest who will be qualified to present victims on the altar, sprinkle the blood, bear it on the day of the great atonement into the Holy of Holies, nor to burn incense morning and evening on the golden altar. To suppose them to attempt it is to suppose them to set the laws of the Mosaic ritual so flagrantly aside, as to make it solecistical to imagine that they will regard the injunction itself of sacrifices and oblations as of any authority.

That there are to be worshipers of idols also among that people, even at the time of Christ's second coming, is foretold by Isaiah ii. 20, 21: "In that day a man shall cast his idols of silver and his idols of gold, which each one made for himself to worship, to the moles and to the bats, to go into the clefts of the rocks, and into the tops of the ragged rocks, for fear of the Lord, and for the glory of his majesty, when he ariseth to shake terribly the earth." The whole imagination of these writers is thus a dream that has sprung from a desire to give an air of probability to their false notions respecting the Emperor of France and Antichrist.

6. There is no proof that the Man of Sin is to seat himself in a temple of God at Jerusalem, in order to be honored as divine. A temple erected without authority from God, and for ends that are not consistent with his will, would not be a temple of God. As, then, there is not to be a true temple of God at the time that Antichrist goes there, he plainly cannot seat

himself there in one. It is not probable that the Man of Sin will select Jerusalem as the scene of that act of impiety. His seating himself in the temple of God, and showing himself that he is God, is exhibited not only as his greatest act of wickedness, but as having for its aim the reception of divine honors from his subjects. In order to that he will naturally select as the scene some capital in his empire where he has his court, where his subjects throng in the greatest numbers, and where those dwelling at a distance may have the readiest access to him. To go to Jerusalem would be to go where no worshipers except his immediate attendants and his army could present to him their homage. Dr. Tregelles holds that it is in the temple at Jerusalem that he is to seat himself: "The Holy place is that in which this abomination of desolation will be set; this, of course, means the temple of God at Jerusalem," p. 105. But the abomination of desolation is not the Man of Sin. This is clear, from the fact that the time of its intrusion into the Holy Place, by which is meant, not the temple edifice, but the courts of the temple, was immediately before the commencement of the siege of Jerusalem by Titus, as is seen from Christ's injunction to his disciples, that when they saw that abomination standing in the Holy Place, they should flee to the mountains, implying that the siege of the city would not then have commenced. In order to see the abomination of desolation established in the courts of the temple, it was necessary that they should be at the city and at points from which the temple courts were visible; and that they might flee from the city it was necessary that it should be unbesieged.

7. These expositors furnish no proof that there is to be a great persecution of the true worshipers by the Man of Sin in Palestine, when he goes there to make war with the Jews. That it is to be a time of unparalelled tribulation, we are distinctly forewarned; but the trouble is to be of the same kind as that which signalized the siege of Jerusalem by the Romans; the trouble of internal factions and of external war. There was no persecution of the Jews by Titus on account of their peculiar religion. The war was a mere ordinary war to crush the nation into subjection. And there is no hint that the war of the eighth king, the Antichrist, on the Israelites at Jerusalem, will be anything else than a fierce, merciless and bloody assault on the nation to break up its organization and drive it again into exile. That is the picture drawn of the trial by Zechariah: "And it shall come to pass that in all the land, saith the Lord, two parts therein shall be cut off and die; but the third shall be left therein. And I will bring the third part through the fire; and will refine them as silver is refined, and will try them as gold is tried. They shall call on my name and I will hear them; I will say, it is my people; and they shall say, the Lord is my God," chapter xiii. 8, 9. This seems to imply

that none are to die but the unbelieving. The factions and strifes of the wicked may be as violent as the feuds and contests were of the Zealots. They may be as great a source of terror and suffering as Antichrist will be. In like manner it is foreshown in Isaiah, that the slaughter and destruction at that crisis, vast as they are to be, are to be confined to the incorrigible: "For behold the Lord will come with fire and with his chariots like a whirlwind, to render his anger with fury, and his rebuke with flames of fire. For by fire and by his sword will the Lord plead with all flesh, and the slain of the Lord shall be many. They that sanctify themselves and purify themselves in the gardens behind one tree in the midst, eating swine's flesh, and the abomination and the mouse shall be consumed together, saith the Lord," chapter lxvi. 15–17. This destruction, moreover, is to be by the direct hand of God and his attendants; not the work of Antichrist and his host.

The aim of the eighth king who is to make war on the Lamb, in Palestine, is not to be to persecute the Jews and force them to worship him as God, but to intercept their re-establishment in their land, drive them again into exile, and thereby confute the faith they and the whole body of Gentile believers will at that crisis hold and profess, that Christ is to come in the clouds and assume the sceptre of Israel, and judge and destroy all his and their open and avowed enemies. The great question to be determined by the invasion of Palestine and the neighboring countries, is not to be, whether the Man of Sin is to be worshiped or not; but whether Christ is to come in his glory, assume the dominion of the world, and destroy all his organized enemies; and the power represented by the beast in its last form, will attempt to determine that by force of arms, and will be hurled to the lake of fire by Christ's own hand, while his army will be consumed by the brightness of his coming, and the breath of his mouth. Rev. xvi. 14–16; xvii. 11–14; xix. 19–21.

I might point out other errors in these authors, but these are sufficient to show the utter untenableness of their system.

CHAPTER XIV.

There is no proof that an Image is to be set up by Antichrist in a Temple at Jerusalem—That Notion is derived by these Writers from Apollinarius—The Absurdity of the Views of the Image held by Dr. Tregelles, Mr. Baxter and others—The reason that Apollinarius assumed that an Idol or Statue was to be placed in the Temple, and that he with others maintained that Sacrifices are to be offered there; that there the Abomination of Desolation is to be Exhibited; and the other Peculiarities of their Constructions of Daniel—The Ground on which he and others Interpreted the 1260, and 1290 Days, as the measure of Antichrist's Career.

There is no indication in the prophecy that an image or idol is to be set up in the temple in which Antichrist is to seat himself. The notion of such an image is a fiction of the commentators from whom these modern writers derive their views. Some of them represent that the shape, which they hold is to be the abomination foreshown by Daniel, is to be that of the Man of Sin himself. Others intimate that it is to be the image of the beast.—Rev. xiii. 14, 15. Tregelles, p. 153. Baxter, pp. 200, 207.

Hippolytus makes no allusion in his work on Daniel, to the introduction of an image into the temple which he held Antichrist is to rear in Jerusalem, and make the scene of the worship which his minions are to pay him. That notion, however, was held by

Apollinarius of Laodicea, who in the fourth century obtained some celebrity as an opponent of Porphyry, and a commentator on the Scriptures. His works are chiefly lost, but the passage I am to give is preserved in Jerome's Commentary on Daniel. The error of Eusebius in respect to the seventy weeks, lay according to Jerome, in his assuming that the term anointed, or Messiah Prince denoted the chief priests and princes or rulers of the Jews who led the captive people back from Babylon to Jerusalem and their successors there to the birth of Christ; and in consequence of that misjudgment, reckoning the sixty-nine weeks from the edict of Cyrus, which terminating according to his mistaken calculation, at Christ's birth, led to the assumption that the seventieth week was disjoined from the sixty-ninth by a space of thirty years. Apollinarius ran into the still greater error of assigning the whole seventy weeks to the ages that immediately followed Christ's crucifixion, instead with the exception of the last half week, preceding them. It was this untenable assumption that prompted Jerome to reject his theory.

"But Apollinarius dismissing all inquiry in respect to past times, directed his search to the future, and adventurously wrought out a judgment in regard to events that are altogether uncertain: which, should those who are to live after us, find are not verified according to his calculation, they will be under the necessity of seeking another explanation, and will arraign him as a teacher of error. He said then: 'During four hundred and ninety years, sin and all the excesses that spring from sin, are to be *repressed;* after which good is to come, and the world is to be reconciled to God at the advent of his Son. For from the going forth of the word when Christ was conceived of the Virgin Mary unto the forty-ninth year; that is, the end of the seven hebdomads, there was a waiting for the repentance of Israel. But after the eighth year of Claudius Cæsar, the Roman arms were arrayed against the Jews. For, according to the evangelist Luke, in the thirtieth year of his age in the flesh, the Lord began to preach the Gospel; and according to John (through three passovers), he afterward spent two years; and after that six years of Tiberius are to be reckoned, and four of Claudius Cæsar, sirnamed Caligula, and eight of Claudius: that is, together forty-nine years, which make seven hebdomads of years. But when four hundred and thirty-four years have revolved, Elias shall come, who, according to the words of our Lord, is to restore the heart of the fathers to the children; and in the last hebdomad, during three years and a half, Jerusalem and the temple are to be built, and Antichrist is to come, and is to sit in the temple of God; and after he has fought against the saints, is to be put to death by the Spirit of the Lord. And so it is to be that the half week will confirm the Covenant of God with the saints; and again the half will proclaim the cessation of sacrifices under Antichrist, who will place the abomination of desolation, namely, the idol and statue of his own god, in the temple; and the Jewish people, who have spurned the truth of Christ, and accepted the lie of Antichrist, will be overwhelmed with the utmost desolation and doom."

Jerome adds moreover:

"Apollinarius asserts that he adopts this *conjecture* of the times, because Africanus, a writer on chronology, testifies that the last hebdomad is to be at the end of the world: which cannot be; inasmuch as it implies that ages that are continuous are to be divided. And besides it contradicts the prophecy of Daniel, *according to which all times are coupled together in an* uninterrupted line." *

* Apollinarius Laodicenus omne præteritorum temporum se liberans questione, vota extendit in futurum, et periculose de incertis profert sententiam. Quæ si forte hi, qui post nos victuri sunt, statuto tempore completa non viderint, aliam solutionem quærere compellentur, et magistrum erroris arguere. Dicit ergo: In quadringentis nonaginta annis, peccata omnia, quæ ex peccatis oriuntur vitia, comprimenda; post quæ ventura sint bona et reconciliandum Deo Mundum in adventu Christi filii ejus. Ab exitu enim verbi, quando Christus de Maria generatus est usque ad quadragesimum nonum annum, id est finem septem hebdomadarum, Israelis expectatam pœnitentiam. Postea vero ab octavo Claudii Cæsaris anno, contra Judæos Romana arma correpta. Tricesimo enim juxta Evangelistam Lucam anno ætatis suæ, cepit in carne Dominus evangelium prædicare, et juxta Joannem Evangelistam, per tria paschata duos postea implevit annos; et exinde sex Tiberii supputantur anni, et quatuor C. Cæsaris cognomento Caligula; et octo Claudii, id est, simul anni quadraginta novem, qui faciunt hebdomadas septem. Cum autem quadringenti triginta quatuor anni, post hoc fuerint evoluti; id est, sexaginta duæ hebdomadæ, tunc ab Helia, qui venturus est juxta sermonem Domini Salvatoris, ut restituat cor patrum ad filios, in ultima hebdomada ædificandum Hierusalem et templum per annos tres et semis; venturum que Antichristum, et juxta Apostolum sessurum in templo Dei, et interficiendum Spiritu Domini Salvatoris postquam contra sanctos dimicaverit; atque ita fieri ut media hebdomada confirmit testamentum Dei cum Sanctis, et rursum media cessationem victimarum esse pronuntiet sub Antichristo, qui ponet abominationem desolationis, id est, idolum et statuam proprii Dei in templo, et erit extrema vastitas et condemnatio populi Judæorum, qui spreta veritate Christi, receperunt Antichristi mendacium. Asserit autem idem Apollinarius hanc se temporum capere conjecturam, quia Africanus, Scriptor temporum, cujus super expositionem posui, ultimam hebdomadam in fine mundi esse testatur; nec posse fieri, ut junctæ dividantur ætates, se et omnia sibi juxta prophetiam Danielis esse tempora copulanda."—*Jerome on Daniel ix.*

It is apparent from this that Dr. Tregelles and those of his school drew from Apollinarius their notion that an image of the Man of Sin, of the beast, or of some other deified object, is to be set up in the temple at Jerusalem; and that he himself or that image is to be the abomination of desolation.

It is obvious also that it was from Apollinarius that they derived the idea that the putting a bar to sin, predicted of Christ, Daniel ix. 24, was not accomplished by him in his death on the cross, but was to follow his crucifixion and resurrection. Apollinarius held that that act was especially to mark the four hundred and ninety years, that followed Christ's crucifixion: when he supposed he would appear again, and introduce a reign of righteousness and peace. Dr. Tregelles, and his school, hold that that interception of sin from its penal effects is still future, and is not to be consummated till Christ comes at the close of the present dispensation.

Mr. Baxter's representation also, that the postponement of the seventieth week till Christ's second coming, was because the Jews rejected him, is in like manner to be traced to Apollinarius, who held that the first seven weeks from Christ's conception, was a period in which the question was put to trial whether Israel would repent or not: and that at the close of that forty-nine years the destructive judgments on the nation commenced in the war of the Romans, and the forbearance of God was thereafter restricted to the Gentiles. Mr. Baxter's views on that point are at least essentially those of Apollinarius.

The views held by Dr. Tregelles, Mr. Baxter, and others, respecting the idol or statue that, according to their representation, is to be set up by Antichrist at Jerusalem; and the notion that it is to be an image of the beast, Apoc. xiii. 14, 15, are absurd as well as false. The image of the beast was a mere symbol, and the representative of the Catholic hierarchies of the ten kingdoms, united in one organization with the Pope as their head. The gift of life to the image accordingly, that it should both speak, and cause that as many as would not worship it should be killed, was a mere symbol of the analogous acts which that Catholic hierarchy was to exert in its sphere as an organized body of ecclesiastics, modelled after the civil government of the Roman imperium under the emperors denoted by the seventh head, after it had been restored from its deadly wound; Rev. xiii. 14, 15. The abomination that causes desolation, is not an idol. The supposition that the introduction into the temple grounds of an idol by the Man of Sin, as some of these writers hold, or as others deem by the Romans, could be the reason that God should abandon the temple and its courts to desolation, is forbidden by the consideration that it would not be the crime of the Jews, but of their enemies. The abomination of desolation was not the work of the Romans, but of the Jewish people themselves; and consisted in the profanation of the temple and its courts by the bloody faction of Zealots who took possession of the whole site, a short time before the siege of the city began, and converted it into a fortress, and made it the scene of violence, bloodshed, and every species of wickedness of which that impious band was capable. And that was the construction placed on it, Josephus represents, by the Jews themselves, who witnessed it. "Daniel wrote in regard to the supremacy of the Romans, and ἐρημωθήσεται, that they should lay waste our country." *Jud. Ant. Book x., c. xi.* 7. He says again: "There was a prediction that the city should be taken, and the sanctuary burned by an enemy at a time when a faction should rise, and their own hands should pollute the sacred inclosure." *De Bello Jud., Book iv. c. vi.* 3. The notion of these writers that the abomination of desolation is yet future, and is to be the work of the Man of Sin, is thus against the express teachings of the prophecy, and against Christ's representation that its period was to be that of the invasion of Judea by the Roman armies, a short time before the city should be besieged.

As there is no intimation in the Scriptures that an image is to be set up by Antichrist in the temple of God, in which he is to seat himself, and exhibit himself as God; how was it, it is natural to ask, that Apollinarius and others were led to the belief that an image is to be placed by Antichrist in the supposed temple at Jerusalem, and that that image, whether of himself or some other being, is to be the abomination of desolation? It was undoubtedly from the fact that Antiochus Epiphanes who, in that age, was held to be a precursor or type of the last Antichrist, on his conquering Jerusalem, and taking possession of the temple, introduced an image of one of his deities into it, and made it an object of worship. As he was regarded as a symbol of the Antichrist who is to appear in the last age of this dispensation, it was natural that they should assume that he is to act a part in its chief respects like that of Antiochus Epiphanes in all the impieties toward God, and atrocities toward men, of which that merciless tyrant persecutor, and slaughterer of God's people, and violater of the temple, was guilty. That they held that Antiochus was the type and forerunner of Antichrist, is seen from the following passages from Jerome on Daniel. He says in commenting on chapter xi. v. 21:

"Thus far the order of history is followed, and no dispute exists between Porphyry and ourselves. But what follows to the end of the book, he interprets of Antiochus Epiphanes, brother of Seleucus, and son of Antiochus the Great, who after Seleucus, reigned eleven years in Syria, got possession of Judæa, and prohibited and profaned the rites enjoined by the laws of God, as is detailed, along with the wars of the Macchabees, in the remainder of the eleventh and in the twelfth chapters.

"But our writers regard all these things as foreshown of Antichrist, who is to appear in the last times. . . . And as many of the things which we are yet to expound, are applicable to the career of Antiochus, they choose to regard him, as a type of Antichrist, and what took place but partially under him, as to have its full completion in Antichrist. . . . For as the Saviour had in Solomon and other saints types of his coming; so it is justly believed that Antichrist had Antiochus the worst of kings, who was to persecute the saints and desecrate the temple as a type of him." . . .

"And he shall do what his fathers have not done (verses 37, 38)."

"Porphyry treats this at large; but I briefly. For our writers interpret it more justly as denoting that at the end of the world this is to be done by Antichrist, who is to have his descent from a small people, the Jews, and is to be so humble and despised, that regal honor will not be given to him; and he will obtain the supremacy by artifice and fraud, and the arms of the Roman people will be assailed by him and broken. And he will do this because he feigns he is the prince of the league; that is, of the law and covenant of God." *

* Hucusque ordo historiæ sequiter, et inter Porphyrium ac nostros nulla contentio est. Cætera, quæ sequntur usque ad finem voluminis, ille interpretatur super persona Antiochi, qui cognominatus est Epiphanes: frater Seleuci, filius Antiochi Magni qui post Seleucum undecim annis regnavit in Syria, obtinuitque Judæam, sub quo Legis Dei persecutio, et Macchabaeorum bella narrantur. Nostri autem hæc omnia de Antichristo prophetari arbitrantur qui ultimo tempore futurus est. . . . . Cum que multa, quæ portea lecturi et expósituri sumus, super Antiochi persona conveniant: typum eum volunt Antichristi habere, et quæ in illo ex parte præcesserint, in Antichristo toto esse complenda. . . . . Sicut igitur Salvator habet et Salomonem et cæteros sanctos in typum adventus sui; sic et Antichristus pessimum regem Antiochum qui Sanctos persecutus est, templumque violavit, recte typum sui habuisse credendus est. . . . . Fecitque, quæ non fecerunt patres ejus. Hæc Porphyrius sermone latissimo prosecutus est: quæ nos brevi compendio diximus. Nostri autem et melius interpretantur et rectius, quod in fine mundi hæc

In accordance with this view of Antiochus Epiphanes as a type of Antichrist, Hippolytus, Apollinarius, Jerome and others ascribe to Antichrist acts of the same kinds, both towards God and towards men, as the Jewish and other historians ascribe to Antiochus. Thus the author of Macchabees relates:

"And Antiochus turned, after he had smitten Egypt in the year B. C. 170; and passing into Palestine, advanced to Jerusalem, and entered into the sanctuary in haughty insolence, and seized the golden altar, and the candlestick, with all its furniture, and the table of presentation, the vessels of libation, the veil, and the golden ornaments on the front of the temple, and broke them in pieces. He also took silver and gold and precious vessels, and the hidden treasures which he found, and carrying all away, returned to Syria. He made a slaughter of the people also, and spoke in great pride. . . . And after two years he sent the curator who had charge of tributes into the cities of Judea. And he came to Jerusalem with a great crowd, and deceitfully addressing the people with pacific words, and gaining their confidence, he made a sudden onset on the city, and struck it with a severe blow, and put to death a multitude of the Jewish population; and took the spoils of the city, and set it on fire, and demolished its houses and the wall around it. And he built up the city of David—Sion—with a high and strong wall, and massy towers, and made it a fortress; and they placed there a

sit facturus Antichristus, qui consurgere habet de modica gente, id est, de populo Judæorum, et tam humilis erit et despectus, ut ei non detur honor regius, et per insidias, et fraudulentiam obtineat principatum, et brachia pugnantis populi Romani expugnentur ab eo, et conterantur. Ei hoc faciet, quia simulabit se ducem esse fœderis, hoc est, Legis et testamenti Dei.—*Comment on Daniel xi.* 21–38.

12

race given to sin, unjust men, who rose to strength there, and made it a magazine of arms, food, and spoil; and they made it a snare, and a means of plots against the sanctuary, and poured out the blood of the innocent in the courts of the sanctuary, and polluted the holy place. And the sanctuary was made desolate like a solitude; its festivals were turned to lamentation, its Sabbaths to a reproach, and its honors to nothing. And King Antiochus wrote to every part of his kingdom that the whole people should be one, and each should relinquish its own peculiar law of religion, and all the races unite in one worship, according to his command. And many of the Israelites consented to that subservience to him, and *offered sacrifices to idols*, and desecrated the Sabbath. And the king sent edicts by messengers to Jerusalem, and to all the cities of Judæa, requiring that they should follow the laws of the Gentiles; and that they should forbid the offering of holocausts and sacrifices, and expiations, in the temple of God; and prohibit the observance of the Sabbath, and feast days. And he commanded that holy things, and the holy people of Israel, should be profaned and polluted; and he ordered the erection of altars and temples and idols, and the immolation of swine and animals that were not clean; and that their sons should be left uncircumcised, and their souls defiled with all impurities and abominations, so that they should forget the law, and change all God's statutes; and that whoever should not obey the will of the king, should be put to death. And he appointed officers over the people, who should compel them to do these things. And they ordered that sacrifices should be offered in the cities of Judæa. And many of the people gathered to them, and forsook the law of the Lord, and did evil. And many of the people of Israel were driven into seclusion, and into the hiding place of fugitives. And on the fifteenth of the month, Chisleu, in the hundred and sixty-eighth year before Christ, King Antiochus erected the abomination of the idols of desolation on the altar of God, and built altars in all the cities of Judæa, and before the gates of houses they burned incense, and offered sacrifices. And tearing the books of the Law of God in pieces, they burned them with fire. And whoever was found having the books of the Lord's covenant, and whoever observed the Law of the Lord, they put to death. . . . And many of the people of Israel resolved with themselves that they would not eat unclean things, and chosing to die, rather than to be polluted with impure food, they refused to break God's holy Law, and were slain."—1st *Macchabees, chapter i.*

A similar account is given by Josephus of the deceits, robberies, slaughters and impieties of which Antiochus was guilty.—*Antiq. Jud., lib. xii., cap.* 3, 4.

The crimes which he perpetrated are thus, in the main, like those ascribed by Irenæus, Hippolytus, Apollinarius and Jerome, to the future Antichrist.

1. Thus Antiochus invaded Judæa and conquered Jerusalem. Antichrist, those writers held, is also to invade that country and conquer Jerusalem.

2. He not only entered into a league or compact with many apostate Israelites, who desired to observe the rites of idolatry, but gave pledges of his favor and protection to the Jewish people at large, in order to draw them into a condition in which he could disarm them, and make them the victims of his avarice and vengeance. Antichrist is also, those writers maintained, to make a league with the Jews, by

which he is to draw them into his power, that he may make them the tools and victims of his ambition.

3. Antiochus soon broke the pledges of peace and protection he had given to the Jewish people, and trampled them down with the most savage fury, and slaughtered great numbers of them. Antichrist, according to these authors, is to perpetrate a similar violation of his covenant with the Jews to re-establish and protect them in their national land. After the lapse of three years and a half he is to break his league and turn and crush and slay them with the most unsparing cruelty.

4. Antiochus not only robbed the temple of God of its golden furniture, and plundered the population of Jerusalem and the other cities, but he gathered vast spoils in Egypt, and undertook to seize the treasure of an idol temple in his own empire. That robbery is also to be the characteristic of Antichrist, who is to lay his hand on the treasures of gold and silver, and precious things of Egypt.

5. Antiochus was eminently a destroyer. He not only laid waste the cities and fields of Judæa, but spread devastation through Egypt and other regions. These authors held that Antichrist is to run a similar career as a slaughterer of men and a devastator of the countries he overruns.

6. Antiochus prevented the Jews from offering in the temple the sacrifices that were enjoined by the divine law, and made the presentation of those offer-

ings an offence punishable with death. Antichrist is also, according to those commentators, to cause sacrifice and libation to cease, and put an end to all the acts of worship that are enjoined by the Most High.

7. Antiochus caused temples to be erected in every city of Judæa, and numberless altars for the worship of his false gods. Those ancient writers maintained that Antichrist is in like manner to build a temple in Jerusalem, in which sacrifices are to be offered for a time, and in which he is at length to seat himself, and demand the homage of his subjects as God.

8. Antiochus set up an idol in the temple in Jerusalem, and required and compelled many to worship it as a deity. Antichrist is, in like manner, those writers affirmed, to set up an image or idol in the temple he is to build at Jerusalem, and compel his subjects to worship it as a God.

9. Antiochus intruded into the temple what those writers regarded as the abomination of desolation; some holding that it was the image of Jupiter which he set above the altar of Jehovah; and some the polluted and impious oblations with which it was served. Antichrist, in like manner, they maintained, is to intrude into the temple he is to erect at Jerusalem the abomination of desolation; some deeming that Antichrist himself is to be that abomination; and some that it is to be the image he is to set up there, and the impious rites with which it is to be adored.

10. Antiochus, in connection with these atrocities, instituted a fierce and bloody persecution of the Israelites, who continued steadfast in their allegiance to God, and consigned great numbers to outrage, slavery and death. Antichrist, in like manner, according to those authors, on breaking his league with the Jews, and prohibiting them from offering sacrifice and homage to God, is to turn and persecute those who refuse submission to his will with relentless fury, and is to put to death the witnesses of Jesus, and a crowd of other believers.

11. Antiochus, by artifices, frauds and violence, drew a large crowd to offer the impious worship which he enjoined. Antichrist, these commentators represent, is to win the multitude to pay him the sacrilegious homage he is to demand of them.

12. As Antiochus perished suddenly while unchecked in his career of wickedness; those writers deemed his death by violence a type of the instantaneous and remediless doom that is to overtake Antichrist in his war on God and his kingdom.

The parallel thus embraces nearly all the acts and characteristics which they predicate of the future Antichrist; and the reason that they imputed them to him undoubtedly was, that they assumed that Antiochus was the type of Antichrist; and thence that whatever specially signalized his career, was to have its counterpart in the ambition and avarice, the devastations and slaughters, the revolting impiety and merciless persecution of the holy and faithful that are in their belief to mark the Man of Sin as he advances through his career to the gates of perdition. For that postulate not only implied, but was equivalent to an affirmation, that such a parallel was to subsist between them; and that was the sole ground on which their prognostications of Antichrist were founded.

That assumption, however, was wholly gratuitous and mistaken. *First*. Because there is no authority for it in the prophecy. There is no intimation in Daniel that the person foreshown, v. 21–30, is a type of the king predicted v. 36–45, who is to exalt himself above God, nor is there any parallel between the actions foreshown of them except that both were to be enemies of God and his people; both ambitious conquerors; and both to engage in war with the king of the south, and to overrun and lay waste Judæa, which was not altogether peculiar to them; for not only were several other kings of Syria involved in war with the monarchs of Egypt, and invaded and plundered Palestine, but Shishak, one of the Egyptian kings, in the reign of Rehoboam, captured Jerusalem and plundered the temple, the palace and the city of their treasures. The sums deposited in the temple as gifts to God were, indeed, repeatedly taken by the kings of Judah and devoted to the payment of tribute or the uses of war: as by Asa, who gave all that he could gather from sanctuary and palace to the king of Damascus, to purchase his alliance against the king of Israel; and two hundred years later the temple hoards were seized by Ahaz, and presented to Tiglath Pileser, king of Assyria, as the price of that monarch's alliance and war on his behalf on the kings of Syria and Ephraim. A like appropriation was made by Hezekiah of the wealth of the temple that had been gathered in the last years of Manasseh, and the first of his own reign, in the form of a tribute to Sennacherib. At length the temple was plundered and destroyed by Nebuchadnezzar. The second temple also, which Antiochus robbed and polluted by his impieties, was in the year B. C. 65, captured and profaned by Pompey; in the year B. C. 54, it was violated and plundered once more by Crassus; and finally, in the year A. D. 70, it was captured and destroyed by Titus: and sixty-five years after, the Jews were banished from Jerusalem by Hadrian, and forbidden to observe the rites of their religion; a Pagan colony was settled in their place, and a fane erected to Jupiter near the site where the temple of Jehovah had stood, and the image of that false God set up in it as the object of worship. Why should Antiochus Epiphanes be considered any more than any one of those Pagans as a type of Antichrist because of his having robbed and desecrated the temple of the Most High, of which they also had been guilty?

Next. But the supposition that he was a type of

Antichrist, is not only without any authority from the prophecy, but is precluded by the fact that no notice is given that he filled that office. For it is a peculiarity of types, that they are formally appointed by God; and the place they fill is made known to those who are required to employ them as such. Thus Adam, as the head of the race, was by divine appointment the type of Christ. The Holy of Holies also was expressly constituted the type of the Holy of Holies in the heavenly temple in which God reveals himself. The expiating sacrifices of the Mosaic ritual were, in like manner, ordained as types of the Lamb of God who takes away the sins of the world: and so also were the high priests who as representatives of Christ, entered into the Holy of Holies annually on the great day of atonement, and presented the blood of the victims that were consuming on the altar as a symbol of Christ's blood which was to be shed for the remission of sin. That no notice is given that Antiochus Epiphanes filled the office of a type of Antichrist, is an indubitable proof therefore, that he held no such place in his career of pride and lawlessness, of slaughter and of sacrilege.

Thirdly. But the groundlessness and error of that supposition are demonstrated in a still more emphatic manner by the consideration that on the point of chief significance no parallel whatever is presented by Antiochus Epiphanes, to the Man of Sin, and Antichrist who is to appear at the close of the present dispensation. For the greatest and most distinctive peculiarity of Antichrist is to be, that he is to exalt himself above all that is called God, and is an object of worship, and is to set himself as God in the temple of God, and as such demand the homage of his subjects. But Antiochus Epiphanes made no such impious pretence in respect to himself. He did not seat himself in the temple at Jerusalem, and proclaim himself God, and extort the homage of his subjects in that sphere. Instead, he asserted the deity of his idol god, and set up his image over the altar of Jehovah, as a rival of him; and enforced the worship of the sacrilegious shape by insults, tortures, and death. As therefore there is no parallel in respect to this most distinctive characteristic between Antiochus and Antichrist, there is the most indubitable certainty that Antiochus did not fill the office of a type of him. Antiochus aimed only at a supremacy over man. Antichrist is to aspire to a superiority over God, the Self-existent and Almighty. All the main grounds on which those ancient writers and their modern disciples proceed in their speculations in regard to Antichrist, are thus swept from beneath them, and their theory left without support.

I now turn to the views on which those early writers proceeded in their interpretation of the great periods of Daniel, as denoting days simply, in place of years.

As Apollinarius held with Africanus, Hippolytus,

Eusebius, Jerome and others, that the days of the seventy weeks of Daniel were representative of a corresponding number of years; why was it that neither he nor they applied that law of exposition to the other periods of Daniel, such as the time, times, and half a time, the twelve hundred and sixty days, and the twenty-three hundred evenings-mornings: and to the forty-two months and twelve hundred and sixty days of the Apocalypse?

The reason doubtless was, that from the false notion they had inherited from the Jews, that the world was to reach its end at the close of the sixth millennium, there was no space left between their age and Christ's second advent for periods of such length as twelve hundred and sixty years. They held that Christ's incarnation took place at or near the middle of the six thousandth year from the creation. This is seen from the following passage from Hippolytus:

"From the birth of Christ five hundred years are to be computed, in order that six thousand years may be completed; and so the end will come. For as in the fifth (thousand) and a half the Saviour was present in the world, bearing the incorruptible ark, that is his own body, John said, *And it was the sixth hour:* that he might point out the half of the day. But the day of the Lord being a thousand years, the half of them are five hundred. For it was not suitable that he should come earlier, for the burthen of the law still continued; nor were the six thousand years completed; but only the fifth and a half; that in the remaining half (millennium) the gospel might be preached in all the world; and the sixth day being completed, the present life may end." *

Such being their belief in regard to the time when the present dispensation was to end, in the age of Africanus only two hundred and sixty, and in that of Hippolytus one hundred and eighty years were in their expectation to revolve, before the Son of God would come in the clouds; and in the age of Eusebius and Apollinarius only a hundred and thirty or forty. On their views, therefore, of the vicinity of the world's final hour, they were constrained to interpret the time, times, and half a time of Daniel, and the forty-two months and twelve hundred and sixty days of John, as simply denoting the periods which they directly express. Had they extricated themselves from the false ideas in which they had been nurtured, that all the predictions of the prophets which remained unfulfilled, were to have their ac-

* VI. . . .*Ἀπὸ γενέσεως οὖν Χριστοῦ δεῖ ψηφίζειν πεντακόσια ἔτη τὰ ἐπίλοιπα εἰς συμπλήρωσιν τῶν ἑξακισχιλίων ἐτῶν, καὶ οὕτως ἔσται τὸ τέλος· ὅτι δὲ πέμπτῳ καὶ ἡμίσει καιρῷ παρῆν ὁ Σωτὴρ ἐν τῷ κόσμῳ, φέρων τὴν ἄσηπτον κιβωτὸν, τὸ ἴδιον σῶμα, λέγει ὁ Ἰωάννης· ἦν δὲ ὥρα ἕκτη· ἵνα ἥμισυ τῆς ἡμέρας ἐπιδείξῃ· ἡμέρα δὲ Κυρίου χιλία ἔτη· τούτων οὖν τὸ ἥμισυ, γίνεται πεντακόσια· οὐ γὰρ ἐνεδέχετο αὐτὸν τάχιον παρεῖναι, ἔτι γὰρ βάρος νόμου ἦν, οὐδὲ ἕκτης πεπληρωμένης· καινοῦται γὰρ τὸ λουτρὸν· ἀλλὰ πέμπτης καὶ ἡμισείας, ἵνα ἐν τῷ ἐπιλοίπῳ ἡμίσει χρόνῳ, εἰς πάντα τὸν κόσμον τὸ εὐαγγέλιον κηρυχθῇ, καὶ πληρωθείσης τῆς ἕκτης ἡμέρας παύσῃ τὸν νῦν βίον.*

complishment in two or three hundred years, they not improbably would have interpreted the other periods of Daniel in the same manner as they did the seventy weeks of that prophet. And had they done so, and verified their construction of the seventy weeks, by a true exhibition of the dates of the commencement and termination of the three divisions into which they were distributed, they would naturally have commanded the acquiescence of the churches of their day, and saved the generations that followed from the false excitements and fatal delusions in which so many have been involved by their inconsistencies and errors.

CHAPTER XV.

Dr. Tregelles' Views of the Symbols of Time—His Error in regard to the Meaning of Shabua, Week.

WITH a share of the objections, I have alleged to the views of these writers, they are probably not unfamiliar. Dr. Tregelles, especially, endeavors in his remarks on Daniel, to evade those that relate to the interpretation of the symbols that are employed as the representatives of time. Let the mode be carefully noticed in which he treats that subject.

"Many," he says, "have adopted a principle of interpretation with regard to designations of time when they are found in prophecy, to which they have given the name of the year-day system. This principle is that in such prophetic designations of time the literal meaning must not be held, but that in *all expressions of periods of time in future events, a day* stands as the representative of *a year*, and all other spaces of time in similar proportion." P. 110.

This statement is at a great distance from accuracy. The question between those who hold what Dr. Tregelles calls the year-day system, and those who reject it, is, not whether *all designations of time that are found in prophecy* are used to denote greater periods than they literally express; but whether those which occur in the *symbolic* prophecies, especially those of Daniel and John, and are given as measures of symbolic agencies, are used in that relation or not. There are several designations of time in the prophecies of Isaiah; but no one supposes that they are symbols of greater periods than themselves; inasmuch as they occur, not in symbolic, but in mere language predictions.

"There are not a few who hold this as an opinion so established in their minds, that they regard it as an undoubted truth, without knowing definitely on what grounds it was adopted. They speak of a *prophetic day*, or a *prophetic year*, as if it were an axiom that these expressions denote the one a literal *year*, and the other a term of three hundred and sixty literal years.

"On this principle they would interpret the designations of time in the Book of Daniel, and in the Revelation:—they thus speak of the 1260 *years* and the 2300 *years*. Of course, if we find distinct Scripture warrant for this assumed canon, we must bow to it, and interpret accordingly. But if this canon is supposed to be a deduction from Scripture, let us examine whether the inference be legitimate, and let the reception or the rejection depend on the grounds of proof.

"It is not, I believe, stated by any that this canon is a subject of direct teaching in Scripture; at least none of the points advanced seem to be relied on as showing this; some of the maintainers of the system, expressly repudiate such a thought.

"Some who have received the year-day principle without inquiry, will be surprised at these admissions of the weakness of that *a priora* evidence by which it is upheld; others may think that too much is surrendered. At all events, it must be owned that this course of interpretation, is not known as an intuitive truth: the early church knew no such maxim: and therefore I hold that it should be shown to be either laid down in Scripture, or else it should be *proved thereby*, before any one can be expected to receive it, and before it is applied to the interpretation of prophetic statements." *Remarks on Daniel*, *pp.* 110–112.

Dr. Tregelles thus affirms here, not only that there is nothing in the Scriptures to authorize the interpretation of periods of time expressed in days as representing a corresponding number of years; but avers "that the early church knew no such maxim," or canon of construction. This is an extraordinary misrepresentation. For the seventy weeks of Daniel ix. 24–27, are expressed as distinctly and exclusively in days, as the period of 1260, or 1290, days is, or the forty-two months. And those seventy weeks were most certainly generally interpreted as symbolizing four hundred and ninety years, the number that corresponds with the days comprised in seventy weeks. Thus Hippolytus in his work on Daniel, says:

"That he might show the time when he was to come whom Daniel desired to see, he said: 'And after seven weeks, there are other sixty-two weeks, which contain the time of four hundred and thirty-four years. For after the return of the people from Babylon, under the leadership of Joshua, son of Josedech, and Ezra, the Scribe, and Zerubbabel, the son of Salathiel, who was of the tribe of David, there were four hundred and thirty-four years to the coming of Christ, that the Priest of priests might appear in the world, and that he who took away the sins of the world might be openly pointed out as John said of him 'Behold the Lamb of God who taketh away the sins of the world.' "*

By the coming of Christ he meant his public manifestation of himself at his entrance on his ministry, as is seen from his reference to John's pointing to him as the Lamb of God.

Here is thus the clearest certainty that Hippolytus regarded the days of the seventy weeks as employed as representatives in the ratio of a day for a year, of four hundred and ninety years: for the seven, and the sixty-two weeks stood for 49 and 434, that is 483 years, to which adding the one week, which he also recognizes, they make 490. Nor was this interpretation of the seventy weeks peculiar to Hippolytus, but was common to him with Julius Africanus, Eusebius, and others, whom Jerome quotes. Thus Africanus, who says:

* XV. *Ἵνα οὖν ἐπιδείξῃ τὸν χρόνον πότε μέλλει παραγενέσθαι ὃν ἐπεθύμει ὁ μακάριος Δανίελ ἰδεῖν λέγει· καὶ μετὰ ἕπτα ἑβδομάδας, ἑξήκοντα δυαι ἄλλαι ἑβδομάδες. αἳ περιέκουσι χρόνον ἐτῶν τετρακόσια τριάκοντα τέσσαρα· μετὰ γὰρ τὸ ἐπιστρέψαι τὸν λαὸν Βαβυλῶνος ἡγουμένου αὐτῶν Ἰησοῦ τοῦ Ἰόσεδεκ, καὶ Ἕσδρα τοῦ γραμματέως, καὶ Ζοροβαβὲλ τοῦ Σαλαθιὴλ, ὡς ὄντως ἐκ φυλῆς Δαβίδ. τετρακόσια τριάκοντα τέσσαρα ἔτη γεγένηται ἕως παρουσίας Χριστοῦ, ἵνα ὁ ἱερεὺς τῶν ἱερέων ἐν κόσμω φανὴ καὶ ὁ αἴρων τας ἁμαρτίας τοῦ κόσμου φανερῶς ἐπιδείκθη, ὡς Ἰωάννης περὶ αὐτοῦ λέγει. Ἴδε ὁ ἀμνὸς τοῦ θεοῦ ὁ αἰρῶν τὴν ἁμαρτίαν τοῦ κόσμου.*—*Hippolytus on Daniel, Section* XV.

"But the angel himself said 'Seventy hebdomads of years; that is four hundred and ninety years from the going forth of the decree, that there should be a response to the enemies of the Jews, and that Jerusalem should be rebuilt; the first year being the twentieth of Artaxerxes, king of Persia."*

Jerome quotes largely from Eusebius, and gives the two dates from which he computed the beginning and close of the seven, the sixty-two, and the one week. I transcribe only sentences which show that he contemplated the weeks of the three divisions as symbols of as many years as they contained days. Thus:

"It does not seem to me to be without a reason that a division was made of the seventy hebdomads, so that seven are spoken of first, then sixty-two; and the last, a single week is added, which is also itself divided into two parts. For it is written, know and understand that from the issuing of the decree, that an answer should be returned, and that Jerusalem should be built unto Messiah the Prince, should be seven hebdomads and sixty-two hebdomads. And after other things which he relates, he adds at the close: And he shall confirm the covenaut with many for one week. It is manifest that this announcement was not made without a reason nor without the inspiration of the angel."†

* Dicit autem ipse Angelus, septuaginta ANNORUM hebdomadas; id est, ANNOS quadringentos nonaginta, ab exitu sermonis ut respondeatur et ut ædificetur Hierusalem. Vicesimum Artaxerxes regem Persarum, annum habere principium.

† Non mihi videtur frustra septuaginta hebdomadarum facta divisio, ut primum diceret septem, deinde sexaginta duæ, et ultima addereter hebdomada una, quae et ipsa in duas partes secta est. Scriptum est

And he proceeds to compute the periods from the issue of the decree of Cyrus, under the false notion that the term anointed—Messiah—denoted the chief priests and princes under whom the captives returned to Jerusalem, erected the temple, and finally built the wall and the city:

"It is to these leaders," he says, "that the prediction refers, in the words: 'From the going forth of the decree that Jerusalem should be built, unto Christ, the anointed Prince, are seven hebdomads, and sixty-two hebdomads, which make four hundred and eighty-three years, counting them from Cyrus."*

The one hebdomad he referred to Christ's ministry and the three and a half years that followed his crucifixion. And the words, "He shall confirm the covenant with many one week, and in the middle of the week victims and sacrifice shall cease," he interpreted as foreshowing—

"That Herod reigning over the Jews and Augustus over the Romans, Christ should be born, who, preaching the gospel three

enim; scies et intelliges ab exitu sermonis, ut respondeatur, et ædificetur Hierusalem usque ad Christum ducem hebdomadas septem, et hebdomadas sexaginta duas. Et post alia quæ narravit in medio, ponit in fine: Et confirmabit testamentum plurimis hebdomada una, Hæc non frustra et absque inspiratione Dei Angelum respondisse manifestum est.—*Jerome on Daniel ix.* 24.

* Hosque significat et vaticinium prophetale, dicens: Ab exitu sermonis, ut respondeatur, et ædificetur Hierusalem usque ad Christum ducem, hebdomadae septem, et hebdomadæ sexaginta duæ: i. e. ut septem hebdomadae, et postea sexaginta duæ, quae faciunt annos quadringentos octoginta tres a Cyro numerentur.

years and a half, according to the Evangelist John, and confirming the worship of the true God through three years and a half, there should be to the Apostles and believers a discontinuance of victims and oblations in the half week that followed the Lord's crucifixion. For what was afterwards transacted in the temple in the judgment of all, was not a sacrifice to God but a worship of the devil." *

I resume the quotation from Dr. Tregelles in which he endeavors to discredit the interpretation of the symbolic periods of Daniel and John, as without any sanction from those prophecies, and as the work of expositors who have little knowledge of the principles on which they proceed, and gratuitously assume what they affect to prove.

"It is true that some expositors show that this principle is needful in their explanations of the prophecies themselves. This really is only a *petitio principii;* a certain exposition cannot stand, unless this canon is *assumed:* therefore it is concluded the canon *must* be true.

"If then the prophecies containing designations of time, do not state any thing on the face of them which supports such a mode of interpretation, we must look elsewhere for the a priora

Quodque infert; Confirmabit enim pactum multis hebdomada una et in dimidio hebdomadis deficiet hostia et sacrificium; sic interpretatur; quod Herode regnante apud Judæam et Augusto apud Romanos, Christus natus sit, qui tribus annis et sex mensibus juxta evangelistam Joannem Evangelium praedicavit et confirmavit veri Dei cultum multis, haud dubium Apostolis et credentibus, quando post passionem Domini in demidia rursum hebdomada, defecit hostia et sacrificium. Quicquid enim in templo postea factum est, non fuit sacrificium Dei, sed cultus Diaboli, cunctis in commune clamantibus.—*Jerome on Daniel ix.* 24–27.

grounds of this opinion. I have then to consider certain passages which are commonly referred to in support of this hypo thesis."—*Remarks*, *pp.* 110–114.

I shall not attempt to shield the parties to whom he refers from the objections he offers to the princi ples on which they proceed. The chief writers of the last fifty years, Faber, Frere, Cunningham, Bick ersteth, Birks, Elliott and others, undoubtedly had no exact understanding of the subject, and greatly embarrassed it by unauthorized assumptions, and unreliable logic. But great as their errors are, it will be seen from the objections I am to offer to the theory held by Dr. Tregelles, that he is at even a greater distance from a just comprehension of it than they were, and that the principles on which he proceeds are as contradictious to the truth as the most mistaken of the postulates and reasonings are by which those authors led great numbers into a wrong judgment in respect to the events that are at hand. He first refers to Num. xiv. 34.

1. Numbers xiv. 34: "After the number of the days in which ye searched the land, even forty days, each day for a year, shall ye bear your iniquities, even forty years."

"This passage speaks of a denounced fact; but in it there is nothing that implies a principle of interpretation. The spies had searched the land of promise forty *days;* and God sentences the murmuring and rebellious Israelites to wander in the wilderness the same number of *years*. In the prophetic part of the verse *years* are literal years, and not the symbol of anything else. Apply the year-day system to this passage, and then forty years will expand into a vast period of *fourteen thousand and four hundred years*."—*Remarks*, *p.* 114.

This is a very awkward misapprehension. No one supposes that years, in the prophetic part of the expression—Num. xiv. 34—are not literal years. It is because they are literal years that the forty days have that ratio to them which literal days bear to literal years. To convert them from literal years into other periods would be to desert the proportion that subsists between days and years. Nor does any one suppose that after the "year-day system has been applied to *the forty days*" interpreting them as denoting years, it is then to be applied also to those *years*, as though they were representatives of forty still different periods as much greater than years, as years are greater than days. For that is the principle on which the ratio of days to years would be applied to years, if they were taken as denoting periods as much greater than themselves, as years are greater than days. The issue of such a process, instead of 14,400 years, would be 5,184,000 years, or 14,400 periods of 360 years each. But no one holds, that in this or other passages in which days are used as symbolic of years, the years they represent are also to be taken as standing for another set of periods, that are proportionally greater than themselves. The imputation of such a feature to the year-day principle is a total misrepresentation.

"All that can be deduced from this passage as to the connection of the terms day and year, is, that as the search of the land had occupied forty literal days, so the wandering in the wilderness should continue forty literal years. Literal years answer to literal days." (p. 114.)

And that is precisely what I affirm of the passage, that the days of the search of the land are used as representatives of the years of the wandering in the wilderness in the ratio which periods of the earth's revolution on its axis bear to the periods of its movement round the sun. It is an example, therefore, of the use of days as the representatives of years, in precisely the manner in which the 1260 days are employed as symbols of a corresponding number of years.

He next refers to the command to Ezekiel iv. 4–6, to lie first on his right side and next on his left, with the explanation:—"I have laid upon thee the years of the iniquity of the house of Israel, according to the number of days, three hundred and ninety days, and the iniquity of the house of Judah forty days. I have appointed thee each day for a year." Of this he says:

"Now this is not a symbolic *prophecy* at all, but simply a symbolic *action* which was commanded by God; and unless there had been the express statement, we never could have known that what Ezekiel did for so many days really represented the actions of so many years."

But as God has informed us that Ezekiel's actions through so many days represented analogous acts or conditions of the Israelites of a corresponding number of years, is it not the part of submission and faith to receive it as a fact, and a fact of so much significance to the people of Israel and Judah, as to make it just and wise that he should apprise them of it? Dr. Tregelles falls into a singular error in alleging that this is not a symbolic prophecy, but simply a symbolic *action;* as though symbolic actions were not prophetic. No misapprehension could be at a greater distance from the fact. The acts of symbols are as truly prophetic as the symbols themselves. Thus, as the beast of ten horns from the sea—Rev. xiii. 1–7—is the representative of that group of kings, and subordinate officials of the western Roman empire that exercised the legislative and executive functions of the ten kingdoms for a long period; so the acts of the beast in opening his mouth in blasphemy against God, and in making war with the saints are representatives of the analogous acts of those rulers in blaspheming the Most High, and persecuting his people. It is the very office, accordingly, of the 1260 days, the forty-two months, and the time, times, and a half, to indicate *the periods* through which *the acts of the great agents* extend, of whose career they give the measure. The 1260 days are not the measure of the *life* of the witnesses (Rev. xi. 3), but of their *testimony* only: and the forty-two months of the beast from the sea (Rev. xiii.), are not the measure of the official life of those whom it represents, but only of their career as conquerors, blasphemers and persecutors of the saints of the Most High. How is it that this great fact escaped Dr. Tregelles' notice? He proceeds:

> "It is true that this is an instance in which a day *symbolically represents* a year, but the way in which this is done is wholly different from any such ground being taken as though in prophetic language the one were used for the other."

The confusion of thought and expression that reign in the last part of this passage is truly lamentable. The question at issue is simply whether, in the verses from Ezekiel, "a day *symbolically represents a year*." That is all that I, and all as far as I know, that others affirm of it. It is all that I allege the passage to prove, and that Dr. Tregelles admits. How could he, in the presence of the words from the lips of God himself deny it? The question, consequently, is not at all whether "the way in which this is done is wholly different from any ground being taken as though in prophetic language the one were used for the other." No one ever advanced such a pretext. The note-taker from whose memoranda this passage was printed, manifestly did not understand the subject sufficiently to give an accurate statement of the point in debate. No one pretends that ground is taken in the use of days as symbolic representatives of years, that in *prophetic language*, the one is used for the other. The question does not relate to "*prophetic language*," but to symbols, which, instead of words, are things, agents, objects, acts, *times*,—realities; not the mere names of those realities. But it is a total mistake to represent that days are not here used as symbolic representatives of years in the same way as they are in the *symbolic prophecies*. The way in which they are here employed is identically the same; the period of the earth's revolution on its axis being employed to represent the analogous period of its movement round the sun. He adds:

> "If, in this passage, *day* meant *year*, or if it were to be interpreted by *year*, what should we find? That Ezekiel was commanded to lie on his left side *three hundred and ninety years*, and on his right side *forty years*." (p. 115.)

This is a sad misrepresentation. He has already admitted "that this is an instance in which a day symbolically represents a year." But that is all that is claimed by those who hold that days when used as a symbol, represent years. For that is the way, and the only way in which they regard a day as standing for a year. How is it then, that Dr. Tregelles, after admitting all that those with whom he is contending affirm, turns round and represents that that is not the relation in which they hold that a day stands for a year, but that what they maintain is, that a day means a year, irrespective of the fact that it is *used symbolically*, to denote that period, and that it is appropriated to that use by the lips of the Most High himself. What confusion of mind! What inacquaintance with the simplest and most essential of the principles on which symbols are used!

In his attempts, to depreciate and caricature this use of days as symbols of years by the bold ascription to it of a meaning that contradicts the sense God himself expressly assigns to it, he exhibits a sad insensibility to the truth and sanctity of the divine word. How full and emphatic the significance was which God attached to it, in these instances, is seen from the fact that the period denoted in each, was verified by his providence. Thus in consequence of the wish of the Israelites to return to Egypt because of the false reports of some of the spies, he prolonged their wanderings in the wilderness through thirty-eight more years, during which the whole of the congregation who had come out of Egypt, with the exception of Joshua and Caleb, were disinherited of Canaan, and consigned to dishonored graves. What an awe-inspiring verification of the truth of the words that had been spoken by the Holy One of Israel! "After the number of the days in which ye searched the land—forty days—each day for a year, shall ye bear your iniquities, forty years."

This sovereign stroke of avenging justice which changed the history so disastrously of two millions of human beings, and was inflicted for the express purpose of showing the guilt and the danger of trifling with the truth of God: Dr. Tregelles contemplates with a sneer, and ridicules it, by the pretence that "the year-day system" if legitimate, is to be applied to the "forty years," as well as to the forty days; by which the "forty years" will be made to "expand into fourteen thousand and four hundred years."—*Remarks on Daniel, p.* 114.

The symbolization of years by days by Ezekiel's bearing the iniquities of Israel for three hundred and ninety days, and the iniquity of Judah for forty days, had an equally exact fulfillment; though their representative direction was retrospective instead of future; a consideration that puts a fresh and impressive seal on the truth and validity of the principle on which the symbol is used: for God places a double sanction on it by employing it in measuring the past as well as the future. The three hundred and ninety days taken as symbols of years, give the length of the period during which he bore with the Israelites from their revolt under Jeroboam, to the date of the seizure in the eighteenth of Nebuchadnezzar of a small group of captives, among whom were, doubtless, some Israelites whose ancestors having fled into Judæa before the fall of the kingdom of Samaria, or subsequently, left their descendants there to meet a doom like that which overtook their fathers one hundred and thirty-five years before.

Thus: From the year of Jeroboam's revolt.........B. C.	976
Deduct the period denoted by the three hundred and ninety days..................................	390
	586

The year when the three hundred and ninety years expired was the five hundred and eighty-sixth before Christ, and the eighteenth of Nebuchadnezzar. Jeremiah lii. 29.

There was a like verification of the symbol of forty days, as the representative of the forty years during which God was to bear with the iniquity of Judah.

Thus: From the reign of Josiah, of thirty-one years......	31
Deduct eighteen; it having been in his eighteenth year that the people made a fresh covenant with God........	18
	13
Add to that the reigns of Jehoiachin and Zedekiah........	22
Add five years from Nebuchadnezzar's eighteenth to his twenty-third year, when Nebuzaradan, the captain of his guard, gleaned the last body of captives that were transported to Babylon, Jeremiah, lii. 30 and they make forty years..	5
	40

Mr. Cuninghame reckons those periods as but one, namely, 430 years, and as extending from the dedication of the temple, in the year B. C. 1020, to the beginning of the siege of the city, B. C. 590, or else from the first passover, after the erection of the temple, B. C. 1018, to its destruction in the year B. C. 588. But he overlooks the fact that the three hundred and ninety years were years of Israel's separate existence; and the forty of Judah, years exclusively of that people. The first is to be dated therefore at the epoch of the revolt of the ten tribes: and the other at the commencement of God's prolonged forbearance with Judah, because of the reformation of that people forty years before the last body of them were carried captive to Babylon.

"III. Another passage which has been used as a basis for this system, is the latter part of the ninth of Daniel: some, however, of the strenuous advocates of the year-day principle, fairly own that it has no bearing upon the question. Its supposed connection arises from the word 'Shabua,' rendered 'week,' having been taken as though it must be simply in its literal meaning seven days. This might be called wholly a question of lexicography; the word itself is strictly, *something divided into, or consisting of seven parts; a heptad, a hebdomad.* Gesenius simply defines its meaning to be a 'septenary number;' he then speaks of its use as applied sometimes to days, sometimes to years: the word itself, however, defines nothing as to the denomination to which it belongs, whether the one or the other.

"In translating, we may use the word 'week' not at all as conceding the point of *meaning of the Hebrew word*, but simply for convenience sake, and requiring less explanation and circumlocution, than any other in common use. I believe that I need say no more to prove that this ninth of Daniel, in no way upholds the year-day scheme."—Pp. 115–117.

But his errors here are as extraordinary and self-confuting, as those into which he fell in respect to the passages in Numbers and Ezekiel.

It is a peculiarity of the prediction of the seventy weeks, Daniel ix. 1–27, not often noticed, so far as I have observed, by those who have given interpretations of it—that it is not a symbolic, but a simple language prophecy, with the single exception of the time which is given as the measure of the years that were to intervene between the edict of the king of Persia, authorizing Nehemiah to rebuild the wall and dwellings of Jerusalem, and the close of the three and a half years that were immediately to follow the crucifixion of the Messiah. And this feature of the prophecy, it is especially important should be understood. For it distinguishes it from all others in the Old and New Testament, and may at the first glance be thought an obstruction to a satisfactory proof that the days of which the weeks consist are employed as representatives of a corresponding number of years. If, however, notwithstanding the fact that the seventy weeks are not associated with any other symbols, but all the agents, acts, and events that are foreshown as to take place in the period which they denote, are expressed in simple language, and their prophetical meaning is their natural grammatical sense; and yet the weeks are employed as symbols of years in the ratio of a day for a year: then much more may we feel it to be certain, that when times are used in prophecies that are confessedly symbolical, like those of Daniel vii. viii. xi., and of John, they are to be interpreted, as representatives of periods that stand to the symbol in the ratio of years to days.

While, then, I hold that the seventy weeks are symbolical: I admit and state it as a fact that the great agents, acts, and events foreshown in it are not; but have their prophetic meaning exclusively in the grammatical sense of the language in which they are expressed. Thus in v. 24, the cutting off of the seventy weeks upon the people and the city, the putting a bar to transgression, sealing sin, making expiation for iniquity, bringing in everlasting righteousness, sealing vision and prophecy, and anointing a Holy of Holies; are acts, the first of God, and the others of the Messiah in his ministry and death; and have their whole meaning in the usual sense of the words in which they are embodied. In like manner, in v. 25, the going forth of the commandment; the restoring and building Jerusalem; the Messiah the Prince; the street and the wall, their building again, and the troublous times; are used in their natural sense, and signify exactly that of which the words themselves are the proper names. So also in v. 26, the Messiah, his being cut off; the people that shall come, and the prince; the destroying of the city and the sanctuary, the ending of them with a flood, and the continuance of the war, till the predicted desolations are accomplished, are all expressed in the simplest language, and have in its ordinary meaning all their significance. The metaphors in the use of cut off, and flood, to denote the suddenness and resistlessness of the power by which the city was to be destroyed, are as clear in their settled meaning as it would have been had it been expressed without a figure. To cut off a person, was in the language of the Hebrews, to strike him violently and suddenly from life. To destroy a city with a flood, was to reduce it quickly and resistlessly to desolation, as an overwhelming deluge bears away the dwellings, fences, and crops of the fields, which it sweeps, uproots the trees, tears up the soil, and spreads the scene with desolation.

And so finally in the 27th verse, the person who was to confirm the covenant, the covenant itself, its confirmation, and the many with whom he was to confirm it; the sacrifice, and oblation, and his causing them to cease; the abomination of desolation, its coming over the battlement, and his pouring destruction upon the desolate, until the full accomplishment of all that has been decreed, are all embodied in the words that are their proper names as persons, acts, and events.

Most obviously then, so far as Christ and his acts and sufferings are concerned, and so far as the act of the Persian king in issuing his decree, and of the Jews in cutting off the Messiah, of the Roman prince and his army, and their acts, and the effects to which they gave birth, are concerned, the prophecy is certainly not symbolical; but a mere language prophecy.

But it will be asked if the seventy weeks are used as symbols on the ground of analogy, why were not the other parts of the prophecy conveyed to us through the same vehicle? The answer is, *First*, Because the great actor himself, his peculiar acts, and the acts also of men, and other events that are foreshown, could not be adequately exhibited through symbols. There are no symbols by which the Messiah in his twofold nature could be represented. There are none that could clearly indicate his peculiar office. There are none that could represent his obedience. There are none, that in the relation of analogy, could symbolize Jerusulem and the temple, so that they could be identified. There are none that could show the coming of a foreign prince and army to the city, and set forth its capture and destruction with the distinctness and certainty of meaning that are requisite in a prediction of such events; and *next*, because if the Messiah and his acts and the other acts and events were symbols, it would be impossible to find any counterpart to them. What could the Messiah himself symbolize? Being God, and God-man, it is impossible that he should be the representative of another being, who must of necessity be a mere creature; for there would be no analogy between him and a mere human and dependent agent. What could his being cut off denote, as a symbol of some catastrophe that was to befall a mere human or angelic person? What could the coming of a prince with an army signify, that differed from itself? What could the destruction of the city and sanctuary foreshow, that bore a mere resemblance to itself? There are no parallel persons; there are no parallel places, acts, and events, that they could symbolize. The prophecy accordingly of agents, acts, places, and events, is from necessity conveyed, not through symbols but through language solely. The Messiah is designated by his official name; his work in obeying and dying on behalf of men is described in the terms that are most suitable to express its true nature: and the coming of a foreign prince and his army, and destroying the city and temple are in like manner foreshown through words merely; and it is necessary that this characteristic should be seen, and the reason that words were employed instead of symbols, understood, in order to a true judgment of its meaning. When justly apprehended, it will be found that the use exclusively of words to indicate the agents, the acts, and the events, is no barrier to the employment of the *time* which is given as the measure of those acts and events, as a representative of a far greater period to which that time bears the analogy that subsists between days and years.

1. The first ground on which Dr. Tregelles endeav·

ors to prove that the word shabua, translated "week," is not used to denote weeks, but years, is, that it does not etymologically mean a week, but simply "something divided into, or consisting of seven parts—a heptad; a hebdomad." That is true; but instead of sustaining, it confutes his interpretation of it as denoting *a year*, as effectually, as according to him, it confutes the view which he opposes—that it is used to signify a week. Inasmuch as shabua, or the word from which it is formed, has, as he affirms, etymologically no special reference to time, and only means something that consists of seven equal parts, it indubitably has nothing in its derivation or form that can any more make it indicate a year than it can make it stand for a week. Taken irrespective of *usage*, it can only mean a thing that is divided into seven equal parts. He, therefore, overthrows himself as effectually as he imagines he does those whose views he regards himself as setting aside by a self-evident proof.

The question, then, whether the word shabua here denotes a week, and not a year, is to be determined by *usage*. As its primary sense is that of seven, or sevenfold, signifying that that to which it is applied consists of seven equal parts; to determine its usage, it must be ascertained whether it is employed to designate periods of time that have that characteristic; and if so, what *the radical* or shortest period is of which it is used in that sense, as the name. And that it is used as a name, of periods of time that consist of seven equal parts, all know and admit. Not an expositor can be found who denies it. Dr. Tregelles, instead of denying it, only affirms that it does not, in Dan. ix. 24–27, denote weeks, but in place of that is an indicative or name of years. But if used as the name of a period of time that consists of seven equal parts, it would naturally be employed as the name of that septemized period—that is, the most radical;—that is, that consists of the shortest times that are united in a septemized whole; and next of that septemized period which was most frequently used in the daily life of the Hebrews. Of that, whatever it is, it would naturally become the distinctive name. But that period is unquestionably the period denoted by the word week, consisting of seven days, or times of the earth's revolution on its axis. That was the first division of time that was instituted by the Most High, and was coeval with the creation: the seventh day from the first being set apart for rest and worship, and the observance of it made obligatory on the first pair and their posterity, through all subsequent time. The introduction of a longer septemized period did not take place, even according to the Hebrew chronology, till more than two thousand years later, at the appointment of the sabbatic years and Jubilees at Mount Sinai. The division of time into weeks was thus not only its first and shortest artificial division into periods, but was a division that from the frequent recurrence of the seventh of its days, which was constituted a Sabbath, was kept continually before the eyes of the antediluvians, the patriarchs and the people of Israel, through their residence in Palestine down to the time of the Babylonian captivity. We may be certain, therefore, that it was used as the name of that division of time, and exclusively, which, being the first, the shortest and the reigning division, impressed itself on the whole surface of life. It accordingly is not employed as a designation of year-weeks, except in the single instance of Jacob's use of Rachel's seven, or week (Genesis xxix. 18, 20, 27, 28), where her seven or week is specifically defined as a seven, or week of years. It is indisputably, therefore, used in that instance symbolically, each day standing for a year. There is no other passage in which it is used to denote seven years. In the appointment of the sabbatical year (Levit. xxv. 4–8), they are not called weeks of years, but sabbaths of years. They are, therefore, used as symbols, each seven days standing for seven years, and seven times for seven times seven years. In every other instance of the word in the Hebrew and Greek Scriptures, except Dan. ix., the term is used to denote literal days. There never was a clearer case, therefore, of the absolutely uniform use of a term. It is employed in every instance of its occurrence in the Bible in the sense I ascribe to it as the name of a seven, or week of days; and owes its use accordingly to denote years in Genesis and

Leviticus, to its being employed as a symbol—the sevens, or weeks being expressly defined as weeks of years. Dr. Tregelles thus has not a solitary passage to verify his interpretation of it in Dan. ix. 24–27, as *literally* denoting a week of years. It is as clear, therefore, as demonstration can make it, that shabua, the term translated week, was used habitually and undeviatingly as the proper and distinctive name of a week of days; and that that is its *literal* sense, therefore, in the pasage, Dan. ix. 24–27. It is thence, by its being employed as a symbol, that the sevens of days signify sevens of years. If Dr. Tregelles denies that it is thus used as a symbol, he must, to be consistent, maintain that the seven days are used *literally* to denote seven years, and exhibit that as its proper sense. But that he cannot prove, inasmuch as there is no example of its use in that sense; and were he to prove it, it would overthrow the construction he now puts on it. If he admits that it is used as a symbol of years, he then abandons the theory respecting it he has advanced, and yields what I maintain.

2. But Dr. Tregelles sees nothing of this; not a glance does he bestow on the usage of the term. Instead, he endeavors to sustain his interpretation of it, by the statement that

"In the present passage it takes its denomination from *years* which had been previously mentioned in Daniel's *prayer*. Daniel had been praying to God and making confession on behalf of his people, because that he saw the seventy *years* which had been denounced as the term of the captivity of Judah, were accomplished; and thus the denomination of *years* connects itself with the answer granted to him. He had made *inquiry* about the accomplishment of seventy *years.* He receives an answer relative to seventy *heptads of years.*" (p. 116.)

This is truly an astonishing misapprehension! There is not the slightest allusion in Daniel's *prayer* to *the seventy years* of the Jewish captivity. Instead of "*inquiring* about the accomplishment of seventy years," the prophet relates that he "*understood by books* the number of the years whereof the word of the Lord came to Jeremiah the prophet, that he would accomplish seventy years in the desolations of Jerusalem," (c. ix. 2.) In place of offering supplication for instruction in regard to that period which he already understood; that for which he prayed was that God would "turn away his anger from Jerusalem and from his holy mountain, and cause his face to shine upon the sanctuary, which was desolate," (v. 16–19.) He did not even ask for the restoration of the captives; for that God had expressly promised; but, on the ground of that promise, he breathed out the fervor of his heart solely for the re-erection of the sanctuary and the rebuilding of the city; and most naturally and wisely, inasmuch as they had not been so specifically promised, and especially because they were indispensable conditions of the resumption of the sacrificial offerings that were types of the suffering Messiah, and of the coming of that great messenger of the covenant to accomplish the expiation of sin. It was accordingly because of his prayer for *the restoration of the temple and its services*, that the revelation that was made to him related so chiefly to the coming of the Messiah, the accomplishment of his expiatory work, and his ascension to heaven. This conspicuous correlation of the revelation to the prayer, Dr. Tregelles unhappily overlooks.

Such is the issue of his attempt to prove that the term he renders, heptad, is not the name of a week of days. What can be more certain than that he is wholly mistaken? What can be clearer than that he does not fully see what his assumptions imply, and has not a glimpse of the principles which he so confidently opposes?

CHAPTER XVI.

Dr. Tregelles errs respecting the Relation in which a Time, Times, and Half a Time are employed—He mistakes in his Views of Daniel xii. 7. His denial that the twelve hundred and sixty days, forty-two months, and twenty-three hundred days are used as Symbols of longer Periods than they themselves literally express—His error in regard to Nebuchadnezzar's Seven Times.

He next endeavors to demonstrate that none of the great periods of Daniel and John are employed as symbols to represent periods that are longer than themselves. Thus he says:

"And now, to consider the principal statements of time to which this supposed canon is applied: They are

I. The time, times and a half, Daniel vii. 25, and xii. 7. The first of these periods is mentioned in the same manner in the book of Revelation xii. 14. In that book also we find a similar period spoken of as forty and two months, xi. 2. xiii. 5, and twelve hundred and sixty days, xi. 3, xii. 6. In neither of the passages in Daniel does this designation of time occur, in the midst of a symbolic prophecy at all; for in ch. vii. the period is spoken of in the plain, literal interpretation of the symbolic horn; which is said to mean a literal king, who shall subdue three literal kings (not described as horns in *this part* of the chapter) into whose hand the saints shall be given for a time, times, and a half a time—three years and a half. If we make these words symbolic, may we not arbitrarily explain away any other expressions of Scripture?"—Pp. 117, 120.

This attempt to divest the time, times, and half a time in Daniel vii. 25, of a symbolic meaning, is marked by much the same inaccuracy as his criticism on Exodus, Ezekiel, and Daniel ix. 24–27. Had he carefully scanned the passage, he would have seen that the acts ascribed to the horn, are not the acts of an animal, but of a man; and properly, because the horn had eyes like the eyes of a man, and a human mouth speaking great things, v. 8. The acts accordingly ascribed to it, are speaking very great things with a human mouth, looking more imperious or haughty than its fellows, making war on the saints, and prevailing against them; which are acts, not of a mere horn, but of an intelligent being and a man. Now the passage that follows, which Dr. Tregelles represents as the plain, literal interpretation of the *symbolic horn* is no interpretation whatever of *its acts*, but a mere repetition of what had before been foreshown of it; namely, that it should be diverse from the other horns, should subdue three kings, should speak words against the Most High, should wear out the saints, and should think to change times and law; all which is what had before been ascribed to it, vs. 8, 20, 21. Its thinking to change times and law, was one of the forms in which its pride, its arrogance, and its ambitious look were to reveal themselves. There is nothing affirmed of it in vs. 24, 25, that is not embraced in the description vs. 8, 20, 21, except that it stood for a king, which had already been implied in the ascription to it of eyes like the eyes of a man, and a mouth and speech. The only additional stroke in the delineation, vs. 24, 25, is the duration of its agency. The time, times, and a half, are measures accordingly, of the acts of the horn as truly as they are of the acts of the king whom the horn represents; and they are therefore symbols, as truly as the horn itself is a symbol. Will Dr. Tregelles deny this? He cannot without a direct misrepresentation of the passage. His pretext accordingly that the designation of time in v. 25, is a mere *interpretation* of what had before been embodied in the description of the horn and his denial that it is a symbol, are equally in antagonism with fact. He adds in regard to Daniel xii. 7:

"In chapter xii. there is no symbol at all; the communicator of truth to Daniel, held up his right hand and his left hand unto heaven, and sware by him that liveth forever, that it shall be for a time, times, and a half. It seems to me as if the solemnity of this oath—by him that liveth forever—would exclude the thought of mere metaphor and symbol. At least I know of no words in Scripture on which emphatic exactitude is more impressed."—*P.* 120.

This implies that if a metaphor or symbol had been used by the angel, it would have divested his oath and affirmation of "exactitude of meaning," and converted them into vagueness and uncertainty. A more sad oversight of the office of metaphors and symbols, and even of letters and vocal sounds, is not often exhibited. Dr. Tregelles seems to have forgotten the very profession to which he is devoted. There is not a word nor letter in his volume; there is not a syllable nor a mark in the manuscripts and editions of the Scriptures he is accustomed to read; there is not a voice that passes from his tongue, nor an accent that reaches his ears from the lips of others, that is not a sign of something that differs from itself; and in hundreds of instances in a thousand, stands for something to which it bears no analogy. Yet amid these vast processes which bespeak more impressively than any other function of the mind, the greatness of an intellectual nature—he flutters and falters at the thought that the Almighty should employ a metaphor or a symbol in revealing his purposes—from the feeling that the novelty and intricacy of such methods of expressing truth must baffle his powers, and plunge him into a whirling sea, where all landmarks are lost, and chart and compass fail. But symbols and metaphors are as easy of interpretation as spoken voices, or literal words. The question to which the angel's oath was an answer was, "How long shall it be to the end of these wonders?" How long a period is to intervene between their beginning and their end? Here the fact is distinctly given, that the time, times, and half a time, are *the measure* of the span between the commencement and the end of these wonders. And as the agents of those wonders are represented by symbols, the period they were to occupy is also indicated by a symbol. But who are the agents of those wonders, and what are the wonders themselves? The agents are the parties who are represented by the eleventh horn of the beast, with the eyes and mouth and speech of a man; and the wonders themselves are the mysteries and monstrosities of its pride, its blasphemies, and its war on God's people. This is seen from the fact, that the period here given that was to pass before the end, is the same as that assigned to the proud boasts, the blasphemies, and the persecutions of the horn, Daniel vii. 8, 20–25; and it began, doubtless, soon after the delivery of the times and law into the power symbolized by that horn; and is to continue till near the time when that power is to be destroyed. It is a symbol, therefore, and its employment here in the oath of the angel, was as legitimate as its use was as a symbol, chapter vii. 25; and as the employment was of the beast, the horns, or any other agent, act, or effect that occurs in the visions of that chapter.

He proceeds:

"But when we turn to the book of Revelation, and see how *variously* this period is expressed, 1260 days, forty and two months, a time, times, and a half, it seems as if care had been taken to prevent all possibility of misconception, whether occurring in symbolic description, or in literal explanation, the same isochronic expressions are repeated."—*P.* 120.

Here Dr. Tregelles alleges the fact that the periods

he specifies are so *variously* expressed, as a proof that they cannot be used as symbols of longer periods than themselves! He forgets that if they are used as symbols, they *must be natural days*, in order that they may bear the requisite analogy to years, which it is their office to represent. The fact that they are days, is an indubitable proof that they symbolize years. But that Dr. Tregelles cannot comprehend. On identically the same ground, he must deny that any other symbol in the prophecy is a representative of a being, act, or event that differs from itself. Was not the monster beast, Daniel vii. 7–11–17–27, a real beast? Did not the prophet see it with his bodily eyes, emerge from the sea and take its position on the land? Did he not see its iron teeth, its brazen claws, its ten horns, and its eleventh horn with the eyes and mouth of a man; and did he not hear it speaking great words? Did he not witness its fierce and bloody acts toward inferior animals and toward the people of God; and finally, see it arraigned, and consigned to the burning flame? Most assuredly, if as Dr. Tregelles affirms, the fact that the times that are used as symbols are real days, proves that they are not symbols; then for the same reason, the fact that the great symbols taken from the animal and material world, were real existences in the visions of exactly the nature which their names import, is a proof that they were not symbols, but were or are to appear in their own proper nature on the earth, and act out the great tragedy that is ascribed to them. Let Dr. Tregelles disprove this if he can. Let him, on the other hand, admit that the great beasts of Daniel were realities, and that they were, nevertheless, mere symbols of other agents that differ essentially from themselves, and he will be obliged, for the same reason, to admit that the periods of time that are used to measure the agency of those symbols, are also symbols, and are employed on the same principle as are the beasts, the horns, and their actions to represent periods that differ from themselves.

"The second passage," he says, (Daniel viii.) "is literally unto two thousand three hundred evenings-mornings! referring to the offering of the daily sacrifice each morning and evening. This also occurs in *an explanation;* so that the symbolic theory (even if it had any true foundation, instead of being, as it is, a gratuitous assumption) *would avail nothing.* The expression seems such as intentionally to exclude all thought of other than real days."—*P.* 121.

This is but another mere assertion which he employs to determine the most important questions against the plain and unequivocal teaching of the prophecy. What an unwarrantable assumption! Who authorized Dr. Tregelles to allege it as a self-evident maxim, that God could not recognise the existence of symbols in the prophecies which he himself interprets, nor use additional symbols to give further knowledge to the prophet and to his people? For these assumptions lie couched in the postulate on which he here proceeds. He first assumes that the twenty-three hundred evenings-mornings are used in such a connection, as to show that they are not employed as symbols; and then infers from that, that the whole theory that times are used as symbols, is groundless, and false. But he is wholly mistaken; first, in the representation that the twenty-three hundred evenings-mornings are used in the *interpretation* of what had previously been revealed. Instead, they were expressly given by the angel as *the measure* of the preceding vision, in answer to the inquiry by one of the holy ones: "How long the vision;" and they are the medium of *a wholly new revelation;* instead of an explanation of what had before been foreshown. He is equally in error in the virtual assumption that the Spirit of God could not, in interpreting a prophecy, recognise it as symbolic, and make the interpretation an express explanation of its symbols. For this prophecy itself is most certainly symbolic; and is as indubitably interpreted by the Spirit as such. This will be seen from an analysis of the vision. The prophet had seen a little horn come up under one of the four horns of the goat, which waxed exceeding great toward the south, and toward the east, and toward the pleasant land. And it waxed great even to the host of heaven, and it cast down some of the host and the stars to the ground, and stamped upon them. Yea, he magnified himself even to the Prince of the host, and by him the daily sacrifice was taken away, and the place of his sanctuary (the sanctuary of the Prince of the stars) was cast down. And an host was given him against the daily sacrifice by wickedness; and it cast down the truth to the ground; and it practiced and prospered. The great agent in this fierce and heaven-daring career, was the sixth horn of the goat; and it was a symbol. The power which it represents was wholly different from itself, in nature, sphere, and agency. Its acts, also, are symbols—namely, its enlarging itself greatly toward the south, and toward the east, and toward the land of the Jews; its shooting itself up among the stars, and casting some of them down to the dust, and trampling on them; and its magnifying itself against Messiah, the Prince of the heavenly world, and taking away the daily sacrifice, and casting down the place of his sanctuary; and finally, its having a host against the daily sacrifice, and casting down the truth to the ground. All these acts are as truly and exclusively symbolic, as the horn that exerted them is. They cannot be literal. The mere horn of a goat could not, acting in the sphere of its nature, conquer the whole of the Persian empire. It could not shoot itself up millions of millions of miles into the arch of heaven, and strike down suns and planets to the mountains and plains of our globe, and trample on them. Our earth, which is but a speck compared to those orbs, could not receive a group of them on its bosom. In like manner, its magnifying itself against the Messiah, and taking away the daily sacrifice, and casting down the place of his sanctuary, are purely symbolic acts, wholly out of the sphere of an animal that has no apprehension of the Messiah; no knowledge of the daily sacrifice which was the type of his vicarious death; and no power to overturn his temple and reduce it to a ruin. All these acts of the horn are *representative* of analogous acts of the power of which the horn was the symbol. Taking away the daily sacrifice leveling the temple with the dust, and casting down the truth to the ground, are as exclusively representative, and denote acts that differ from themselves, as clearly, as striking suns and planets from their stations in the distant realms of space, and treading them into the dust of our globe, denote acts that differ from themselves. The prophecy, then (verses 9–12), is indubitably symbolic. It is expressed altogether through symbols. There is not a syllable in it that fills any office, except in the delineation of its representative agents, objects, acts and effects. What ground now has Dr. Tregelles to interpose and announce, with an authoritative voice, as though he were uttering a self-evident maxim, that the Almighty does not and cannot, in interpreting it, treat it as symbolic? For the whole adaptedness of his argument to the end for which he employs it, lies in that pretext. If he admits that God may use symbols as a medium of prediction, and may interpret them as such, his inference against "the symbolic theory," falls to the ground. But what can transcend that deduction in thoughtlessness and error! God surely has a right to interpret the prediction according to its nature. If he pleased, he had an equal right to employ additional symbols to make new revelations to meet the necessities of the prophet and of his people in regard to this prophecy. What then is necessary to verify the fact? *First*, that he interprets verses 9–12 as symbolic; and *next*, that he employs additional symbols to express the time through which the action of the horn was to extend, and to indicate the event that is to mark its termination, that proceed on the same principle of analogy as that on which the horn, and its acts, the daily sacrifice, and the temple, are employed. The first, is apparent from the interpretation given by the angel of verses 9–12. "Now, the great horn being broken, whereas four stood up for it, four kingdoms—dynasties—shall stand up out of the nation; but not in his power. And in the latter time of their kingdom, when the transgressors are come to the full, *a king* of fierce countenance, and understanding dark sentences, shall stand up. And his power shall be mighty; but not by his own power: and he shall destroy wonderfully; and shall prosper and practice; and shall destroy the mighty and the holy people. And through his policy, also, he shall cause craft to prosper in his hand; and he shall magnify himself in his heart, and by peace shall destroy many: He shall also stand up against the Prince of princes, but he shall be broken without hand" (verses 21–25). Such is the interpretation given of the vision of the horn, of verses 9–12; and it treats it throughout as the representative of an agent, wholly different in nature from itself. Every stroke in the delineation exhibits it as a human being, or line of human beings, and all the characteristics and acts ascribed to it, as those of human beings. He is a "*king*." He has a stern and imperious countenance. He is skilled in artifice and deceit. He is to rise to great power, but not by his own strength; his power being derived from the Roman imperium in the west. He shall destroy wonderfully, and shall prosper in his undertakings. He shall destroy the mighty and the holy people, the Jews. Through his cunning he will cause deceit to prosper; and will magnify himself, and by peace destroy many. And he will also stand up against the Prince of princes. All the acts and achievements thus foreshown of him, are unlike those attributed to the horn. Not one in the prediction has its exact likeness in the interpretation. While they are parallels throughout, each is suited to the nature of the agent of which it is predicated; the spirit, acts and achievements of the king, being in his sphere, what the powers, acts and achievements of the horn are to an animal that has such an aggressive organ as the horn of the goat. Nothing can be more indubitable, therefore, than that the prophecy respecting the horn is interpreted as symbolic.

It is equally certain also that antecedently to that interpretation, and wholly independent of it, two additional symbols are employed in answer to the inquiry of the holy one, for the purpose of showing the length of the period over which the vision extended; and the event that is to signalize its close. Let the reader scan the passage, and he will see that this prediction of time is a new prediction, not an interpretation, as Dr. Tregelles represents of the vision in vs. 9–12:

"Then I heard one holy one speaking; and another holy one said unto that holy one who spake: *Unto when is the vision* of the daily sacrifice and the wicked one that is to lay waste, to give both the sanctuary and the host to be trodden underfoot? and he said unto me: Unto two thousand three hundred evenings-mornings. Then shall the Sanctuary be cleansed," vs. 13, 14.

Here the answer to the question in respect to the period through which the vision extended, and the indication of the event which is to mark the termination of that period, are not explanations of the preceding vision, but are new revelations. Not a hint had before been given in regard to either; and instead of being explained like vs. 9–12, they are left uninterpreted; and they are symbols. The period of time is most indubitably such, as it is expressly given *as the measure* of the horn's acts and the chief effects it was to work; namely, the taking away of the daily sacrifice, the casting down of the sanctuary, and the trampling of the Jewish people under foot. As those acts of the horn and the effects it wrought, like the horn itself, and the ground to which it cast the stars, were symbols, so the period which is given as the measure of their *duration*, must also be a symbol. It cannot be the measure of any thing else, for there is nothing else in the prediction the duration of which can be the subject of such a measure. As the two thousand and three hundred evenings-mornings stand in the same relation to two thousand three hundred years, as that in which the horn stands to the group of agents which it represents; having a general analogy to them; they must for the same reason be interpreted as a symbol. To deny them that office, is to contradict their nature, and imply that God uses them in a sense that is not in harmony with the peculiar laws of the vision, and is suited to baffle and mislead his people.

The cleansing of the sanctuary is likewise a symbol. As the sanctuary itself is a symbol; as polluting and casting it down, are symbols; so most indubitably is its cleansing a symbol. To take the sanctuary as a literal edifice, and its purification as a literal removal of defilements and defacements, by the processes by which ordinary edifices are cleansed, and made fit for the use to which they are appropriated, is to deny to the prophecy its true nature, and materialize it, as though it treated of a mere goat, and other sheer external and physical objects and effects, in place of human agents who act in immediate relations to God, and of impieties of which they are guilty toward him, and atrocities they perpetrate on his worshipers. The casting down and desecration of the sanctuary on the one side, and its cleansing on the other, can no more be taken as literally denoting what the terms philologically mean, than the acts of the horn in upshooting itself to heaven, and casting some of the stars to the ground, can be taken in their mere verbal sense, and not as symbols. The prophecy, vs. 13, 14, is framed on precisely the same principle as that of vs. 9–12, and is to be interpreted by the same law of analogy.

Such is the issue of Dr. Tregelles' attempt to divest this important passage of its symbolic character. Into what more unfortunate blunder could he have fallen! What more decisive proof could he have given that he has failed to master the subjects which he effects to treat with so much accuracy!

He proceeds to Daniel iv:

"In Daniel iv. 16, 23, 32, king Nebuchadnezzar was told that he should be driven from men, etc., till *seven times* should pass over him." This on the year-day theory would be a period of two thousand five hundred and twenty years; longer than from the time of Nebuchadnezzar to the present day; and the term seven times occurs both in the symbolic part of the chapter and the literal, so that the force of words cannot be avoided by any such distinction. Nebuchadnezzar, however, says (v. 28), 'All this came upon the king Nebuchadnezzar.' The prophecy related to literal years; and in literal years it was accomplished. If then, in chapter iv. seven times are seven years, of course the period in chapter vii. is half that number. Thus king Nebuchadnezzar is an unexceptional witness that the prophetic Scripture does not admit the year-day theory."—P. 123.

The only apology for Dr. Tregelles' mistake here, is his inacquaintance with the principles on which symbols are used. The symbols drawn from the animal and material world which have thus far been noticed, are employed in the relation of analogy; and denote agents, objects, acts and events that differ from themselves. But beside these and other kindred symbols, there is a large class that are used, not on the ground of *general resemblance*, but in the relation of identity or absolute likeness. Thus God was never represented in the visions of Daniel and John by a created symbol, but appeared in all instances in his own person, seated on a throne surrounded by insignia of his deity, and attended by hosts of holy intelligences that worshiped him as the creator and ruler of all. Rev. iv. v.; Dan. vii. 9, 10. In like manner, Christ in all instances appeared in the visions in his own person; never by a mere created symbol. And the reason obviously was, that no created being or object could form a suitable representative of the uncreated, all-creating, and infinitely powerful and wise. To have used a creature as his representative, would have been to imply that he was himself a creature, and not the Self-existent. There are numerous instances also in which angels represent angels of their own nature and rank, such as the innumerable millions that stood around the throne of the Ancient of days, Daniel vii. 9, 10; and the throne of the Father and the Son, Apoc. v. 11, 12; and undoubtedly because no other symbol could so adequately indicate their nature, and their relations to God. In other instances, individual angels are employed as symbols of great numbers of men, such as the angel from the sunrising, Rev. vii. 2, the angel invested with a rainbow, ch. x. and the three angels, ch. xiv. proclaiming messages to men. These beings of a higher order are employed, that they may indicate more impressively, the conspicuity, power, and influence of the groups and successions of men whom they represent.

And finally, there are many instances in which men appeared in their own persons in the visions, and represented themselves, because there is no other symbol that could present them in their relations to one another, and to God; and under the sway of the thoughts and affections by which they are to be prompted in the scenes that are foreshown. Such are the kings and their armies at the advent of the

Lamb under the sixth seal, Rev. vi. 15–17 and xix. 17–21, the two witnesses, xi. 3–12, and others. And the reason is, that no other symbol could adequately represent them in the conditions in which those for whom they stand, are to appear. Now the seven times that were to pass over Nebuchadnezzar, were undoubtedly employed as representatives of themselves, because no other was suited to give to him and his court a true indication of the period during which his exile from his palace and throne was to continue. Neither the king nor his people knew any thing of the use of days or times, as representatives of a longer period than themselves. Had the dream and the interpretation given days or times as symbols of a longer period than themselves as the duration of his humiliation, they might have been misunder stood, and led to uncertainty and distrust, especially among the numerous nations and tribes living under his sceptre, whose language was not Chaldaic; yet to whom it appears from the decree addressed to them by Nebuchadnezzar, the dream and its interpretation were made known. It was the part of wisdom, therefore, and righteousness to guard against that danger of misconception by using a period, the exact length of which was well known, and using its name in its natural and established sense, and employing the same period, and the same name of it, both in the prophecy and in the interpretation.

Can Dr. Tregelles gainsay this explanation of the

use of seven times in the prophecy, as well as in the interpretation? He perhaps has never noticed the difference in the relations in which the two great classes of the symbols are employed, and will not be aware of it unless these pages meet his eye. King Nebuchadnezzar, however, is not a witness, exceptional, or 'unexceptional,' that prophetic Scripture does not admit the year-day theory.

He alleges Daniel, as well as Nebuchadnezzar, as showing that he did not regard the periods of time in his prophecies as used as symbols on the principle of analogy, of longer periods than they literally express.

"The next witness is Daniel the prophet himself. In ch. ix. 2, he tells us that he understood by books—the prophecy of Jeremiah—that the Lord would accomplish *seventy years*, in the desolations of Jerusalem. Daniel did not understand the period spoken of by Jeremiah, according to the arbitrary canon which some would now apply to his own prophecies. He understood seventy years to mean seventy years; and not *two thousand five hundred and twenty years*. Thus, this very chapter of Daniel, from which some (even though it is a prophecy free from all symbol) would draw a proof of their theory, supplies decisive evidence against it," pp. 123, 124.

Dr. Tregelles should have been incapable of resorting to a pretext like this. Daniel utters no testimony in ch. ix. 2, or anywhere else, against interpreting the periods of time that occur in the symbolic revelations that were made to him, as symbols, denoting years in place of days. His not regarding the seventy years of the captivity as employed in that relation, to signify two thousand five hundred and twenty years, is surely no proof that the time, times, and a half a time, of ch. vii., and the twenty-three hundred days of ch. viii., are not used on that principle. Does Dr. Tregelles disown the difference between a symbolic and a mere language prophecy? Does he, in a word, mean to deny that there is any diversity between them; and maintain that it is as reasonless and false to interpret a prophecy couched in symbols as denoting agents, acts, and events that differ from the symbols themselves, as it is to interpret mere language predictions as though they were symbols? If not, why does he allege the fact that Daniel regarded the seventy years of Jeremiah as literal years and nothing else; as a proof that periods of time, when used as symbols, were not understood by him and are not to be interpreted by us, as representing periods longer than themselves? If that is not the view which he entertains, his assumptions and conclusions, assuredly, are altogether illogical. If Jeremiah's prophecy was not conveyed through symbols, but mere words, while the revelation made to Daniel, ch. vii., is embodied in symbols, not in words, how does it follow from the fact that Daniel interpreted Jeremiah according to the medium through which his prophecy is expressed; prove that Daniel's own prophecy is not to be interpreted according to its peculiar nature as embodied in symbols; but is to be construed as though it were a mere language prophecy? What utter confusion reigns in Dr. Tregelles' reasoning! Will he clear up this perplexity? Let him turn which way he will, he overthrows himself. If he admits that a symbolic differs from an unsymbolical prophecy, and grants that symbols are to be interpreted as symbols; then he abandons his assumptions and conclusions in this passage. If, on the other hand, he asserts that there is no radical difference between a symbolic and an unsymbolic prophecy, then he contradicts the divine word, and sets aside all the interpretations which the Spirit himself has given of the symbols of Daniel and John. But I am weary of pointing out his misrepresentations and perversions of the prophecy. The reader has ample proofs in the foregoing criticisms, that he is mistaken in all his leading views, and that whatever may be his skill in other spheres, he has not the special qualifications that are requisite for the task which he has undertaken in his volume on Daniel.

CHAPTER XVII.

That Periods of Time are used as Symbols of greater Periods than themselves is proved on a vast scale by Events; as in the Conquest by the Romans of the Greek Empire, their Destruction of Jerusalem, and their Persecution of the Saints.

If the times, the months, and the days of the prophecies of Daniel and John, are employed as symbols of periods longer than themselves, according to the ratio of days to years, the fact of their use in that relation must have been demonstrated by the appearance in the great theatre of the Roman world, of a vast succession of agents, and events that answer to the predictions; and so obviously and fully, as to make it apparent that they are the actors and events that are foreshown in those prophecies. If no such persons, no such agencies, and no such effects have had a place in the western empire and filled it with their presence and their power, during the long round of ages that has revolved since their career must have begun—if days are not used as representatives of years; then demonstratively either that construction of the prophetic periods is mistaken; or else the prophecies themselves are false. If, on the other hand, successions of persons, of exactly the rank, the character and the agency foreshown in the visions, have appeared in that scene, and acted the parts and met the catastrophes predicted of them; and in forms so conspicuous and on a scale so vast, as to prove with the utmost amplitude and certainty that they are the identical beings and events that are depicted and foreshown in those prophecies; then it is clear beyond doubt that those predicted periods, are periods not of days, but of years.

Now the agents, acts and events foretold in those prophecies, are of a nature and of a conspicuity, that render them more easily recognizable, and more susceptive of identification and proof, than any others that appear in the world. The great agents in the tragedies that are predicted, are not unofficial individuals who act in a secluded sphere, where no spectators witness their acts, and no means exist for conveying a knowledge of them to contemporaries, or transmitting it to later generations. Instead, they are personages of the greatest notoriety and celebrity; whose acts are official and public, and who are surrounded by crowds of spectators that behold all their actions, witness every play of their features, and feel impulses in their lives and fortunes, from every step of their procedure. They are emperors and kings; they are conquerors that steep the earth in blood. They are merciless tyrants that crush their subjects with oppression. They are ambitious, usurping and apostate priests, that arrogate the rights of God, and persecute his people. They are great civil and military bodies; vast ecclesiastical organizations, that extend their sway over wide domains, and give law to the nations. They are therefore more easily determinable than any other classes of men, and more sure to leave a record of their names and their deeds. Most of the historians, accordingly, of the civilized world, for the last twenty-five centuries, are occupied by these very actors and their actions. All the archives that have come down from the Assyrian, Babylonian, and Greek empires and the early and later ages of the Roman, relate to them and their achievements; and all the great monuments of art that survive from those times were the work of their hands. To hold that they have not existed; to affirm that their forms and features are not those which are depicted in Daniel and John, is therefore to deny that we have any knowledge of the past; is to denounce the records of history as unreliable and false.

The Roman power, for example, has exhibited all the characteristics, and exerted all the great agencies, that are ascribed to it, except the modifications it is to assume, and the peculiar acts it is to exert that are yet future, and are shortly to precede its final overthrow. Thus it has verified the predictions that like the monster shape, which was employed to represent it, it should be unlike all other civil and military governments; that it should be aggressive, resistless, bloody, and wanton in the oppression and destruction of those whom it assailed and conquered. Like a voracious and insatiable beast, it has crushed its victims with its iron teeth, torn them with its brazen claws, and in its rage and fury, stamped them in the dust. But beyond these general characteristics that marked its career, especially till it had reached the acme of its power, it exerted all the peculiar and distinctive agencies that are ascribed to it, and that have no parallel in any other civil and military empire. Thus, after having extended its conquests over all Italy, and over Carthage at the South, and Gaul, Spain, and Britain at the West and North, it entered the empire of Alexander, and overthrowing the Macedonian horn of the goat, substituted itself in its place, according to the prediction, Dan. viii., and spread its conquests over Asia Minor, Syria, Mesopotamia, Palestine and Egypt; and soon transferred its throne to Nicomedia, and ultimately to Constantinople, and reigned there over the East through a long series of years. On the revolt of the Jews in the reign of Nero, a Roman army under Vespasian, and afterwards under Titus entered Judea, and after conquering and demolishing the inferior cities and fortresses, and strewing the land with slaughter and desolation, besieged and took Jerusalem, destroyed the temple, and swept the few who survived, as with a deluge, into exile and slavery, according to the prediction, Daniel ix. 26, 27, that the people of a prince should come and destroy the city and sanctuary, as with a flood. *And this* was not an ordinary or slight event; nor has it lost its significance by the lapse of eighteen centuries. It was one of the most momentous calamities God ever inflicted on a guilty people. It changed the history not only of the Jewish race through the ages that followed, but of the whole civilized world, and fills a place, and is to answer ends in the divine administration, that are transcended by no others. It was essential as an avenging judgment, to the manifestation of God's righteousness and its appointment, its execution, and the issues that are to spring from it, are to be made known not only to men, but to the universe, and their equity and wisdom be so unveiled, as to prompt the approval and adoration of all holy beings. Otherwise, it would issue in discredit and defeat. And finally, this great act of the Roman power as the instrument of God's justice, is attested in the most ample manner both by the Jewish nation and by the Romans. No fact in the history of the world is more indisputable, none is more widely known. The conquest of Macedonia, Syria, and Palestine, destruction of Jerusalem and the temple, and dispersion of the Jewish nation, fell within the fourth and fifth centuries of the period symbolized by the twenty-three hundred evenings-mornings, and shows that the Roman power was acting at that remote period in the sphere assigned to it by the prophecy of Daniel, and therefore is not restricted in its agency to the narrow space of 1260 literal days that are yet future.

The next great act of that Roman horn, which had sprung up in the limits of the Greek empire, was its waxing great toward the host of heaven, and casting down some of the host and of the stars to the ground and stamping upon them; a gigantic act, indicating unparalleled strength, and ambition, and bespeaking an infuriate rage against the maker of the orbs and his kingdom. What acts of human beings can present a correlation to those assaults on God and his people? The stars of the firmament are symbols of the saints of the Most High, who, it was revealed to his people in a later vision, are to shine as the brightness of the firmament, and as the stars for ever, and ever. The casting down of those stars from heaven and treading them in the dust, represented the dejection of the saints and ministers of the Most High from their sphere in his kingdom on earth by persecution, and consigning them to dungeons, to the mines, and to the block. And this had its fulfillment in the persecutions of the people, and especially the ministers of the Christian churches by Diocletian, Galerius, and Licinius. The audacity of those monsters was in their sphere, what the towering arrogance and rage of the horn was in its war on the stars. They are not to be envied for their discernment and taste, who see nothing of the dazzling light in which the rights of God and the dignity of his true worshipers, on the one side; and the impiousness of his usurping enemies on the other, are set forth in this symbolization. What mere word-picture could approach it in the strength and grandeur in which it presents the greatness and sacredness of God's prerogatives; the place his true children hold in his regards; and their audaciousness in sin who tread his truthful worshipers in the dust! And this fell within the first third of the twenty-three hundred days; and shows again that the Roman power was in that distant age, fulfilling the work of persecution and impiety, that was foreshown of it. No facts are more indubitable than that the emperors of the east exerted the acts and wrought the effects here ascribed to them. They are recorded by the pens of a great number of writers, Pagan as well as Christian; the decrees of Diocletian consigning the churches to demolition, the Scriptures to the flames, and the ministers of the word to the mines, the stake and the block, are still in existence. No one has ever questioned their genuineness. No one has ever denied the truth of the narratives in which these events have descended to us. To doubt them, is as reasonless and absurd as it were to doubt that Diocletian, Galerius, Licinius, and other persecutors of that class were ever invested with power in the Roman empire, or had a place among its population.

The next impious act of that horn, was its magnifying itself against the Prince of the host, and taking away from him the daily sacrifice, and casting down the place of his sanctuary; having a host against the daily sacrifice, and casting down the truth to the ground. This had its fulfillment first in the arrogation by Constantine and his successors of the right to legislate over the church which belongs only to Christ, and next in the rejection of his work of expiation, and substitution in its place, of superstitious rites, relics, idols, and other inventions of men as a ground of justification. And the prophecy presents in these symbolic acts, a true picture of that usurpation of Christ's rights, and rejection of him as the sacrifice for sin. For as the literal taking away of the daily sacrifice, and casting down of the place of his sanctuary, while the Mosaic institute was existing and obligatory, would have been to debar worshipers from the offerings and services which were the medium to them of their faith and their acceptance. So the preclusion of Christian worshipers from looking to Christ's blood for redemption, by false doctrines and vain and impious rites; and closing or destroying the edifices in which a true homage was presented to God; was taking Christ from them as their expiation, and debaring them as individual churches and communities from worshiping him. And this impious work, which who, apart from the prediction, could have foreseen or deemed possible, was wrought by Constantine and his successors in the fourth, fifth, sixth, and following centuries, and spread like a courtly fashion, through the whole empire. They were introduced by them and their civil subordinates; not by the ministers of the church. A large body of the saints of the Most High resisted them for a period, and thousands and thousands were persecuted and consigned to martyrdom for their faithful denunciation of them, and unfaltering maintenance of the word of God and of the testimony of Jesus. At length superstition, the homage of relics, images and saints in the eastern empire; and in the western especially, the idolatry of the mass, were legalized and enforced by the clergy themselves, and became, and have continued to be, to the present day, the religion of the Greek and Latin churches. In what other form could this astounding apostacy from God have been presented in such strength, and clothed in such awful hues! It is a direct rejection of Christ and his redemption, and the substitution of a false and impious system in their place! The question whether this prophecy has been fulfilled, is therefore of immeasurable moment. It is the question whether Christ really occupies the place which the Scriptures assign him in the work of redemption! It is the question whether the religion of the Greek and Catholic church is the true or a false religion! There is certainly no dearth of means for deciding that question.

That the war on Christ and his sacrifice, and the introduction of a superstitious and idolatrous religion took place in the age to which I have referred, is certain from the most ample testimony of the historians of the period, the decrees and enactments of the emperors themselves, and the acts and canons of ecclesiastics. And their agency in this apostacy, in place of being denied, has been admitted and approved by the whole Greek and Roman church through all the ages that have followed. Those great acts of revolt from God are indisputably, therefore, the fulfillment of this prophecy. That such exact coincidences with it are not its accomplishment, is impossible. No other apostacies of the kind have ever taken place in the Roman empire. No other events can be denoted by the symbols, consistently with the laws of analogy. If these are not their fulfillment, it were vain to look for their verification. The supposition that this concurrence of the events with the prediction, is no proof that the events are those that were contemplated in the prophecy, is an impeachment of God's truth and rectitude. It implies that his word and providence are deceptive in regard to millions of the most conspicuous and influential agents, and events, and through a period of many ages of the world; and if assented to, must naturally destroy all faith in the other prophecies. Let those who are venturing on such an arraignment of God, pause and arrest the dread imputations on him that are passing from their lips.

The next great prediction respecting the Roman

power, is that of the fourth trumpet of the Apocalypse, in which the fall of the western emperor and his associates in the government, is foreshadowed by the obscuration of a third part of the sun, and a third part of the moon, and a third part of the stars, by an obliterating stroke that divested them of their power to give light during a third part of the day, and a third part of the night. The third part of the sun is the symbol of the emperor of the west, after the loss of a large share of the dominions that had belonged to his predecessors; and the third part of the moon and of the stars, of the inferior officials of the western imperial government. Their loss of the power of giving light, represented the divestiture of Augustulus and his subordinate officers of their civil and military authority. And this had its fulfillment in the year 476. Neither Augustulus nor the great officers of his court, were put to death, but he being forced to resign the throne and take the station of a dependent, all who were associated with him in the government, were, by his abdication, deprived of their offices, and reduced to the rank of mere subjects.

With the fall of Augustulus, the seventh head of the beast, the symbol of the imperial power fell, and gave place to the Gothic kingly sovereignties that had conquered the western empire; and each grasping the part that had fallen under its power, erected a kingdom for itself, in independence both of its associate monarchies, and of the eastern empire; a change of the greatest significance, and without any parallel in the revolutions which befell the empires that had preceded the Roman. On the overthrow of the Assyrian empire, instead of being divided into separate kingdoms under independent monarchs, it was added to the dominions of the conqueror. On the subversion also of the Babylonian empire, it was incorporated in that of the Medes and Persians. Theirs was in like manner appropriated by the Greeks to themselves; and on the conquest of the vast territories of the Greeks by the Romans, instead of erecting new and independent kingdoms, they held the whole under their own despotic rule. But the subversion of the western Roman empire was not the work of a single people, but of a group of foreign nations, each acting independently in a great measure of the others, and appropriating to itself whatever domains it could seize and hold, and giving the sceptre into the hands of the chief to whom they already owed allegiance, and by whom they had been led to their conquests.

And this momentous change, marked by the greatest peculiarities, and conspicuous as the orbs of heaven compared to ordinary events, was the division of the Roman empire into ten separate kingdoms, predicted through the toes of Nebuchadnezzar's image, and through the diadems on the horns of the beast of the Apocalypse from the sea, ch. xiii. 1–5. The diadems are symbols of kingly power. The disappearance of the diadems from the heads, denoted that the orders of rulers symbolized by the heads, had passed from existence, and their presence on the horns, indicated that the sovereignty had been grasped by the kings of whom the horns were the representatives. These events answer in the most exact and impressive manner to the symbols. To deny that they are the events contemplated by the prophecy, is in effect to impeach its truth. If an exact accordance of events of the greatest moment, and the greatest notoriety, with a prediction, and their standing in the gaze of the whole civilized world for ages, is no proof that they are the events the prophecy foreshows, what can possibly have any claims to be considered as the verification of a prediction? The supposition of such a concurrence without a fulfillment, especially in a case in which thousands of millions of the most influential actors in the civilized world, and ten thousand times ten thousand millions of acts of the greatest significance and notoriety are concerned, is a self-contradiction too palpable to meet the assent of any who truly apprehend its meaning.

CHAPTER XVIII.

Dr. Tregelles' Denial that the Kings denoted by the ten Horns rose at the time of the Conquest of the Roman Empire by the Goths—The rise and career of the Power denoted by the eleventh Horn, demonstrates that the 1260 days are Symbols of an equal Number of Years—It is proved also by the Prophecy of the second Beast and the Image.

THAT the kings foreshown in these prophecies, are the kings that rose contemporaneously with the conquest of the western empire by the tribes that appropriated its territory to themselves, is indeed denied by Dr. Tregelles and others, under the representation that writers who have attempted to identify the ten kingdoms, have fallen into errors, and that no means exist for a clear demonstration that ten rose into being at, or near the period of the fall of the imperial rule. He says:

"The tenfold division of the Roman empire (even if we had a right to exclude the eastern half), could never be definitely pointed out, whether in the early centuries or since. The lists differ exceedingly, and very frequently countries wholly disconnected with the Roman empire are introduced, simply because in later days they have been upholders of the popedom."—*Remarks on Daniel, p.* 68.

But the mistakes into which writers have fallen, generally from gross inattention to the prophecy, are no proof that the kings denoted by the horns did not enter on their career, as the sovereignty passed from the line denoted by the last imperial head of the beast. It is not supposed that they all sprung into power at the moment when Odoacer, the chief of the Heruli, displaced Augustulus, and assumed the sceptre of Rome. Most of them entered the empire in the early part of the fifth century, and had established themselves in France, Spain, northern Africa, and Italy, long before the fall of Augustulus. The Lombards, Heruli, and Ostrogoths had occupied Pannonia and Noricum, a considerable period before they invaded Italy. That there were ten hordes, or communities that invaded the western empire, established themselves in the possession of territory, and instituted or perpetuated a kingly rule for a considerable time, is as indisputable as any of the events of that period. That several were soon to fall, was foreshown by the prophecy. That great changes subsequently took place by the encroachment of the tribes on one another, is no proof that the original number was not ten. That the western empire continued under the dominion of a group of kings from that age onward, without any considerable exception of territory, is as indisputable as it is that it is now under the sway, with the sole exception of Switzerland, of independent monarchs, and of lines generally that trace their lineage back through centuries. When a dynasty has fallen, as once in England, and five times in less than a century in France, it has not issued in the substitution of a republic for a monarchy for more than a short period. The change of the line has not essentially altered the principle of the rule.

And these kings have acted the *parts* ascribed to them in the prophecies of Daniel and John. Thus they and the governments of which they were severally the heads, gave, and there is reason to believe, before the close of the seventh century, the saints of the Most High and the times and law into the hand of the power denoted by the eleventh horn: accredited the impious pretensions of that apostate church, and executed its behests in the persecution of the true worshipers. They have opened their mouths also in blasphemy against God, and blasphemed his name, and his tabernacle, and them that dwell in heaven; by assuming the right to legislate over his prerogatives, his word, and his church; by representing the temples of idolatry as his tabernacles, and exhibiting the saints that dwell in his presence, as entitled to worship and as accepting the homage that is addressed to them by men; and finally, they have made war on the saints, and have overcome them. Among the kingdoms that now subsist, or that have subsisted in the western Roman empire, there is not one, the rulers of which did not perpetrate this blackest and most impious of crimes against both God and man; and most of them have been the scenes of bloody and exterminating persecutions without very long intervals, for eight hundred, or a thousand years. There is not a principal city that has not been the scene of the martyrdom of God's witnesses. There is not a place of concourse that has not resounded with the shouts and execrations of their accusers and murderers, as they were dragged from their dwellings to be buried in dungeons, or given to the flames. What must be their blindness who can shut their eyes to these indisputable facts, and maintain that there is no evidence that these audacious persecutors, whom it is impossible that any others should exceed in atrocity, are the bloody kings whom the prophecy represents were to make war on the saints, and prevail against them. They succeeded in silencing the voice of dissent from their false doctrines and impious worship in Britain, France, Spain, Portugal, Italy, and Germany, for a long series of centuries. Is it probable they can ever prevail against them on a greater scale at a future period; and especially if, as these writers hold, their work is to be consummated in the short space of three years and a half? If proofs so vast and extended through a thousand or twelve hundred years, are no evidence that they are the monsters that the prophecy contemplates, it is absurd to imagine that any demonstration that could take place in a brief period, could identify their future successors as the individuals that fulfill the vision.

Dr. Tregelles attempts to draw a confirmation of his views from Daniel ii.:

"From the vision of Daniel ii. and that of chapter vii. we may see that the ten kingdoms do not arise until a certain process of deterioration (the mixture of clay with iron) is complete; and that these kingdoms, when all developed, have not any protracted course before them. Just as the sovereignty out of which they sprung, was secular, so were they of course also secular. Whatever have been the changes in the Roman earth, as yet we have not seen the definite tenfold division; indeed had we seen it, we could have expected nothing other than the appearance of the last horn, and the judgment of the Son of Man at his coming."—P. 67.

Dr. Tregelles overturns instead of supporting his construction by this appeal to Daniel. The iron of the legs and feet of the image, represented the monarchs and nobility whose power was inherent, or inherited from their predecessors. The clay is interpreted in the prophecy as denoting the seed of men, that is, the unnoble, the common people who were to be intermingled with those symbolized by the iron, but were not to cleave to them. Now Dr. Tregelles holds that when that intermingling of the clay with the iron in the structure of the governments of the ten kingdoms takes place, it will show that they have reached their last stage, and that the last horn, by which he means Antichrist, has appeared, and the advent of the Son of God arrived. But if the intermingling of the common people with the nobility in the structure of the government, is a signal that those great events have taken place, they must have taken place ages ago. The mingling of the people at large of a kingdom in the structure of the government, is manifestly the symbol of their taking a part in the creation of their rulers by the elective franchise. The nation that exercises that function, selects its rulers, and gives them the power by which they exercise the government. This is indisputable, inasmuch as there is no other form in which they can, as a people, have a part with the supreme rulers in the government. They cannot all, nor generally be officials. There would then either be no subjects, or but a small minority, which has never yet been, nor ever can be the condition of a monarchy. If, then, as Dr. Tregelles represents, the admission of a people to the right which the mixture of the clay with the iron denotes, is a proof that the last three and a half years of this dispensation have come, that Antichrist has revealed himself, and that the Son of God has appeared in the clouds; then those great events must already have occurred, and in ages long past. For Great Britain has had a representative government, in a large measure, for hundreds of years. France had a parliament or states general many centuries ago; Spain has for ages had her cortes; and within the last fifteen years France has extended the right of suffrage to all her male adults, and made it the basis of her imperial government. The new constitution of Italy rests the monarchy of that kingdom on the same foundation; and the right of representation is conceded in some degree, it is believed, to a share of the population in every kingdom within the limits of the old western empire. Had Dr. Tregelles avowed the belief from these facts, that Antichrist has manifested himself, and the Son of God has come in power and great glory, he would scarcely have offered a more palpable contradiction to fact, than he has in denying that the western Roman empire has been divided into ten kingdoms according to the predictions of those prophecies, and that the ten kings have acted the part for ages which the pen of inspiration ascribes to them.

There has been an equal verification of the prediction Dan. vii. 8, 20–25, in the rise and career of the eleventh horn of the beast. That horn is the symbol of the pope in his two fold office of bishop and monarch. A century or two passed, after the kings had entered on their reign, before the pope made such advances in his arrogations of power as a prelate, and in the subjection of the clergy and people to his sway, that he was able to take that attitude of superiority and dictation toward the rulers of Italy, Gaul, and Germany, that led on to the aspirations, cabals, intrigues, and usurpations by which he at length won or constrained the concession to him of a territory, and assumed the title and insignia of a civil monarch as well as the head of the Roman church. Having reached that position by a long train of deceits, impieties, and violences, he then began in the most open and audacious manner to act the part ascribed to him in the prophecy;—speaking great words against the Most High, usurping authority over his laws, and persecuting and wearing out his saints. He blasphemed the Almighty by proclaiming himself to be his vicegerent on the earth; by arrogating power to rescind his laws; to introduce new methods of redemption; to install new intercessors, and new objects of worship in heaven; to license every species of sin; to disgrace and obstruct every true belief, and every form of virtue; and to crush by oppression and tortures, and sweep to the grave by fire and sword, all who refused submission to his imperious will. And he pursued that course of antagonism to God, and tyranny to men, for eight or ten centuries; never for an hour repressing his blasphemies, or pausing in his work of torture and slaughter, except when met by a recoil from the millions who were groaning under his merciless sway. What pencil can paint in colors that are just to the truth, the gigantic atrocities that have marked his career! Who can count the many myriads whom he consigned to promiscuous slaughter in the wars which he prompted on the Albigenses, the Waldenses, the Bohemians, the Huguenots and others? Who can enumerate the multitudes whom he has driven into exile, torn on the rack, and burned at the stake? Who can sum up the agonies with which he has wrenched the hearts of the long train of generations that have dwelt under his rule? Who can estimate the millions on millions whom he has led down to the gates of eternal death? It is madness to deny that this arch wretch who has maintained this war on God and his worshipers through such a series of ages, is the monster fiend drawn in the prophecy under the symbol of the little horn! All his hideous features, all his haughty attitudes, all his dragon-voiced utterances, all his bloody deeds answer to the picture that is there given of him. If he is not the power denoted by the horn, it is vain to imagine that the prediction can ever have a fulfillment. No human being can possibly in his peculiar sphere, transcend him in wickedness. No short-lived torturer, like the Antichrist for whom Dr. Tregelles and his associates look, could approach him in the number of his victims or the misery with which he could wrench and rend them. All the believers that will be in life on the earth in the persecution that is yet to come, will probably not be a tithe of the millions whom the pope in his war on the people of God has consigned to the grave.

There has been a like verification of the prophecy of the papal power under the symbol of the second beast with two horns like a lamb, and the speech of a dragon, Rev. xiii. 11–18. Its horns represent his two fold power as a bishop and a king. He in its presence, exercises all the power in kind of the ten-horned beast. The power of the first beast was not the power of a civil and military sovereignty only; but also of a blasphemer, and a persecutor of the saints. The papal sovereignty arrogated all those prerogatives and exercised contemporaneously with the first beast, a civil government, and blasphemed God, and persecuted his saints. But the most important act ascribed to him, is his prompting the people of the ten kingdoms by means of false miracles, to erect an image to the beast that had been wounded by a sword and revived: and his giving life unto the image, so that it could speak and persecute those who refused to worship it. As the beast was the symbol of that combination of rulers, of which the emperors denoted by the seventh head were the chiefs: so the image of that beast was not a literal statue, but an organization of ecclesiastics after the model of the civil government of the empire, embracing all the ranks of the clergy of the ten kingdoms, and having the pope as its head. His giving life to the image and causing it to speak, was his infusing into that structure a power by which it became an active and influential agent, spake with an authoritative voice, and caused those who refused to honor it with the veneration and submission it demanded, to be put to death. That this prediction had a fulfillment in the eighth, ninth and subsequent centuries, is as indisputable as any other fact in the annals of the papacy. The bishop of Rome was for near two centuries after the rise of the Gothic kings only the head of the hierarchy of his own Italian patriarchate. He was acknowledged as the successor of Peter, and in rank the first bishop of the church; and was consulted as of high authority on questions of doctrine and discipline; but his decisions were advisory only, not legislative and judicial; and became authoritative only by adoption and ratification by princes and councils. The bishops were elected by their clergy, and the metropolitans by their bishop; and all questions between bishops, were determined by provincial or national councils.

But after the erection of the papacy by Pepin and Charlemagne into a civil kingdom, in the eighth century, the popes began to aspire to *an ecclesiastical dominion* over the other kingdoms. They represented their decrees as of universal authority; they claimed the right of making all appointments to benefices. They arrogated the determination of all ecclesiastical questions; and in order to give effect to their pretences, procured the forgery of a great body of letters and documents in the name of earlier popes and princes, which exhibited them as exerting legislative and judicial authority over the whole church, and represented princes and prelates as acknowledging that jurisdiction; and those false documents they inserted among the canons, and thereby constituted them a part of the ecclesiastical laws. By these atrocious means, the popes made rapid accessions to their power, and though meeting for a time a stern resistance from individuals and hierarchies, after a struggle of two or three centuries succeeded in their aim, and brought the whole church of the ten kingdoms into the most abject subjection to their despotic sway. They arrogated the appointment to all offices. They assumed the determination of all causes. They usurped an absolute supremacy over all laws human and divine. They claimed that their decrees and judgments were of divine authority. They extorted an oath of allegiance to them from all who held offices in the church. They asserted a similar supremacy also over the monarchs and princes of the ten kingdoms, and affected to give them their crowns; when refractory, released their subjects from their allegiance; and when able, wrenched their sceptres from their hands. And finally, as the climax of these lying and impious usurpations, they caused that as many as would not worship this image of the beast, by assenting to its arrogations and yielding to its will, as though it were divine—to be put to death. And it was *in this sphere*, not as the mere bishop of Rome, but as the absolute and despotic head of the whole church, that it instigated and carried on its bloody persecutions in every part of the ten kingdoms from the time of Gregory VII. through the centuries that followed, and swept millions, who refused submission to its will, to the grave. The annals of the Roman Catholic church, and the civil history of the ten kingdoms, are in a great measure occupied for six or eight centuries with these monstrous usurpations and tyrannies; and it was the towering height to which they rose, and the horrible demoralization and misery to which they gave birth, that prompted the revolt of Zwingle, Luther, and the Reformers generally of the sixteenth century. It was against this image of the beast; this lawless and bloody imperium in the church, by which Christ was thrust from his throne, his word was divested of its authority, and the pope was exalted to an absolute despotism over the whole domain of religion, and against this alone, that the battle was fought by the Protestants at the Reformation; and it was by extricating themselves from the thrall of this monster tyranny, that they reinstated themselves in the freedom of the sons of God. Their whole debate with the Catholics related to the question, Who is the law-giver of the church? The Protestants held that God is alone its legislator, and his word the sole rule of its faith and worship. The Papists gave that place to the pope and his decrees. The fulfillment of this prophecy, is thus one of the most indubitable, one of the most conspicuous, and from the atrocity of the crimes that entered into its tragedy of lies, of false miracles, of blasphemies, and of blood, one of the most portentous that has taken place of the revelations made in Daniel and John.

There is not one that transcends it in the singularity of the events foreshown ; in the vast combination of agents that united in giving it existence ; nor in the magnitude and awfulness of the results that have sprung from its agency. That it fills the place I have indicated, none will venture to deny, unless blinded by gross ignorance, or warped by invincible prejudice.

I might allege additional proofs that the Roman civil, military, and religious power in the eastern empire is symbolized by the sixth horn of the goat; and that the eleventh horn of the beast, Daniel vii. and the second beast, and the image, Rev. xiii. are symbols of the papal power in some of its shapes; and that that power came into existence and entered on the career ascribed to it many ages ago, and thereby demonstrate still more amply that the time, times, and a half a time, the twelve hundred and sixty days, and the forty-two months which are given as the measure of its agency, are used as symbols of a corresponding number of years; but it is unnecessary to add to the evidence I have already alleged. No certainty can be more ample than that the power denoted by the eleventh horn of Daniel is the papacy, that it began its career some twelve centuries ago, and that it is rapidly advancing to the catastrophe in which its war on God and man is to meet its end.

CHAPTER XIX.

The Errors of these Writers in respect to the Division of the Roman Empire into the eastern and western—Their mistaken Notion that the four Kingdoms of the Greek Empire are to be revived.

These writers have fallen into an important error in respect to the division of the Roman Empire into ten kingdoms; maintaining not only that it has not yet taken place, but that it is to embrace the eastern or Greek empire, as well as the western or Roman. Dr. Tregelles says:

"In Daniel ch. vii. we see that the whole of the Roman earth is to be divided into ten kingdoms; these ten being found in its whole extent, the east as well as the west. The four parts of Alexander's empire formed a considerable portion of the eastern half of the Roman territory: and as we see here (ch. viii.) those four existent as kingdoms at the time of the end, it only follows that four kingdoms out of the ten will be identical with the parts into which the third empire was long ago divided. A horn springs out of one of those parts, *it may be described in a general manner*, as in ch. vii. as rising from one of the ten kingdoms, or else in a much more definite way as in this chapter, in which we see even what part or direction of the Roman earth will give him his origin."—*Remarks on Daniel, p.* 82.

Here is not only a sad absence of proof, but a very unfortunate cluster of misapprehensions. He exhibits the four kingdoms of Alexander's empire, as four of the ten kingdoms of the Roman empire foreshown Daniel vii. 8. No misconception could be more inexcusable. The four kingdoms of Alexander's empire ceased as they were successively conquered by the Romans, and their territory was incorporated in a mass in the Roman empire.

The ten kingdoms of Daniel vii. did not come into existence until four to five hundred years after the overthrow of the last of the Greek kingdoms; and they had their scene exclusively in the western empire, of which in the main, the Romans were masters before they extended their sovereignty into Asia.

Dr. Tregelles represents also that the four Greek kingdoms are to exist at the time of the end. The prophecy utters no intimation of that nature. What it teaches is, that in the latter time of those kingdoms, when transgressors had accomplished their work, a king of fierce countenance, symbolized by the sixth horn of the goat, should stand up, and should destroy the mighty and the holy people, and should magnify himself against the Prince of princes. And it is *that, the Roman*, not the *Greek* power which it is foreshown is to continue to the end, ch. xi. 36–40. He asserts that the sixth horn that sprung from the head of the goat may be described in a general manner as in ch. vii. as rising from one of the *ten kingdoms* whose kings are symbolized by the horns of *the beast!* That is to offer a direct contradiction to the prophecy. The sixth horn sprung, it is specifically affirmed, from the head of the goat, by pushing one of the four horns from its place. There is no intimation that a twelfth horn, as Dr. Tregelles' interpretation implies, sprung up on the head of the beast, and displaced one of the preceding ten. What can be more manifest than that Dr. Tregelles, instead of framing his construction in conformity with the prophecy, employs himself in interpolating and modifying the prediction to bring it into harmony with his preconceived theory?

Mr. B. W. Newton presents the same views. He says:

"The first king of Grecia has arisen and has fallen; his four successors also have reigned; but they too, have passed away, and *their kingdoms have vanished*—without the king of the fierce countenance having appeared, of whom it is declared, that he shall arise *in the latter time of their kingdom.* Has, then, this prophecy been falsified? It has not. The eighth chapter throughout its whole course declares, that its burthen respects the time of the end when the transgressors shall have come to the full. . . . These four kingdoms, therefore, *must be revived.*

"We know from the preceding chapters that the whole Roman empire, and therefore *that* part of it within which those kingdoms fall, is to be revived. We know also that the eastern as well as the western branch is to be divided. All, therefore, as to this, that we learn additionally from the eighth chapter is, that four of these divisions will be the kingdoms which passed from Alexander's successors into the hands of Rome; that is to say, Greece, Egypt, Syria, and the rest of the dominions of Turkey."—*Prospects of the Ten Kingdoms.* 1864, *pp.* 117, 118.

"The legs of the image corresponding with the division of the Roman empire into eastern and western, would lead us to expect that five kingdoms will ultimately be found in the eastern, and five in the western part of the Roman dominions. The eighth chapter of Daniel places it beyond a doubt that Greece, Egypt, Syria reaching to the Euphrates, and the rest of Turkey both in Europe and Asia, will form four of the eastern kingdoms."—*Prospects of the Ten Kingdoms. Ed.* 1864, *p.* 50.

Here is the same error as is held by Dr. Tregelles, in respect to the meaning of the expression, "In the latter time of their kingdom when the transgressors shall have come to the full;" that is, shall, have reached the acme of their impieties, and become ripe for destruction. Each treats it as though that time was *not* the time when the rulers and people of the four kingdoms had reached the climax of their iniquities, and were about to be smitten by the hand of avenging justice; but a period two thousand years later, and as though the transgressors who had wrought the full measure of sin that they were to be permitted to perpetrate, were not the inhabitants of those kingdoms, but were transgressors of a different race or races, existing in a distant age, and in a remote part of the world, who will have had no participation in the crimes of the rulers and people of the four kingdoms! But what can be more false and preposterous? The language of the prediction is, "in the latter time of *their king-*

dom": not ages after their kingdom had vanished from existence: and "when the transgressors shall have filled the measure of their sins;" that is, the transgressors of those kingdoms, and especially those of the Jews, who had apostatized from Jehovah, to idols—not transgressors of a different lineage, a different country, and a different age, who had no connection whatever with the Greeks or Jews of that period. The sense which I have expressed is indubitably that of the passage. The construction advanced by these writers, not only has nothing to support it, but it perverts what it professes to explain by the interpolation of a wholly foreign and false element! What an expedient to give a show of truth to their groundless theory!

Their version of the prophecy is confuted also by the prediction that immediately follows, that a king of fierce countenance should interpose, who should rise to great power, and should destroy among others, the people of the saints; that is, the Jewish people; and should stand up against the Prince of princes, that is the Messiah; as this shows that the power denoted by that king was to conquer the Jewish nation, and to set itself up against the Son of God; and therefore was to subsist and continue its agency through a long tract of ages; for these predictions had their fulfillment in the conquest of Judea by the Romans, the destruction of Jerusalem and the temple, the dispersion of those of the Jews that survived, throughout the empire; and finally in the arrogation by that power of authority over Christ's kingdom, and attempt to subvert it by setting aside his expiation, and substituting a work of man in its place. And it is to continue that war on Christ till the close of the vision at the end of the twenty-three hundred evenings-mornings, which are representatives of twenty-three hundred years.

There is not a hint in the prophecy that the four Greek kingdoms are to be revived. The pretence is as preposterous, as it would be to assume that Babylon, Persia, and the Greek empire in the form it bore under Alexander are to be revived; or that the whole Roman history is to be acted over again. How can those four kingdoms be recalled into existence? To reproduce them, the Greeks themselves must be resummoned into life, and reinstalled in the sovereignty of Asia Minor, Syria, and Egypt. The organization of new governments in those countries over their present populations, and by either their present rulers, or by sovereigns of a different lineage, would not be a revivification of the four Greek kingdoms. There is a government now existing in Egypt, in Syria, in Asia Minor, and in Greece. Are they the four Greek kingdoms into which Alexander's empire was divided? No one will be so rash as to affirm such a solecism. And if they are not, how could the erection of new monarchies by races that are not Greeks, be a revival of Alexander's empire?

Mr. Newton regards the legs of Nebuchadnezzar's image, as indicating the division of the Roman *empire* into two equal parts, and thence infers that at least four of the dynasties symbolized by the toes are to be in the eastern, and the others in the western empire. No misapprehension could involve the symbols of the prophecy in more inextricable confusion and contradiction to each other. In the postulate on which he proceeds in that theory, he overlooks the fact that the office of the metals of the image is not to represent *the territories* over which the several dynasties reigned, but simply to symbolize the human beings who exercised the sovereignty of the empires. Thus he says:

"As regards the four metals which composed this image, almost all expositors agree that they represent the successive *empires* of Chaldea, Persia, Greece, and Rome. . .

"If then the iron legs of the image denote the *whole* Roman *empire*, why do expositors, after admitting this, suddenly forget their admission when they begin to treat of the divided parts, and write as if *half* only of the Roman empire were represented? If a whole is to be divided, we must divide that *whole*. Nothing but error can ensue, if we divide only half. Yet this is the mistake that has been committed. The eastern half of the Roman empire has been forgotten."

"If the terms of the vision had been adhered to, and the ten final kingdoms had been sought in the *whole* Roman Empire, the modern theory of interpretation could never have existed: for it is based upon the extraordinary fallacy that *half* of the Roman empire, is the Roman empire."—*Prospects. Edition* 1864, *pp*. 14, 15, 16.

He thus in the first place falls into the error of assuming that that which the iron represents, is the Roman *empire* or *territory*, instead of the rulers who were to hold its sovereignty, and exercise its government. His theory is accordingly wholly groundless, and in contradiction to truth. As the iron is not the symbol of territory, but only of supreme and subordinate rulers, the fact that it was distributed into two legs, is no proof whatever that the empire which they were to sway was also to be divided into two equal parts. This single consideration overthrows the theory he advances with so much assurance.

In the next place, his assumption implies, that the division of the Roman empire into the eastern and western, was coeval with the origin of the empire itself. For as the legs of the image were separate from each other throughout their whole length; if their separation implies and proves that the Roman empire was in like manner to be divided into two equal parts; then it also proves that that separation subsisted from the beginning of the empire. But that is in contradiction to fact. The separation of the empire into the eastern and western did not take place until eleven centuries and a half, after the rise of the Roman power. Near seven centuries passed before the conquest of the Greek kingdom of Syria and Egypt was completed.

In the third place, his assumption involves other

consequences that are equally false and preposterous. Thus, if the legs of the image indicate a division of the Roman empire into two equal parts, then for a like reason the arms and shoulders attached to the breast should imply a division of the Median and Persian empire into two equal parts: and on the same ground, the thighs of the image also must be taken as symbols of a division of the *Greek* empire into two similar parts under different dynasties; while the unity of the belly, must represent with equal effect, that no such division was to exist! On that principle the four legs also of the monster beast which represents the Roman power, would symbolize a fourfold division of the Roman empire. Not a glance does Mr. Newton appear to have cast at the self-confuting results to which his assumption thus leads. There is no more reason for assuming that the legs of the image denote a division of the empire into two parts, than there is that the legs and wings of the lion symbolized a division of the Babylonian empire into an equal number of kingdoms; or that the legs of the bear, the leopard, the monster brute, or the ram and the goat indicate that the territories over which those whom they represented reigned, were to undergo a like division into separate dominions. The reason that legs were given to these symbols, was, not to foreshow that the territories which were their scene were to be distributed to a like number of sovereignties; but was in order that being perfect in organization and shape, according to their several natures, they might be suitable representatives of the analogous combinations of human beings, whom it was their office to symbolize. Had the image been with but one leg it would have implied that the power it represented, was mutilated, and incapable of the acts that are ascribed to it. Had the ten-horned beast been without four legs, it would have carried a proof in its organization, that the power it denoted, could never exert the vast and resistless activities that are foreshown of it. Instead of such deviations from truth, which would have defeated the object of the visions, the symbols were all perfect according to their several natures, and some of them were endowed with supernatural organs, as wings, in order that they might present a fit exemplification of the exact and full adaptation of those whom they represented, for the extraordinary agencies they were to exert. The view advanced by these writers is accordingly wholly groundless and untenable.

On the other hand, the construction which refers the ten kings symbolized by the toes of the image, and the horns of the beast to the western empire exclusively, is not only unembarrassed by objections, but is sustained by the most unanswerable certainties.

The dragon of seven heads and ten horns, Rev. xii. 1–4, and bearing diadems on the heads, was the symbol of the Roman power from its origin, down to the fall of the western empire: and all the lines of supreme rulers which the heads symbolized, had their seats in the western Roman empire: and Rome continued to be the capital of the empire down to the separation of the west from the east, in A. D. 395; and from that time held its place as the capital of the west, till the fall of Augustulus, and the extinction of the imperial rule. The beast from the sea, Rev. xiii. 1–5, having seven heads and ten horns, and bearing diadems on the horns, represents the Roman power exclusively in the western empire from the fall of the imperial line to the coming of Christ. The horns denoting the ten kings who, having conquered the territory of the western empire, usurped each the government of the domain it had grasped; and bore the diadem as the badge of its supremacy in its kingdom. This is clear, *first*, from the consideration that as the eastern emperor did not lose his sceptre on the fall of the western dynasty, but continued to reign as independently as before, he cannot be symbolized by the seventh head of the beast, which had lost its diadem: as that would be inconsistent with the fact that he continued in possession of his sovereignty; but must be held to have been still represented by the seventh diademed head of the dragon, which remained the symbol of the Roman imperial power in that part of the empire in which it still subsisted.

And *second*, from the fact that ten horns actually rose in the western empire, and continued for a considerable time and acted the part that is foretold of them. Of this, as I have already shown, as ample proof exists as of any of the events of that period. And *third*, from the fact that the eleventh horn rose up among them a century or two after they came into power, and has sustained itself among them, and acted out the tragedy of fire and blood that is foreshown of it in the prophecy. There is not a fact in the history of the last thousand years of more indisputable certainty than this. And *fourth*, from the consideration that the ten horns of the scarlet beast from the abyss, Rev. xvii. 3–14, are without diadems, and obviously because they are not to be independent sovereigns, but are to give their power and strength to the beast in its last form, in which it is the symbol of the eighth king. For if the horns which bore the diadems on the emergence of the beast from the sea, Rev. xiii. 1–5, are not the symbols of the kings who have reigned during the last thirteen or fourteen hundred years, it is apparent that no such kings as those horns denote are ever to hold the sovereignty of the western Roman empire. As the kings that are to reign after the beast rises out of the abyss, ch. xvii. 8–14, are the last that are to reign, and they are not to wear diadems; if those who preceded them are not the kings whom the diademed horns, ch. xiii. 1–5, represent, what can be more certain than that no such kings are ever to hold supreme power in the western empire?

The persuasion of these writers that a part of the kingdoms into which the Roman empire is divided, lie in its eastern division, is thus wholly mistaken.

CHAPTER XX.

Their Error in regard to the Time of Christ's Advent—The Translation of the Hundred Forty-Four Thousand—The Wise Virgins—The Man-child.

ANOTHER subject on which they entertain notions that are groundless, and likely to betray those who embrace them, into expectations that are to prove delusive, and will recoil on them with a disastrous power, is the time of Christ's advent, and the translation of the 144,000 sealed persons, Rev. vii. 1–8; and xiv. 1–5. I quote from Mr. Baxter:

"Whenever Louis Napoleon shall have confirmed the seven years' covenant with the Jews, the point will then be settled that from the date of that event, there will only be seven years and two and a half months to elapse before the glorious descent of Christ upon the earth at the battle of Armageddon, to slay the impenitent, and introduce the millennium.

"It might then at first sight, be thought that the resurrection and translation of the saints, which is to take place at Christ's advent, would not occur sooner than the termination of the same period of seven years and two and a half months, since we are told that it is not till 'the Lord himself descends from heaven that the dead in Christ shall rise first, and we which are alive and remain, shall be caught up together with them in the clouds, to meet the Lord in the air, and so shall ever be with the Lord,' (1 Thess. iv. 16.) It would, however, be an error thus to suppose the resurrection and rapture of the saints to occur at so distant a period after the date of the covenant; inasmuch as they are clearly declared in the prophecies to take place rather more than two years after the covenant.

"The advent of Christ is shown to occupy about five years in its accomplishment, and to be effected in two stages. He first comes from the highest heavens into the air, and then the raised and translated saints are immediately caught up to meet him, (1 Thess. iv. 17), and consequently the hosts of Satan, the prince of the power of the air, are cast down from the air into the earth, and proceed (after an interval) to carry on through the agency of Napoleon, the Antichrist, the final 3½ years' persecution against the unready Christians who have been left behind upon this globe (Rev. xii). Meanwhile, Christ, with his raised and translated saints remains invisibly in the air, in the pavilion cloud, until *after* that 3½ years' tribulation (Matt. xxiv. 29, 30), and then suddenly displays the sign of the Son of Man in the heavens, and openly reveals his bright glory and majesty to the astonished inhabitants of the world below. At this point he sends forth his angels to gather to him in the air, all the saints that are found on the earth, including the surviving foolish virgins, and those who have been converted since the first translation, and he then 'raines a horrible tempest of fire and brimstone' upon Antichrist's hosts and all the ungodly, but sparing some of the least hardened, especially among the Jews and heathen. This spared remnant constitutes the holy seed, or nucleus of the population of the earth during the subsequent millennium, and with descendants will compose 'the nations of them that are saved,' who will be governed during the thousand years by Christ and his glorified, raised, and translated saints, these latter living principally in the heavenly Jerusalem, and visiting the earth daily, in order to exercise rule over the successive generations of its mortal unglorified inhabitants." Pp. 283, 284.

"The diagram prefixed to this chapter shows the period of the ascension of the literal day man-child, or wise virgins, to be two years and from four to six weeks after the date of the covenant. This is demonstrated by deducing from the year-day fulfillment of Daniel and Revelation during 2595 *years* from 722–4 B. C. to 1871, A. D., what their future literal day fulfillment will be during 2595 *days*, that is, seven years and two and a half months from the date of Antichrist's approaching seven years' covenant with the Jews, until his destruction at Christ's descent at Armageddon."—P. 296.

As I have already shown, that the chronology on which he proceeds in his theory of the 2595 years, is a mere fiction; that the theory of a double fulfillment of the prophecies is equally false; that the notion of a covenant between Louis Napoleon and the Jews is idle and sacrilegious; and that the pretext of determining the exact distance of Christ's coming, and other events from the date of that imaginary covenant, is a delusion; it is not necessary that I should repeat the proofs that they are errors. With their overthrow as sheer interpolations and misrepresentations of the prophecies, the whole fabric of Mr. Baxter's eschatology falls to the ground.

He runs into several other mistakes, which it is important should be understood. The first is the representation that two translations of saints are foreshown in Rev. xiv.:

"Two distinct translations or removals of living saints from the earth at Christ's coming, are plainly described in literal day, Rev. xiv.; the first being an earlier and smaller ingather ing than the second, and consisting of the 144,000 persons, called the *first fruits*, v. 4, who are caught up *before* the fall of Babylon and Antichrist's subsequent 3½ years' persecution; the second being composed of all the saints found on the earth *after* Antichrist's 3½ years' persecution, and who are called the harvest." (Rev. xiv. 15; vii. 9.)—P. 297.

I shall not now enter into the question whether the 144,000 are to be translated or not; nor if they are, whether it is to be before or after Christ comes in the clouds of heaven; but simply point to the fact that Mr. Baxter gives no proof, that those who are to be the subjects of the harvest, are at the period when they are reaped, to be translated to the skies. There is nothing in the passage to sustain that construction. Their being harvested is like the gathering of ripened grain from a field, in order to their preservation and appropriation to the ends for which they are redeemed; but whether they are to remain in the natural life for a time, or be immediately transformed from mortal to immortal, is not indicated. Moreover, if they are to be released from the sentence of death, and changed to immortal, it does not follow that they are forthwith to be transferred from this world to another. There is no authority for such a persuasion.

He has no ground for his representation; that Christ is to come and remove those whom he denominates the wise virgins, several years before the great tribulation of the Israelites, when he is to interpose visibly for their deliverance. He says: "The general descriptions of Christ's second advent, intimate that he comes to remove the wise virgins at a time of comparative peace and prosperity; and then comes after a short interval of awful tribulation, to gather up the remnant of saints, and to destroy Antichrist and the unrepentant."—P. 200. And he refers to Matt. xxiv. 37, and Luke xvii. 28, as representing the second advent as occurring at a period of general quietude and prosperity.

There is no intimation, however, that the wise virgins are to be removed from the earth, either before Christ's coming and raising the holy dead, or afterwards. They are to be admitted to his kingdom at the marriage supper of the Lamb, which is immediately to follow the resurrection of the holy dead, and is to consist in their exaltation to the relations to Christ and stations in his kingdom, which they are to occupy in their glorified life. Matt. xxv. 1–12; Rev. xix. 5–9. But there is not a hint that they are then to be removed from the earth; nor is that supposition consistent with the parable. If Christ and his risen saints are to withdraw from the earth, and pass into heaven, how are the unwise virgins to have access to the door in the skies, through which he is to enter the scene of the supper, and plead to be admitted among the guests? They plainly are to remain on the earth, as Christ himself is.

The great tribulation, moreover, foreshown Daniel xii. 1–3, and Matt. xxiv. 15–31, is a tribulation of the Israelites, not of Gentile believers, nor of the unbelieving generally. There is indeed to be a great tribulation of Gentile believers, as is impressively foreshown in the vision of the innumerable multitude of palm-bearers of all nations, Rev. vii. 9–17, who had come out of great tribulation, and washed their robes and made them white in the blood of the Lamb. But the period of this Gentile tribulation will probably be the same as that of the Israelites, as each is doubtless to be caused by the beast, the false prophet, and the dragon, who are to league together in war, on those who refuse submission to their impious will, and maintain allegiance to God.

Most of the Israelites who will be likely to return first to Palestine, reside in Europe. Who will obstruct their migration and make war on them, unless it be the rulers of the ten kingdoms, and the monarch of Russia, who, as the head of the Greek Church, is symbolized by the dragon? Besides, both tribulations are to precede Christ's coming and intervention for the deliverance of his people. There is also to be a season of great agitation and terror to the unsanctified of all nations; but it is to be of a different nature from the tribulation of believers, and at a later time, as it is to be caused by the signals of his approach to judge and destroy them.

Immediately *after* the tribulation of those days

with which Israel is to be overwhelmed, Dan. xii. 1–7, "shall the sun be darkened, and the moon shall not give her light, and the stars shall fall from heaven, and the powers of the heavens shall be shaken; and then shall appear the sign of the Son of Man in heaven. And then shall all the tribes of the earth mourn; and they shall see the Son of Man coming in the clouds of heaven with power and great glory." "Then shall be distress of nations and perplexity, men's hearts failing them for fear, and for looking after those things which are coming on the earth," Luke xxi. 25–26; and Christ indicates that this is to *precede* the deliverance of his people, for he adds, "When these things begin to come to pass, then look up, and lift up your heads, for your redemption *draweth nigh*," v. 28. Mr. Baxter is wholly mistaken, therefore, in representing that Christ is to come and translate those whom he denominates the wise virgins, who he holds are to be a vast host, before the great tribulation. They are not to be exempted from that trial: which has for its object the test of their fidelity, by which it shall be seen by all eyes that they are his true disciples and meet to be openly received and acknowledged as such, and admitted to his kingdom.

That the unbelieving multitude will go on in thoughtlessness and presumption till the signals of Christ's coming startle them from their delusions, Math. xxiv. 37, does not imply that the people of God are not at that juncture to be overwhelmed with persecution. So far from it, the persuasion that their condition is hopeless, that the powers that are making war on them are sure to prevail and extirpate them from the earth, will very probably be one of the false beliefs that will serve to lull the fears of the unbelieving, and prompt them to give themselves up to worldliness and revelry.

He is equally without authority for his representation that there are to be two companies of 144,000 each, that are to be translated to the skies. He says:

"It should be observed that the righteous dead, who are raised up at the first stage in Christ's coming, are entirely distinct from the 144,000 who are then translated, because none of the sealed 144,000 will ever have undergone death. In the literal day fulfillment of the seals during the final 1840 days (or about five years), the 144,000 mentioned in Rev. vii. consist entirely of *Jews*, who are preserved and caught up in the *second* translation *after* the three and a half years' great tribulation. Thus there are two separate companies of 144,000 translated saints; the one in Rev. xiv., consisting chiefly of Gentiles caught up in the first translation, and the other in Rev. vii., being composed exclusively of Jews caught up in the second translation."—P. 300.

What ground has he for this representation? Not a particle. It is a sheer figment. That the 144,000 of ch. vii. are the same as the 144,000 of ch. xiv. is not simply indicated by their number, but is made indubitable by the identity of the name on their foreheads. The 144,000, chapter vii., are said to be sealed with the seal of God on their foreheads, and that seal is shown in ch. xiv. to be the name of God written on their brows. The inscription on each is the same, and its impression on them answers to the office of sealing, which was to mark and identify persons or things as belonging to him, whose name was stamped on them. That the persons sealed, ch. vii., were of the tribes of Israel, is no proof, as Mr. B. intimates, that those whom they represent are *Jews;* that is, all of one tribe, instead of twelve. Instead, it proves that they are not; inasmuch as *the twelve tribes*, if used as symbols of the descendants of Jacob, would undoubtedly symbolize themselves,—that is, each 12,000 denoting 12,000 of their own tribe; and accordingly there would be eleven times as many sealed of the other tribes as there would of the tribe of Judah. But those sealed out of the twelve tribes are not used as symbols of themselves, but as representatives, on the ground of analogy, of bodies of Christian believers, precisely as the being sealed is a symbol of an effect that differs from itself; the inscription of the name of God on their foreheads indicating that those whom the sealed represent are to be made to give as conspicuous and indubitable proof that they are the true children of God, as would be formed by the inscription by the finger of the Almighty, in characters of light, of his name on their foreheads.

His views of the man-child, and of the relation of

the man-child to the 144,000 sealed, is still more preposterous and revolting. He says:

"The coming of Christ in the air, the resurrection of the sleeping saints, and translation of the 144,000 wise virgins (or man-child, Rev. xii. 5,) are about two years and from four to six weeks after the Covenant.—Rev. xiv. 1–5; Thess. iv. 16.

"This event is shown in many passages of Scripture to take place *before* the three and a half years' great tribulation, and the precise time of its occurrence is discovered by the chronological position of the rapture of the man-child, in the literal day fulfillment, being ascertained from its chronological position in the year-day fulfillment. The different visions of the seals, trumpets, and vials, etc., in Revelation, are fulfilled first, on the year day scale, within about 1872 years; and secondly, on the literal day scale, within about 1872 days; and the second fulfillment is a miniature fac-simile of the first, the relative order of events in each fulfillment being almost exactly the same. Thus as the year day of rapture of the man-child is evidently the ascension of Christ in A. D. 29–33, at the distance of 1838 to 1843 years *before* the end of this dispensation in 1871–2; therefore, the literal rapture of the man-child, which incontrovertibly denotes the ascension of the wise virgins, will be at the distance of from 1838 to 1843 days, that is, rather more than five years before the end. And as the end of this dispensation will be seven years and two and a half months, or 2595 days after the date of the covenant, therefore the ascension of the wise virgins will thus be from 752 to 757 days; in other words (allowing an ample margin to avoid particularity as to a precise day), two years and from four to six weeks *after* the date of the covenant."—Pp. 77–78.

After building such a towering structure out of materials fabricated wholly by his fancy—what a dainty scrupulosity he exhibits in avoiding "particularity as to a precise day," and reserving an "ample margin" to himself of "two weeks," within which the sublime event he affects to foretell is to take place! Who is there whom such a dream would not discredit? He not only proceeds on the unauthorized assumption that there is to be a covenant between Louis Napoleon and the Jews; that the period of the covenant is to be seven years; that there is to be a double fulfillment of the symbolic prophecies; and that the year day fulfillment furnishes him with an infallible clue to the time and length of the literal day fulfillment which he anticipates;—but he treats one set of symbols as representatives of another with which it has no connection whatever, and perverts and caricatures them with a measure of inconsideration and audacity that was never transcended. Thus, he exhibits the wise virgins as the same as the 144,000 sealed. What has he to justify this assumption? Nothing whatever. The characteristics of the wise virgins, who were but five in number, are that they went forth to meet the bridegroom; that they had oil in their lamps; and that though they slumbered immediately before the bridegroom approached, yet on hearing the announcement that he was coming, they trimmed their lamps, and going out, joined the marriage train, and entered with the bridegroom to the supper. There is no intimation that extraordinary means had been employed to prepare them to fill that office, and that they were admitted to the supper because they had before given peculiarly eminent proofs of their attachment to Christ. On the other hand, it is expressly foreshown that the 144,000 sealed are to receive the impress of the Almighty's name on their foreheads by an extraordinary agency; that their sealing is to signify that they have given the most indubitable proof of their inflexible allegiance to God; and that they are, on the ground of their truthfulness and spotlessness, to be distinguished from all that preceded them by the intimacy and grandeur of the relations to Christ to which they are to be exalted. What can more emphatically show that they not only are not the same as the wise virgins, but are immeasurably to transcend them in their sphere in this life, as they are in the glory with which they are to be distinguished in Christ's kingdom on the earth!

But his confusion of the man-child, Rev. xii. 1–5, with Christ, is still more mistaken and revolting. In the first place, the vision of the man-child was prophetic of the future; not historic of the past. Mr. Baxter's assumption that the man-child was Christ implies, therefore, that Christ was, or is, again to become incarnate, and to be exposed to be put to death by enemies, and then once more ascend to the throne of heaven; and that implies that his redemptive work at his first incarnation was inadequate to the salvation of men, and needs to be supplemented by another humiliation, persecution, and death. For how could he any more ascend to heaven after a second incarnation, without passing through death and a resurrection, than he could at his first assumption of our nature? Moreover, if Mr. Baxter's theory that the prophecies are to have a double fulfillment is legitimate, then the second incarnation, persecution, death, resurrection and ascension of Christ, which he implies is foreshown under the symbol of the man-child, is again to be repeated; and so, for aught that can be shown, in an endless series. Such is the portentous result to which Mr. Baxter's false construction would lead, were it legitimate. But though he sees nothing of this, it is but a specimen of the misapprehensions and misrepresentations that pervade his views of the prophecies. The man-child was not the Son of God, but a human being, and the symbol of a human being; and his being caught up to God and to his throne did not betoken a literal translation to the presence and throne of the Almighty, but was a symbol of the assumption of the place and prerogatives of God by the person denoted by the man-child, in much the same manner as the Man of Sin is to usurp the rights and place of God in his relations to men, and claim the homage that is due only to him.

So much for the chief errors that are put forth by Mr. Baxter and others, cited by him, in the volume under notice. I might point out many other misconceptions and misconstructions, that wrest and deface the prophecies; but I have adduced sufficient proofs of the superficiality and untruthfulness of the system they maintain, and prefer to turn to the Scriptures and inquire what the great events are which they most surely reveal, as to precede and attend Christ's advent, and the establishment of his kingdom on the earth.

CHAPTER XXI.

The point to which the Fulfillment of the Prophecies has advanced—The Fifth and Sixth Vials—The Prophecies yet to be accomplished—The Sixth Seal symbolizes the Descent of the Powers denoted by the Wild Beast of Ten Horns to Hades—The Prediction of its return in a new form, and resumption of the Throne of the Western Roman Empire—The Renationalization of the Catholic Hierarchies—A fresh persecution of the true Worshipers.

WHAT, then, is the point which the fulfillment of the prophecies, especially of the Apocalypse, has reached? What are the great events that are yet to take place before the coming of Christ? And what are the peculiarities of the dispensation he is to institute on his assuming the sceptre of the earth?

I.

The fifth vial of the Apocalypse was poured, there is reason to believe, at the period of the revolution in France and several other of the ten kingdoms in 1848. All the great features of that event correspond to the prediction. The vial fell "upon the seat of the beast." The movement in France, Italy, and Germany was directed against the old arbitrary Catholic monarchies, symbolized by the beast; denying the validity of the despotic power which they claimed as inherited from their predecessors, and aiming to wrest it from them, and substitute representative governments in its place. "And his kingdom was full of darkness."

This was eminently true of the nations that suddenly, and without forethought, precipitated themselves into that abyss of distraction and anarchy. After having driven several monarchs from their thrones, and forced others to grant constitutions that admitted their subjects to the elective franchise, and pledged to them prerogatives and privileges they had never before enjoyed; they failed to act with the harmony and energy that were necessary to secure those concessions; and weakening themselves by divisions, betrayed by traitors, and resisted by those in whose hands the supreme power was held, they became so bewildered and paralyzed, that the monarchs and other chiefs who wielded the soldiery, easily baffled them in their struggles for emancipation, and reinstating themselves in the arbitrary power they had lost, soon repressed or crushed the multitude with a sterner sway than they had before ventured to exercise. And this disappointment filled vast crowds in France, Italy, and Germany, with mortification, chagrin, and rage. "And they gnawed their tongues for pain, and blasphemed the God of heaven, because of their pains and their sores, and repented not of their deeds." Rev. xvi. 10, 11. And this is the temper, in a large degree, of the population of those and the other Catholic kingdoms at the present day. They writhe under the despotic rule that is exercised over them, and kept in subordination only by force, are ready whenever an opportunity presents itself, to spring upon their masters, and strike them from their thrones. Another shower from this vial may ere long rouse them to a more effective effort to gain their rights.

II.

The sixth vial has also been poured, and is still pouring on the great river Euphrates. Scarce a symbol of the Apocalypse has been more sadly misconstrued than this. Expositors, almost without an exception, have maintained that the Euphrates denotes the Turkish empire; and thence have assumed that the drying up of the waters of the river symbolizes the decay of the Turkish power. This misconception is founded on the pretext that the waters of that river are employed, Isaiah viii. 7, 8, as a symbol of the army of the king of Assyria. But no error could be greater. That prophecy is not symbolic: it is conveyed exclusively through language, and its grammatical is its predictive sense. It is by a metaphor, not by a symbol, that the waters of the river are declared to be the king of Assyria and all his glory, to indicate that the Assyrian monarch, with his armed host, was to sweep over Judea, like a flood from the Euphrates, that should submerge all its vales and plains, and strew them with desolation. The use of a metaphor to exemplify the resistless power of the Assyrian invader, is no ground for the assumption that under the sixth vial, the Euphrates is employed as a symbol of the Turkish power. No postulate could be more mistaken and preposterous. How does the fact that the river in Isaiah is used by a metaphor to illustrate the power of Assyria, prove that in the Apocalypse it is employed as a symbol of Turkey? Moreover, as the symbol of the vial is taken from the capture of Babylon by Cyrus, and is designed to indicate the analogous method by which the Babylon of the Apocalypse is to be overthrown, the supposition that the Euphrates is the symbol of the Turkish power, implies that the decay of that power, is to be the occasion of the subversion of the Catholic hierarchies of the ten kingdoms of the western Roman empire! No two things, however, can be more utterly disconnected with each other. How is the fall of the Turkish empire to occasion the fall of Babylon the great? Are kings from the east to invade the western kingdoms and overturn their nationalized hierarchies, as Cyrus by the diversion of the river from its channel, entered Babylon, and forcing his way into the palace, slaughtered the monarch and his courtiers? Nobody can believe it.

The Euphrates is the river on which ancient Babylon stood. As it passed through the centre of the city, Cyrus by turning its waters from their channel, marched his troops along its bed, and mounting the stairways from the water, and finding the gates at their head unbarred, entered the streets with little obstruction, and conquering the guards and putting the monarch and his attendants to the sword, became master of the city and empire. From this act the symbols of the vial are taken; the Babylon which Cyrus conquered, being the representative of the mystical Babylon of the Catholic Church: the waters of the river which were essential to the safety and support of the city, symbolizing the kindreds and nations that sustain an analogous relation to that apostate Babylon as the means of her subsistence and strength; waters being expressly exhibited as the symbol of "peoples, and multitudes, and nations, and tongues," in their relations to her as her subjects, ch. xvii. 15. The drying of the waters denotes the alienation of the Catholic multitude from her sway; and the kings of the east who conquered Babylon, symbolize the leaders who are to withdraw the Catholic crowd from attachment and submission to her imperious rule. This is indubitably the meaning of the symbols. It lies on their face, and like the glow of a noonday sun on a landscape, presents all its objects in their true forms and relations to one another. The symbols and the event are an exact parallel to each other. Moreover, the truthfulness of this construction is verified by a vast, conspicuous, and active alienation of the Catholic population from the nationalized hierarchies of the ten kingdoms, as they are united in the image of the beast in a single structure, with the pope as its head. This recoil from the pope and the vast organization of prelates, priests, and other officials, of which he is the chief, that claim absolute dominion over the churches, and over the whole population, and demand on penalty of perdition, submission to their imperious will—pervades in a great measure, not only Rome and Italy, but France, Spain, Portugal, Belgium, and Germany. In Sardinia, Florence, Sicily, and Rome itself, where it is most fully developed, it is not a rejection of the Catholic religion, but rather a revulsion from the usurped and despotic dominion asserted over them by the pope and his train of hierarchies. This is in harmony with the symbol. The water of the river continued to be water after it was turned from its channel, though it no longer gave security to Babylon, or ministered to its wants. So the alienated Catholics continue to be Catholics, though they no longer uphold the pope and his train of officials.

This coldness, aversion, and hostility to the Catholic priesthood, is to become, we may justly presume, far more general, and rise to greater intensity, and is to prepare the way for the denationalization and overthrow, at length, of the hierarchies; as the drying of the Euphrates rendered ancient Babylon accessible to her besiegers, and led to her being conquered by Darius and Cyrus. That the vial has not yet been fully poured, is manifest from the fact that the unclean spirits like frogs that appeared immediately after the vial, are not yet gone forth from out of the mouth of the dragon, and out of the mouth of the beast, and out of the mouth of the false prophet, to gather the kings of the earth together to the battle of the great day of God Almighty. It is the loss of its hold on the faith of the people, and perhaps its dejection from its place as a nationalized body, that exciting alarm for its existence, is to prompt it, and its associate powers, the dragon and wild beast, to send forth its emissaries to gather the kings together to intercept Christ from establishing his kingdom on the earth.

III.

Among the predicted events that are not remote, and that are to give birth to consequences of the greatest moment, the first undoubtedly is, that modification of the sovereignties of the ten kingdoms which is indirectly signified by the *implied* descent of the wild beast into hades; and directly by the specific prediction of its ascent from that world, and reassumption of supreme power. Rev. xi. 7; xvii. 8. The beast ascends out of the abyss; that is, hades, the world of the dead. This implies that it had undergone a syncope, or suspension for a period of its living power; and is a natural and striking symbol of their loss by the rulers whom the beast represents of their authority, detrusion from their thrones, and deprivation of their lives.

That the abyss from which the wild beast is to ascend is the world of the dead, is shown by the repeated use of the term to denote that realm. Thus it is employed in that sense, Rom. x. 7: "Say not in thy heart; Who shall ascend into heaven: that is to bring down Christ: ἤ τις καταβήσεται εἰς τὴν ἄβυσσον; τοῦτ᾽ ἔστιν Χριστὸν ἐκ νεκρῶν ἀναγαγεῖν, or who shall descend into the abyss: that is, to bring up Christ from the dead." The abyss is thus indubitably the world of the dead, or scene where spirits who have departed from this life have their abode. It is a real place, therefore, and Christ at his death descended there; for it was from among the dead that he returned to life. It is used accordingly, Acts ii. 31, as synonymous with hades, which is the usual name of the world into which the spirits of men pass at death. David being therefore a prophet, and knowing that God had sworn to him by an oath that in respect to the flesh Christ was to come of the fruit of his loins, to sit upon his throne; having the gift of foresight, ελάλησε περι τῆς ἀναστάσεως τοῦ Χριστοῦ ὅτὶ οὐ κατελειφθη ἡ ψυχὴ ἀυτοῦ ἐις ἅδου, ουδὲ ἡ σὰρξ ἀυτου εἶδε διαφθοράν—he said "in regard to Christ's resurrection, that his soul should not be left in hades, nor his flesh see corruption." The abyss and hades are names, therefore, of the same place, to which the spirits of men pass when separated from the body by death. Hades is the term also employed in the Septuagint, Psalm xvi. 10, from which this passage was cited by the Apostle. The abyss of Romans x. 7 is, therefore, the name of identically the same world of the dead that is in other places denominated hades. It is used in that sense also in the Septuagint, Genesis xxxvii. 35; Ezekiel xxxii. 27, and other passages.

This sense of abyss is confirmed by its use as the special name of that division of the invisible world, in which demons, or fallen spirits have their prison. Thus the many demons who had possessed the man of the region of the Gadarenes, on being expelled from him, implored Christ that he would not command them, *ἐὶς τὴν ἄβυσσον απελθειν*, to go into the abyss, which implies that that abyss is to be the scene to which they are to be consigned forever when Christ comes and puts an end to their war against his kingdom on the earth. It is the name also of the invisible world in which Satan and his legions are to be shut and sealed during Christ's millennial reign on the earth. "And the angel seized the dragon, the serpent who was of old, who is the Devil and Satan, and bound him a thousand years, and cast him *εἰς τὴν ἄβυσσον*, into the abyss, and shut and put a seal above him," Rev. xx. 3. It is accordingly called v. 7, *ἡ Φυλακὴ αυτοῦ*, his prison.

And *finally*, this is corroborated by the fact that when abyss is employed in the New Testament to denote a recess in *the earth*, it is defined as having its place in its depths, in contradistinction from the invisible realms in which the spirits of the dead, and Satan and his legions have their abode. Thus under the fifth trumpet, the abyss of which the angel of the meteor had the key with which he opened its gates, that the smoke of the abyss might rise into the atmosphere, is defined as *το Φρέαρ της ἄβὑσσου,* the pit of the abyss; that is, a passage descending from the surface, and terminating in a deep chasm below; as is shown by the emergence of the smoke from the abyss into the atmosphere; and in so vast a volume as to fill the air and overcloud the sun, Rev. ix. 1–3. In like manner when in the Septuagint the word abyss is used to denote the deep of the ocean, or the ocean itself, as Gen. i. 2, and vii. 11, it is clear from the context that it denotes the ocean of our world; not a vast deep or abyss in some other sphere.

It is manifest, therefore, that the abyss into which the wild beast is to descend, when for a time it ceases to be on the earth, and from which it is subsequently to ascend, is the world of the dead; not a deep or abyss on the earth. And from that it is manifest that the catastrophe by which it is to be hurled from its throne, is the symbol of a stroke by which the monarchs, magnates and others whom it represents, are to be struck from life. This is self-evident from the consideration that no human beings pass from this world into hades, except by death. It would be a contradiction to the nature and office of that world, to suppose individuals of our race conveyed there and made its tenants in their natural, corporeal life. In accordance with this wherever the usurping and apostate powers are represented as put to death, the death inflicted on them is a literal, not a spiritual or metaphorical death. Thus the delivery of the wild beast, Dan. vii. 9–11, to the burning flame, by which its life was destroyed and its body consumed, symbolizes the corporeal destruction of the human persons who are represented by the beast: the slaying of the armies of the beast at the battle of Armageddon, is to be a literal slaughter; for the birds are to feed on them: and the burning of the persons who are to constitute Babylon the great at her destruction, is to be a literal burning.

These great events are undoubtedly future: and the first in the train—the descent of the powers denoted by the wild beast to hades, is, it is abundantly clear, that which is symbolized under the sixth seal by the earthquake; the darkening of the sun and moon; the fall of stars; the disruption and uprolling of vapors in the atmosphere; and the flight of mountains and islands.*. This group of symbols, has in-

* Though aware from my earliest study of the Apocalypse that the ascent of the beast from the abyss was still future, and led on several occasions to refer to it as one of the most important events that is to precede Christ's advent; it was not till five or six years ago when I entered on the preparation of a volume not yet published, that I reached the

deed since 1789, been interpreted by many as having met its fulfillment in the French revolution. It is, however, altogether mistaken. There was no such

conclusion that the movement by which the precipitation of the beast to hades is to be wrought, is that of the political revolution symbolized by the earthquake of this seal. That dejection of the beast, not being like its return, *directly* foreshown, it was not unnatural to infer that it was to occur, like many other great events, without a formal symbolization of its cause. On a fresh analysis however of the symbols of the seal, it became apparent on the one hand, that they present no parallel to those of the first, fourth and fifth vials, notwithstanding a seeming similarity of the effects of the first vial to the agitation and disorder produced by an earthquake; and of the blackening of the heavenly orbs, to their obscuration by vapor and smoke, occasioned by the volcanic action which upheaves the ground; and therefore that they have no reference to the overthrow of the French monarchy in 1789; and on the other hand, that the political revolution symbolized by the earthquake will naturally precipitate the persons denoted by the beast to the realms of the dead.

The following passage from the xxvii. chap. of the Coming and Reign of Christ, published in 1858, presents the views I then entertained of the descent of the beast to hades, and its return and resumption of its throne:

"A revolution of the civil governments of the ten kingdoms is to take place, probably at or near the close of the sixth vial, in which the old monarchies are to fall and be succeeded by new chiefs of perhaps an elective or military order, and they and the whole empire are to be under a common chief or emperor, as at the time of the vision, before the sovereignty passed from the heads to the horns."

"The wild beast, chap. xiii. 1–10, represents the civil and military rulers of the Roman empire from its origin down to near the end of the period denoted by the forty-two months. The beast of chap. xvii. is the symbol also of the civil rulers of that empire, but at a later stage, and after the beast of the first period has died, as it were, and returned from hades to a new life, and in an altered form. The beast of chap. xiii. rose out of the sea. The beast of chap. xvii. is to ascend out of the abyss, overthrow at that period, of the whole circle of monarchies in the ten kingdoms, and reduction of all ranks and individuals to the same level; as is symbolized in this vision. The only monarchy that fell by the agitation and uprising of the people, was that of France. The revolutions that were excited at near the same epoch in Italy and Holland, and subsequently in Switzerland, and parts of Germany, were the work, not of the population of those countries, but of the conquering armies of France, and the arbitrary dictation of the ruling powers at Paris. Nor has there been any such general subversion of the governments of western Europe since the close of the French revolution. Though the fall of the French monarchy in 1848, and the temporary paralysis of others, seemed like a descent into the world of the dead, that diminishing of vitality was not common to the whole circle of monarchies, and was soon followed by as firm an establishment nearly of the old dynasties, as they had enjoyed before.

The events predicted here are of the greatest signi-

hades, the invisible world, where the devil is to be cast and imprisoned, chap. xx. 3, and where the spirits of the unsanctified abide. This indicates that before assuming the form which it is to wear at the period to which chap. xvii. refers, *it is to perish*, and is to return to life in its last shape, as it were by a resurrection. The angel said of it accordingly, 'the beast that thou sawest, was and is not, and shall ascend out of the abyss—hades—and go into perdition;' and he represents its reappearance after its destruction, as exciting the astonishment of the nations over which it is to rule."

ficance. As the objects that are taken as symbols, comprise all the great constituents of our solar system, the earth, with its islands, mountains and air; the sun, the moon, the stars,—their universal blight, and divestiture of power to perform their natural functions, or disappearance from the scene; indicate that in like manner, the whole of the monarchies and other forms of government in the western Roman empire are to be overturned, and the population reduced to confusion and anarchy. The quaking of the earth, the obscuration of all the luminaries of heaven, the uprolling of the clouds and the flight of islands and mountains, bespeak a like overthrow and obliteration of the powers of the political world. Not one in the ten kingdoms will survive.

Nor is this catastrophe, unexampled and stupendous as it is to be, incredible or unlikely in the judgment of many who reason from the great movements that are in progress among the nations. It, or a change much like it, is in fact anticipated by thousands and myriads of the leading actors in the politics of Europe, and observers of the direction in which the principles and passions that give them their hue are tending.

There is not a government in western Europe that is not liable to be overthrown, and suddenly, by a popular movement. The whole group of dynasties rests in a measure, on a volcano, that may at any crisis explode, and open a gulf that will swallow them up. When, however, that is to take place no one can foresee. Powerful agencies are at work to retard, and if possible intercept it; but unexpected causes may precipitate it at a moment when it is least looked for.

The ascent of the beast from the abyss does not imply that the combination of human agents whom it symbolizes, is to be the same throughout, or in any degree, as those whom the beast represented at the moment of its descent into hades. They will doubtless be not simply in a large measure, but absolutely, different persons; and far more fierce, bloody, and impious than their predecessors. Its truculence is shown by its scarlet color, and its impiousness by its being covered with names of blasphemy. The blasphemous epithets of the beast that preceded it, chap. xiii. 1, were confined to its heads. The vision of this chap. xvii. 3, thus foreshows that the whole body of the officials whom the monster symbolizes, as well as the supreme rulers, are to arrogate the rights of the Almighty, and traduce his name, his sanctuary, and the saints who dwell in his presence in heaven.

The civil and military organization represented by the beast, as it ascends from the abyss, is to differ essentially from that of the empire under the beast before its descent into hades. Ten kings are still to reign; but in place of absolute sovereigns, they are to give their power and strength to an imperial chief, who, from the supremacy to which he is to be exalted, is called the beast itself; the whole sovereignty being lodged in his hands, and the kings being his subordinates and instruments. This is doubtless the reason that no diadems were seen on the horns. That no crown was seen on the brow of the imperial chief, doubtless was that he is to claim to be God: God never appearing crowned, and because of its inconsistence with his self-existence and independence. Crowns are given only as rewards, and are badges, therefore, of a derived authority. Jehovah's office and authority are underived.

Whether the kings are to give their power and strength to the imperial chief from constraint, because he has conquered their territories, or voluntarily, because they need his concurrence and aid to keep their subjects in submission, is left in uncertainty. Both may have a place in the reasons that are to prompt them to take the attitude of subordinates and dependants. Their surrender of their sovereignty to him bespeaks an overpowering motive, whether it is to spring from the instability of their thrones, or from his all-grasping and resistless power.

The first function of the beast after its emergence from hades, is its bearing the woman named Mystery, Babylon the Great, the mother of harlots and abominations of the earth, Rev. xvii. 3–6. Her seat on him indicates that she is nationalized and acting in conjunction with the imperial chief, whom the beast denotes, as his instrument; while he, it is apparent from ch. xi. 7, is to be the great agent in shedding, at her beck, the blood of the saints with which she is to become drunk. The woman is the symbol of the Catholic hierarchies, united in a single structure under the pope, as symbolized by the image modelled after the beast under its seventh head. She is to be nationalized, fostered, and armed with power to carry her aims into effect, as being just what she is—Mystery, Babylon the Great, the mother of harlots and abominations of the earth ;—not as a profligate who is softened to penitence, and reformed ; but with all her infuriate passions raised to greater intensity than ever before, eager to win the crowd to drink of her execrable cup, and burning to steep her lips in the blood of those who refuse to yield to her sorceries.

The crowd, whose names are not written in the Book of Life, are to contemplate the beast on its emergence from hades, in its new form, with wonder and astonishment. They are to be aware that the power which it denotes had existed for a long series of ages before. They are to know that there was a time when it was not ; and when like the dead who have passed into the invisible world, it was regarded as struck forever from existence here ; and yet on its reappearance they are to see, with amazement at the unexpectedness and singularity of the event, that it is the same sovereign power as had before reigned over the empire, and been represented by the beast that had gone down to hades.

All these characteristics of the beast, the woman, and the crowd that is to contemplate them with admiration, are depicted ch. xvii. 1–10, and in the following verses :—" The beast that was and is not, even he is the eighth [king,] (not head, as many writers imagine—the noun with which eighth agrees, being *Βασιλευς,* king, not *Κεφαλή,* head, which is feminine), and is of the seven ;" that is, of the same order as the absolute sovereigns of the whole empire, who were the rulers of previous ages symbolized by the seven heads of this beast. " And he goeth into perdition." Instead of perpetuating his power, and transmitting it to a long line of successors, he is to perish in the war he is to wage, along with his vassal kings, on the Lamb.

It is apparent from this delineation of the beast and the woman, that on the rise of the imperial monarch, symbolized by the beast, from hades, the Roman Catholic hierarchy is to be nationalized throughout the ten kingdoms. This is shown by her seat on the beast. She is to be sustained by it in the position in which she is to exert the acts ascribed to her. It is clear also from her cup and her intoxication with blood, that an attempt is immediately to be made by her to allure the whole population of the empire to partake of her sorceries and idolatries : and that on meeting with dissent and resistance, a bloody and remorseless persecution is to be instituted, to drive the reluctant into submission, or else to exterminate them by the sword. That implies that the Protestant establishments of Great Britain, France, and other parts of the ten kingdoms are to be denationalized, and all other faiths, rites, and forms of worship beside the Catholic proscribed and treated as a crime against the Church and State.

And this persecution by the Papacy will be the natural consequence of her restoration to power. It will be but the resumption of the ambitious schemes which she had often endeavored to carry into effect before. She will not have relinquished her pretext that she is the vicegerent of God,—she will not have abandoned any of her arrogations of the right to dictate the faith and worship of men. Her long experience of the inefficacy of persecution to convert her dissenting subjects to her creed, will not have lessened her belief in its rightfulness or utility; nor diminished her delight in torturing and slaughtering the unoffending and holy. Her iron heart will not have been softened to pity, nor touched with horror at the barbarities to which she has for ages been addicted. Her principles will remain as false, her ambition as boundless, and her rage against God and his people as infuriate as ever; and she will act them out with an eagerness, and on a scale proportioned to the flush of hope with which the unexpected recovery of her lost power will inspire her.

It will be equally natural and certain that the true

people of God will meet this attempt of the Church and State to force them into apostacy, with a prompt and unfaltering resistance, and will assert and declare the rights of God, on the one hand, which the persecutors will claim have become theirs; and on the other, will expose and denounce the false principles, the execrable superstitions, and the impious idolatries of the apostate church, with a truthfulness, fidelity, and power, that will be suited to the exigency; and will be ready to lay down their lives, rather than swerve from their allegiance to God. He will not leave his children to apostatize from him. He will not allow his truth to fall unproclaimed and unvindicated. He will raise up witnesses like the martyrs of former ages in fearlessness and steadfastness; he will send forth teachers and leaders like Moses, like Elijah, and like Paul, whose spirit, whose wisdom, and whose courage will fit them for the crisis, and enable them to vindicate and glorify his name, and abash and confound their enemies.

The certainty that the events foreshown under this seal are still future is of the greatest importance, in respect to the question, whether Louis Napoleon fills the office, and has the destiny which they ascribe to him, who regard him as symbolized by the seventh head of the beast, and as to become the great persecutor of the church, and the Antichrist. As he, as the Emperor of France, is a horn of the beast, if he continues in life and power until the great moment arrives in which the seal is to receive its fulfillment, he will of necessity go down with all the other monarchs and magnates of the ten kingdoms, to hades; and if once lodged there, cannot return to seize again the sceptre of France, bring the other kingdoms into subservience to himself, and act the part of the last persecutor, and of Antichrist. What more effective confutation of the preposterous notion that he is to fill that office can be conceived than is thus furnished by this vision? Whatever else may happen, he is most certainly to be swept from the scene either before, or at the descent to the abyss of the powers denoted by the beast. However much he may accomplish ere his doom comes, he is to be precluded from all the offices and agencies in the ten kingdoms that are to follow the rise of the new-modeled beast from the abyss. Should he go on in a career of aggrandizement for twenty years; should he extend the domain of France to the Rhine; should he gain by policy or power a determining influence over Spain and Portugal; should he hold Italy in a position of subjection; should a revolution take place in Great Britain that should weaken her to such a degree as to compel her at his beck to nationalize the Roman Catholic Church; he yet would achieve nothing that would constitute him the great agent who is to be the persecutor and Antichrist, *after the fall of the old and the rise of the new dynasties*. But I shall recur to this subject in a later chapter.

The truth of the construction I have placed on the vision, the certainty that it has not yet had its fulfillment, and the greatness and momentousness of the events that are to spring from its accomplishment, will become more and more apparent as I advance in the consideration of the prophecies that are to have their verification after the fulfillment of the sixth seal has taken place.

CHAPTER XXII.

The questions to be debated between the Witnesses and the Imperial Chief, the Kings, and the Catholic Hierarchy, that are to rise to power at the ascent of the wild beast from the abyss, and persecute them—Great changes to be wrought in the views of believers and others, in respect to the nationalization of Churches—The death of the Witnesses: their resurrection and ascension to Heaven—The effect of these events on the persecutors.

THIS fearful strife, these gigantic struggles, of the two parties, are accordingly distinctly foreshown in other passages, and intimations given of the great question that is to be the subject of the conflict. It is to be; not whether the Scriptures are a divine revelation: not whether men owe a homage to the Creator: not whether subjects are bound to render obedience to rulers in their proper sphere: but the far higher question; Who is God? Who is the rightful law-giver and ruler of the church? Jehovah? The Lord Jesus Christ who has all power in heaven and on earth? Or the imperial chief of the ten kingdoms, and the Roman Catholic pope and heirarchy? For the arrogation of authority over God's worshippers, and over his laws by the civil rulers and Catholic hierarchy, implies that their prerogatives in that sphere are higher than God's—that they have a right to dictate the faith and worship of those of his creatures who are their subjects; to set aside his appointments, and institute a false method of redemption, and a false worship in place of his; and to force those under their power, to yield submission to their will; or else to punish their refusal by torture and death. If God is the sole law-giver of the church; if his rights and authority are supreme, and independent of the concurrence of civil rulers, and ecclesiastical officials; then when rulers and ecclesiastics assume the right of legislating over his laws, and his creatures in their immediate relations to him; to set aside his appointments, and dictate a faith and a worship that have their ground solely in their will; and enforce them by the greatest and most fatal penalties that are within their reach; they plainly arrogate what belongs exclusively to the Most High. They assume, in fact, that he has no rights, no title to homage, except by their sufferance. And that assumption of his place and prerogatives will lie at the foundation of the nationalization, or legalization of the Catholic hierarchy, at the crisis to which Rev. xvii. refers; and of all the measures which the civil rulers and the Catholic powers will take to force their subjects to submit to their sway. It is the postulate that is the basis of all the church nationalization of the past and of the present time; whether it be Catholic, Greek, or Protestant. In attempting to dictate the faith and worship of their subjects, the rulers assume that their subjects owe them allegiance in the sphere of religion; that they have dominion over the consciences and the religious obligations of those under their rule: and that disobedience to their dictates, is a crime of as great enormity, as apostasy from God, and punishable with the same great and lasting penalty.

This question, therefore, it is intuitively certain, will be raised and debated with the greatest earnestness and energy, when the Catholic church is renationalized by the imperial chief and the kings of the ten kingdoms, and attempts by tricks and artifices, and tortures and death, to drive dissentients into submission to her will, or to exterminate them from the earth. There will be no ground but God's exclusive right to legislate over religion, appoint the method of redemption, and enjoin the faith and worship of men, on which his true people can justify themselves in yielding implicit obedience to him, and rejecting with execration and horror the false methods of salvation, the false doctrines, and the idolatrous worship, invented and enforced by the Catholic powers. If they admit that civil rulers and nationalized hierarchies have a right to determine what the faith and worship of their subjects shall be; and punish resistance to their will by the penalties which God annexes to the greatest crimes that human beings commit against him: they can have no just reason for their repulsion of the system that is enforced on them. Their concession of the rights the persecuting powers are to arrogate, would be a confession of their guilt in refusing obedience to them; and an acknowledgment of the justice of the doom to which their rebellion is to consign them.

This question will therefore become invested at that crisis, with the highest significance; will fill the whole sphere of vision, and will be debated with the utmost fullness and vehemence. This is shown by the prophecy, ch. xi. of this great contest; in which its nature is more largely unfolded. They who are then to maintain their allegiance to God, and be martyred for their fidelity, are denominated witnesses; and persons who prophecy; that is, proclaim and verify the revelations which God has made on the one hand, respecting his rights, his will, the measures he has instituted for the salvation of men, and the faith and worship he enjoins; and on the other, respecting the rise of identically such persecuting civil rulers, and prelates, as are assailing them; the guilt of their pride, their apostasy, and their malice; and the doom to which his justice consigns them. It is to be for the word of God, and for the testimony of Jesus, like the prophet, Rev. i. 9., that they are to be arraigned; and it is to be for their inflexible adherence to that word and testimony, and rejection of the impious claims of their persecutors, that they are to be condemned and put to death.

Let us endeavor to conceive of the struggle that

will naturally take place in Great Britain, for example, when the Protestant establishments are struck to the ground; the Catholic hierarchy is reinstated in unrestricted authority, and armed with power to give effect to its decrees; and in its pride and audacity in evil, undertakes to prohibit all freedom of faith and worship, and demand that all churches and individuals shall enter her communion, partake of her rites, and offer her idolatrous worship. And we shall see that a strife of intellect and of feeling, will arise, that has no parallel in the struggles and revolutions of past ages. It may indeed be thought improbable and impossible that such a change can take place, either in the policy of the rulers, or the principles and inclinations of the people. So far, however, from being impossible or improbable, there are causes already in existence, that if combined under favorable circumstances, will naturally give birth to that result. There is already a large infusion of Catholics in the population of England and Scotland, who are in a measure organized, and ready to act in concert at any important crisis. A very considerable portion of the clergy of the establishments, and a large part of the members of the state churches, are deeply imbued with the superstition and faith of popery, and would in an exigency, like that of a change of the national church from Protestant, to Catholic, feel little hesitation in joining the latter.

The majority of the lower orders have little interest

in religion, and would be likely to give their adherence to that which is most kindred to their ignorance, their superstition, and their lawlessness. Whether the revolution is to spring spontaneously from causes that lie in the British mind, or is to be the work, in a measure, of influences from without, it may naturally take a shape that will carry the majority of the nation to the side of Roman Catholicism. If the government be paralyzed in a degree by disasters in war, or embarrassed and endangered by a foreign Catholic power; how possible it is that that power would demand as a condition of the continuance of the royal line on the throne, and the preservation of the aristocracy, the adoption of the Catholic as the state religion; and that that condition will be acceded to by the monarch and nobles for the sake of preserving the throne and the nominal independence of the kingdom? If, as is far more probable, the monarchy and aristocracy are endangered by a domestic revolution; how possible it is that the proffer of universal suffrage on the one side, and of Catholic nationalization on the other, will combine such a multitude as to carry the scale in favor of Catholic supremacy? That there will be a numerous and powerful party on the side of the Catholics embracing the universities, the cathedrals, all Puseyites and semi-Romanists; and a large part of the merely worldly officials in the church, a leading share of the aristocracy, and a great body of the middle and lower ranks, no one can doubt; and if to that be added the weight of a foreign power, on whose will the continuance of the monarch and nobility should be in a measure dependent, victory would naturally declare on the side of the Catholics.

While this great question is in determination, and still more after the Catholics have regained their lost inheritance of universities, cathedrals, churches, and bequests of every description, and reëntered on the work of crushing the nation into submission to its behests, a contest of the most impassioned vehemence will naturally arise in respect to the principles on which the persecutors proceed; and in which their false doctrines and bloody purposes are to be repelled. It is not in human nature that it should be otherwise. There will be many apostates from the ranks of those who had professed to be Protestants; there will be many cowards: there will be a still greater number who will care little whether the persecuted or the persecutors are in the right. But there will be not a few who will not cower to the enemy, and sacrifice conscience, truth, and God's favor, and brave eternal death, to escape the momentary rage and malice of the foe whom they know the Almighty himself is quickly to confound and dash to perdition. At his bidding thousands and thousands will spring to their feet, like the dead from the sepulchre at the summons of the last trumpet, and take the attitude and fill the office of witnesses of his word and of the testimony of Jesus. A multitude of books and essays, it may be presumed, will be published, thousands of discourses will be uttered; myriads of harangues, arguments, and appeals be employed to win those who waver, or repress the bold and unyielding. And the contest will go on, doubtless for a considerable period. A revolution so fundamental and far-reaching, is not to be the work of a few days nor a few seasons. No greater reversal ever took place in the views of a body of men, than is to be wrought in those who become the witnesses of Jesus at that crisis, and lay down their lives rather than swerve from fidelity to him. There probably is not at this moment a solitary individual in Great Britain, who is prepared to fill the office of a witness and martyr for Christ, as it is to be filled by those who are at that juncture to yield up their lives for his sake. Most certainly the members of the establishments generally, and the great body of those who dissent, or are without settled opinions, have not the remotest suspicion that the great question that is to be at issue at that crisis, is to be—Who is the Supreme; the Almighty, or the civil and Catholic rulers? Who has the right of legislating over the conscience? Who has the prerogative of prescribing faiths and worships? To whom does it belong to institute a method of redemption for the guilty? The general impression unquestionably is, that that right belongs, in a degree at least, to the state and church; that the church is the ally of the state, and is to be upheld and invested with power to enforce her faith and discipline as the auxiliary of the government and the engine of public good. It is not suspected that the assumption of such a power is an arrogation of the inalienable rights of God, and is one of the greatest impieties of which men are ever guilty. A total revolution, therefore, is to be wrought in the views of God's own children, who have previously assented to the nationalization of the church, and the dictation by rulers and ecclesiastics of their faith, their rites and their worship, to their subjects; that will require with many, a long and fierce struggle with prepossessions, party prejudices, cherished friends, and worldly interests ere they reach the truth in its greatness and sacredness, and are prepared to give their adhesion to it at the price of their lives. Some will fall; some will falter: but the true people of God will at length see and embrace the teachings of his word with untrembling hearts, and will be ready for the consequences that may result from their fidelity.

That the witnesses who are to be put to death and their believing friends who are to sympathize with them, are to have a full knowledge of the truths on which they proceed, and of the errors and impieties of their persecutors, is apparent from the fact that they are to be fully aware that they are the individuals whose martyrdom is foreshown in the vision,

Rev. xi., and are to die in the full expectation of being at the end of three years and a half from their martyrdom raised from death to immortality and glory. That they and their associated believers, are to cherish and avow that persuasion, and that it is to be fully understood by their persecutors, is clear, from the care those who put them to death are to take, to conform all their measures to the prophecy of their death, their non-burial, their exposure to the gaze of spectators, and their resurrection at the end of three years and a half. Those extraordinary steps will undoubtedly be taken by those whose office it is to slay and preserve them, in the hope and expectation that the prediction of their resurrection will not be verified, and that its non-verification will demonstrate that they are not the true witnesses of God, but hypocrites and fanatics; and their prediction be thereby confuted, that the Son of God is soon to come in the clouds, and assuming the sceptre of the world, consign the powers that are hostile to him to perdition. Why should the martyrs be slain in the same place and on the same day; why should they be preserved unburied, and in a condition in which they may be inspected by whoever pleases, unless it be that they may be identified as the persons who were put to death as witnesses for Jesus? And why should the people assemble at the scene where they lie, on the day in which it is predicted their resurrection is to take place, unless it be to test the truth of the prophecy, and be able to show that it is confuted by their remaining under the power of death? Nothing can be more evident than that that is to be the aim and hope of the persecutors; and nothing is more certain, therefore, than that the martyrs are to be fully aware that they are the witnesses who are foreshown in the Apocalypse, ch. xi., and that they are to avow and proclaim that conviction, so that their death, non-burial, and resurrection in the presence of a crowd of their enemies, shall be a proof on the one hand, of the truthfulness of their office as witnesses for God, and on the other, of the error, impiety, and doom of their persecutors. And this implies that the subject is to be discussed with great thoroughness, and for a long period, and that the witnesses and the believing who are not called to die for their faith, are to enjoy eminent aids of the Spirit, and be raised to a largeness and perfection of knowledge, a strength of faith, and a fearlessness of man, immeasurably beyond what the renewed ordinarily attain.

And this is indicated in the great promise: "And I will give unto my two witnesses that they may prophecy a thousand two hundred and three score days clothed in sackcloth. These are the two olive trees and the two candlesticks standing before the God of the earth;" that is, the receivers of the means of light, symbolized by the oil, and the agents of sustaining and diffusing that light symbolized by the candlesticks. "And if any man will injure them, fire proceedeth out of their mouth, and devoureth their enemies. These have power to shut heaven that it rain not in the days of their prophecy, and have power over waters to turn them to blood, and to smite the earth with all plagues as often as they will," v. 3–6. It is as prophets that they are to exert these great acts; that is, as messengers of God's will, proclaiming the great truths he has revealed in his word respecting the work of redemption, and uttering the forewarnings he has given of the judgments with which he is to overwhelm those who make war on him and his kingdom. This prediction indicates that they are to have special gifts and eminent aids of the Spirit, and are to act a part toward the persecutors, like that which Moses acted toward Pharaoh, and Elijah toward Ahab, between whom the question debated was the same as that which is to arise between the witnesses and their antagonists; namely, Who is supreme; Jehovah or the idols of Egypt; the Lord God of Israel, or Baal? And it is to be determined by Jehovah himself, as it then was, not by men.

What momentous events the prophecy thus foreshows! How unexpected at the present moment by the people of Great Britain and the other European States? There is not one of a thousand probably, even of those who look for the speedy coming of Christ, who anticipates this bloody strife, and on a question that lies so wholly out of their ordinary sphere of thought. The leading writers on the subject, Cuninghame, Faber, Elliott, Cumming, and others, having maintained with the utmost assurance, that the prophecy had its fulfillment ages ago, have betrayed the church generally into that false belief. But it is to be recalled from that delusion. The misrepresentations of those authors are to meet a just appreciation, and the truth again win the eyes and ears of the intelligent and impartial, and be received in its greatness and awfulness.

"And when they shall have finished their testimony, the beast that ascends out of the abyss, shall make war against them, and shall overcome them, and shall kill them, and their dead body shall be placed in the street of the great city which is spiritually called Sodom and Egypt, where also their Lord was slain." v. 7, 8. The period of their testimony is to be twelve hundred and sixty days: which being used as a symbol in the relation of analogy, denote twelve hundred and sixty years. It is only by this close of the period, that the time is to be known when it commenced, there being no other means of determining its beginning. The prophecy only foreshows its length and the event that is to mark its close. That their martyrdom has not yet taken place, is a conclusive proof therefore that the twelve hundred and sixty years have not yet expired.

The great city in whose street their dead bodies were placed, was Babylon, which is the symbol of the Catholic hierarchies in that organization which is represented by the image. This is seen from the appropriation of the epithet *great* to that city, in the visions, and to that city alone. ch. xiv. 8, xvii. 5, xviii. 2, 10, 16, 18–21. The broad street of Babylon, was like the market places of Greek cities, the chief scene of concourse and commerce. It symbolizes, therefore, that part of the persecuting hierarchy which is to hold the central place in that body, and be the seat of its most important functions. Where that is then to be, whether in Italy, France, or Great Britain, is left unrevealed.

"And they of the peoples and tribes, and tongues and nations, shall look on their dead bodies three days and a half, and shall not suffer their dead bodies to be put in a supulchre." v. 9. This foreshows that the whole empire will have its thoughts fixed on them during the three years and a half of their lying in death; and implies that the great doctrines they had taught, the exposition of this prophecy they had uttered, and the expectation with which they had died, that they should speedily be raised to a fresh and immortal life, to the confusion and overthrow of their enemies, will be the theme of continual consideration and debate during that period. Persons from different parts of the empire are daily to go and gaze at them, discuss the peculiarities of their faith, and express their estimate of their character, and their belief or unbelief of their restoration to life.

"And they that dwell on the earth rejoice over them, and exult, and will send gifts to one another; for these two prophets tormented them who dwell on the earth." v. 10. This indicates that while the people of the empire generally will regard them as mere hypocrites or dupes, whose expectations of a public vindication by the Most High himself by a resurrection to glory, is to be disappointed, and consign them to ridicule and scorn; they are still to be objects to them of great interest; and while hating them, they are to be haunted by a secret dread that the prediction of vengeance on their persecutors they had uttered, may prove true.

And when the day of their predicted resurrection arrives, the curiosity, the concern, the anxiety, of the multitude, instead of subsiding, will be raised to far greater intensity. A crowd is to assemble in the scene where they lie, consisting largely of their enemies, but embracing, also, it cannot be doubted, many of their friends, who will wait for the time that is to determine the truth or falsehood of the prophecy. What hours will those be of uncertainty, of dread, of terror to some of the enemies, of scoffs and mockeries to others; but of awe, of faith, and of joy to the believing. No moment can exceed it in the depth of feeling the infinite interests that are to be decided by the event will excite.

At length the moment of deliverance comes. The Spirit of life from God enters into their dead bodies, and they stand on their feet. And great fear falls upon them who see them; and they hear a great voice from heaven, saying unto them, "Come up hither. And they ascend into the sky in the cloud, and their enemies behold them." v. 11, 12. Who can paint the impressions that amazing spectacle will make on those who witness it? What other deliverance of his children of which the world has ever been the scene, carried with it so resistless and sublime an expression of God's approval? What other seal set on the brows of those whom he redeems, ever indicated with such strength and resplendence that they are his? What other testimony from the lips of the Almighty ever conveyed such confutation and doom to his enemies, as that restoration of his martyrs from death and elevation to life and glory in his kingdom will bear to their persecutors! No bosom will be untouched: no spirit will remain unawed. No one will doubt the reality of the resurrection. It were to doubt the truth of his own eyes; to reject the resistless testimony of his consciousness. No one will persuade himself that the revivification of the martyrs, and their assumption to heaven, are not the work of God. No one will doubt that it is the identical event foreshown in this prophecy. And none will fail to see how majestic a vindication it forms of the martyrs; and with what terrific emphasis it speaks the condemnation of their murderers. Great fear will fall on all them that see them, whether friends or foes; and that awe and terror will spread through the whole empire, and seize every heart: for in the same hour there is to be a great earthquake, and a tenth part of the city is to fall; and in the earthquake seven thousand men of name are to be slain; and the remnant are to be affrighted and give glory to the God of heaven." v. 17. These effects will naturally spring from an intervention of the Almighty bespeaking in such an awe-inspiring manner his presence, his power, his fidelity to those who trust in him, and proclaiming in such tones the certainty that he will fulfill all the pledges of protection and deliverance he has given to his true worshipers, and all his threatenings of vengeance on those who make war on him and his kingdom.

The earthquake is the symbol of a political revolution, and foreshows that under the impressions of this interposition of the Almighty to redeem his witnesses, and baffle and confound the powers denoted by the beast and by Babylon; the people of at least one of the kingdoms will rise and throw off their allegiance to the king who holds the sceptre over them. The tenth part of the city that is to fall, is the hierarchy of one of the ten kingdoms; and doubtless of that in which the political revolution denoted by the earthquake is to take place, and give birth to a new form of government. The fall of the hierarchy, is to be its fall from nationalization. The overthrow of the State, is to involve the overthrow of the State-church.

That seven thousand men of name are to be slain by the earthquake, indicates that the revolution is to involve a civil war in which the chief officials of the government that is overthrown are to perish by the sword. That the remnant are to be affrighted and give glory to the God of heaven, shows that the current of popular feeling is to turn with such violence against the persecuting party in the state and in the church, as to fill them with terror who would otherwise be disposed to avoid engaging in the contest, and lead them to an open and unreserved acknowledgment, that God has irrevocably determined the question between the martyrs and their persecutors, and that his deliverance of his true worshipers, and condemnation of his enemies, are worthy of his righteousness, his wisdom and his power.

The testimony, the death, and the resurrection of the witnesses are thus to form an epoch in the annals of the earth. They are to have the greatest conspicuity. The knowledge of them is to be carried to every bosom in the civilized world, and to thousands and millions of the Pagan and Mahometan races. They are to work the most radical, the most comprehensive, and the most momentous revolution in the views of the true worshipers themselves, that ever took place, in respect to the incommunicableness and sanctity of God's rights, and the guilt of the arrogation of his place and prerogatives by human rulers, and ecclesiastics: and are to give rise to a train of consequences of the greatest significance; prompting in a degree on the one side, the dragon, the wild beast, and the false prophet, to the measures they are to take to retrieve their cause from the shock it will have received; and exciting the multitude on the other, in defiance of their will, to make the war on Babylon the great in which she is to fall from her nationalization and perish.

CHAPTER XXIII.

The end of the Second Woe, or Fall of the Turkish Power—The Seventh Trumpet—The great events foreshown under the first five Seals—The Predictions under the Sixth—The Seventh Seal—The Trumpets—The Vision, chap. xii. of the Woman and the Dragon—The War of Michael and of Satan—The Vision, chap. xiii. of the Wild Beast from the Sea—The Beast from the Land and the Image—The Visions of ch. xiv., xv., xvi.

I.

After the prediction of the death, resurrection, and ascension of the witnesses, and of the impressions that are to be made by those events on the spectators, the prophecy adds: "The second woe is past. Behold, the third woe cometh quickly," ch. xi. 14. The second woe is that under the sixth trumpet, of the two hundred millions of horsemen from beyond the Euphrates, who were to kill a third of the men by fire and smoke and brimstone from the mouths of their horses, and were to leave the rest of the worshipers of demons and of idols, who survive the plague, as demoralized and incorrigible as they found them, Rev. ix. 14–21. Faber, Cuninghame, Elliott and others have maintained with great positiveness that the second woe terminated at the battle of Zenta, in 1697, or the peace of Carlowitz, in 1699. No persuasion was ever built on a more unsubstantial foundation. The

Turkish power is still in existence, and is still as false, as barbarous, and as bloody in proportion to its strength, as it was on its entrance into the Eastern empire. It is at this moment making a savage war on its Christian subjects in Candia. The unparalelled slaughters, tortures, and degradations, it was commissioned to inflict, will not have reached their end till that monster which breathes fire from its mouth, and torments with its serpent's sting, is struck from existence.

There is no intimation that the fall of the Turkish rule is to be the effect of the great miracle wrought in the Western Roman empire, by which the truth of Christianity, as held and taught by the witnesses, will have been demonstrated, and the falsehood and impiousness shown of Roman Catholicism, Mahometanism, and all other religions which are the work of men. It is to take place at near the same time,but is to be the effect, doubtless, of a different cause; and probably of conquest by a foreign power; as the fall of the present government by a domestic revolution, while a great majority of the people remain the disciples of Mahomet, would not necessarily draw after it the release of the nominally Christian population from the degrading vassalage in which they are held. How could a mere division of the empire into three or four independent Mahometan kingdoms, naturally prompt a reinstatement of Christian churches, families, or individuals, in the religious freedom and civil franchises into which they will emerge, when the woe with which they have for so many ages been smitten reaches its end? As the dragon which retreated to the north on the fall of the Eastern empire in 1453, is to reappear on the scene, and act in concurrence with the wild beast and false prophet in summoning the kings to the great battle of God Almighty, Rev. xvi. 13–16, it is probable that Russia, whose monarch is now the head of the Greek communion, will make himself master of Constantinople, and extend his dominion over Asia Minor, Armenia, and Mesopotamia. On becoming the monarch of those territories, he will naturally nationalize the Greek Church, and divest the Mahometan population of power to persecute the professors of the Christian faith.

The overthrow of the Turkish rule and extinction of Mahometanism will be events of great significance. What a tragedy that people have acted for eight hundred years! What an exemplification their career presents of what man is, under the sway of a false religion that licenses all the brutal elements of his nature, and imbues him with the mercilessness and malice of a demon! What ghastly proofs will the sins and miseries to which their religion has given birth form of its falsehood and malignity! And how just, how wise, how gracious will it be in God to strike it to annihilation! Who can appreciate the benignity of the change to the fifteen or eighteen millions of Greeks, Armenians, and others who are to be released from bondage to the power which has made it its office for so many generations, to reduce them to the lowest physical degradation, and steep them in the most execrable moral pollution!

II.

Immediately after the announcement, "The second woe is past. Behold, the third woe cometh quickly," the seventh trumpet sounded; and a group of events of the greatest moment was foreshown. "And the seventh angel sounded. And there were great voices in heaven saying, 'The kingdom of the world is become our Jehovah's and his Messiah's, and he shall reign forever and ever.'" The loud voices in which this was uttered were from the lips of angels, and show that they are to be aware of the great measures of Christ's administration that are then to commence. That those voices were the voices of angels is seen from the peculiar expression, "Our Lord's"—that is, "our Jehovah's and his Messiah's," in which they designate Jehovah as *their* Jehovah, and Christ, not as theirs, but *his* Messiah. They were not redeemed spirits, therefore, of whom Christ is the Messiah, but were unfallen angels who do not need redemption. The reign of Christ, on which he is now to enter, is to be in this world, and in person; not merely by a providence, or by the Spirit. He is to come in the clouds, so that every eye shall see him, and reign as conspicuously as he now reigns in heaven.

The predictions that next follow were uttered by the elders. "And the four and twenty elders who sat before God on their thrones fell on their faces and worshiped God, saying, We give thee thanks, O Lord God Almighty, who art, and wast, and art to come; that thou hast taken thy great power and reigned," v. 16, 17. What beauty marks this adoring celebration by the redeemed, of God's righteousness and wisdom in asserting his rights, and exercising the sway over the world to which his infinite power, knowledge and goodness entitle him! What an understanding of his ways it bespeaks, what confidence, what submission, what joy! "And the nations were angry [at thy sway]; and thy wrath is come, and the time of the dead, to judge and give the reward to thy servants, the prophets, and the holy, and those who fear thy name, small and great; and to destroy those who corrupt the earth," v. 18. This is a prediction of the great measures of retribution which Christ is to institute at the commencement of his reign. The period of forbearance will have passed: the time to inflict his wrath will have come, and the time of the dead, to judge and recompense his servants, the prophets and the saints; to judge and reward the living also that fear his name, small and great; and to destroy the corrupters of the race. The resurrection and reward of the holy dead and the living saints, on the one side, is thus foreshown, as to take place under the seventh trumpet; and on the other, the judgment and destruction of the corrupters of the nations. Through what period that trumpet, under which the last woe on apostates and persecutors is to be inflicted, is to extend, is not indicated. As the trumpet, however, is immediately to follow the close of the twelve hundred and sixty years, its period is probably the thirty years that are to intervene between the twelve hundred and sixty days and the twelve hundred and ninety, that are to extend on to the time when the sanctuary is to be cleansed by the extirpation of the worship of creatures and the mass. What the order is to be in which these events are to take place, is not here foreshown, but is in a measure indicated in other passages.

This prediction is followed by the announcement, that the temple of God was open in heaven, and the ark of his covenant was seen in his temple. "And there were lightnings, and voices, and thunders, and an earthquake, and great hail," v. 19. That the inner temple was open, and the ark of the covenant seen, denotes, doubtless, that the mysteries of his former administration, in which, though he reigned in the greatness of his power, he allowed the nations to rebel and rage against him, are finished; and he is thenceforth to reign visibly to men on the earth, make the reasons of his procedure understood, and complete the redemption of those whom he has chosen unto life. The predictions that follow are made through symbols. Lightnings, and voices, and thunders are symbols of analogous utterances and explosions of the thoughts and passions of men. An earthquake is the symbol of a great and violent political revolution, in which a government is overthrown. And great hail symbolizes sudden and resistless inflictions on men, that resemble the dash of heavy hailstones on plants and trees. Whether these terrific excitements and retributive strokes are to be in a chief measure consequent on the startling and overpowering disclosures made through the death, resurrection, and ascension of the witnesses, is not intimated. They probably are to be; as those events produced so profound a conviction in the spectators, that the witnesses were true worshipers of God; and that their forewarnings of the destruction of their persecutors would be verified; that an insurrection immediately took place in one of the ten kingdoms which overthrew the monarchy, consigned the nobles to the sword, and hurled the Catholic hierarchy from its nationalization; it may be expected that similar excitements and revolts from the ruling power will take place in one or more kingdoms in which there is a considerable number of Protestants. Whatever the extent may be to which these agitations and revolts are to go, the power denoted by the wild beast is likely at this crisis to have other cares beside superintending the migration of the Jews to the Holy Land! It is the desperation with which the danger to his throne, resulting from his successless war on the witnesses, is to inflame him, that will drive him to gather his forces together to make war at Armageddon on Israel, and on the Son of God.

III.

Hitherto there had been no symbolization in the Apocalypse of the great civil powers that were to rise and persecute the people of God. The event foreshown under the first seal was a rapid enlargement of the church in the century or two following the vision. That indicated by the second, was the distraction of the church by ambitious and contentious prelates. Under the third was revealed a famine of the bread of life, wrought by the substitution by the clergy of asceticism and other unrequired works, in the place of faith in Christ as the condition of acceptance with God. And under the fourth, were foreshown the apostasy of the clergy to relics, and idol worship, the invocation of saints, and the sacrifice of the mass; and their enforcement of those deadly doctrines and rites on the church. Under the fifth, the revelation was first clearly made in the prophecy that the people of God were to be put to death by them that dwell on the earth, but without indicating whether it was to be by factions, or by the ruling powers.

The prediction under the sixth seal is of the greatest significance. Through a group of symbols taken from the material world, it is foreshown that the supreme and the inferior powers of the empire are to be overthrown by commotions and revolutions, and the monarchs, princes, and hosts armed against Christ, smitten with dismay and terror by the advent of the Son of God.

"And I looked when he opened the sixth seal, and there was a great earthquake. And the sun became black as hair sackcloth, and the whole moon became as blood. And the stars of heaven fell to the earth, as a fig-tree shaken by a great wind casts her unripe figs. And the clouded heaven was separated (into parts, and borne away) like an uprolled scroll, and the mountains and islands were moved from their places. And the kings of the earth, and the great men, and the commanders of thousands, and the rich and the mighty, and every bondman and freeman hid themselves in the caves, and in the rocks of the mountains, and said to the mountains, and to the rocks: Fall on us, and hide us from the face of him who sits on the throne, and from the wrath of the Lamb; for the great day of his wrath has come, and who is able to stand." Rev. vi. 12–17. A great earthquake denotes a violent political revolution. The blackening of the sun, and the bloodiness of the moon, which result from a loss of power to give light, foreshows that the monarchs symbolized by them, that had before ruled the empire, are to be divested of their power to go on with the functions of their office. The fall of the stars signifies the fall of princes and nobles from their stations; the disruption and uprolling of the vapors of the sky, the dissolution and disappearance of the great civil organizations of the empire; and the removal of mountains and islands, the reduction of all to the same level.

The consternation of the kings, the great men, and the commanders of thousands, and all inferior ranks, and flight to the mountains to escape the wrath of the Lamb, foreshows that at the close of this series of commotions and catastrophes, the Son of God is to appear in the clouds of heaven, to execute his wrath upon his enemies.

It is a question, therefore, of the greatest moment, whether those of these predictions which precede the last, have already been verified, or whether their accomplishment is yet future. They have been interpreted by many writers of the French revolution: and it has been assumed that the political agitations and upheavals symbolized by the earthquake, and the loss by the monarchs and princes of their power, denoted by the darkening of the orbs, are to continue at intervals down to the advent of Christ. It is undoubtedly, however, a mistake, and a mistake that has had a most misleading influence on their views of the prophecies that follow. That a large share of the events foreshown by these symbols is yet unaccomplished, is unquestionable. The Son of God most certainly has not yet come in the clouds of heaven. The kings of the earth, and the great men, and the commanders of thousands, have not yet gathered together at Armageddon to make war on the Lamb. The governments of the ten kingdoms have not universally fallen, and left their subjects in anarchy. And though a great earthquake denotes an event much like the uprising of the French people at the revolution; and the loss by the sun and moon of the power of giving light, might aptly symbolize the loss by the king, and others of the Bourbon family at that juncture, of the power of going on with the functions of royalty; and the fall of stars might naturally indicate the dejection of princes and nobles from their stations; yet as the other symbols drawn from the natural world had no counterpart in that revolution, and instead of several groups, separated from each other by long intervals, consist of a single cluster that are naturally connected with each other; they undoubtedly are all yet future. And this is confirmed by the entire difference of *the objects* on which the symbols of the seal acted, from those of the first six vials, which unquestionably had their fulfillment in the French revolution, the wars to which it gave birth, and the political and religious strifes that sprung from it at a later day.

The symbols of the *seals* represent catastrophes that are to befall the *rulers* of the empire. But those of the first four and the sixth *vials* denote inflictions that are to fall on the *subjects* of the beast, instead of the beast itself. The fifth was poured on *the throne* of the beast, but had its chief effect in shrouding its subjects in darkness, and causing them to gnaw their tongues for pain.

The symbols of the seals were unlike those of the vials also in *nature*, as well as the direction in which they acted. There was no earthquake under the first six vials. The darkening of the sun and moon under the sixth seal, betokened the loss by the supreme rulers of the power of discharging their functions as monarchs. The effect of the fourth vial on the sun—the symbol of a monarch—was to cause it to scorch men with great heat, and prompt them to blaspheme; which is wholly different from the effect of the seal. There was no rolling up of the disparted heavens as a scroll under the vials, nor removal of mountains and islands.

Under the seals, there are no symbols of bloody strifes and wars. But the symbols of the second and third vials, are symbols of the massacres of the French population during the reign of terror, and of the vast slaughters of their armies, and the armies of the nations they assailed, in the twenty years of conquests and defeats that began with the revolution. As the symbols of the seal and of the vials are thus unlike each other; the events they foreshow, and their times, it is evident, are in an equal degree to differ from each other.

This is confirmed, moreover, by the fact that the

period of the seal is to be the period of the wrath of the Lamb, which is to follow the seventh trumpet, and of the sealing of the servants of God, which, though it is to take place after the martyrdom of the witnesses, is to precede the advent of the Son of God. This will be more fully shown when I come to notice the vision of the sealing of God's servants, ch. xiv. 1–5.

The opening of the seventh seal was followed by voices, thunders, lightnings, and an earthquake, which foreshow the revolution that took place at the overthrow of the Pagan emperors by Constantine, and legalization of the church by the state. The first four trumpets were then blown, by which the conquest and devastation of the western empire by the Goths, and the fall of the imperial rule are foretold. Under the fifth trumpet the war of the Saracens is revealed; and under the sixth, that of the Turks, whose career is to continue to the slaying of the witnesses, and the sound of the seventh trumpet.

IV.

After the seventh trumpet, follows the vision, ch. xiii., in which the supreme powers of the Roman empire from their origin, are represented by a great red dragon of seven heads, and ten horns, and seven diadems on his heads, down to the fall of the western empire, and thereafter the imperial rule of the eastern empire, till its overthrow in 1453.

Next follows the symbol of the wild beast from the sea, having seven heads and ten horns, and upon his horns ten diadems, and upon his heads names of blasphemy, representing the sovereignty of the ten kings in their several kingdoms, into which they divided the western Roman empire, on their overthrow of the imperial rule.

To that succeeds the vision of the second beast from the earth, having two horns like a lamb, but speaking like a dragon, and symbolizing the twofold power of the papacy; while the image it caused to be made represents the Catholic hierarchy formed by the union of the whole body of ecclesiastics in the Roman churches under the headship of the pope.

Chapter xiv. contains the vision of the Lamb standing on Mount Zion; the angel soaring through mid heaven with the Gospel: the angel announcing the fall of Babylon; the third angel uttering a warning against worshiping the beast and its image. It is then foreshown that the period of that warning is to be a period of persecution.

Next is the vision of one like a Son of Man, throned on a white cloud, and reaping the harvest of the earth; and that is followed by the vision of an angel gathering the vintage of the earth, and casting the clusters into the wine-press of God's wrath. These events, foreshown ch. xiv., are indubitably to take place *after* the martyrdom of the witnesses, and the sounding of the seventh trumpet.

V.

The vision of the seven angels that were to bear the vials, *follows* in ch. xv., and of the pouring of the vials in ch. xvi., *although the events the first six vials denote, have unquestionably already in the main taken place; while the slaughter of the witnesses and the sounding of the seventh trumpet are still future.*

What is the reason, it is natural to ask, of this arrangement of the visions in an order so different from that in which the events they foreshow are to have their accomplishment? This question has met no satisfactory answer from expositors. Instead, they have run into extraordinary errors in their expositions; some asserting that the vials are all contemporaneous with each other; some that they are contemporary with the sixth seal; and others that they are included under the seventh trumpet. But those constructions are in the utmost degree mistaken. The reason that the vials occupy the place that is assigned them in *the order* of the visions, is undoubtedly, that *a previous symbolization of the great powers denoted by the seven-headed and ten-horned beast, the second beast and the image*, was necessary in order that it might be understood *whose subjects they were on whom the vials* were to be poured. How could the guilty parties on whom the plagues of the vials were to descend, be identified, if it had not been shown in the vivid colors of the xiith and xiiith chapters, what the powers are to which, instead of Jehovah, they pay their supreme homage! After the delineations of those visions, the predictions in ch. xiv. of the great changes that are to take place in the conditions and acts of the true worshipers after the resurrection of the witnesses, and the prophecy of the harvest and vintage, it is apparent who they are on whom the vials are to fall, and what the crimes are that are to draw on them those fearful retributions.

It is undoubtedly also for a similar reason, that the description of the scarlet beast that is to ascend out of hades, and of its relations to the woman Babylon, is reserved to ch. xvii. The student of the prophecy gains thereby a far clearer and more emphatic conception of the character of the power represented by the beast and by Babylon, and of the justice of the doom that is to be inflicted on them than he otherwise would.

A knowledge of these great features of the prophecies, I have thus pointed out, is of the utmost moment to the comprehension of what follows. Let the reader then carry in his mind the fact that the sixth seal is yet future; that the catastrophe it foreshows is that by which the powers denoted by the wild beast are to be borne down into hades; that on its ascent from the abyss, the supreme Sovereignty is to be held by an imperial chief; that the ten kings are to become subordinates to him; that he is to nationalize the Catholic Church in all the ten kingdoms; that at the instance of that Church he is to persecute and slay the witnesses; that the great question to be debated between the witnesses and their persecutors is to be: Who is of supreme authority in religion? Who has the right to institute a method of salvation, enjoin rites, and appoint a worship? Jehovah; or the civil and ecclesiastical rulers of the empire? That the witnesses are to assert the exclusive right of God to legislate in the sphere of religion; and denounce their persecutors as arrogating his prerogatives in assuming power to appoint the faith of his subjects, and making war on him and his kingdom; and are to forewarn them of their impending destruction: that they are to indicate that they are the witnesses whom it is foreshown, are to be put to death; and express the belief that God will raise them to immortal life: that their murderers are to follow the intimations of the prophecy, respecting their non-burial, and their exposure to the public gaze: that their restoration, therefore, to life and assumption to heaven, are to form an overwhelming demonstration that they are the true children of God; and are to carry that conviction to the spectators and others; and that that is to be followed by commotions and agitations, in the ten kingdoms, and by the spread of the feeling through the empire that the Catholic is not a true, but an apostate Church. These great teachings, and the fact that the predictions of ch. xii–xvii. are not arranged in the order in which they were and are to be verified, but are grouped together in the manner they are, that there might be a clearer indication of the agents and acts which they reveal; are thus of great moment to just views of the fulfillments that have already taken place, and that are approaching. It is only by knowing what the principles are, that are to be determined by the slaying and resurrection of the witnesses, and the effects which those events are to produce in the convictions of the believing and unbelieving, that a just estimate can be formed of the occurrences that are to fill up the period from that epoch to the coming of Christ.

CHAPTER XXIV.

The Emission of unclean Spirits—The Sealing of the Servants of God—The flight of the Angel bearing the Gospel—The fall of Babylon—The third Angel uttering a warning not to worship the beast, nor the image—The destruction of Babylon.

I.

ONE of the great events that is to follow the death of the witnesses, and probably the seventh trumpet, is the emission of the unclean spirits after the pouring of the sixth vial on the Euphrates. "And I saw from the mouth of the dragon, and from the mouth of the beast, and from the mouth of the false prophet, three unclean spirits like frogs; for they are spirits of demons working wonders, that go to the kings of the whole inhabited world to gather them to the battle of that great day of God Almighty. Behold I come as a thief. Blessed is he who watches, and keeps his garments, that he may not walk naked, and they may see his shame. And they gathered them in the place which is called in Hebrew Armageddon, Rev. xvi. 13–16. The dragon's reappearance here, and sending forth an unclean spirit to coöperate with the spirits that proceed from the mouth of the wild beast and of the false prophet, shows that the power he represents, is to have a common interest with the imperial chief of the western empire and the pope, in the war they are to wage against the kingdom of God; and the reason is, doubtless, to be, that the question at issue is to be whether the monarchs of the earth have the right to dictate the religion of their subjects, and make the Church the instrument of the State. As the monarch of Russia is the head of the Greek church; he will have as deep a concern in that question, as the powers symbolized by the wild beast and false prophet. This movement of those powers to unite the hosts of the whole civilized world to put down the kingdom of God by force, is probably to be first prompted by the alienation of the Catholic crowd from the pope's hierarchy, and the assaults made during the progress of that alienation, on the assumption by civil rulers of authority over religion. But as the agency of the spirits is to continue to the battle of Armageddon, a very considerable time will pass before it will reach its climax. The kings are not to be gathered at Armageddon till near the day of the battle. That such a measure should be adopted and pursued through a number of years, indicates a deep alarm for their supremacy by the powers whom the dragon, the wild beast and the false prophet denote. As the object of the gathering at Armageddon is to be, to break up the Jewish community which will have reëstablished itself in Jerusalem, it implies that at the period when these spirits enter on their work, a body of Jews will have returned to Palestine with the purpose of re-erecting a kingdom there; and that the true worshipers of God in the ten kingdoms who take his word as their guide; and are animated by the spirit of the martyrs, will hold and teach that Christ is to appear as their Messiah, reinstate them in their relations to him as a covenant people, and destroy the powers denoted by the beast and false prophet, by a miracle, as he had wrought a miracle to restore the slain witnesses to life. Why else should such a measure be adopted, to defeat the party of the martyrs and the Israelites? Believers generally, it is obvious from this, are at that crisis to receive the teachings of the Scriptures respecting the restoration of the Jews, and Christ's reign over them. It bespeaks, therefore, a vast advance of the Church in the knowledge of those subjects, and the great scheme of Christ's administration. The fact that such a stupendous miracle will have been wrought to call the dead witnesses to life, and demonstrate that they were true worshipers of God, will be one of the reasons doubtless that the demon spirits will attempt to work miracles to convince the multitude that they have as high a sanction of their procedure, as the witnesses had of theirs. The spirits are to be embodied doubtless in human beings, through whom they may work their behests, as in the time of Christ's ministry, they exerted their power through those of whom they took possession; using their organs of motion and of speech as though they were their own; imbuing them with thoughts; exciting them to passion; and wrenching them with bodily convulsions and tortures. The effects to which they will give birth, will all lie within the sphere of their own nature, and theirs whom they make their victims; yet they will to the spectators, doubtless, wear the air of miracles, and terrify and delude them. All this implies that the impression made by the witnesses, and of those who succeed them in the testimony of Jesus, are to be so effective, as to demand the most subtle and vigorous antagonism to counteract them. If no serious dangers are to threaten the dragon and his associates; if there are no powerful forces to be met; why should they employ such a dark and deluding enginery to secure themselves from defeat?

II.

Another group of agents is to rise contemporaneously, it is probable, with the demon spirits, of directly the opposite character and sphere; their office being to unfold in a decisive manner, and vindicate the rights of God, and prompt the true worshippers to render him a just allegiance. These are symbolized by the angel ascending from the east having the seal of the living God.

"And I saw four angels standing at the four corners of the earth, holding the four winds of the earth, that wind shall neither blow on the earth, nor on the sea, nor on any tree. And I saw another angel ascending from the sun-rising, having the seal of the living God. And he cried with a loud voice to the four angels to whom it was given to injure the earth and the sea. Saying: Injure not the earth, nor the sea, nor the trees, until we can seal the servants of our God on their foreheads. And I heard the number of the sealed, a hundred and forty-four thousand were sealed of the whole race of the sons of Israel." Rev. vii. 1–8.

This vision foreshows one of the greatest and most effective of the measures God is to employ to raise his people to a full knowledge of his rights and their relations to him, and arm them with wisdom, steadfastness, and faith to meet the great trials to which they are to be exposed from the artifices of the demon spirits, and the rage and malice of the wild beast and the sorceress Babylon. The angel is the symbol of a group of men who are to fill an office towards the true worshipers, that is analogous to that of impressing the seal of God on their brows. The resplendence of the angel, and the conspicuity of his ascent from the east, and flight through the arch of heaven, indicates that those whom he represents, are to be men of extraordinary gifts, and are to perform their work in the presence and gaze of the whole empire. The office of the seal, was visibly to mark those on whom it was impressed, as the servants of God, so that all spectators could identify them as his. They were not *constituted* his servants by the sealing, but the sealing *marked and identified* them as his. The inscription on the seal which was impressed on the forehead, we learn from chapter xiv. 1., was Christ's name, and the name of the Father. That which the sealing denotes therefore, is, that an agency is to be exerted by those whom the angel symbolizes, on those represented by the sealed, by which it shall become as indubitable and conspicuous that they are God's servants, as it would be if his name, and the name of Christ, were stamped by a seal on their foreheads. This implies most emphatically, that a special necessity is to exist for a public and indubitable manifestation that they are his true servants. Why should the Most High employ such an extraordinary measure to bring out in the most conspicuous form the reality and unalterableness of their allegiance, if there is no peculiar occasion for it? The summoning of a group of extraordinary agents to exert such an influence on the sealed, most assuredly indicates that the effect to be wrought, is essential both to God's vindication, and the vindication of his servants. There is, therefore, to be some powerful antagonism to be overcome, some special danger, against which his people will need to be guarded; and that necessity is to spring, doubtless, from the loud and imperious denial by the beast, the image, and the demon spirits, that the witnesses, and those who concur with them, are true worshipers; and endeavor by delusive pretexts, and false miracles, to draw them either into doubt or apostasy. The question to be at issue, is therefore to be essentially the same, as it was in the conflict of the witnesses with their persecutors who usurped the rights of God, and claimed the homage as due to them, which belongs only to him. This is seen indubitably from the delineation of their peculiarities, ch. xiv. 1–5. "These are they who have not been defiled with women: for they are pure. These are they who follow the Lamb wherever he may go. They have been redeemed from men, a first offering to God and the Lamb; and in their mouth no falsehood was found; for they are spotless." The women of the Apocalypse who present the cup of enticements to men, and endeavor to seduce them, are the woman Babylon and her daughters, who are symbols of the Catholic hierarchies. To be defiled by them is to assent to their claims of authority, to receive their false doctrines, and to unite in their superstitious and idolatrous worship, and thereby reject God as the sovereign of the church, and Christ as the sacrifice for sin. That the sealed had not been defiled with those women, signifies, that they had never consented to their impious claims, never entered their communion, never united in their worship, but had shunned them as apostates and enemies, and maintained an unfaltering allegiance to God. Many others who are the children of God, may have belonged to nationalized churches, and held that rulers of the State have the right to legislate over their subjects, in their relations to God. The sealed will never have sanctioned in any manner those consummate errors, but will have recognized, proclaimed, and vindicated the prerogatives of God with truth and fidelity. They will stand, therefore, in the attitude of direct and strenuous antagonism to the vassals of the beast and its image; bearing the name of God on their foreheads, as the worshipers of the beast and the image bear their marks on their faces or their hands. The sealed will give their whole homage to God, according to his perfections, his rights, and his will: the vassals of the beast and image, will give their homage exclusively to those usurping and blaspheming powers, according to their impious claims to authority, and demands of a worship.

There will be ample scope, therefore, for the agency that is symbolized by the act of the sealing angel. Far truer, more comprehensive and impressive views of the sanctity and the inviolableness of the rights of God are possible, than have hitherto been attained. Just in proportion as the grandeur of his perfections is seen, the vastness of his empire, the subordination to him of all creatures, the boundlessness of the interests that depend on the efficiency of his government, and the wisdom and righteousness that mark all his ways—just in that proportion will the feeling be deepened of the sacredness of his prerogatives, and the necessity of his asserting and maintaining them, in order to his own glory and the well-being of his kingdom. In all these directions there is room for far clearer, higher, and more transporting thoughts. On the other hand, the larger, and truer the apprehensions become of the impiousness of the powers denoted by the beast and the image in arrogating the place and rights of God; demanding a worship of themselves, and treating those who pay a true homage to him, as traitors and apostates, that deserve torture in this world, and eternal perdition in the next, the deeper will be the execration with which the authors of that gigantic impiety, and the impiety itself will be contemplated, and the more instinctive and resistless the abhorrence with which they will be shunned. The guilt of the sin, and the boundless miseries to which it has given birth, in the debasement and ruin of the multitude, and in the oppressions, outrages, and murder of the children of God, may be painted in colors far more vivid, and with a fullness far more ample, than any in which they have hitherto been drawn. And how suitable to God to employ these extraordinary and efficacious means to impart that higher knowledge to his people, and vindicate himself and them in the eyes of the universe? Warred against, and blasphemed as he is by the usurpers of his throne, it behoves him to set forth all the great truths that concern his attributes and his rule, in a light so dazzling, that no one can fail to see them. It befits him to confute all the calumnies of his enemies in such a form, that all shall be constrained to see their true character, and the mouth of falsehood and malice be hushed into eternal silence. Who can doubt that this great measure of the divine administration, so peculiar, and so grand, will prove an immeasurable blessing to those who feel its power? That not only will the sealed be raised to far higher intelligence, steadfastness, and fidelity, than they would otherwise reach, and meet a more glorious reward; but that millions may be withheld by it from apostasy, sheltered from dangers, and led on to crowns of immortal life?

The period of the suspension of the winds, during which the sealing is to take place, is probably that which is to follow the resurrection of the witnesses, and is to be occupied by the first, second, and third angel, immediately before the destruction of Babylon. The purpose for which the winds are to be held, is to give opportunity to those whom the sealing angel represents, to warn, teach, and prompt believers and others to abstain from allegiance to Babylon, and resist her deceitful and malicious arts.

That the reward of the sealed is to be in a measure peculiar to them, is seen from the fact that they alone could learn the song which they sang before the throne, and before the living creatures and the elders. No others, therefore, are to be presented by Christ to the Father, that will have the same distinctions. Their diversity from others may be, not simply that they are the first offering of the kind; but that no others can ever give such proofs as they will have given, of fidelity to God. Their salvation will have been completed, at their assumption to the divine presence; as they are said to have been redeemed from men, a first offering to God and to the Lamb. As they will have been freed from the curse, and admitted to the most intimate relations to Christ, they will doubtless have been changed from mortal to immortal, and in that relation, will be the first who are distinguished by that mode of redemption from death; while the harvest is to consist of the living that are thereafter, at the close of the great tribulation, to be redeemed by a change from mortal to immortal.

When this assumption to the tabernacle of the vision is to take place, is not indicated. That it is not to be before the resurrection of the holy dead, seems implied by the presence of the living creatures and elders in the vision, ch. xiv. They were present also in the vision in which the fall of Babylon is celebrated, ch. xix. 1–4, which is immediately to precede the resurrection of the saints and marriage of the Lamb. If the sealed are exalted for a time to the tabernacle in the heavens, what an impression it must make on the church that remains on earth, and on the whole world! What a majestic testimony to the truth and beauty of their allegiance! What a throb it must send through the hearts of the true worshipers who survive! What confirmation it will yield to their faith, their steadfastness, and their love! What dismay and consternation will seize the persecutors and their vassals! As God is to manifest his approval of the witnesses who are to lay down their lives for his word, by raising them from death to glory and thrones in his kingdom, why should he not grant a like signal of his acceptance of the sealed, who will have given equal proof of their allegiance, by changing them to immortal, and raising them for a period to his visible presence in the skies?

III.

The vision of Christ standing with the 144,000 on Mount Sion, was followed by the flight of the angel through mid heaven, having the everlasting Gospel to proclaim to those who dwell on the earth, and to every nation, and tribe, and tongue, and people, saying with a loud voice, " Fear ye God and give him glory, for the hour of his judgment is come; and worship him who made heaven, and earth, and the sea, and fountains of waters," ch. xiv. 6–7. The period of this angel is manifestly not only after the death and resurrection of the witnesses, but after the seventh trumpet; inasmuch as the angel announces that the hour of God's judgment, which is to commence with that trumpet, has come, ch. xi. 18. The angel is the symbol of men; and the announcements he makes, and the summons he utters, represent the great messages they whom he symbolizes are to address to men. That they are to proclaim the Gospel to those who dwell on the Roman earth, and to every nation, and tongue, and tribe, and people, implies that their number is to be very great—myriads and tens of myriads. Otherwise such an emphatic proclamation of the Gospel to all nations, and warning to turn from the worship of God's works to the homage of him, could not be accomplished except in a long period. The time of this great measure will be immediately after the hour has arrived of God's judgment under the seventh trumpet.

What a stupendous change this mission of so many thousands to the whole Christian, Mahometan, and Pagan world, bespeaks! A total revolution will manifestly have been wrought in the church that remains faithful to God in respect to his future administration over the world. Now the number who look for Christ's speedy coming and reign on the earth, is comparatively small. Then no doubt will remain whether those great measures are foreshown in the Scriptures, and hold a most essential place in the divine purposes. Every believing heart will turn to him with the most fervid interest, the deepest awe, the loftiest joy, and consecrate itself without reserve to his service, and be willing to meet the self-denials and persecutions that are to try the fidelity of his people. How clearly this indicates that the great political changes which are to take place at the opening of the sixth seal, the rise of the beast from the abyss, the renationalization of the Catholic hierarchy, and the persecution, martyrdom and resurrection of the witnesses, will have been the means, through the aids of the Holy Spirit, of opening the eyes of the church to the true teachings of the Scriptures on these and other subjects; and raising them to a lofty knowledge, a filial subjection, and a joyful consecration to him. Yet these results are such as might be expected from such confutations of the errors they now cherish, such necessities of re-studying the divine word, such fresh and stupendous verifications of its truths, such fearful perils, such crushing trials, such interventions of God to rebuke and confound his enemies, and such miracles for the deliverance of his witnesses and servants. Thanks be to his name that he is to rouse his people from their slumbers, break from them the shackles of misconception and delusion in which they are now held, and breathe the all-enlightening and transforming power of his Spirit into their hearts.

This vision thus foreshows that before God begins to inflict the destroying judgments of the seventh trumpet, he is to call the whole race to a direct and emphatic decision whether they will worship him, and accept his mercy, or not. He is to raise up a host of messengers of eminent knowledge of his word, of great conspicuity, and of extraordinary power, whom he will send forth to all nations and kindreds, to proclaim to them the Gospel, summon them to pay their homage to him, and warn them that he is about to judge and retribute them according to their deeds. While he thereby gives them an opportunity, if they will, to embrace his salvation, he will place them in a condition that will oblige them to show in the most decisive manner what their dispositions towards him are, and make it manifest to men and to the universe, that if they reject him, and persist in the worship of creatures and idols, the doom he is to assign them will be just to them, befitting his truth and righteousness and wisdom, and essential to the well-being of his kingdom. The announcements, the arguments, the exhortations, and the appeals of these messengers, will undoubtedly be of great power, and make profound impressions on myriads and millions of hearts. Their mission is manifestly to fill a place of great significance in the divine administration. It is to show in a sublime manner God's readiness to forgive and redeem all who bend in submission to his sceptre, and accept forgiveness and life through Christ. None will perish except by their own voluntary act. It is to put every individual in a condition to cause him to manifest in a direct and specific form, whether he will recognize and honor Jehovah as God alone, the creator and possessor of all; or will give his allegiance to idols; and it is to summon him to this decision in the presence of the indubitable and miraculous proofs that he is God, which he will have given in the resurrection of the witnesses, and their assumption to heaven, and in the confutation of the usurping and persecuting powers denoted by the wild beast and Babylon, by the sealing angel, and those on whose foreheads he is to impress the name of Christ and the Father. For all these great measures of the Most High, and of men, will be known not only to the population of the ten kingdoms, but to all other civilized nations, and in a large degree, doubtless, to all the kindreds and tribes of the earth; and they will be understood and recognized as fulfillments of these prophecies respecting them, the witnesses, the sealing angel, the host whom he seals, and the messengers symbolized in this vision. These ministers of God will also carry in their bosoms a perfect consciousness that they severally are the persons whom the prophecy foreshows; and feel the self-possession, the strength, and the faith which that assurance will naturally inspire; while those on whom they act will be touched in a measure with a like conviction that they are those whose advent and work in the predicted scene are depicted in these visions. The utterances of those, we may justly believe, who make this last proclamation of the Gospel in such extraordinary conditions, will not be faint, formal, and unimpassioned deliverances of their message, but earnest, fervid, awe-inspiring, and of a power that will befit the crisis. Who can doubt that myriads and millions will be touched by the summons, and hasten with loving and adoring hearts to the Saviour?

IV.

The event next announced is the fall of Babylon: "And another, a second angel followed, saying, Great Babylon has fallen, has fallen, which made the nations drink of the infuriating wine of her fornication," v. 8. Great Babylon is the symbol of the Catholic hierarchies in their nationalization by the imperial government. Her fall is to be her dejection from her station as a state establishment; by divesting her of the authority and support she had derived from the civil sovereignty of the empire, and leaving her to her own resources for sustenance, and the enforcement of her decrees. She will retain her organization after her fall, and endeavor to force her subjects to continue in allegiance to her, as is seen from the next announcement. Her power, however, to persecute to death, it would seem, will have ceased at the resurrection of the witnesses; as her time, times and a half during which she is to wear out the saints, will then reach their end. But though retaining her pride, her imperiousness, and her malice, she will be restrained within a narrower sphere, and compelled to take the place of a weak auxiliary of the beast, instead of its equal and master. Her final destruction is to be postponed to a later period.

Her fall is thus to be an event of the greatest moment, and is to bespeak a vast change in the structure of the civil government, and in the sentiments of the people at large toward her. For her overthrow, it is seen, ch. xviii. 9–19, is to be the work of her subjects; not of the imperial chief, the kings, or the nobility. This implies that the power of determining the measures that are to be pursued in regard to her, will have passed in a great degree into the hands of the people; not by anarchy, for the civil government is still to exist in much strength, but through the elective franchise, and the force of the popular will. What a stupendous revolution this indicates! The crowd are not only to be alienated from Babylon, as is foreshown by the drying up of the Euphrates, but the way is to be prepared by that dislike and disgust, for leaders answering to Darius and Cyrus, the kings of the east, who will directly assail, and at length conquer and destroy her. The wine of her fornication, of which she is to cause the nations to drink, symbolizes the enticements and sorceries by which she is to win, or drive the multitude to receive her false doctrines, enter her communion, and offer her worship of creatures and idols. Her being thrown down from her connection with the state because she had acted that impious and corrupting part, shows that her pretext that she is the vicegerent of God, and is sanctioned by him in her idolatries and atrocities, is then to be seen to be false. The cunning of her deceits, and the artifice of her miracles will be discerned and appreciated; and instead of being any longer upheld or endured, she will be detested and repelled as a monster of hypocrisy, of malice, and of blood. This violent revulsion from her by which she is to be severed from the state, is doubtless to be the consequence of her brutal war on the witnesses, her hardihood under the overwhelming proof their resurrection is to form that she is an apostate, and is doomed to destruction; and her imperious attempts after all her refutations and rebukes, to continue her tyranny over those who are within reach of her power. The testimony the witnesses are to utter against her; the miracle by which God is to deliver their dead bodies from her power, and reward their fidelity by exalting them to his heavenly presence, the agency of the sealing angel in impressing the name of Christ and of his Father on the brows of his servants; and the peculiar and unparalleled proofs those servants are to give of their allegiance; must manifestly make the most powerful impressions on her vassals to rouse them to this struggle, without which they will be unable to free themselves from her galling tyranny.

This proclamation of her fall by a host of great and conspicuous messengers, shows that it is to be regarded as an event of the greatest import to the church and the world. The heralds of her fall, though the messengers of God, will probably proceed from the capital where the doom of her denationalization will naturally be made public by the imperial chief, in concurrence, perhaps, with the will of a representative legislature of the empire; and they will characterize her as having made the nations drink of the intoxicating cup of her idolatry. And how justly may they exult over her overthrow! They will understand a thousand times better than we do, the guilt of her apostasy, the impiousness of her blasphemies of God, the fury of her rage against his worshipers, the millions on millions whom she will have put to a cruel death for their fidelity to him, and the countless multitudes whom she will have led down to eternal destruction. What joy will swell their hearts that her bloody career is over; that no more victims are to be buried in her dungeons; no more wrenched on her rack; no more given by her remorseless hands to the flames. How will the tidings of her fate ring through the world! How many thousands will repeat the exclamation: "She has fallen, she has fallen, great Babylon, which made the nations drink of the infuriating wine of her idolatry," and with what dismay and terror will it strike her and the baffled crowds that still follow in her train!

V.

A group of messengers are next to go forth whose office is to utter a warning of the doom that is to fall on them who thereafter worship the beast and its image. "And another, a third angel, followed them, saying with a loud voice, 'If any one worship the wild beast and its image, and receive its mark on his forehead, or on his hand, he shall even drink of the wine of the wrath of God poured an unmixed wine into the cup of his indignation, and shall be tormented in fire and brimstone before the holy angels and before the Lamb. And the smoke of their torment ascends forever and ever. And they have no rest day and night who worship the wild beast and its image, and whoever receives the mark of its name. Here is the patience of the saints, who keep the commandments of God and the faith of Jesus. And I heard a voice from heaven saying: Write; Blessed are the dead who hereafter die in the Lord: yea, saith the Spirit, that they may rest from their labors, but their works follow with them." Ch. xiv. 9–13.

This angel also is a symbol of a body of great and conspicuous men, who are to fill the office toward the church, and the population of the empire which he filled in the vision. That he followed the angels that preceded him, implies not simply that his flight was in the same direction, but that instead of being separated by a vast interval, they were near each other, as though when the first descended below the horizon in the west, the second began to mount the eastern sky, and when he passed in the track of the setting sun beneath the line of vision, the third shot up the opposite arch of heaven. As they are thus to follow one another in quick succession, their work will occupy but a brief period. This warning and prophecy is to be addressed exclusively to the inhabitants of the ten kingdoms; and it indicates that though the Catholic hierarchy denoted by the image will have fallen from her nationalization, she will still continue an organized body, and will go on presenting her intoxicating cup to those within her reach, and endeavor to beguile or constrain them to worship her and the wild beast, and receive a mark on their forehead or hand that will identify them as hers. To worship the beast and its image is to approve and ratify their arrogations of the place and rights of God, and trust and honor them as of higher authority than he. After all the miracles God will have wrought in proof of his exclusive deity, and all the demonstrations that will have taken place that the beast and Babylon are usurpers and apostates, many will still cleave to them from the love of sin, from party spirit, from unbelief, from worldly ambition, and from hatred of God. What blindness; what unyielding hardihood! The doom denounced on the incorrigible bespeaks their guilt in worshiping creatures, and creatures of the vilest and most execrable character, as of the greatest possible impiousness; and God accordingly concentrates in the threat of eternal punishment in the most ignominious and devouring form, the greatest possible motive drawn from the dread of evil, to awe and terrify them into a repulsion of the false worship demanded by the beast and its image. It will accordingly be seen in the clearest light, that those who at this crisis revolt from him and give their adoration to creatures, cannot be withheld from apostasy by the prospect either of endless blessedness or of endless misery: and that infinite righteousness, wisdom and truth, therefore, demand that they should be left to their choice, and the retributions it is to draw after it. They deny his title to reign; they blaspheme his name; they attempt to wrench the sceptre from his hands, and thrust him from his throne. He therefore verifies his deity, his holiness, and his goodness, by adjudging them to a destruction by which their sin and misery will be forever made the occasion of his showing forth his perfections in a more dazzling resplendence, and binding his holy subjects to him in a more fervid and joyous allegiance.

These fear-inspiring warnings are to be rendered necessary, the prophecy indicates, by a violent attempt of the persecuting powers to force not only those who nominally belong to the Catholic communion, but the true worshipers to yield obedience to their impious behests. "Here," it is announced, "is the patience of the saints who keep the commandments of God and the faith of Jesus. And a voice from heaven said: Write, Blessed are the dead who hereafter die in the Lord; yea, saith the Spirit, that they may rest from their toils, and their works follow with them." This warning is therefore to be followed by a furious and bloody persecution, by the imperial and kingly power, with the concurrence of the Catholic hierarchy; for though she will have been separated from the state, yet from the fact that the aim of the persecutors is to drive the people of God to worship the image of the beast—that is, the Catholic hierarchy in its connection with the pope—as well as the beast itself, it is apparent that the Catholic power, though without authority to enforce its decrees, is to act in concurrence with the civil rulers. The servants of God *generally* are, therefore, at this crisis, to be put to as severe a test of their fidelity to him, as the witnesses were, when arraigned and compelled to choose betwixt apostatizing, or yielding up their lives. Revolt from God or death will now be the alternative presented to all. What grandeur marks the intervention of God by a voice announcing the blessedness of those who, after this warning, die in the Lord; that is, on his behalf, in expression of their allegiance to him! What a thrill of strength and courage that assurance from the lips of the Almighty will shed through the hearts of his trembling children! In how many bosoms those gracious words will be treasured up! By how many joyous voices they will be repeated, and made to resound through the whole empire! It is immediately before this great crisis, probably, that the sealing of the servants of God is to take place in the fervor and invincibleness to which their fear and love of him will be raised; and possibly they are to be the persons symbolized by this angel, who are to utter the denunciation of eternal death on those who apostatize, and the promise of eternal blessedness to those who lay down their lives rather than swerve from their fidelity to God. In what fulness and beauty their adherence to him will shine! How indubitably it will be seen that they are meet to be admitted to his kingdom! They are to rest from their perilous and exhausting labors; but their works are to follow with them; that is, they are to be received by the Almighty to his kingdom *as martyrs* who are forever to be crowned with special distinctions in his presence, because of their steadfastness here in truth and righteousness.

The witnesses, it is thus foreshown, are not to be the last of God's children who are to be subjected to martyrdom. A far more general and terrible persecution is to take place after the fall of Babylon, in which the character of the two parties will be raised to the most emphatic contrast, and God will indicate by his own gracious voice, his approval of his faithful children; while he will speak in accents of terror the doom that awaits his incorrigible enemies. And this great strife is to fill an important place in the divine administration, by showing in the most resistless light that those whom he accepts are truly renewed after his image, and prepared for admission to his kingdom; for having maintained their allegiance under the greatest temptations to falter to which they could be subjected, how indubitable it will be that no trial they can afterwards meet can be of any power to shake their adherence to God. And this demonstration, in all its greatness, is to be indispensable in order to the differing administration that is to be instituted at Christ's coming, under which the race is to be sanctified, and saved without being carried through the trials that are so conspicuous a feature of the present dispensation. The reality and unalterableness of the renovation of those whom he now redeems, set forth with such strength and grandeur by the martyrs, will carry the assurance to every bosom in the universe, that those whom he saves without subjecting them to similar trials, are equally renewed, and raised to a fervor and steadfastness of love, that render their allegiance indubitable through eternal ages. It is thus seen again, from this vision, that the great question on which the conflict of the people of God with their persecutors is to proceed is: Who has the rights of law-giver over the church? Whose prerogative is it to institute a worship, appoint a method of salvation, and demand a homage of men? The arrogation of that prerogative by the civil rulers, and Catholic priests, is clearly the vital principle of all their legislation over the Bible and the church, and all their persecutions of the true worshipers. It is also seen that the messengers who are to utter the warnings of this vision are to be aware that they are the persons whom it foreshows; and that the whole church, and perhaps the population generally of the empire, will be impressed with the fullest conviction that their ministry is the fulfillment of this prophecy. After the slaying of the witnesses, the heralding of the Gospel to all nations, the announcement of the fall of Babylon, and the sealing of the servants of God, the church will be in no uncertainty as to the point which the accomplishment of the prophecy has reached.

VI.

That a considerable period is to intervene between the denationalization of Babylon, and her final destruction, is indicated by the violent persecution of the saints, in which, in conjunction with the wild beast, she is to engage after her fall. It is implied also in the deeper depth of degradation and malevolence to which she is to sink after her severance from the state.

It is at this period, undoubtedly, that she is to receive the shock of the seventh vial. "And the seventh poured his vial into the air, and a great voice came from the temple from the throne, saying: It is done. And there were lightnings, and voices, and thunders; and there was a great earthquake. The like had not been since men were on the earth: such an earthquake, so great. And the great city went into three parts; and the cities of the nations fell.

And great Babylon was remembered before God, to give to her the cup of the wine of the vehemence of his indignation. And every island fled, and mountains were not found. And hail, great in weight as talents, descended from heaven. And the men blasphemed God for the stroke of the hail, for its stroke was very great." ch. xvi. 17–21.

Lightnings, voices and thunders, denote analogous commotions in the world of men. An earthquake is a symbol of a sudden and violent revolution in which the whole mass of a nation is thrown into anarchy, and the government overturned. This upheaval of the population in passionate and resistless revolt, is manifestly to extend through the whole empire; as the Catholic hierarchy which is to be co-extensive with the ten kingdoms, and which though denationalized, is to retain its organization up to this vial, is now to be rent into three parts, and every island is to flee, and all mountains disappear.

As the great city is the symbol of the Catholic hierarchy, modeled after the form of the imperial government under Jovian and his successors, having the pope as its head, its division into three parts, denotes that the Catholic priesthood is to be separated into three parties; Italian perhaps, French and German. It implies therefore, that Babylon will at this disruption, lose the support of two-thirds of the hierarchies. The cities of the nations which are also to fall, are the nationalized hierarchies in the

Catholic and Protestant kingdoms that lie out of the western empire: such as Holland, Denmark. Prussia, Sweden, perhaps Russia also, and Greece. The effusion of the vial into the air, indicates that it may act in one direction as well as another.

What the event is that is to prompt to this universal revolution, is not specified. It may be an attempt of the civil power to renationalize the Catholic hierarchy. That it is in some way to have a direct reference to that church, is manifest from its issuing in its disruption into three parts; and its being followed immediately by its annihilation. If the overthrow of the imperial government and the monarchies of the ten kingdoms, is to be the condition of the extermination of the Catholic priesthood, the determination of the people to extricate themselves from that power, may lead them to revolutionize the imperial and kingly sovereignties.

It is doubtless to be after a defeat of the Catholic hierarchy in a stuggle of some kind to reinstate itself in authority that the angel, ch. xviii., is to descend from heaven and proclaim again that she has fallen, and announce that her destruction is nigh. "And I saw another angel come down from heaven having great power, and the earth was lightened with his glory. And he cried with a strong voice, saying: She has fallen, has fallen great Babylon, and become a habitation of demons, and a station of every unclean spirit, and a station of every unclean and hated bird; because all the nations have drunk of the inflaming wine of her fornication, and the kings of the earth have committed fornication with her, and the merchants of the earth have grown rich from the strength of her luxury." Ch. xviii. 1–3. The splendor of this angel bespeaks the momentousness of the errand on which they whom he represents are to come! They are to light up by their conspicuousness and glory the whole atmosphere of the empire. Their voice is to ring through every vale, and reverberate from every steep and hill; and they are to proclaim not only that Babylon has fallen, but that she has become the habitation of demons, and a watch post of every unclean spirit, a station for every unclean and hated bird; that is, she is to wear a more haggard and ghastly aspect than before, and is to sink to a lower abyss of debasement and malignity, than she reached in the days of her luxury and power. All pretence to a religious character is to be abandoned, and the attitude and air assumed of an odious bird of prey; of an unclean spirit, whose office it is to defile; and of a demon whose work is to torture and destroy; and she is to employ herself in endeavoring indiscriminately to steep those within her reach in the putrescence of her own pollution; and wreak on them her insatiable malice. What a picture of exasperated and reckless wickedness! She is to reach such an extreme of shamelessness, malice, and fury, that the unholy themselves who meet her glance, will recoil from her as from death's horrid shape. How righteous in God thus to allow her to reveal the full venom of her heart, and leave her at length to turn her poisonous fangs upon herself! She is to be given up to make evil her good, because she had spent her life in seducing the kings and princes to sin, and drenching the nations with the cup of her abominations. Yet some of God's people are still to continue in her communion! "And I heard another voice from heaven, saying: come out of her my people, that ye partake not of her sins, and that ye receive not of her plagues; for her sins have accumulated unto heaven, and God has remembered her iniquities." v. 4–5. How clearly it is seen from this, that the warning of the third angel against offering any farther worship of the beast and its image, is to be needful to guard even some of God's children against that sin! Some, though they may not formally have honored those usurping powers, may by remaining in their communion, give a tacit sanction to them, and expose themselves to be drawn into her sins, and made to share in her punishment.

A voice from heaven now enjoins those who have suffered from her sorceries and tyranny, to destroy her as she had destroyed them. "Give unto her as she also gave," that is, without mercy; and double to her double according to her works. Into the cup into which she has poured, pour to her double. In one day her plagues shall come, death, and sorrow, and famine; and she shall be burned with fire," v. 6, 8. Her destruction is accordingly to be the work of the people on whom she had wreaked her malice; not the monarchs and princes. Though her annihilation is to involve the death of those generally whom she represents, the pope, it is seen from ch. xix. is to survive: "And the kings of the earth who had lived luxuriously with her, when standing afar, for fear of her torment, they shall see the smoke of her burning, shall lament and mourn for her, saying, Alas, alas! the great city Babylon, the mighty city; for in one hour has thy judgment come. And the merchants of the earth weep and lament for her, because no one buys their merchandize any more; they who have grown rich by her shall stand afar for fear of her torment, weeping and lamenting, saying Alas, alas! that great city which was clothed in linen and purple and scarlet, for in one hour so great riches are destroyed. And a mighty angel took a stone, like a great millstone, and cast it into the sea, saying, Thus with violence shall the great city Babylon be cast down, and shall not be found any more." Vs. 9–21.

What a group of stupendous events is thus foreshown under the seventh vial, and the vision of the angel repeating the announcement: "She has fallen, has fallen, great Babylon, and become a habitation of demons, a watch-post for every unclean spirit!"

What revolutions of the civil governments are here foreshown, which expositors have universally overlooked! What a solution the presumed defeat of the Catholic hierarchies in an effort to regain their lost power, furnishes of the exasperation in wickedness to which they are to be excited by their despair!

VII.

On the destruction of Babylon, adoring acknowledgments of God's righteousness and power were uttered by the heavenly hosts. "After these I heard as a loud voice of a great multitude in heaven, saying, Halleluia [that is, Praise Jehovah]. The salvation, and the glory, and the power of our God; for true and righteous are his judgments: for he has judged the great harlot, who corrupted the earth with her fornication, and has avenged the blood of his servants from her hand! And again they said, Halleluia! And her smoke ascends for ever and ever. And the four and twenty elders and the four living creatures fell and worshiped God, who sat on the throne, saying, Amen. Halleluia." Ch. xix. 1–4.

The loud voice of the great multitude was from the lips of angels, as is seen from the chant of acquiescence in their hymn that followed from the elders and living creatures, who are symbols of the redeemed in heaven.

What grandeur marks this expression of their

assent and joy at the destruction of that apostate and malignant power! What a sense it bespeaks of God's rectitude, and wisdom, and goodness, in consigning her to that doom! What an understanding of her wickedness and her guilt! What a feeling of the necessity that God should thus vindicate himself from her aspersions and put an end to her war on his people! It is their lofty intelligence, their spotless purity of heart, and the glow and fervor of their benignity, that will prompt them thus to approve of his delivering her over to shame and perdition through the ages of ages. And how sublime is the Amen of acquiescence from the living creatures and elders, who represent the unnumbered hosts of the ransomed in the skies! How clearly this chant shows that these great measures of God's avenging justice are fully known to all the inhabitants of heaven; and that their effect is to bind them in firmer attachment to his service! The perpetuation of her punishment through endless ages, is to be as necessary as her punishment at all. To strike her to annihilation, would imply that God could not uphold and reign over her for ever in her fallen condition, wisely and gloriously to himself. Her punishment will be perpetual, because she will for ever persist in sin; and because her perdition is for ever to be overruled to his glory, and the well-being of his kingdom. This again indicates that a boundless significance is to attach to her destruction. Her doom is to be public and visible. She is to be "tormented with fire and brimstone in the presence of the holy angels and of the Lamb," and the smoke of her burning is to ascend up for ever and ever, ch. xiv. 10, as a signal of the folly and madness of her sin; and a token of God's righteousness, truthfulness, and power.

CHAPTER XXV.

The Man of Sin—Return of a part of the Israelites—Resurrection of the Holy Dead—The change of the Living—The binding of Satan—The Advent of Christ, and Battle of Armageddon.

I.

It is at this period, there is reason to believe, that the Man of Sin and Son of Perdition is to develope himself, and set himself up as the object of worship. That his revelation of himself is not to take place until after the destruction of Babylon, and extinction, in the main, of the Catholic faith and worship, is seen from the warning immediately before her annihilation, ch. xiv. 8–11, against worshiping the beast and its image, and receiving its mark on the forehead, or hand. The Catholic religion is therefore to continue to be the religion of the persecutors and the unbelieving, so far as they have a faith and worship, down to the hour when the popular rage strikes the priesthood of that fallen church from its organization and from life. It is to be at that moment accordingly, when the imperial chief and the kings being left without any religion, which they can enjoin on their subjects, and the multitude continuing more alien from Christ than they are to be from Roman Catholicism, which they will have just swept from the earth;

that the Man of Sin will attempt to furnish his subjects with a new religion, by the pretext that he himself is God, and has a supreme title to worship. He is to treat Christ as a deceiver, and Christianity as a fable; as is seen from his making war on the Lamb, ch. xvii. 14; as though that Almighty Being had no power to protect his followers. And he is to do according to his will; exalting himself, and magnifying himself above every God; and speaking marvellous things against the God of gods, and he is to prosper in that career of conquest and self-aggrandizement, till the indignation denounced against the Israelites is accomplished. Dan. xi. 36–39; 2 Thess. ii. 3, 4.

Monstrous as this deification of himself will be, it is so far from being improbable, that it may naturally, in a measure, spring out of the false metaphysics of Kant, Schelling, Hegel, and Coleridge, that have spread their deadly venom through almost the whole mass of the educated on the continent of Europe, and largely in Great Britain; their most distinctive doctrine being the denial of God's personality, and substitution of a material or ideal pantheism in his place. When the Man of Sin blasphemes the God of gods, as being but an idea, and existing only in the thoughts of men, he will utter nothing that will shock the disciples of those impious hierarchs; nor will he when he claims to be himself divine and entitled to worship; as it will be but asserting of himself, what they hold to be true of all, each one being on their theory, an element in the universe of matter, or thought, which according to them, is God. And he is to prosper in his arrogation of the name and place of God till the indignation which is to be poured on the Israelites reaches its close. He will succeed in his false miracles. He will have the co-operation of the unclean spirits of Satan. He will gain a host of worshipers.

II.

It is probably at this time—or perhaps at an earlier day—that the Israelites will begin to return, and re-establish themselves in their own land. The exact period of their re-gathering, and the attitude the nations are to maintain toward them, is not defined in the prophecies. It is only foreshown that they are to re-establish themselves in Palestine, and in Jerusalem, before the imperial chief of the western Roman empire shall make war on them. Zech. xiv. 1–9. The fact that he and the kings of his empire are at the prompting of the unclean spirits to proceed there with their armies, to intercept them from erecting a kingdom, of which many of them will believe Messiah, descending from heaven, is to become the king, implies that they will have returned in such numbers that a powerful force will be necessary to conquer them, and drive them again into exile. What period is to pass after the commencement of their return, before he invades Palestine, is not revealed, nor what the motives are to be, that are to prompt the king of the south and the king of the north to make war upon him. Dan. xi. 40. Their aim, probably, is to be to prevent him from encroaching on their own territory, as well as from conquering Palestine. The king of the south is doubtless, the king of Egypt. The king of the north, though he may have conquered Armenia and Mesopotamia, is probably the monarch of Russia; as he is to come with many ships, which no other northern power could employ in approaching Palestine. Where his conflict with them is to take place, is not indicated, except that it is not to be in the land of Israel. He is to march into the countries, and is to overwhelm and pass through; and he is to march into the goodly land, and many of the Israelites shall fall. But these shall be delivered from his hand;—Edom and Moab, and the chief of the children of Ammon. v. 4. The goodly land, is the land of Israel. As he is not to invade that land until after he has fought the king of the south, and the king of the north, his battles with them are not to be in the territory that belongs to Israel. They are to be in Philistia, therefore Phenicia, or perhaps upper Syria. This is confirmed by the fact that he is not to invade Egypt, until after his contests with them, and his first invasion of the territory of the Israelites. He is to rule over the treasures of gold and silver, and over all the costly things of Egypt; and the Lybians and Ethiopians are to be in his steps. v. 42–43. Nothing is said of his demanding submission to himself as God, or seating himself in a temple at Jerusalem. One of his chief aims is doubtless to be, to augment his territory, and increase his power, though his wish in that may also be to aggrandize his fame as a warrior, and thereby give a bolder color to his demand of worship from his subjects.

But his main object in conquering Palestine and Jerusalem, it is clearly indicated by the gathering together of the kings and their armies to make war on the Lamb at Armageddon, is to be to prevent the fulfillment of the numerous prophecies that God is to recall his ancient people from their dispersion, re-establish them as a nation, and constitute Christ their king, and the king of all the earth, and destroy the persecuting and idolatrous rulers, who are arrayed against him. He will deem himself, doubtless, under an imperative necessity of confuting those predictions, from the resistless impressions made by the witnesses, the sealing angel, the sealed, and the martyrs, that are to suffer at the period of the third angel's warning against the worship of the beast and its image. To remain a careless spectator of these powerful assaults, he may feel will be tamely to surrender his throne; while, as he will anticipate no conflict with any but a human power, he may flatter himself that the conquest of Palestine, Syria, and Egypt, will be an easy task.

III.

After the hymn of the angels, the living creatures, and the elders at the destruction of Babylon, " A voice came from the throne, saying: Praise our God all ye his servants, and ye who fear him both small and great. And I heard as a voice of a great multitude, and as a voice of many waters, and as a voice of mighty thunders, saying, Halleluia! that the Lord God Almighty has reigned. Let us rejoice, and exult, and give glory to him; for the marriage of the Lamb has come, and his bride has prepared herself." ch. xix. 5–7. The voice from the throne is a summons from the angels, doubtless to the servants of God on the earth, and all who fear him small and great, to praise him. That it is from the heavenly hosts, is apparent from their denominating God " our God;" and that it is addressed to the servants of God on the earth, is seen from the appropriation to them of that name, which is exclusively theirs, and from their consisting of persons of all ages, the small and the great, which is a distinction that is known only to a race like ours, not to angelic orders of being. This call of all his people on earth to praise him, implies that a great epoch is reached in the divine administration that demands a grateful and adoring recognition from his children, of every age and rank, who remain in the natural life. The response from the earth, like the voice of a great multitude, like the voice of many waters, like the voice of mighty thunders, indicates the number of the renewed on the earth is to be immense; and shows, therefore, that the Spirit of God will have breathed his quickening influences on his true worshipers, during their long struggles with the persecuting powers; given them wisdom and fidelity in the instruction of their families, heard their prayers, and made the word of truth from their lips, efficacious to vast numbers of the nations to whom they have addressed the testimony of Jesus. What sublimity breathes in their answer! They glance first at the reign of God in the ages that are past, and then to the more wondrous measures of the administration he is about to institute: "Halleluia that the Lord God Almighty has reigned! Let us rejoice and exult, and give glory to him; for the marriage of the Lamb has come, and his bride has prepared herself." v. 6–7. How clearly this implies, that they are to understand all the great steps of God's government over his people, and over his enemies; and see with what grounds they are fraught, of joy and thanksgiving. And how distinctly this proves that they are to be aware of the great events that are next to take place: the resurrection of the holy dead, and their installation in the offices they are thenceforth to fill in his kingdom. The Lamb's bride is the symbol of the risen and glorified saints, and his marriage with them, their exaltation to the kingly and priestly stations which they are to occupy in his kingdom. Ch. xxi. 9–10.

"And it was given to her that she should be robed in fine linen, bright and pure, for the fine linen is the rightousness of the saints." Her investiture with those robes is the symbol of her justification. "And he said unto me, write; Blessed are they who are called to the supper of the marriage of the Lamb." v. 9. Those called to the supper are not the bride, but living saints, and those doubtless who are to be transformed from mortal to immortal, and fitted thereby for admission to the most intimate relations to Christ in his kingdom on the earth.

IV.

Immediately before the resurrection of the holy dead, it would seem from the vision, ch. xx. 1–3; Satan and his legions, are to be bound, and banished from the earth for the period denoted by the thousand years. "And I saw an angel descending from heaven, having the key of the abyss, and a great chain in his hand. And he seized the dragon, the ancient serpent, who is the devil and Satan, and bound him a thousand years, and cast him into the abyss, and shut and set a seal on it, that he might not seduce the nations any more, until the thousand years should be finished; and after them, he must be loosed a short time." Satan is here the representative of the whole body of fallen angels of whom he is the chief. The abyss is the invisible world, the realm of the unholy dead. His dejection into that deep, and confinement there, denotes that he is to be precluded from access to men during the thousand years, and intercepted from his war on God's kingdom. The thousand years are the symbol of three hundred and sixty thousand. There is no more reason for assuming that the thousand years are not employed as representatives of a greater period that bears an analogy to them, than there is for assuming that Satan is not the symbol of any fallen angel but himself; or that his being bound with a great chain and cast down into the abyss, and sealed there, are not symbols, but denote merely, that though an incorporeal being, he is to be literally bound with a chain, and literally shut up in an abyss, by material barriers. The vision is symbolic, and the period is used as a symbol, as truly as the chain, the binding of Satan, his dejection into hades, and his imprisonment there are. What a stupendous event this is to be! How benign to the living race on the earth! They are to be relieved in an instant by this great act of the Son of God, from the assaults of that gigantic wretch, who will through all preceding ages have wreaked his malice on every generation, and every individual that has come into being, and been the prompter of all the crimes into which they have been led, and the author of the degradation and misery with which they have been overwhelmed. But as he and his legions sink into the depth of hades, that terrific tempest which will have raged through so many thousand years, will subside into a calm. Silence, serenity, peace, will shed their balmy power over every nation and every heart.

V.

The resurrection of the holy dead, there is reason to believe, is to take place immediately after this chant of the servants of God that remain in life on the earth. It is implied in the marriage supper of the Lamb, which is then to be celebrated; as those who are called the bride are they who are to be raised from the dead. It is implied also in the non-appearance of the living creatures and elders in the visions that follow the chant, ch. xix. 1–3, on the destruction of Babylon. As they are symbols of the spirits of just men made perfect, their presence in that character, after their resurrection, would be precluded. That their resurrection is to precede Christ's coming in the clouds to judge and destroy his enemies, is seen from the consideration that they are to come with him, ch. xix. 11–14; Thess. iv. 14; Zech. xiv. 5. Their resurrection is accordingly foreshown, chap. xx. 4–6, immediately after the binding of Satan. "And I saw thrones; and they sat on them, and judgment was given to them; and the souls of those who had been beheaded for the testimony of Jesus and for the word of God, and whoever had not worshiped the wild beast, nor its image, and had not received the mark on their forehead, and on their hand. And they lived and reigned with Christ the thousand years. But the rest of the dead lived not until the thousand years should be finished. This is the first resurrection. Blessed and holy is he who has part in the first resurrection. Over them the second death has no power, but they shall be priests of God and of Christ, and shall reign with him a thousand years." This is thus expressly declared to be the first resurrection; a resurrection exclusively of the holy dead, and a corporeal resurrection; for it is to be a resurrection, among others, of those who had been put to death under the reign of the beast and its image, for the testimony of Jesus, and for the word of God. When they first met the apostle's glance, he called them souls—conscious human spirits, which was descriptive of them while disembodied by death. Their resurrection was their investment with incorruptible and glorified bodies. That their resurrection is to be corporeal is seen also from the prediction that the second resurrection is to be of that nature. As the second resurrection is to be from the grave and death, so also is the first. The saints thus raised to life were then installed in their offices as kings and priests by the gift to them of judicial authority; and they entered on their reign with Christ. The rest of the dead are not to live until the thousand years are finished.

What an amazing display of the knowledge, the power, and the grace of the Redeemer this instant summons of innumerous millions from the ruins of the grave to a glorious and deathless life will form! What a moment to the raised will it be of wonder, of adoration, and of joy!

VI.

It is foreshown by Paul that in intimate connection with this great event, the living saints are to be changed to immortal. "The Lord himself shall descend from heaven with a shout, with the voice of the archangel and the trump of God, and the dead in Christ shall rise first. Afterwards, we who are alive and remain, shall be caught up to meet the Lord in the air; and so shall we ever be with the Lord," 1 Thess. iv. 16–17. Those who are thus to be caught up to meet the Lord in the clouds, we learn from 1 Cor. xv. 51–54, are at their assumption to be changed from mortal to immortal. "Behold I show you a mystery. We shall not all sleep, but we shall all be changed. In a moment, in the twinkling of an eye, at the last trump, for the trumpet shall sound, and the dead shall be raised incorruptible, and we shall be changed. For this corruptible must put on incorruption, and this mortal must put on immortality. So when this corruptible shall have put on incorruption, and this mortal shall have put on immortality, then shall be brought to pass the saying that is written: Death is swallowed up in victory."

The passage from Thessalonians implies that there is to be an interval between the resurrection of the dead and the transformation of the living; επειτα rendered in the common version, *then*, that is next, being equivalent to *afterwards*. That the change of the living is not to be strictly contemporaneous with the resurrection, is shown also by the prediction that the dead in Christ shall rise first; that is, before the transformation of the living. How long the interval between them is to be is not revealed. The translation of those who are changed to the cloud in the air is doubtless in order to their being judged and accepted. The throne of the Almighty will be in the heavenly temple in the atmosphere, as it was in the visions.

This transformation of the living is obviously that foreshown under the sixth seal, when, after the sealing of God's servants, who are to be the first on whom this renovation and exaltation of nature is to be conferred, he saw a great multitude, whom no one could number, of every nation and tribes and peoples and tongues, standing before the throne and before the Lamb, and clothed in white robes, and having palm branches in their hands. And they cry with a loud voice, saying, The salvation to our God who sits on the throne and to the Lamb! And all the angels stood in the circuit of the throne, and of the elders, and of the four living creatures, and fell before the throne on their faces, and worshiped God, saying, The blessing, and the glory, and the wisdom, and the thanks, and the honor, and the dominion, and the might to our God forever and ever. Amen!" ch. vii. 9–12 That this vision of the transformed is to have its accomplishment soon after Christ's advent, is seen from the announcement by the angel that "these are they who came out of the great tribulation, and washed their robes and made them white in the blood of the Lamb." The delineation which follows of their reward, is of ineffable beauty. "Therefore are they before the throne of God, and serve him day and night in his temple. And he who sits on the throne shall dwell in a tabernacle with them. They shall not hunger any more, nor thirst any more, neither can the sun strike them, nor any heat, because the Lamb who is in the midst of the throne shall guide them, and lead them unto the fountains of the waters of life; and God shall wipe away every tear from their eyes."—Ch. vii. 15–17.

What transcendent events these are to be! How clearly they bespeak the introduction of a new dispensation! With what emphasis they indicate that the multitude of the sanctified on the earth at the time of Christ's coming is to be innumerable; that his power to redeem will have been manifested with ineffable glory during the long struggle of the persecuting powers to crush his kingdom into extinction! What wonder will thrill the breasts of the living on finding themselves instantly freed from the sentence of death, and the blight and wreck brought on them by the fall; raised to that integrity, that beauty, that glow of nature that belongs to immortals, and entering on a spotless, blissful, and undecaying existence! What grandeur of power, wisdom and love marks this new method of deliverance from the curse of sin! What a proof it is to form of the efficacy of Christ's expiation, and the glory of his righteousness! It is in this mode, doubtless, exclusively, that men are to be raised during the thousand years into the freedom from evil that is then to distinguish the sons of God.

VII.

Soon after the resurrection of the holy dead, and the marriage supper of the Lamb, the Son of God is to descend with his risen saints, and destroy the wild beast, the kings and their hosts who will have gathered together to the battle of the great day of God Almighty. It is foreshown, Daniel xi. 44–45, that after the king who deifies himself has conquered Palestine, Egypt, Ethiopia and Lybia, "tidings out of the east and out of the north shall disturb him. Therefore he shall go forth with great fury to destroy and to lay waste many, and he shall place his regal tent between the seas and the holy and beautiful mountain, and he shall come to his end, and none shall help him." The tidings out of the east are doubtless to come from Edom, Moab, and Ammon, and those from the north from the hosts of Russia in Upper Syria, or on the Euphrates; and are to indicate that fresh forces are gathering against him to snatch his conquests, especially Palestine, from his hands. He is therefore to go forth from Egypt with great fury, to destroy those who assail him, or who he may fear are ready to revolt from him; and will at length proceed to Idumea, where he and his army are to be struck to perdition by a power, and in a form he will not have anticipated, though forewarned by the word and the people of God.

"And I saw heaven opened, and behold a white horse, and he who sat on it is called faithful and true, and in righteousness he judges and makes war. And his eyes were as a flame of fire, and on his head many diadems, having a name written which no one knew but he, and he was clothed in a garment dyed with blood. And his name is called the Word of God. And the armies which were in heaven followed him on white horses, clothed in fine linen, white and pure. And from his mouth proceeds a sharp sword, that with it he may smite the nations. And he shall rule them with an iron sceptre, and he shall tread the wine-press of the wine of the vehemence of the wrath of God Almighty. And he has on his garments and on his thigh a name written, King of Kings and Lord of Lords.

"And I saw an angel standing in the sun. And he cried with a loud voice, saying to all the birds that fly in midheaven, Come, gather ye together to the great supper of God, that ye may eat flesh of kings, and flesh of commanders of thousands, and flesh of mighty men, and flesh of horses, and of them who sat on them, and flesh of all, both freemen and slaves, both small and great.

"And I saw the wild beast, and the kings of the earth and their armies gathered together, to make war with him who sat on the horse and with his army. And the wild beast was taken, and the false prophet with it, who wrought wonders before it, with which he deceived those who received the mark of the wild beast, and those who worshiped its image. And they two were cast alive into the lake of fire which burns with brimstone. And the rest were slain with the sword which proceeded from the mouth of him who sat on the horse, and all the birds were filled with their flesh," ch. xix. 11–21.

He who sat on the white horse is the Son of God. The armies of heaven, which followed him, are the risen and glorified saints; as is indicated by their white robes, which are the symbols of their justification, and show that in the interval between their resurrection and their descent from heaven with Christ, they had been presented by him to the Father, and accepted as his. The false prophet is the pope, as is seen by his having wrought wonders before the beast, with which he deceived those who received the mark of the beast, and worshiped its image. Having lost his power at the destruction of his hierarchy denoted by the image, he appears here, as far as is seen, without any train. His sympathies are to be with the beast, though that monster has set himself up as God; and they are to perish together by being taken and cast alive into the lake of fire which burns with brimstone. Where their destruction is to take place is not here indicated. It is, however, it would seem from Isaiah xxxiv., not at Jerusalem. There is no intimation in the prediction of Christ's descent on the Mount of Olives, Zech. xiv. 5, that the beast or his armies are then to be there; and no hint that the fires by which they are to be consumed are to fall on that scene. Instead, the Israelites in the city are, on the occurrence of the earthquake, to flee from it into the new-formed valley extending to Azal; which implies that the upheaval and cleaving of the ground are the only dangers to which they are to be exposed. Armageddon, in the great plain of Esdraelon, having been the scene of two great battles, is used doubtless as the symbol simply of a place of great slaughter. The site of the battle in which the beast and his armies are to perish is undoubtedly in Idumea, whither after his return from Egypt he may go to add to his conquests that country, which had before escaped his hands, Dan. xi. 41. It is foreshown in Isaiah, that that is to be the scene of God's vengeance in the year of recompenses for the controversy of Zion. "For my sword reeks in the sky; behold it shall come down upon Idumea, and upon the people of my curse to judgment. The sword of the Lord is filled with blood; for the Lord hath a sacrifice in Bozrah, and a great slaughter in the land of Idumea. And the unicorns shall come down with them, and the bullocks with the bulls; and their land shall be soaked with blood, and their dust made fat with fatness. For it is the day of the Lord's vengeance, the year of recompenses for the controversy of Zion. And the streams thereof shall be turned into pitch, and the dust thereof into brimstone, and the land thereof shall become burning pitch. And it shall not be quenched night nor day; the smoke thereof shall go up forever. From generation to generation it shall lie waste, none shall pass through it forever and ever." Isaiah xxxiv. 5–10. This is confirmed by the prediction, Isaiah lxvi. 23–24, that those who repair to Jerusalem from sabbath to sabbath, to worship before Jehovah, shall go forth and look upon the carcasses of the men that have transgressed against him; for their worm shall not die, neither shall their fire be quenched; and they shall be an abhorring unto all flesh." And this is in harmony with the prediction, Zech. xiv. 12–15, that the plague with which the Lord will smite all the people that have fought against Jerusalem, is to be a consuming of their flesh while they stand upon their feet, and a consuming of their eyes in their sockets; and a consuming of their tongues in their mouths. The plague of the horse, and of the mule, and of the camel, and of the ass, and of other beasts that shall be in their tents, is to be the same as of the men. Such a wasting of the flesh, and of the eyes, and of the tongue would be the effect which a sudden envelopment in volcanic fire would produce.

That Idumea is to be the scene of this burst of avenging fire on the foe, is shown also, Isaiah lxiii. 1–6: "Who is this that cometh from Edom, with dyed garments from Bozrah; this that is glorious in his apparel, traveling in the greatness of his strength? I that speak in righteousness, mighty to save. Wherefore art thou red in thine apparel, and thy garments like him that treadeth in the wine vat? I have trodden the wine-press alone, and of the people there were none with me; for I will tread them in mine anger, and trample them in my fury, and their blood shall be sprinkled upon my garments, and I will stain all my raiment. For the day of vengeance is in my heart, and the year of my redeemed is come. And I looked, and there was none to help, and I wondered that there was none to uphold. Therefore mine own arm brought salvation unto me; and my fury it upheld me; and I will tread down the people in mine anger, and make them drunk in my fury, and I will bring down their strength to the earth." Bozrah is a city of Idumea. The treading of the wine-press denotes the same destruction of the beast and his armies as is couched under the symbol of the attle of Armageddon. It is into a lake, therefore, of fire and brimstone that is to gush up from the burning depths of Idumea, that the beast and false prophet are to be cast; and it is there that their unconsuming bodies, and theirs who are to perish with them, are forever to welter;—monuments of God's avenging justice; and objects of horror and execration to all the generations of the holy, through eternal ages. Isaiah lxvi. 24.

CHAPTER XXVI.

The New Creation of the Heavens and Earth—The Judgment of the Living Nations—The Return of the Israelites who still remain in Dispersion—The Means by which the Race is to be Delivered from Sin—The events that are to follow the Thousand Years of Christ's Reign—The Release of Satan, the Revolt of a Multitude—Their Destruction—Satan's Doom—The Last Resurrection and Judgment—The Surrendry of the unfallen Worlds to the Father—Christ's Everlasting Reign on the Earth, and the continued Redemption of Men through endless ages.

THE new heavens and new earth beheld by the prophet were undoubtedly symbolic, as the former heaven and earth had been repeatedly used as symbols. This is confirmed by the absence of the sea. As the earth is to be inhabited after its new creation, a sea will be as necessary to vapors, rains, fountains, streams, and vegetable and animal life, as it is now. The new heaven, therefore, represents rulers of a new order, the earth subjects of a new character, and the absence of the sea, the freedom of the nations from the storms of revolution and war.

The period of the new creation of the heavens and earth is to be that, it appears, which is to intervene between the deliverance of Jerusalem from the beast and his armies that will have conquered it, and the entrance of the risen saints on their reign. The first is seen from Isaiah; the last from John. "For behold I create new heavens and a new earth; and the former shall not be remembered nor come into mind. But be ye glad and rejoice forever in that which I create; for behold I create Jerusalem a rejoicing, and her people a joy. And I will rejoice in Jerusalem, and joy in my people; and the voice of weeping shall be no more heard in her, nor the voice of crying. There shall be no more thence an infant of days, nor an old man who shall not fill his days; for a child (he would be who) should die an hundred years old; and one who should be a sinner a hundred years old would die accursed." Isaiah lxv. 17–20. The renovation of the atmosphere and earth is to take place at the same period as the renovation of the living saints; and the change is to fit them for the abode of beings that are immortal. There is to be no more sorrow, no more death in infancy, no more premature old age. The same picture is drawn in the Apocalypse of the condition of the race at the descent of the New Jerusalem. "And I John saw the holy city New Jerusalem, coming down from God out of heaven, prepared as a bride adorned for her husband. And I heard a great voice out of heaven saying, Behold the tabernacle of God with men! And he will dwell with them, and they shall be his people, and God himself shall be with them, their God. And God shall wipe away all tears from their eyes; and there shall be no more death, neither sorrow nor crying; neither shall there be any more pain, for the former things are passed away. And he that sat upon the throne said, Behold I make all things new. And he said unto me, Write, that these words are true and faithful." Ch. xxi. 2–5.

What a sublime act of mercy! What a divine gift! Though the race is still to come into existence mortal, and none are to become immortal except by a change of their nature; yet none are to die; none are to suffer; none are to weep; and manifestly, therefore, none are to sin: for how, if sin and death continue to reign, can there be no pain, no crying, nor sorrow? Those who have their birth under that dispensation will accordingly come into life in essentially the state corporeally in which Adam and Eve were created—susceptive or capable of death, but not subjected to it, because they will be preserved from sin; as the first pair would have been exempted from it had they maintained their allegiance. In what majesty will the attributes of Christ appear in this deliverance of the countless generations of the millennial ages from the curse of sin! How adequate he will be seen to be to the work he has undertaken! In what resplendence beyond the present thoughts of men will his immeasurable love then appear!

II.

That it is to be after the investiture of the risen saints, with their offices as kings and priests, that the living nations are to be judged, is seen from their being sent forth as Christ's messengers to gather his elect from the four winds from one end of heaven to the other. Matt. xxiv. 31. This is foreshown in the vision of the reaping of the earth, ch. xiv. 14–16. "And I looked, and behold a white cloud, and upon the cloud one sat like a Son of Man, having on his head a golden crown, and in his hand a sharp sickle. And another angel came out of the temple, crying with a loud voice to him that sat on the cloud: Thrust in thy sickle and reap; for the time is come for thee to reap; for the harvest of the earth is ripe. And he that sat on the cloud thrust in his sickle on the earth, and the earth was reaped." The being seated on the cloud was undoubtedly a risen and glorified saint. He is said to be like a son of man, to show that he was a human being. That he had been raised from the dead, justified, and glorified, is seen from his golden crown. He is not the Son of God, manifestly from his being directed by an angel when to thrust his sickle on the earth, which is unsuitable to the eternal Word; and from his foreshowing that his angels, *i. e.*, messengers, are to gather together his elect. In the parable of the wheat and tares also, the good seed are the children of the kingdom, the harvest is the end of the age, and the reapers are—not men—but angels—messengers. The being on the cloud represents, therefore, the whole body of the glorified saints. How suitable this office is to the lofty powers with which they will be endowed; the intimacy of their relations to Christ; and their interest in the living saints whom they are to gather to his presence. Their gathering before his throne, is to be in order to their being judged, accepted, and admitted to his kingdom according to Christ's prediction, Matt. xxv. 31–36: "When the Son of Man shall come in his glory and all the holy angels with him, then shall he sit upon the throne of his glory; and before him shall be gathered all nations; and he shall separate them one from another, as a shepherd divideth his sheep from the goats; and he shall set the sheep on his right hand, and the goats on the left. Then shall the king say unto them on his right hand: Come, ye blessed of my Father; inherit the kingdom prepared for you from the foundation of the world. For I was an hungered, and ye gave me meat: I was thirsty, and ye gave me drink; I was a stranger, and ye took me in; naked, and ye clothed me; I was sick, and ye visited me; I was in prison, and ye came unto me. Then shall the righteous answer him, saying: Lord, when saw we thee an hungered, and fed thee; or thirsty, and gave thee drink? When saw we thee a stranger, and took thee in; or naked, and clothed thee? Or when saw we thee sick, or in prison, and came unto thee? And the king shall answer and say unto them: Verily inasmuch as ye have done it unto one of the least of these my brethren, ye have done it unto me." How clearly this indicates that this judgment is to be preceded by a violent persecution according to the prediction, Rev. xiv. 9–13, that during the denunciation by the third angel of the wrath of God on all who worship the beast, or its image, the people of God are to be put to a decisive test of their fidelity to him; and will when called to that alternative, give up their lives for his sake. Others whose blood is not shed, are to be imprisoned or robbed of their property and left without relief, to suffer the miseries of hunger, sickness, and desertion. It implies, too, that the interval between that persecution and this judgment, is to be but brief, as both the persecuted and persecutors will still be in life.

III.

Immediately after the harvest, the vintage is to take place. "And another angel came out of the temple which is in heaven, he also having a sharp sickle. And another angel came out from the altar who had power over fire, and cried with a loud voice to him who had the sharp sickle, saying: Thrust in thy sharp sickle, and gather the clusters of the vine of the earth; for her grapes are fully ripe. And the angel thrust his sickle into the earth, and gathered the vine of the earth and cast it into the great wine-press of the wrath of God; and the wine-press was trodden without the city, and blood came out of the wine-press, even unto the horse-bridles, by the space of a thousand six hundred furlongs." Rev. xiv. 17–20.

The grapes are symbols of the wicked; their being reaped and cast into the wine-press of God's wrath, denotes their being gathered together, and their being violently destroyed; the blood of the grapes symbolizes their blood; and the extensive surface which it flooded to such a depth, bespeaks the vastness of the multitude who are thus to be consigned to destruction. This vision is parallel with the judgment of the wicked in the parable, Matt. xxv. 4–46. "Then shall he also say unto them on the left, Depart from me, ye cursed, into everlasting fire, prepared for the devil and his angels; for I was an hungered, and ye gave me no meat; I was thirsty, and ye gave me no drink; I was a stranger, and ye took me not in; naked, and ye clothed me not; sick and in prison, and ye visited me not. Then shall they also answer and say unto him: Lord, when saw we thee an hungered, or athirst, or a stranger, or naked, or sick, or in prison, and did not minister unto thee? Then shall he answer, saying: Verily I say unto you, inasmuch as ye did it not to one of the least of these, ye did it not to me. And these shall go away into everlasting punishment; but the righteous into life eternal."

This judgment of the righteous and wicked, is to be the judgment of the living exclusively; and of those on the one side who, during the persecution of the worshipers of God immediately before, will have given the most decisive proofs of their allegiance to him, by bearing in steadfastness the outrages to which they are subjected by the beast and its image; and of those on the other, who will have shown in an equally indubitable form, by withholding all sympathy from the sufferers for Christ's sake, that they are approvers of the beast and its image. It will be confined, therefore, to the nations in which a persecution has taken place; and of those we may believe there will be millions at least of the young, who will not be included in these sentences, inasmuch as they will not have made any decisive manifestation of either a true friendliness, or hostility to Christ's persecuted people.

As the judgment of the several nations will doubtless take place successively, it will occupy a considerable period.

IV.

The Israelites who are in exile at the time of Christ's advent, will, after the destruction of the persecuting powers, and the conversion of the nations, and contemporaneously with the new creation of the heavens and the earth, be recalled to their national land. "And I, (because of) their works and their thoughts, it is meet that I should gather all the nations and the tongues, and they shall come and see my glory, (*i. e.*, his visible presence at Jerusalem); and I will set among them a sign; and I will send survivors of them to the nations, Tarshish, Pul, and Lud, drawers of the bow, Tubal and Javan, the distant isles which have not heard my fame, and have not seen my glory; and they shall declare my glory among the nations. And they shall bring all your brethren from all nations, an oblation unto Jehovah, with horses and with chariots, and with litters, and with mules, and with dromedaries, to my holy mountain Jerusalem, saith Jehovah; as the children of Israel bring the oblation in a clean vessel to the house of Jehovah. And also of them will I take for priests and for Levites, saith Jehovah. For as the new heavens and the new earth which I create, stand before me, saith Jehovah, so your name and your seed shall stand." Isaiah lxvi. 19–22.

It is clear from Isaiah xxxv, and Jeremiah xxxi. 8–9, that this restoration is to take place contemporaneously with the renovation of the heavens and earth; as the deserts are to be changed to fruitfulness and watered with springs, to supply them on their journey. It is shown also, Isaiah xi. After predicting that the Messiah with righteousness shall judge the poor, and reprove with equity the meek of the earth, and shall smite the earth with the rod of his mouth, and with the breath of his lips shall he slay the wicked; and righteousness shall be the girdle of his loins, and faithfulness the girdle of his reins; the prophet adds: "The wolf also shall dwell with the lamb, and the leopard shall lie down with the kid, and the calf and the young lion and the fatling together; and a little child shall lead them. And the cow and the bear shall feed; their young ones shall lie down together; and the lion shall eat straw like the ox. And the sucking child shall play on the hole of the asp, and the weaned child shall put his hand on the cockatrice's den. They shall not hurt nor destroy in all my holy mountain: for the earth shall be full of the knowledge of the Lord, as the waters cover the sea." The whole of the material and animal world will thus be freed from the curse at this epoch, and reinstated in its pristine innoxiousness, and subordination to man. And the Gentile nations, it is seen from their aiding the Israelites on their return, will have been brought to faith in Christ.

It is then added: "And it shall be in that day that the Gentiles shall seek unto the root-sprout of Jessie, which stands as a signal to the nations, and his rest—that is his place or station—shall be glorious. And it shall be *in that day*—when the Gentiles shall seek to the root of Jessie—that Jehovah shall stretch out his hand the second time to recover the remnant of his people, that shall be left, from Assyria, and from Egypt, and from Pathros, and from Cush, and from Elam, and from Shinar, and from Hamath, and from the islands of the sea. And he shall set up a signal to the nations, and shall assemble the outcasts of Israel, and bring together the dispersed of Judah from the four wings of the earth." v. 10–12.

It is to be after the destruction, therefore, of the antichristian powers, not before, as Dr. Tregelles, Mr. Newton, and other writers of their class maintain; and after the nations have been brought to look unto Christ as their Redeemer, and contemporaneously with the renovation of the earth and air, that this great summons to return to the land of their forefathers is to be borne to the scattered sons of Israel. The nations that had held them in bondage, and trampled them down for ages, are to turn and joyfully bear them back as a sacred offering to Jehovah; and miracles, like the drying of the Red Sea and of Jordan, are to be wrought to remove obstructions to their progress homeward. Isaiah, ch. ix., 15–16. xxxv. 1–10.

This is to be one of the greatest and most majestic of the measures of the new administration Christ is to institute. What a multitude of promises it will fulfill! What an exemplification it will form of his power and sovereignty! How suitable to the grandeur of his attributes, that instead of suffering that people to be wrested from his hands by the malice of Satan, he should make their revolt, and the long ages of their abandonment to blindness, incorrigibleness and misery, the occasion of a higher manifestation of his wisdom and grace in their salvation! What a vastness and comprehensiveness mark his purposes of mercy toward them, compared with the thoughts of men! After ages of revolt in the most impious forms, and punishment by the direst degradation and wretchedness, how clear it will be that their redemption thereafter in their unending generations, is the work of his sovereign love! As they are to be exalted to intimate relations to him, and to fill offices of great significance toward the rest of the race, Micah iv. 6–8, the spotless rectitude to which they are to be raised, the fervid love with which they are to glow, and their joyous activity in his service, will make them a more illustrious monument than the saved of any other nation, of the riches of his power, wisdom, and grace.

The measures by which the race is to be delivered from sin and its curse, and raised to lofty intelligence, unsullied rectitude, and unalloyed blessedness, under the reign of Christ, are to have a peculiarity and greatness suited to their ends.

1. Of these, the first is to be the visibleness of his presence and reign. Instead of remaining on the throne of heaven, and revealing himself only by his providence and word, he is to enthrone himself on Mount Zion, Ps. ii. 6, 7, and manifest himself in his glory to the eyes of all the inhabitants of the earth, receive their awed and rapturous homage, and bless them with his voice and smile. The impressions made by this revelation of himself, will transcend all others in greatness and beauty. Some

indeed, with an inconsideration that is surprising, deny that his visible presence can have any adaptation to disinthrall the beholder from darkness, insensibility, and unbelief, because the renovation of the mind is the work of the Holy Spirit. But that is wholly to misjudge, first of the condition of those to whom he is thus to manifest himself; and next of the effect which the sight of his person, the accents of his voice, and his acts of righteousness and grace will produce in the hearts of the renovated. Those over whom he is to reign in visible glory are to be renewed, not impenitent and hostile; and the convictions and realizations wrought in them will naturally be of the highest adaptation to give power and strength to their affections toward him. To imagine that he will be beheld by them without impression; or that his presence will only stun and bewilder, or awaken selfish fear, is to betray the grossest ignorance both of him and of themselves. Is there a renovated person on earth that could meet the glance of that Almighty Being, to whom he owes his salvation, behold the glory with which he is invested, and hear his gracious voice, without a gush of awe, of gratitude, of love, of adoration, that would fill all the depths of his spirit! It cannot be. Why did God reveal himself visibly to Adam, to Enoch, to Noah, to Abraham, to Job, to David, to Isaiah, to Jeremiah, to Ezekiel, and other prophets, if that manifestation of himself had no adaptation to penetrate them with a conviction of his being, his perfections, his right, and his dominion; and rouse their holy affections to the most vivid energy? Why did Christ reveal himself to Paul; why did he raise him to Paradise, and disclose to him the mysteries of his reign there, if it had no suitableness beyond all other means, to augment his knowledge, to add fervor to his love, and give strength to his faith, that he might be fitted for the labors and conflicts of the ministry assigned him, in which he was to meet the scorn of unbelievers, and the rage of the persecuting? It was because of the peculiarity and greatness of the truths disclosed to him, and the inerradicable impressions made on his heart, that those visions were employed to mould him for the service to which he was called. The power of Christ's visible presence in his reign on earth, will be far, far greater to exalt mankind in knowledge, to raise them to perfect faith, and to inspire them with the holy affections in their loftiest forms that become their relations to him. The first dazzling beam from his countenance will put an eternal end to unbelief. No one will ever again doubt his existence, question his deity, or hesitate to recognize and adore him, as the Creator, the Ruler, and the Saviour of men. The chants of the living creatures, the elders, and the angels in the divine presence, may be taken as exemplifying the resplendence of thought, the comprehensiveness of knowledge, the fervor of adoration, the rapture of joy, that are to characterize the homage of the living who are to bend in his presence in his reign on the earth.

2. The life-giving influences of the Holy Spirit are to be poured on them in measures wholly unparalleled in the present age, and to endow them with prophetic gifts. "And it shall come to pass, after (the restoration of Israel) that I will pour out my Spirit upon all flesh, and your sons and your daughters shall prophecy; your old men shall dream dreams, your young men shall see visions; and also upon the servants and upon the handmaids in those days, will I pour out my Spirit." Joel ii. 28, 29. They will not be left to their own powers, great and refined as they may be, in their search after knowledge, and endeavors to instruct their families, and associates; but will enjoy the enlightening and elevating aids of the Spirit, and receive accessions to their intelligence and impulses to their love, in that miraculous form.

3. They are to be freed from the tempting power of Satan. Bound in fetters and hurled with his legions down the depths of hades, he will be precluded from exerting his malignant agency on men, blinding their minds, suggesting to them false and impious thoughts, inflaming their passions, and luring them to destruction. Who can appreciate the greatness, the benignness, the joyfulness of this deliverance! In the struggles of the renewed now against evil, their

battle, we are taught in the Scriptures, is not exclusively with themselves and their fellow beings, but with spirits from the abyss. "For we wrestle not against flesh and blood, but against principalities, against powers, against the rulers of the darkness of this world, against wicked spirits" in aerial regions; that is, the hierarchies of hell, who are carrying on a war wherever they can, against God and his kingdom.

What a calm will settle on the world when he is dashed to his prison! All the infinite brood of evil thoughts he injects into the minds of his victims, all the tempestuous excitements of passion, all the envy, and hate, and rage, and revenge, he engenders in their bosoms will vanish with him; and order, serenity, and peace, spread their mild dominiom over the world.

4. They will be freed from all the disorders of a fallen nature with which the renewed are now left to struggle. The body and mind will be in harmony with each other; the intellect and will invested with authority over the thoughts and affections, and all the functions of life be unobstructed and healthful. What a contrast to the disarray, the weakness, the confusion, the antagonism, that now reign in those who have reached even the highest measure of santification!

5. They are to be exempted from exhausting toil, from pain, from sorrow, and from death. No pangs

are ever to wrench their bodies; no anguish ever to wring their hearts; no darkness ever to settle on their brows. There is to be no more curse. Their life in immunity from bodily and mental evils, will be like the life of holy immortals.

6. Immense accessions will be made to their knowledge of God, his purposes, and his kingdom. They will be acquainted with the boundlessness of the realms over which he reigns; they will know the numerous orders and countless multitudes of the intelligences that dwell in them; the nature of the government under which they are placed; their history, their interest in our world, and the manner in which the revolt, the perdition, and the salvation of men are made to contribute to their instruction, their trust in God, and their joy in his service. He has built his empire on a scale commensurate with the wants in this relation, of the redeemed through eternal ages. Great as their attainments will be, they can never grasp all that will be within their reach. Fresh disclosures will continually be made to them of the infinite multitude of great events that take place in the distant abodes of the blessed; and revelations of future events will come to them from time to time, that will fill their hearts with wonder, adoration, and love.

7. They are to enjoy the presence and the aids of the risen and glorified saints. What the offices are which those exalted beings are to fill, we know only

from their titles. They are to be kings and priests unto God and to Christ, and shall reign with him a thousand years. A king is one who is invested with a sovereignty over men: a priest is one who intervenes between men and God, presents to him symbols of their homage, and bears back to them the responses he returns to their acknowledgments, their thanksgivings, and their supplications. What the form is to be in which they will fill these ministries, is not revealed to us. It is enough for us to know that it will be of a greatness and beauty suited to the sanctitude and majesty of God, and the loftiness of their nature; and will form a fitting expression of their love, their gratitude, and their fidelity. What a transcendent prerogative to enjoy the presence, the guidance, and the love of such illustrious beings: to hear the exposition of God's rights and laws from their lips, to receive his messages through their ministry, to be made partakers of their wisdom and their faith, and be led on by their hands, in the paths of eternal life!

8. How benign will the impression on the heart be of such a peaceful, holy, and blissful world, lighted up by the presence of Christ, compared to the distractions, the weaknesses, the sins, the miseries, the darkness and death, that now reign here! Our conceptions now of what a world of intelligences, raised from the ruins of sin to perfect knowledge, holiness, goodness, and bliss, are but vague and faint.

Those who dwell under the sceptre of Christ, will behold in it a spectacle of ineffable beauty; worthy of his boundless power and wisdom; and shedding a vivifying, and joy-inspiring light over all the domains of his illimitable empire.

VI.

"When the thousand years are expired, Satan shall be loosed out of his prison, and shall go out to seduce the nations that are in the four corners of the earth, Gog and Magog, to gather them together to battle, the number of whom is as the sand of the sea And they went up on to the breadth of the earth, and surrounded the camp of the saints and the beloved city. And fire descended from God out of heaven, and devoured them. And the devil who seduces them, was cast into the lake of fire and brimstone, where are also the wild beast and false prophet, and they shall be tormented day and night for ever and ever." Ch. xx. 7–10. What a proof this fresh plunge of millions into sin, will form that all the holy submission, all the loving trust, all the spotless obedience of the preceding ages, was the work of the sovereign power of the Spirit! He has but to withdraw his renewing and sanctifying gifts, and the generation that next comes into existence in the natural life, will revolt under the impulses of Satan, as those do now who are left to the unobstructed sway of that tempter. It is to manifest this truth with an awe-inspiring power, doubtless, that this revolt after such ages of obedience is to be permitted. On the other hand, in what a lurid light will the unmitigated malice, the unquenchable hate of Satan appear in his renewal, the moment of his release, of his war on God and his kingdom! How clear will it be that no punishment can ever soften his obdurate heart, no sense of the infinite ruin that follows in his train, will ever check his insatiable desire to plunge more millions and other worlds to destruction; and that the safety, therefore, and peace of the universe require that he should be hurled back to the lake of fire that was kindled for him, and lie there in chains through his endless existence!

VII.

The doom of Satan and his legions, is to be followed by the resurrection and judgment of the unholy dead. "And I saw a great white throne, and him who sat on it, from whose face the earth and the heavens fled, and no place was found for them. And I saw the dead, small and great, standing before the throne; and books were opened; and another book was opened which is of life; and the dead were judged from the things written in the books, according to their works; and the sea gave up the dead who were in it; and death and hades gave up the dead who were in them, and every one was judged according to their works. And death and the grave were cast into the lake of fire. This is the second death, the lake of fire. And as any one was not found written in the book of life, he was cast into the lake of fire," ch. xx. 11–15. This is the resurrection of the rest of the dead who were left in the grave at the first resurrection, or are to descend there after that event, under the avenging judgments by which the enemies of Christ, of that period, are to be destroyed; or those of Gog and Magog who are to revolt after the release of Satan. And that they are all to be unholy, is seen from the absence of any intimation that any of their names are written in the book of life. They are to be judged according to their deeds, as they are written in the books first opened. The opening of the book of life seems to have been to show that their names were not written there. Death and the grave, that are the doom in this world of sinners, are then to be cast into the lake of fire, with those over whom they had had dominion, and are no more to have a place on the earth. What an epoch in the annals of the world! As mankind are to continue in an endless series of generations, it indicates that the sentence of death brought on them by the fall, is to be absolutely repealed. They are to be placed in a relation in that respect to the law, in which they would have stood, had the first pair continued in innocence, and secured thereby the holiness and blessedness of all their posterity. The infinite greatness and glory of Christ's expiation and righteousness, are now to manifest themselves in that transcendent effect. There not only is to be no more death. There is to be no more liability to it. All that are thereafter to come into being are adjudged unto life, on account of Christ's obedience; as on account of Adam's disobedience, all were adjudged to death.

VIII.

Having thus reigned on the throne of the universe, until he has put all his enemies under his feet, Christ is then to return the sceptre of the heavenly worlds to the hand of the Father, and thenceforth reign only over the redeemed race of men. "Afterward the last band (is to be raised from the grave) when he is to deliver up the kingdom to God even the Father, when he shall have put down all rule and all authority and power. For he must reign till he has put all enemies under his feet. The last enemy that shall be destroyed is death. For he hath put all things under his feet. But when he saith all things are put under him, it is manifest that he is excepted, who did put all things under him. And when all things shall be subdued under him, then shall the Son also himself be subject unto him that put all things under him, that God may be all in all. 1st Cor. xv. 24–28. The kingdom he is to resign to the Father, is not the kingdom of this world; as he is to reign here through the ages of ages. Dan. vii. 13–14,

18, 27; Luke i. 33; Rev. xi., 11; but is the dominion of the heavenly worlds which he received at his exaltation to the right hand of the Father, and is to exercise till all enemies are put under his feet. What a height and depth of righteousness, of wisdom, and of truth, mark this measure of the eternal Word! Having taken the place of a subject by his incarnation, he is, on the final conquest of all his enemies, to resume it. Among his enemies is death, because of its dominion over his subjects; which, therefore, if not abrogated, would imply that his obedience and expiation were inadequate absolutely to deliver them from that doom. And he is to continue in that relation of subordination to the Father, and yield obedience in it through eternal ages! This full and final repeal of the sentence to death on all who come into being after his millennial reign is closed, it is thus manifest is essential to the full accomplishment of his work. He would fail of giving perfect salvation from the effects of the fall, were he not to abolish death, the penalty of sin, as well as sin itself, of which it is the retributive infliction. During the present dispensation he sits with his Father on his throne. Ps. cx. 1; Heb. 1–3. viii. 1. During his millennial reign on the earth, the Father is to sit with him on his throne. For the new Jerusalem, the symbol of the glorified saints, is to be the tabernacle of God with men, and he is to dwell with them, and they are to be his people, and God himself is to be with them, their God. The throne of God and the Lamb is to be in it, and the Lord God Almighty and the Lamb are to be, by the mode in which they will manifest themselves, its temple, and are to lighten it with their glory. Rev. xxi. 3, 22, 23; xxii. 1–5. Instead of reigning separately, they are then to reign conjunctively, as they now do in heaven. The Father will thus during that period, publicly give in the presence of the universe, his sanction to all the measures of Christ's administration, as he now gives it in heaven. But on the close of the millennial reign, the Father is to resume the sceptre of the heavenly worlds, and Christ is to be in subordination to him; and for reasons of the greatest moment. Two governments, entirely independent of each other, would be inconsistent with the unity of God, the equal rights of the Father and the Son, and the obligation of all intelligences to worship them both as divine. To suppose Christ to be an absolutely independent sovereign of the human race, would be to suppose that mankind would thenceforth owe no homage except to him. But that would be to divest the Father of his title to the submission, trust, love, and obedience that are his due from men. It would imply also that the Son no longer owed allegiance to the Father. But the Son is in his human nature, legitimately and necessarily, a subject of the Father, and cannot be released from fealty any more than any other individual of the race.

He moreover owes allegiance to the Father in his divine nature also, from his voluntarily taking the station of a servant by becoming incarnate, and placing himself under obligation to render obedience in his whole person, as God-man.

This great change in the administration of the universe is thus to spring from the unity of the God-head, and the equal title of the Father and the Son to the full love and homage of all creatures. What a grandeur of truth, and wisdom, and righteousness invests it! In what sanctity the divine rights appear! With what care are the prerogatives of God, and the obligations of creatures guarded from misapprehension! No knee in heaven can refuse to bow to the Son, and acknowledge him to be Lord, to the glory of God the Father, because he reigns only over the race of men; for he is not to be divested of his rights as Jehovah, by that limitation of his special dominion. No human tongue can refuse to recognize and glorify the Father, because he especially reigns over the hosts of heaven; for he will not have relinquished his sovereignty over the earth, but will forever exercise it in the presence of his Son, to whom he has given it as his kingdom. No child of earth will deem it unsuitable to adore and serve the almighty Word, because he has united himself to one of our race, and taken the place of a subject, and is forever to reign in that subordination to the Father. Instead, his stooping to become incarnate, and obey, and die for men, itself gives him a special title to their homage and service ; and constitutes a peculiar and infinite ground of obligation, to love and glorify him. How just to the Father, is the relation that is thus to be assumed by the Son! How suitable to Christ! How majestic his condescension in taking the place of a servant! What strength and beauty are to mark his testimony to the rightful supremacy of the Father! In what a dazzling light will his subordination through eternal ages appear in the eyes of the universe! How will it be felt that his obedience surpasses in greatness and significance, that which any other being can render! And how will the beauty and sublimity of his example, give truthfulness and fervor and constancy to the love and fidelity of all other holy beings!

CHAPTER XXVII.

The Grandeur of Christ's Purposes—The Contrast which the mistaken views of the Writers I have cited present to his designs—The Faults of other Expositors of the Prophecies—A Considerable Period is yet to pass before the Coming of Christ—The Verification of the Sixth Seal will indicate the approach of the great Events that are to follow the Reconstruction of the Fallen Monarchies, and will give birth to vast Changes in the Faith of the true Church—The Certainty that Louis Napoleon cannot survive the Sixth Seal, and therefore cannot be the Antichrist.

Such are the great events that are to precede and attend the coming of Christ; and such is the dispensation he is then to institute over the race. How suitable to him! How transcending the thoughts, not only of the errorists whose misconceptions and misrepresentations I have been confuting; but of the more evangelical of the expositors of the prophetic Scriptures. Before I dismiss them let me recur to the position of the Louis Napoleon party, to the views of the Evangelical Church, and to the changes that are to be wrought in the faith of believers before Christ comes and assumes the sceptre of the earth.

1. A sadder spectacle of narrowmindedness, misjudgment, and delusion, than that presented by the writers whose misapprehensions and perversions of the word of God I have pointed out, is not often ex-

hibited. Not one of their peculiar theories but vanishes into air under the test of a just criticism. Not one of the most cherished and vaunted of the novelties, which give substance and hue to their system, that is not either in antagonism to the teachings of revelation, or without any authority from them. Not one which they attempt to sustain by external testimony, that is not in contradiction to the facts of history. Such is their theory of the wild beast; their scheme of chronology; their views of Louis Napoleon; their notion that the seventieth week of Daniel is yet future; the doctrine several of them advance that the chief prophecies of Daniel and John are to have a double fulfillment, and all the other elements of their system. On the other hand, they have failed to catch even a glimpse of a long succession of events of the most momentous character, that are to take place antecedently to the coming of the Son of Man. They appear to be wholly unaware that the catastrophes foreshown under the sixth seal are yet future, and confute their confident persuasions in respect to the career of Louis Napoleon. The great events that are to mark the period of the seventh trumpet and seventh vial seem scarcely to have attracted their notice. The fancy cherished by them with so much ardor, that all the great actors of the twelve hundred and sixty years are to reappear on the scene and react their tragedies in the last twelve hundred and sixty days of this dispensation, leaves them no room for the great judgments and deliverances which God has assigned to the period that is to intervene between the seventh trumpet and the advent of the Messiah. Their errors are thus, not of a slight and harmless cast, but are fundamental, and adapted in a high degree to bewilder the unlettered and fanatical, and give a fresh impulse to the jeers of the unbelieving and hostile. It becomes those, therefore, who hold the testimony of Jesus, to point out their character, and put the church on her guard against them.

2. The fact is becoming more and more apparent that of the numerous books that have been published on the prophecies of Daniel and John, of Isaiah, Jeremiah, Ezekiel and Zechariah, within the last fifty years, a large part have been fraught with great and mischievous errors. The speculations of writer after writer, from Woodhouse, Faber, Cuninghame, and Frere, down to the present time, have been confuted by events; and their prognostications met so often with confutations that rendered them ludicrous, that thousands have been led wholly to repel the subject in incredulity and disgust. Where lies the cause of their misconceptions and misrepresentations? In a measure, doubtless, in some of the writers in a sanguine and rash temper, which exposed them to extravagance and delusion. But those faults, though very conspicuous in Faber, Frere, Cuninghame, Irving, Cumming, and others, furnish no solution of the most important of the mistakes, into which they

have run, inasmuch as they had in their hands ample means of guarding against them and discerning and verifying the truth. The chief reason of their errors lay in their proceeding on preconceived and arbitrary theories, and neglecting to inquire into the principles on which the symbols and figures of the prophecies are employed, and to define and exemplify the laws by which they are to be interpreted. There is no statement of any one of the leading laws of symbolization in any of the writers of Great Britain, from Woodhouse to the Louis Napoleon school; nor a trace of any thorough knowledge of the peculiarities of tropical language. Their theories and expositions are consequently in a high degree conjectural and vague, dreamy and arbitrary. The most farfetched and mistaken constructions are put forth with the greatest confidence; and the most irrelevant passages, and arguments employed to sustain them. It is not a matter of surprise, therefore, that they have fallen into great mistakes, and run in many instances into extreme delusions. There can be no exposition of the prophecies that is at once truthful and susceptive of a clear and satisfactory demonstration, unless it is framed by the laws of the media through which they are conveyed, whether symbols, figures, or untropical language, according to their respective natures, and their usage in the Scriptures. Had the writers whose volumes are occupied to such an extent by inaccuracies, extravagances, and not unfrequently mere caricatures, qualified themselves for the task of expositors by a careful culture of those essential branches, they would never have fallen into the errors that now disfigure their pages. When will the hour come that those who undertake to unfold the great things of God's word, will recoil from so momentous a work while unfurnished with the elementary knowledge that is indispensable to their success? When will the time arrive, that those who desire instruction in regard to the prophecies will demand that the authors who solicit their patronage shall openly state what the great principles are on which they proceed, and indicate the passages in the divine word by which they regard them as authenticated?

3. It is manifest from the great series of events that is yet to precede the coming of Christ, that a very considerable period is to pass before that epoch arrives. The calculations of such writers as Faber, Cuninghame, Frere, Elliott, and others of that class, and of the Louis Napoleon school, in respect to the time of his advent, or any of the events that are to precede it, rest altogether on a false basis, and have already been confuted by divine providence: and the like fate will overtake all others that may, like theirs, be framed for the purpose of sustaining a preconceived theory, and producing a sensation. There are no means now of determining when the 1260 years of Daniel and John began: nor will there be till the

great event—the death of the witnesses, which is to mark their close, takes place. What the distance of that event is from the present hour, is unknown, and for the present, indeterminable. It must, however, be a considerable series of years; as the overthrow and reconstruction of the monarchies of the ten kingdoms will doubtless occupy a period of some length. Though the tendency of the general mind throughout the whole of western Europe is manifestly in the direction of far more democratic institutions; yet there are no decisive signals of a speedy explosion that will precipitate the present governments into the gulf of destruction. It may be hastened by a sudden catastrophe, such as the death of a leading monarch, that should give birth to a struggle of rival aspirants for the throne, and lead, first, perhaps, to a republic, and then to a military despotism, and contribute, like the French revolution of 1848–1851, to generate similar changes in other kingdoms. Instead of that, it may be the effect of a succession of measures that shall gradually transfer the supreme power from the monarchs and magnates to the people.

4. When the sixth seal has its accomplishment in the engulfing of the monarchies, it will show in the most indubitable manner, that the reconstruction of the ten kingdoms, and institution of an imperial rule, are not far off. That emergence of the wild beast

from the deep in its last form, will demonstrate with equal certainty, that the renationalization of the Catholic church and the persecution of the witnesses are at hand. That those stupendous events are to require more than a brief period, seems certain from their extraordinary nature, and from the fact, that during their progress, a greater revolution than has ever yet taken place is to be wrought in the views of the true worshipers, both in respect to God's exclusive right to legislate over the faith of men, and of the great scheme of administration he is to institute over the world, at Christ's coming. On the one side, all the false and impious arrogations by the persecutors, of dominion over the faith and worship of their subjects, will be openly and resolutely rejected; and on the other, all the mistaken notions that now prevail respecting the continuance of the present dispensation, till a point is reached at which the work of redemption is to end; that the nations are to be converted by the agencies and instrumentalities exclusively that are now employed for the purpose; and that heaven alone is to be the scene of Christ's personal reign through eternal ages, will be universally abandoned and repelled by the believing church; and the great doctrine so clearly taught in the Scriptures, and so glorious to him, and propitious to the world, of his personal reign on the earth, be embraced with a full intelligence of its significance, joy at the destiny it unfolds to the race, and a fervid readiness to consecrate themselves with all their energies to the conflicts and toils to which they are to be summoned, and especially to the great work assigned them, of testifying for God, vindicating his rights, and proclaiming the glad tidings of his grace and the warnings of his wrath to the nations. This vast change of faith and expectation cannot be wrought in a moment. It is more likely to demand a considerable series of years. What a host of gifted and faithful teachers; what arguments, what appeals, what contests with antagonists, will be requisite to achieve that stride in the knowledge and appreciation of the truth! What effusions of the enlightening, convincing, and renovating Spirit, will be needful to give efficacy to their labors!

5. Whenever the catastrophe of the monarchies foreshown under the sixth seal, may take place, whether soon or after a considerable period, nothing can be more certain than that if Louis Napoleon continues in his imperial seat till that crisis, his political career will then end. As he is now a conspicuous and aggressive horn of the wild beast, if he retains that place till the earthquake cleaves the ground beneath his throne, and the thrones of his associate kings, and precipitates him into hades, he can never return to regrasp a sceptre, and make himself the despotic chief of the ten kingdoms.

Facilis descensus Averni.
Noctes atque dies patet atri janua Ditis;
Sed revocare gradum, supernasque evadere auras,
Hoc opus, hic labor est.*

This will be conceded by all who assent to the interpretation of the abyss out of which the wild beast is to ascend, Rev. xi. 7; xvii. 8, as hades, or the world of the dead; inasmuch as he could not return to a corporeal life on earth, except by a resurrection, which cannot take place; as none of the dead, except the witnesses, are to be raised before Christ comes; and their resurrection is to be not before, or at, but after the rise of the beast from the abyss; while none of the unrighteous are to be raised until thousands of years after the earthquake of the sixth seal.

Though the abyss is unquestionably used, Rom. x. 7, to denote the world of the dead; as it was there that Christ's soul was not to be left; and thence that it was to be brought back to life; and though it is clear also, that it is the prison of Satan and his legions, as it is the name of the place to which the demons, Luke viii. 31, intreated that they might not

* Easy the passage down to hell's dark realms,
And open wide its portals ever stand;
But to retrace the slippery steep, and climb
Back to high heaven's free air and light serene,
A baffling struggle that, a fruitless toil.

be sent; and the realm in which Satan is to be imprisoned during the thousand years; yet as the pit of the abyss from which the smoke and the locusts of the fifth trumpet ascended, Rev. ix. 2, was an abyss on the earth; and as abyss in Greek answers to the Hebrew term denoting the ocean, and is used in that sense in the Septuagint, Gen. i. 2; vii. 11, it may be thought possible that abyss is used with that meaning, Rev. xi. 7, and xvii. 8; and that as the great sea, Dan. vii. 2, was employed as a symbol of the nations in the anarchy and strife out of which the rulers denoted by the beasts arose; so here the abyss out of which the wild beast is to rise is a symbol of the people of the ten kingdoms in the agitation and anarchy into which they are to be thrown by the earthquake and other catastrophes of the sixth seal. Should it be assumed that it here denotes the sea, and is used in that relation, it still will remain equally clear that Louis Napoleon cannot be the person who is to rise to the throne of the *new empire*, act the part of persecutor and Antichrist, and perish at the battle of Armageddon. For although on the supposition that the sea is the symbol of the people of the western empire in a state of revolution, in which Louis Napoleon is to lose his sceptre; it would not necessarily follow that he must also lose his *life* by that catastrophe, and thereby be precluded from a return to power; it is yet clear from the nature of the revolution symbolized by the earthquake, that his loss of office and power, if he loses them at that crisis, must be final. For the effects wrought by the earthquake under the seal, plainly imply that the movement of the people which it represents, is to divest the monarchs and subordinate officials of all their authority, and reduce them, if they escape death, to absolute powerlessness. The sun and moon, their symbols, are no longer to give their light; the stars are no longer to hold their place in the skies; and the mountains and islands are to be removed from their stations and disappear. This clearly indicates that every grade of officials is to be intercepted in its functions, and sink into the condition of unauthoritative subjects. That is shown also by the description of the wild beast, Rev. xvii. 8: "The beast which thou didst see was, and is not, and shall ascend out of the abyss, and go to destruction." There is accordingly to be a time between the period when it was, and the epoch of its ascent from the abyss, in which it literally is not to be. It is therefore, for a space, to be absolutely struck from existence. If Louis Napoleon, then, is to be a horn of the beast, when it meets that catastrophe, it is manifest that should he still remain in *life*, he is to be wholly stripped of office and power, and to remain in that condition as long as the reign of anarchy continues. And this renders it altogether impossible that he can reinstate himself on the throne, and grasp the dominion, not only of France, but of the whole western empire. The reasons for which the sceptre will be wrenched from his hands by the people will, it may justly be presumed, be such as will prompt them to prevent him from resuming it.

Apart from that, however, the age he has already reached, renders it certain that he cannot remain in power, nor in life during the long period that is to elapse between the return of the beast from hades and the battle of Armageddon; when those whom that symbol represents are finally to perish. He has already entered his fifty-eighth year. How long a time is to pass before the overthrow of the monarchies of the ten kingdoms, there are no means of determining. The sixth vial, there is reason to believe, is still to be poured for a considerable space; as the subjects of the Catholic hierarchies have not yet become alienated from it in a degree that answers to the drying of the waters of the Euphrates; which bespeak the general disseverance from the pope and his train of priestly officials, of the Catholic populations, whom the waters of the river denote. That may indeed be hastened, and perhaps consummated by a deprivation of the pope of his civil power; yet probably some years would still be required, should that take place, to give full effect to it in Spain, Portugal, Belgium, Bavaria, Austria, and even Italy and France. But a still longer time will be requisite probably for the far greater change that is to be wrought in the views of the people of the ten kingdoms, by which they are to be prepared to rise against their civil rulers, hurl them from their stations, and either release themselves for a time from all government, or else hold the power that is exercised in their own hands. How broad a space is to intervene between the overthrow of the present monarchies, and the rise of the beast from the abyss and organization of a new imperial government, cannot be foreseen; nor how long a period, after the reorganization of the imperial rule, is to be occupied in the renationalization of the Catholic hierarchy, in the rise of the witnesses, their testimony, their arraignment, their slaughter, and their death-sleep to the day of their resurrection; but it will undoubtedly be a considerable series of years. Let it be supposed that ten revolve betwixt the present time and the ascent of the beast from the abyss;—it may be less: it may be fifteen, twenty, or more;—and that ten more intervene between that event and the resurrection of the witnesses, they would carry Louis Napoleon—on the supposition that he continues in life—beyond his seventy-eighth year. Already struck as he is in a degree with the effects of age, no one can deem it likely that he is still to survive, and with an energy equal to the demands of his station, through that long period.

But the resurrection of the witnesses is to give birth to *another earthquake* that is to shake down the hierarchy and monarchy of one of the ten kingdoms, and spread consternation through the whole empire. That event is to be followed by the fall of the Turkish power; and probably through the aggression of Russia, which may involve a war with France and other western kingdoms, unless it should take place at a crisis when the maintenance of their own thrones requires their exclusive attention. The fall of Turkey is to be quickly followed by the seventh trumpet, under which there is to be a third earthquake that may again overturn the monarchy of France, as well as of the other kingdoms. And that is to be succeeded by the seventh vial, under which another and greater earthquake is to occur, that is to divide Babylon into three parts; and that is to be followed by her destruction, the development of Antichrist, the return of a large body of the Jews, the war of the beast and kings in Palestine, and their destruction at the battle of Armageddon. Can any one persuade himself that Louis Napoleon, after reaching his seventy-eighth year, should his life be prolonged for a time, is still to continue in power and activity, through the political and religious revolutions that are still to occupy thirty or forty years beyond that epoch, and not improbably more, before the end? The supposition is absurd. If he survives the fall of the monarchies under the sixth seal, it is still as certain from his age that he must reach his end long before the manifestation of Antichrist, the war in Palestine, and the last great battle, as it is that he will, if he perishes in the revolution under that seal.

Whether then the abyss from which the wild beast is to ascend is the world of the dead, or the deep of the sea; and if the sea, then a symbol of the nations in the commotions of a political revolution in which their monarchies are to be overthrown, it is as evident as the event itself can make it, that Louis Napoleon cannot be the personage who is to be the Antichrist, and perish thirty, forty, or fifty years after, at the battle of Armageddon.

To the supposition that the abyss from which the wild beast is to ascend is hades, it may perhaps be objected that it would be a deviation from the course of nature to recall the persons denoted by the beast that descends to the abyss, to another corporeal life here, and give them to resume the official stations and prerogatives they had before held. To this it may be replied, first, that that deviation from the established course of nature, is no proof that hades is not the scene from which the beast is to return. For that symbolization does not deviate more widely from nature than many other symbols; such, for example, as the gift of wings to the lion and leopard of Daniel's visions; of four heads to the leopard; of seven heads and ten horns to the dragon and wild beast of the Apocalypse; to the dragon a tail of such length as to sweep down stars to the earth; to the goat the power to pass by successive leaps from the Propontis in western Asia to the Eulæus in Persia, without touching the ground; and to its sixth horn a height so great that it struck the orbs of heaven to the earth. Those organs and acts are at as wide a distance from nature as the descent of the beast to hades, and its return to a fresh life and agency, would be.

Its return, however, from hades does not imply that the persons who are to constitute the organization it represents at its emergence, are to be identically the same that formed the body of rulers it symbolized at the moment of its dejection to that world. They may, and doubtless will, be a wholly different group. This is seen from the fact that the beast is the symbol of the *line* of kingly and inferior rulers, from the rise of the ten Gothic kingdoms, through all the ages to its final destruction. As the death of individual monarchs, princes and lower functionaries, has been no obstacle to the perpetuation of the *lines* of rulers; so it is not any obstacle to the representation of the successive *groups* in the lines by the same unvarying symbol. Thus, when the seventh head of the beast received its deadly wound in the death of Julian, the healing of the wound did not involve the restoration of Julian himself to life, and to the sceptre. The healing consisted simply in substituting Jovian, a wholly different person, in the place of Julian as the imperial chief of the Roman power. In like manner, the ascent of the wild beast from hades, will not involve the restoration to life and power of the identical persons who are the rulers of the ten kingdoms at the moment of their overthrow under the sixth seal; but simply denotes that another group of persons will succeed to their places, with important modifications of their relations to each other, and to their subjects, and will thence perpetuate the power in its essential prerogatives and characteristics, which the beast that had perished had represented.

The design of such a departure from nature, in this as in other instances, is, to indicate the extraordinariness of the career those great agents are to run, and the singularity of the modifications and catastrophes through which they are to pass. And this it is expressly foreshown, is to be the effect of the return of the wild beast from hades. "And they who dwell upon the earth, whose names are not written in the book of life from the foundation of the world, shall wonder when they look upon the beast that was, and is not, and yet is." Rev. xvii. 8–9. Their astonishment is to arise from their seeing in their very presence the power denoted by the wild beast, which after having subsisted for ages, had for a period been struck from existence. It is to be as unexpected, therefore, and as startling a deviation from the course the crowd are to anticipate, as it would be if it had taken place by a resurrection from the dead.

CHAPTER XXVIII.

The Agents by whom the Monarchies are to be overthrown—The Motive that is to prompt them to that Measure—The Effect of the recent Struggle between Prussia, Austria and Italy, on the Policy of the Rulers—A knowledge of these Themes important to all classes—The joy-inspiring Prospect that is unfolding to our Race.

1. But who are the agents by whom the monarchies are to be overthrown? A knowledge of the actors in that tragedy, is necessary in order to a just estimate of the tragedy itself. They are not then to be foreign assailants, and conquerors; but the populations of those kingdoms, and subjects of those monarchs. This is seen from the earthquake, the symbol of the revolution in which they are to be struck from their thrones, and consigned to hades. For as the sun, moon, and stars, which give light to the earth and rule its days and nights, its seasons and years, are manifestly from their analogy, the representatives of the kings, nobles, and other officials who rule the population of the ten kingdoms, and determine in a resembling way, their social and political condition; so, on the other hand, the earth on which those heavenly orbs exert their power, is the symbol of the population of the ten kingdoms on whom the kings, princes, and other officials exercise

their corresponding functions as rulers. They present in those relations, an exact analogy to each other. Accordingly as in an earthquake it is the vapor, gas, smoke, and ashes thrown up from the depths of the earth into the atmosphere, that obscure the sun, moon, and stars, and intercept them from transmitting their beams to the earth; so in the political upheaval which the earthquake denotes, it is the people themselves who are to exert the acts by which the monarchs, and others who have held authority over them, are to be divested of their power and struck to inaction. Instead of being wrought by a voluntary abdication of their places and prerogatives, it is to be the work of violence; as the disruption and disarray of the ground in an earthquake, is the work of explosive forces that have their place in the depths of the earth itself. Foreign nations are to be but spectators of the scene in place of such actors as were the great conquerors of former ages,—Nebuchadnezzar, Cyrus, Alexander, Cæsar, Mahomet, Ghengis Khan, and Napoleon, who subverted the monarchies they overthrew, not by spoken or written decrees, but by battles and conquests. There is no symbol in the vision of the sixth seal of an armed force, until the appearance of the Son of Man in the clouds at the last great battle, which is to be at the distance, probably, of forty or fifty years from the catastrophe denoted by the earthquake.

It is clear, therefore, that the unofficial population

of the ten kingdoms, are to be the agents in the violent movements symbolized by the earthquake, by which monarchs and other officials are to be thrust from their stations and borne down to hades; and the measures they are to take to work that effect, are to be essentially the same in the whole group of kingdoms; the earthquake representing the nature of the agitation it is to assume in each.

What then is to be the new force or prerogative by which the multitude are to rise to supremacy, and deprive the kings, magnates, and other authoritative ranks of their political power, and release themselves from the bonds of the old governments, inaugurate for a time a reign of anarchy, or institute a new rule? The sphere in which they are to act in achieving that change, is undoubtedly that of a democracy. The political power is to pass from the hands of the hereditary rulers, to that of the people; and not silently by the spontaneous concessions or wishes of those who are to descend from stations of authority, but by the resistless will of the crowd.

But how is the democracy to acquire that power to set aside their hereditary rule, and institute another in its place? It is doubtless to be by the right of suffrage, obtained either by the concession of the monarchs and parliaments, or by assumption by the people and exercise irrespective of law, as a natural and inalienable prerogative.

And that may naturally result from the views of

right and equality that are now extensively enter tained by the unfranchised ranks. The doctrine that all men are by nature equal in respect to social and political prerogatives, and entitled to a voice in the enactment of the laws on which they are to rely for the protection of their persons, liberty, and property, is not only held by a large part of the educated in Great Britain, France, Germany, and Italy, but has become one of the most fundamental and influential elements, in the popular theories of rights and governments, and is rapidly gaining disciples wherever it is proclaimed, and inclining or constraining some of the monarchs and parliaments, to yield it either absolutely, or in such a degree, that a point may naturally be at length reached, at which the population generally, will obtain the prerogative of electing their rulers, and thence determining the laws by which they are to be governed.

That this view of the sphere, in which the multitude are to act at that crisis, is just, is farther seen from the express prediction, Daniel ii. 41–43, that clay, the symbol of the common people, in distinction from iron, the representative of the monarchs and other hereditary officials, is to be mixed with the iron, in the formation of the image of the Roman power in its last stage, when the feet and toes hold supremacy. "As the toes of the feet were part of iron, and part of clay, so the kingdom—or ruling power—shall be partly strong and partly brittle.

And, whereas, thou didst see iron mixed with miry clay, they (who are denoted by the iron) shall mingle themselves with the seed of men," that is with those, who instead of being like themselves of hereditary rank, are mere subjects. That admission, however, of the crowd, to a measure of political power by the right of suffrage, instead of strengthening, is to weaken the monarchs and nobles. "But they shall not cleave one to another, even as iron is not mixed with clay." And the reason is, not simply that the aims and interests of the two parties are to be in a measure antagonistic; but, in perhaps a greater degree, because of the inadhesiveness of the particles of the clay to each other. The mass being brittle, will be easily broken into pieces and reduced to dust, and thence will fail of the ends for which it was assigned a place with the iron. This is accordingly a prophecy that the accession of the multitude to the right of suffrage, in place of giving stability to the governments, and yielding to the people the benefits they anticipated, is to give birth to antagonisms between the two classes, break the populations into factions, and issue at length in the overthrow of the monarchies and a reign of anarchy.

The union of these two classes in the European governments, has hitherto taken place but partially. It is the basis thus far, only of the monarchies of France and Italy. Prussia, it is said, lately proposed its adoption in Germany, in order to the election of a diet for the formation of a new constitution for the empire; but the war of the summer has issued in the dissolution of the old confederation, and the erection of another by Prussia, the constitution of which, so far as it has one, instead of being submitted to the suffrage of the people, is dictated by her as conqueror. A party in Spain is agitating for the gift of suffrage to the people, and the introduction of free institutions: and great and ardent efforts are in progress in Great Britain to extend the franchise to large classes that now have no part in the election of members of Parliament, or city and county officials.

It is probably in the inauguration and promotion of this great change in the structure of the governments, that Louis Napoleon is to exert his chief influence in generating the causes and occasions that are to issue in the overthrow of the monarchies. He is not to dash them to the dust by victories on the battle-field. He is not to wrench from them their power by feats of diplomacy. He has created, and is creating and organizing a force against them a thousand times stronger, in the gift to his subjects of the elective franchise, and prompting its introduction in other nations; as the crowd when aware of the power with which that implement arms them, will turn and strike his throne from beneath him, if he survives a considerable period, and the thrones of his compeers, and dismiss their occupants to the realms of the invisible world.

2. What are the motives that are to prompt the people of the ten kingdoms to that measure? Essentially the same, undoubtedly, as those that led the French nation, in 1789–92, to overthrow their monarchy; and that have roused that people so frequently since, and those of Spain, Italy, Germany, Hungary, Greece and others, to rise against their kings and rulers, resist their rule, and seek to institute a government more favorable to their personal rights, and the free pursuit of the great ends of life; namely, their degradation to a condition little better than that of serfs; subjection to a despotic rule, that disposes of their persons and lives regardless of their wishes and their well-being; wanton oppression; the probability of vassalage to the end of life; and the certainty that there is to be no essential amelioration of their condition till a reformation is wrought in the government under which they have their lot. This piercing sense of injustice; this revolt from the arbitrary and remorseless sway of despots, has its grounds in the deepest depths of our nature; it is instinctive, inerradicable, and irrepressible, and by a law of necessity, when violently goaded, asserts itself, and like a fettered giant roused from slumber by tormentors, breaks forth with irresistible fury, dashes the oppressor from his seat, and tramples him in the dust.

3. What are to be the effects of the recent struggle between Prussia, Italy and Austria, on the policy of

the rulers towards each other, and towards their subjects, and on the conditions and dispositions of their populations towards them? Are the nations whose relative positions are so greatly changed, now to live in harmony with each other? Are there to be hereafter no causes of discontent, jealousy, or ambition? No impulses, from disappointment and mortification to revenge? No rivalries for power? No schemes of lawless rule? Is it to be the policy of the several governments in the new relations in which they are placed, to grant such ameliorations in the conditions of their subjects as shall meet their urgent wants, inspire them with contentment, and bind them to their respective monarchies with the bonds of an unfaltering loyalty? No one aware of the position of the rulers in relation to their subjects, the policy which they deem it necessary to pursue to preserve their places and power, and the dissatisfaction, the passion for relief from crushing burthens, and the projects of revolution and power that have a place in the breasts of a large part of the lower and middle classes, can persuade himself that such genial results are to spring from the sudden aggrandizement of Prussia, the disarray of Austria, the successes of Italy, and the unexpected and annoying position of France. The same jealousies and rivalries that have heretofore existed between the great nations, the same necessities to the governments of a sway that has its ground in a large degree in military force rather than law; and the same causes of dissatisfaction, restlessness, and resistance to an oppressive rule, are still to exist in at least as great strength as heretofore; and the drift of the general mind, it is clear from the forces that are acting on it, is to continue to be in the direction of representative governments and free institutions rather than otherwise, and with an increasing celerity and power. Should peace continue for a considerable period, no essential mitigation can take place of the burthens to which the inferior classes are subjected for the support of the governments. Let it, for example, be supposed to be the wish of France to maintain amicable relations with her neighbors, how can she diminish in any large degree her standing army, or her navy? The stability of her government depends on the strength and loyalty of her war forces. Were Louis Napoleon to reduce those on the land to a few regiments, and those on the water to a few ships, his inability to repel a powerful assailant from without would put his independence in jeopardy; and his inadequacy to repress the restlessness and ambition of the lawless within, would issue in the subversion of his throne. Surrounded as France is by envious, resentful and aggressive nations, her self-preservation will prompt her to maintain the vast armaments to which she owes her present safety. A like necessity will naturally compel Prussia to continue a vast military array, in readiness at all times to act aggressively or defensively, as danger or ambition may suggest.

How is she to assure herself of security from France, Southern Germany, Russia, unless she has a standing army of sufficient strength to defend her independence? Or how is she to control the large bodies of newly-acquired subjects, to whom her rule is distasteful and humiliating, unless she has a power at her command adequate to make her will the law? In like manner, Southern Germany, Austria, Italy, Spain, Portugal, Great Britain and Russia are to be under a necessity of continuing their present military establishments. Large bodies of troops, great warlike armaments, expensive administrations, and a resistless, and in a measure a despotic sway, will be, in the judgment of the rulers, indispensable to the continued stability of their governments; and they are sure, therefore, to carry that policy to an extent beyond what is necessary, rather than restrict themselves to such limits as to endanger their power. The result, therefore, is naturally to be, that not a single government of the whole group will sit lightly on its subjects. Vast expenditures, exorbitant taxation, crushing oppression, arbitrary and cruel conscriptions for the army and navy, by which all the prospects and hopes of millions will be blasted; and the wanton sacrifice of the well-being of the multitude to the safety and honor of the rulers, are therefore to be the characteristics of their rule generally hereafter, and in a higher degree, not improbably, than heretofore. The causes of disquiet and alienation from the monarchies are to continue and augment in number and ascerbity; and deepen and exascerbate the desire for relief, by the substitution of cheaper and more popular governments.

This feeling is to be nourished and strengthened also by the far more general diffusion that is to take place of political knowledge among the lower classes. The whole of Europe is to be put in possession within a few hours of their occurrence, not only of all the great events of her division of the globe, but with almost as much speed of all of which this country and this continent are the scene, and feel at the same instant their exhilarating or fear-inspiring impulse, and be touched with the same sympathy and joy, if they are favorable to human rights and happiness; and clouded with the same regret and indignation, if they are unjust and malign. The whole civilized world is thus to be the spectator of all that is taking place in its several divisions, and keep pace in knowledge and feeling with the strife that is to rage between the rulers and ruled. A revolution in Paris in Berlin, in Vienna, or Rome, will flash its lurid, or its cheerful light, as it may be contemplated, in a day to every capital and city from the Mediterranean to the Arctic Sea, and like an earthquake that should shake and upheave that wide domain, beget in millions of bosoms the same fierce passions, and prompt to similar deeds of violence and blood. There is thus a preparation for a simultaneous revolution in the kingdoms of Western and Southern Europe that has never existed before. What the issue of the recent war is to be, is not yet seen. That the present peace is to be more than brief, is not probable. Whether short or long, it will be appropriated, there is reason to believe, to measures that contemplate another struggle more bloody and disastrous to the well-being of the nations than that which has just closed.

4. How obviously it is the duty of those who wish to escape the fearful evils that are coming on the nations, to study these great themes, make themselves acquainted with the teachings of the divine word in regard to them, and, disinthralling themselves from the indifference on the one side, and the false views and fanatical expectations on the other, which hold possession of so many minds, be ready by a just intelligence and a steadfast faith to meet the conflicts to which they are to be called without faltering, and without alarm.

5. How joy-inspiring, how sublime, are the prospects of the race as they are portrayed in the prophecies I have been unfolding, compared with the notions that are generally entertained! What a morning will that be that is to break upon the world, when the Son of God flashes the light of his presence on the scenes which man has so long been steeping in blood and blasting with desolation; and hushing in a moment the tempest of ambition, rage and malevolence that reigns in the breasts of men into silence, and

dashing his irreclaimable enemies to destruction, converts the surviving nations to spotless rectitude, imbues them with perfect love, and freeing them from temptation, from suffering, and from death, gives them to dwell under his sceptre in peace and blessedness! How adapted to the necessities of man! How essential to a perfect redemption! How consonant to the infinite price which he paid for their deliverance from sin and from death! How suitable to the grandeur of his attributes! With what effulgence it is to invest his eternal reign!

www.ingramcontent.com/pod-product-compliance
Lightning Source LLC
LaVergne TN
LVHW021242110826
845150LV00002B/392

* 9 7 8 1 4 2 5 5 6 1 2 9 1 *